The Heart of Jerusalem

The
Heart
of
Jerusalem

by Arlynn Nellhaus

edited by Toni Katz Drew

John Muir Publications

Design/Production by Thin Air Graphics, Santa Fe, NM
Cover by Peter Aschwanden
Maps by Janice St. Marie
Typography by Shadow Canyon Graphics, Evergreen, CO

Published by: John Muir Publications
                  P.O. Box 613
                  Santa Fe, NM 87504

Library of Congress Catalog Card No. 87-043164
ISBN: 0-912528-79-6

Distributed to the booktrade by: W.W. Norton & Company
                                     New York, NY

Printed in the United States of America

Dedication

To Abi, Adel, Ami, Andrew, Aviva, Batia, Chaya, David, Eli, Ezra, George, Gershon, Harry, Jeff, John, Jonah, Malkah, Marie- Claire, Marcia, Mary, Miriam, Muriel, Mordechai, Morty, Moti, Nassar, Rachelle, Rafik, Rahel, Rebbe Chaim, Rosita, Sue, Teddy, Tovah, Uli, Wolff and the people of Jerusalem.

The Tale of Jerusalem

A shepherd died and left his land to his two sons. One son was unmarried and lived alone at one side of the land on one side of a hill. The other was married and had three children and lived on the other side of the hill.

The brothers raised wheat and divided it equally.

One night, the unmarried brother woke up in the middle of the night and thought, "Why should I have an equal share when my brother has a wife and children to take care of?"

He went outside and took sheaves of wheat from his allotted half and under the moon and stars went over the hill and placed the sheaves with his brother's half.

Later that night, the other brother woke up and thought, "My brother is all alone. He has no one to take care of him — no wife, no children. He needs more than I do."

He picked up sheaves of wheat and under the moon and stars went over the hill and placed the sheaves with his brother's half.

In the morning when the brothers woke up, to their surprise, each had the same amount of wheat as before.

The second night the same thing happened. First one brother went over the hill carrying sheaves of wheat under the moon and stars, and then the other did the same thing.

The third night, it so happened that each of them awoke at the same time and started over the hill from their different sides at the time.

At the top of the hill, they met. Suddenly, they realized what the other had done and why each one of them still had just as much grain as before.

The brothers dropped their sheaves of wheat, threw their arms around each other and cried tears of joy over their mutual love.

Because of this love, expressed under the moon and stars, God declared that his city, Jerusalem, the city of brotherly love, would be built on that spot.

Table of Contents

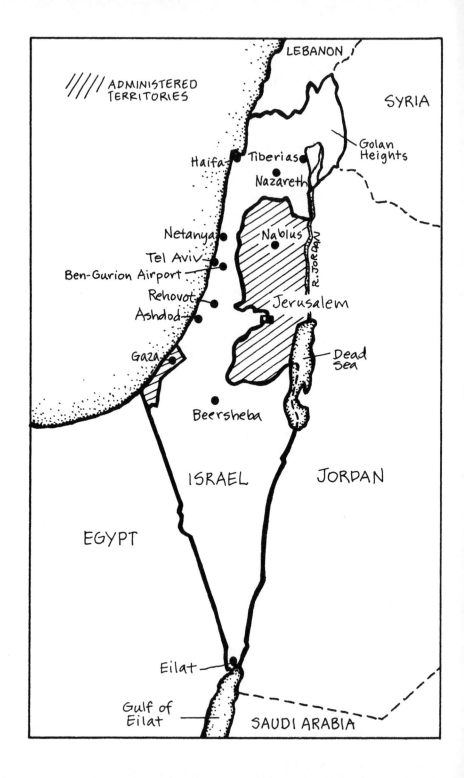

Introduction:
This Year in Jerusalem

How to Use this Book

This book is for persons who come to Jerusalem for a few days, six weeks or a year. It is for those who arrive for the first time or the 15th. It is for those who never have been to Jerusalem and who dream about it.

It describes the sites that give Jerusalem soul and that tourists from all over the world flock to see. But it tells more than of the emotional impact of a visit to the Western Wall or the glowing beauty of the Dome of the Rock.

The book, also, is a picture of the Golden City as a living, modern, urban area. Jerusalem is known as "the heavenly city", but its earthliness is fascinating, too. So this book, also, is about Jerusalem's "everydayness" and offers shortcuts on how a person can deal with and enjoy that aspect of life in this unique city.

Even in an ancient city of heavenly inspiration, visitors need to know such practicalities as how to find a place to stay, how to remain healthy or how to shop when bargaining is required. This book will answer these kinds of questions.

And there is more to learn in these pages — information about the treasures in little-known museums, about the city's living pageantry, about how to chomp on sunflower seeds like a native, about when to go dancing in the streets, and about the plethora of events and occurrences that give Jerusalem heart.

After all, as the 115th Psalm said more than 2500 years ago, "The heavens are the heavens of the Lord and the earth he gave to humans." And heavenly Jerusalem really does exist on earth.

The Setup

Part One is for every traveler to Jerusalem. It contains basic information on how to get there, health considerations, money management, hotels, restaurants, and, of course, in Jerusalem, the city's ever-present history.

Part Two, the touring section of the book, is arranged in four sections. The first provides seven day-long itineraries for visitors with but one week in Jerusalem. The second is for tourists who are lucky enough to have two weeks to spend exploring the Holy City. The third describes less well-known sites, of interest to anyone who has the leisure to stay on as a temporary resident, or who chooses to substitute these sites for those suggested in the one- and two-week itineraries. The fourth section describes the cycle of celebrations that you can join in throughout the year in Jerusalem.

Part Three describes how life is conducted in Jerusalem. The information is intended to guide the long-term tourist to housing, acquaintances, exercise, books, heat, and telephones. This part of the book also is for those of you who won't be staying on, but want to imagine what it would be like to do so. It fills out a picture of the Golden City for the curious and adventuresome, as well as those who feel they have "come home to Jerusalem", and who, indeed, will be staying a while.

Since this is a book to be used in Israel, I figure we should do things the way Israelis do. We use the Hebrew, *rehov* for "street" and *kikar* for "square". Addresses appear as they are given in Hebrew: Street, Name, Number, as in Rehov Alfassi 23.

If the location of certain places reads a bit vague, that is a local idiosyncrasy. Street numbers aren't always to be found, but the place in question usually is in plain sight once you get to the spot. And Jerusalem's downtown area simply is called "the centre", which, as a carry-over from British Mandate years, usually is spelled in English style.

Historical Dates

Following that same logic, instead of referring to an event as having happened in 250 B.C. (Before Christ), it appears in the book as 250 B.C.E. After all, non-Christians don't measure time from the birth of Jesus, but Jews, to prevent historic chaos, designate an event as happening B.C.E., Before the Common Era, or C.E., Common Era.

So 250 B.C. and 250 B.C.E. are the same date.

Hebrew Pronunciations

There isn't an exact science involved in transliterating Hebrew into English. But in general, when you read "ch" as in "Chanukah" and "kh" as in "khan", the pronunciation is with a guttural "h". And almost all Hebrew words get the accent on the last syllable.

Telephone Numbers

All telephone numbers in this book are for Jerusalem unless an area code precedes it. Therefore, unlike many publications about the city, you won't see Jerusalem's area code 02 before a Jerusalem number.

I don't include telephone numbers of many places to which I refer. Making a reservation at certain cosmopolitan, high-priced restaurants, or calling the Egged Bus Company for information, or a taxi company for a driver, are among the few situations in which Bell's invention works efficiently here. Many a business place doesn't even advertise its phone number. Calling businesses is often pointless. You usually will be given no information and told to come in. Business — even the business of gathering information — is conducted face to face.

Fluctuating Prices

Israel's three-digit inflation devastated the country's economy in the early to mid '80s. By 1986, inflation was reduced to a "mere" 20 percent. What the situation will be in the future is hard to predict. Therefore, prices given in this book are an approximation.

"Bruchim Haba'Im" — Welcome

In a recent book, Elie Wiesel wrote that one doesn't go to Jerusalem, one returns to Jerusalem. He meant that Jerusalem is, if not a real home, the spiritual home for millions.

In Hebrew, the expression is that one goes "up" to Jerusalem. It is meant figuratively that in Jerusalem a person reaches a higher spiritual level, but it happens literally. Travel to the city by bus or car from the Ben-Gurion Airport, and at a certain point, the driver has to downshift. The highway now climbs upward through rock-ribbed, pine-covered hills. A bus struggles and sounds winded. An air of expectancy envelops the passengers.

Some four sharp turns to the right and then the left have to be maneuvered along this winding road that clings to the hillside. Next to the last turn, a sign made up of shrubbery on a low slope to the right of the road announces, *"Bruchim Haba'im"*: "Blessed is your arrival."

Once more left and right and suddenly, you are out of the countryside. You have arrived in Jerusalem. Whatever existed in your dreams: this is the reality.

The city's yellow stone buildings top its half-mile-high mountain under a blank, blazing blue sky. The colors of Jerusalem's stone buildings give the city its other name, "the Golden City", by subtly changing from pink to white to golden as the sun rises and sets.

Crowning one slope is the ancient Old City, home to almost 3000 years of religious history of three major faiths, girdled by its towering stone walls. It is divided into four unequal quarters — Armenian, Christian, Jewish and Moslem. At the foot of the Old City, climbing stepwise up a slope from the Hinnom Valley is the City of David, the even more ancient Jerusalem that King David built on earlier settlements.

Beyond the Old City's walls and narrow lanes is, to the west, a modern appearing, sometimes seemingly medieval, but always Middle-Eastern style Jewish city; to the east is its Arab, more bucolic, more graceful version.

Jerusalem's beauty, despite its occasional ugliness and dreariness, strikes you the moment you arrive. It is a churning city, driven by a hothouse ambience.

Maps from the Middle Ages show Jerusalem as "the navel of the world". Today, Jerusalemites are convinced they truly live in the center of the world, that any other place would be dull. In agreement are Jewish teenage girls in skimpy spaghetti-strap tops, Orthodox Jewish men in wide-brimmed beaver hats and white knee socks, and teenage boys lugging Uzis and dressed in green army uniforms. Holding the same opinion are Arab men wearing white gowns and checkered *keffiyehs* around their head and Arab women in embroidered, long black dresses. Of the same view are myriad priests: white-robed Dominicans, brown-garbed Franciscans, Green Orthodox with flat-topped black headdresses and billowing black robes, and Armenians with pointed black headdresses and billowing black robes.

They, and seemingly endless other varieties of humanity, have deep roots in Jerusalem. Jerusalem pulls them to itself like a magnet. Jews alone have come from more than 70 countries. Jerusalem is their lodestar. They and the city are inextricably entwined. While Jews comprise Jerusalem's predominant population, they are but a part of the city's mosaic to which each group's culture, religion and history adds a vital piece.

Yet, you wonder why these dissimilar people have gathered to live in one place. And you wonder even more why it was this particular, rugged, rocky place that logically has no justification for existing. No seaport, river or major commercial crossroads give Jerusalem an easy explanation for being.

Although arid and barren, it has been fiercely fought for. It has been conquered 37 times and destroyed 18. Yet, it manages to rise time and again, through some inexplicable determination on the part of the people who love it. Jerusalem's citizens often have been forced to leave, but they have never abandoned it.

What made the city was God — people's faith that God touched this mountain and, that on it, they are as close to God as they can be and still keep their feet on the ground.

For Jews, Jerusalem is their eternal capital, its name on their lips with their prayers. While to Jews, God is everywhere, God's home is within Jerusalem's Temple Mount. Jews stand before the Western Wall, the remaining structure of the destroyed Second Temple, and feel they are in God's presence.

For Christians, Jerusalem is where their Lord was crucified and resurrected. The city means both pain and joy to them. They can share his agony as he fell on the Via Dolorosa and can walk in his footsteps as he made his way to his crucifixion at Golgotha. They can see his tomb and feel the glory of his resurrection.

For Moslems, it is from Jerusalem that Mohammed rode his winged horse on his Night Journey to visit Allah in heaven, and it is in Jerusalem that "the great gathering" will take place on the Last Judgment Day.

It is these three great religions, Christianity spinning off from Judaism and Islam spinning off from both of them, that built Jerusalem, the Holy City. Christians and Moslems did so literally, stone by stone. Jews, for almost 2000 years, only could do so spiritually. In their hearts and minds, Jews made a holy temple of all Jerusalem.

On modern maps, the city resembles an amoeba with wiggly protrusions from a central glob, creeping up hillsides and down into valleys. Only slightly more than 400,000 residents inhabit its hills and valleys. For a great city, one that persists in the world's headlines and thoughts, it is quite small. Its "centre", its downtown area, is little more than a few unpretentious blocks wide.

But what makes today's Jerusalem great is that it is open to believer and non-believer alike. It takes no special faith to feel Jerusalem's warmth and electricity.

Six days of the week, the city percolates. Available to all is a surge of excitement over its history stretching back for millennia, the visual impact of its ancient sites and colorful people, and especially the radiation of the city's sense of purpose and heightened emotions.

Focus of Jewish pilgrimage for two millenia, The Western Wall is visited by thousands daily.

That purpose is hard to define. Perhaps, simply, it is Jerusalem's determination to live. As for those emotions, they are out there like a flag. They are waved, not bunched up and carried close to the chest. Jerusalem is about feelings. Jerusalem wears its heart on its sleeve.

Then, after six days of super-charged activity, comes the seventh day. The Jewish Sabbath arrives at sunset on Friday. Jerusalem stops running. Even the signal lights rest. Jerusalem now is still, reflective and otherworldly. Now it truly is the Holy City, the City of Peace. And time quietly crawls.

Then, at Shabbat's end when three stars can be seen in the sky Saturday evening, it is as if someone hit a switch and gave the city a jolt. The fire is back.

My adoration of Jerusalem didn't spring from love at first sight. I had visited it during two trips to Israel. The first visit was during an international conference for women writers. We spent the first week in Jerusalem, and our hosts made sure we saw the city. I managed also to do quite a bit of exploring on my own. Five years later, I merely was in and out of the city in order to join a group to climb Mount Sinai.

On both visits, Jerusalem left me feeling uneasy. My senses were overwhelmed by a tidal wave of impressions. I couldn't absorb the colorful sights, the cacophony of sounds and the often pungent odors. My mind focused on the city's ugly side: its decrepit buildings, its beggars, its littered sidewalks. I felt more at home in boisterous Tel Aviv and sedate Haifa.

Still, when I first saw the Western Wall, that holiest of Jewish places, my emotions surprised me. I felt a link I hadn't expected to that place and to my people. Seeing the Wall, I saw 4000 years of Jewish history — my history. At the Wall, I knew the thrill of being part of the chain of "stiff-necked" people that has said yes to life, no matter what.

Another five years passed. I was granted a leave of absence from my job. Where in the whole world to spend my year? I already had lived in Paris, which I adored, but I wanted to go someplace new. Rome? Bombay? Rio? I wanted to know them all, but I decided on Israel. For years, I had been curious to know what it would be like to live there. But where in Israel? On a kibbutz? In Haifa or Tel Aviv, where I had friends?

I mulled over my options, and out of them, the one I had considered least of all at first, Jerusalem, emerged as my choice. As a journalist, I thought I ought to be in the heart of the country. But my real reason was curiosity. Why was it that every person I knew who had visited Jerusalem waxed ecstatic over it and, yet, I didn't feel that way? Had I overlooked something during my visits? I seemed to have missed something, and I wanted to find out what.

Without knowing anyone in Jerusalem, having only the name of a woman who rented out rooms, I began my trip.

At Ben-Gurion Airport, after an exhausting flight, I argued with a taxi driver over how much he was going to charge to drive me the 20 miles to Jerusalem. Finally, I decided I was too tired to worry about it. I climbed into his car, taking the seat beside him, as he directed. No more than three minutes later, the taxi driver, a stocky man of about 35, with dark skin, heavy black, straight eyebrows and black curly hair, was carrying on an animated discussion with me. A native Jerusalemite, he talked of his Yemenite ancestry and his views on democracy, Arabs, the government, peace and war. I forgot about being tired. By seven minutes later, he had invited me to spend a Shabbat with his family. Already, I was liking Jerusalem better than I ever had.

Still, as the months passed, I tried to keep Jerusalem from possessing my heart. But bit, by bit, love grew. I still saw beggars, dog droppings on the sidewalks and makeshift, impoverished neighborhoods. But my eyes opened to inviting courtyards, the grace of quiet streets, flaming sunsets day after day and the view from a height of the barren, mysterious Judean desert scratching at the city's edge.

I fell in love with Jerusalem through unexpected peeks into Jerusalemites' way of life. One occurred when I was strolling through the Israel Museum, heard music and followed it to its source. It came from a radio belonging to the janitors. The sounds were of North African Jewish music, and the men, vacuum cleaner and brooms beside them, were dancing and laughing right there in the exhibit hall.

I loved the freedom they had to interrupt their work day, to enjoy life and turn a museum into a living, spontaneous repository of culture. Other moments touched me, such as when I smelled the perfumed air of springtime that begins with white almond blossoms in February and culminates with saucer-size roses in May.

And I felt love for Jerusalem when a teenager, standing in front of me in line for a pay phone, overheard me say something to a friend about telephone tokens. Thinking I had none, she turned and offered me one of hers. It was an example I encountered over and over of generosity between strangers.

Many months after I met Ezra on that taxi ride from the airport and got to know his wife and five children, he said to me, "In Jerusalem, you are never alone." The message was, "In Jerusalem, you always are with family."

It is a boisterous, unruly family from which you can hide little. I sat on a bench outside a laundromat doing my Hebrew lesson while I waited for the washing machine cycle to end. Next to me was an attractive young woman, also waiting for her laundry. As I wrote in my notebook, she leaned closer, read my notebook, waved an index finger and admonished me, "You made a mistake." She then corrected my writing and gave me a mini-Hebrew lesson. Only in a world where there is a feeling of family even between strangers could her act have been not only acceptable, but expected. I obviously needed help; of course, she would give it.

This family isn't always loving. But the conviction remains that disputes are within family; and, families argue sometimes, so it's no big deal.

With "family" around you, to paraphrase Ezra, how can you be alone in Jerusalem?

Most of all, I fell in love with Jerusalem when, to my surprise, I realized I felt at home. The city had embraced me. It made me, as it has and always will to so many others, feel I belonged. As those words of Elie Wiesel said, I hadn't arrived in Jerusalem: I had returned.

It can happen to you, too — even if you are here for a short time. You can find in Jerusalem, if not your physical niche, your spiritual niche. And this doesn't depend on a formal religious view; it depends on an attitude. To accomplish this, abandon your preconceptions. Drop your defenses. Be like a child. Open your eyes and ears, your mind and your heart. And you will find yourself agreeing with the anonymous person who wrote in 1601, "O Jerusalem, my happy home."

Ultra-orthodox Jews and an Arab conducting business in the Old City.

Part One:
What Everyone Needs to Know

Chapter 1:
Getting There

Getting to Israel

Israel Government Tourist offices in the United States and your own travel agent can offer the most help in figuring out how to get to Israel. But do your own independent browsing through advertisements in the travel section of a newspaper such as the Sunday New York Times. You might find some bargain flights.

Most travelers fly to Israel, and this is the simplest way of getting there. But being shoehorned into an airplane seat not only makes for an abominable experience, but the speed of the flight trivializes cultural differences between countries. We have no time to repack the cultural baggage we carried with us onto the plane. While in flight, we have little opportunity to intermingle with persons from other countries and allow a bit of them to rub off on us. By the time the plane lands, we haven't had the chance to absorb introductions to the new lifestyle we will face. A tendency is to think that because we covered such great distances in such a short time, the differences between people's backgrounds can be conquered as easily. But it isn't so.

An antidote to jet travel for anyone with a sense of adventure, money and time is to fly to one of several Mediterranean cities in Europe, Cyprus or Turkey and then sail to Haifa.

Getting into Israel

Holders of valid American and Canadian passports receive a free three-month visa on arrival. To study or work in Israel, you will need to obtain a visa from an Israeli Embassy or consulate before arriving. If you plan to travel to an Arab country other than Egypt, ask that your passport not be stamped when you go through passport control on arrival. All other Arab countries will not allow you to enter on a passport that indicates you have been to Israel. Visas to Egypt may be obtained in Israel. A visa for any other Arab country must be obtained before entering Israel.

Currency

Any amount of foreign currency can be brought into Israel. After passing through passport control at Ben-Gurion Airport, change some of your money or traveler's checks for Israeli *shkelim*. (*Shkelim* is the plural of the Israeli unit of money, the *shekel*. A *shekel* is divided into 100 *agarot*). Grab a cart for your luggage. Hang onto it, and while you wait for your luggage to be unloaded, get in line at the bank counter. Banks charge a small commission to cash traveler's checks.

Persons who are staying in Jerusalem for a considerable amount of time will want to read Chapter 16 "To Your Health: Physical and Financial".

Health Requirements

Israel doesn't require special immunizations for entry, but your doctor might have some recommendations. One might be that you have a shot of gamma globulin for protection against infectious hepatitis, which is prevalent in the Middle East, but not notably a problem in Israel. Gamma globulin's effectiveness lasts from three to four months. If you are planning an extended stay, there may be no point in getting the shot.

Your doctor also might advise you to take anti-malaria medication. While the disease no longer is a problem in Israel, *per se*, the World Health Organization has been warning travelers that mosquitoes carrying the disease are able to fly enormous distances.

Getting to Jerusalem

To travel the 20 miles from Ben-Gurion Airport to Jerusalem, take a *sherut*, a seven-passenger taxi that doesn't depart until it's full. If you arrive by ship in Haifa, find a *sherut* that goes directly to Jerusalem, rather than only to Tel Aviv. Going to Tel Aviv wouldn't be a disaster, only more expensive and longer, because you would have to take a second *sherut* from there.

About Bringing the Children

If you are considering bringing your children along for a visit, take into consideration that commercial excursions aren't targeted for children. The talks, inevitably packed with historical information, could be as dull as oatmeal to them.

Consider hiring your own tour guide for the family. Also, track down Marcia Kretzmer's book, *Adventure in the Holy Land — A Guide for Children and Their Families*. It is aimed at children eight to 13 years old.

Persons who plan a lengthy stay in Jerusalem and wish to enroll their children in school should see "Youth Has Its Day" in Chapter 15.

Boning Up and Packing Up

A list of recommended reading appears in the Appendix. A list of what to bring appears in the Appendix.

JERUSALEM SCENE:

Rehov Yafo, the main throughfare in and out of Jerusalem, roars with cars, trucks and buses pushing, pushing to get through the congestion. Seen one day, standing on a tiny island dividing traffic lanes, was a bearded, young man dressed in the black coat and pants and highcrowned hat of a Hasidic sect. He wasn't watching for an opening in the traffic so he could make a dash across the busy street. Instead, he calmly stood there reading to himself from a prayer book, as though the cars, trucks and buses didn't exist.

Traffic bore down on either side of him and passed no more than inches from his elbows and toes. Exhaust fumes fouled the atmosphere. The weight of rumbling, heavy trucks made the ground shake, and the man's side locks, curling in front of either ear, quivered from the rush of air.

But for the man, he wasn't on a traffic island; he was in a world he had created for himself. For him, there wasn't traffic, there wasn't noise, there wasn't even time. There was only God.

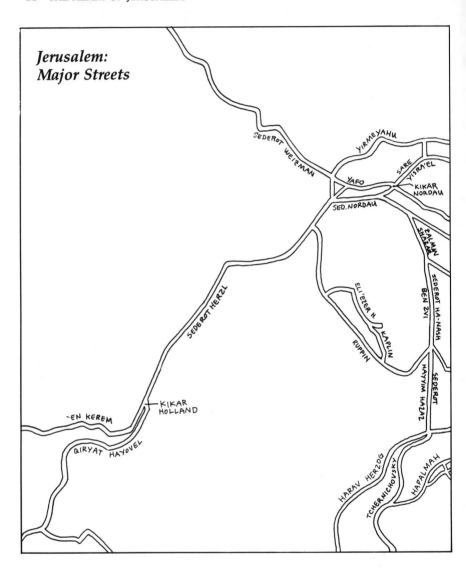

Jerusalem:
Major Streets

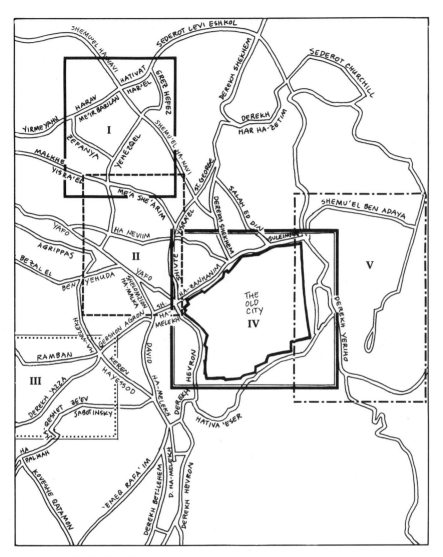

Neighborhoods

I   Bucharan
II   Mea She'arim and Nahalat Shiva
III   Rehavia
IV   The Old City
V   Mount of Olives
     Kidron Valley

Chapter 2:
Facts of (Jerusalem) Life
People, Time, Places,
Terrorism — What to Wear

To deal with Jerusalem knowledgeably, a few facts about it in terms of people, time, places and, yes, terrorism, need to be digested beforehand.

The Chosen People

Like Israel itself, the people of Jerusalem (ah!) are vivacious, pushy, loving, loud. To me, the city merely would be a collection of historic stones without this warm, unruly knot of humanity.

This is a joke Israelis tell on themselves:

A woman is conducting a survey. She encounters a Russian and she says to him, "Excuse me, what is your opinion on the meat shortage?"

The Russian answers with his own question, "What is an 'opinion?' "

She approaches a woman, who is an American, and says, "Excuse me, what is your opinion on the meat shortage?"

The American answers, "What is a 'shortage?' "

The surveyor approaches another person. This one is an Israeli. "Excuse me," she asks, "what is your opinion on the meat shortage?"

The Israeli has his own question, "What is 'excuse me?' "

Time out. Israeli soldiers take a break at an outdoor cafe near Ben-Yehuda Mall.

One of the most fascinating aspects of Jerusalemites is their diversity. Even those whose families have lived in Jerusalem for generations retain their ethnic and religious distinctions. Others have come to the City of Peace from the corners of the earth. Pick a place on the globe and you are likely to find Jews with origins there. Christians have left such homelands as Armenia, Greece, Egypt, Ethiopia, England and the Soviet Union. Moslems have come from around the Mediterranean Basin and beyond.

Jews, ethnically, fall into two main groups: Sephardi and Ashkenazi. The word, "Sephardi", strictly speaking, means "Spanish". Originally, it referred to Jews who had lived in Spain before the expulsion of 1492 and their descendants. Sephardi has come to refer to Jews from Moslem countries as well. Another term used to describe these Jews is "Oriental". A better one would be "Afro-Asian".

Ashkenazi Jews are those whose roots are in Northern and Eastern Europe. The cultural separation and increasing amalgamation between Ashkenazim (the plural of Ashkenazi) and Sephardim is an important Israeli dynamic. Centuries of separation have created political and social conflict. Amalgamation is producing understanding, an equalization of opportunity and, in the case of "inter-marriage", the "new" Israeli.

Add to these, Jews who can't be pigeonholed, like those from India, Ethiopia or South America. A Jew from Colombia has a Hispanic culture, but what if his parents came from the Soviet Union? How would a census taker classify him? A peculiarity of Israeli attitudes is that any Jew whose native language is English is referred to as "an Anglo-Saxon", even though that person's family emigrated to an English-speaking country from Minsk and that to an American Jew, "Anglo-Saxons" were the people he perceives as wanting to keep his family out. Now, by a twist of perceptions, he's stuck with that label!

Besides the ethnic classifications, Jews also fall into religious divisions. This consideration is important in Jerusalem which has a growing population that is highly observant religiously. While neighborhoods often have their ethnic cast, they also lean toward degrees of religious observance.

The range of observance is wide. It goes from Jerusalemites who disparage any form of organized religion to the ultra-Orthodox who are so adherent to the printed word of the Jewish Bible and their interpretation of it that they don't even recognize the existence of the nation of Israel.

Another religious element to be reckoned with is the existence of Hasidic "courts". Spiritually, Hasids are the descendants of an alternative form of Judaism that sprang up in Eastern Europe in the 1700s. They gather around a leader, forming a "court". Usually, leadership is passed on from father to son, forming a dynasty. Many Hasidic courts exist, each with its own leadership. Among Hasidic courts are those that are tolerant of less observant Jews and those that demand total conformity. Hasids add yet another level of interplay between religious beliefs.

But for Bureaucracy

The edges of Jerusalem's mosaic become rough now and then and scrape against each other. Sometimes it seems as if differences that exist in the city's population have their greatest opportunity to be played out in the realm of the bureaucracy. Descriptions of dealings with Israeli bureaucrats often sound like battle communiques, and on occasion you may feel as if you are facing the guns.

Dealing with a bureaucracy is especially difficult for foreigners. But dealing with business matters in a foreign country is no simple matter, whatever the country. I lived illegally in Paris almost an entire year. Getting my identity card turned into an endless wait in line. I simply gave up.

We forget that things are easy at home because we know the language and our way around (although a New Yorker who has tried to deal with City Hall would dispute that statement). Amazing as it may seem to Americans, foreigners complain that they find the United States confusing and frustrating.

We, as visitors, don't know the way things work in Israel. Added to that is Israel's overlay of Turkish, British, Israeli and sheer Levantine custom. And, yes, things don't necessarily go smoothly even for the knowledgeable. After all, a low-level functionary, especially, may feel powerful only when he's on the job. He may need to demonstrate that power.

It is best to look on life's occasional hassles in Jerusalem as a drama to watch, a Near-Asian game to observe. Don't sweat them; consider them a quaint local custom (which they are). Remember, a smile to the functionary who stands in your way will go further than a shout.

On the other hand, there are spontaneous demonstrations of warmth and hospitality that can make life in the Golden City buoyant and easy.

So, keep your sense of humor. Learn the Arab word, *"Inshallah"*, which means, roughly, "Trust in fate", and the Hebrew expression, *"Ma l'assot?"* With its usually accompanying helpless flap of the hands, the latter means literally, "What to do?" but really says, "There's nothing you can do about it, so forget it."

Have handy in your Hebrew repertoire, *"B'vakasha"* (Please), *"Todah"* (Thanks) and *"S'lee-cha"* (Excuse me).

Above all, face Jerusalem as if you were embarking on a grand adventure. You are. It may be the greatest of your life.

JERUSALEM SCENE:

Uli, a handsome, wiry, darkskinned sabra of Yemenite descent, has unlimited enthusiasm for Israel.

"I was in Europe for three months," says the 25-year-old native Jerusalemite. "When I came back, I kissed the ground. There is no place else for me."

He even talks about his army unit with great affection. Serving with it is an honor, he says, not a task.

But one year when he was called for his annual return to his unit, he had a troubling dream a few nights before he was to report to duty. In his dream, he was sent home from performing his military service with no feet. He was greatly worried. Was the dream an omen, perhaps?

He told his commanding officer about the dream and asked if he could postpone his return. In another country, Uli would have been laughed at or locked up. Probably both. In Israel, his commander reflected a moment and then said, "All right. Come back later."

Time

Time in Jerusalem, "the navel of the world", is treated differently than in any other city. First of all, let's examine the week.

There's good news and bad news in the Israeli week. Bad news first, and that is the weekend lasts only one day. Shabbat, equivalent to our Saturday, is all there is to the weekend. Sunday is business as usual. But since stores and businesses close by mid-afternoon on Fridays, Israelis stretch the weekend to one-and-a-half days.

Of course, if you are a tourist, you shouldn't worry — every day is a weekend. And with Jerusalem's stores locked up tight for Shabbat, there is one less day to spend money in gift shops (unless you go to East Jerusalem or the Arab section of the Old City where you can shop on Saturday).

Keep in mind that with three strong religions in Jerusalem, from Friday through Sunday is somebody's day of rest. Moslems close shop Friday, Jews Saturday and Christians — Arab, Greek, Armenian, Syrian and others — on Sunday.

The six-day business week can mean good news, however, for people staying in Jerusalem a while. Since our Sunday is a regular business day in Israel, it can be looked on as a bonus in which to get time-consuming bureaucratic matters out of the way. An errand to the bank or a government office could kill a morning. So, since it is possible to start your business or pleasure on Sunday, when Monday rolls around you are entitled to feel as if you have gained a day, and so the week stretches ahead generously.

But shopping and other business matters have to be planned to accommodate afternoon closings during the week. In addition to everyone in Jewish Jerusalem calling it quits early on Friday afternoon, each business has its day to be closed at least one other afternoon a week. (See "Shop Warn" in Chapter 7.)

While all these openings and closings may seem convoluted and Levantine, Israelis are totally practical when it comes to names of the days of the week. Except for Saturday, which simply is Shabbat, the rest of the days are numbered in Hebrew. Sunday is "first day", Monday is "second day", Tuesday is "third day" and so forth. But most shop owners use the English names of the days when they deal with tourists.

Another practicality of life in this part of the world is the afternoon siesta. The workday starts early, but most businesses close around 12:30 p.m. and reopen at 3:30 or 4 p.m. Big supermarkets, department stores, shopping malls and a few other places are exceptions to this tradition.

Recently, city government has been trying to put the squeeze on local custom and convince business people to keep their doors open straight through the day. So far, most working people have insisted that this is the Middle East, not Chicago, and they will hang on to their siesta.

Anybody who can, takes a nap. Avoid calling people between 1 and 4 p.m. You might awaken a snoozer, which isn't nice to do.

Places

To find your way around Jerusalem, one of your first acquisitions should be a good street map. But locating a street on a map doesn't solve the problem of finding such a street in the real world.

A former *Time* magazine bureau chief used to complain that with all the buildings constructed of Jerusalem stone, every corner looks alike. He never could tell where he was. "The buildings want to be incognito," he insisted.

Making matters worse is that street signs rarely stand on street corners. Instead, they usually are blue and white plaques, written in Hebrew, Arabic and English, found on the sides of buildings. (Some of the big boulevards have lighted street signs, but these are rare exceptions.) Often, shrubbery has grown up in front of these plaques. Occasionally, they aren't to be found at all. You will feel like a detective searching for them. With only your map to guide you, you will have to make an assumption or ask for help from a passerby.

With a street located, the matter of an address can be another mystery. Numbers appear on little squares somewhere on a building's facade or gate. In business areas, one number will serve for several establishments.

One source of help in locating addresses, at least on a map, is the Government Tourist Office at Rehov King George 24.

Terrorism

Inevitably whenever I am preparing to go to Israel and I mention my plan to friends, they respond first with silence. Then their eyes get big, and finally they pop the question, "Aren't you afraid?"

My first indignant reaction is to compare Israel with other places in the world and the current disasters striking them. "Is Jerusalem being bombed almost daily like Paris? Are drivers on the highways afraid someone will shoot them — and for no apparent reason, as in Los Angeles?" Or, I ask, "Can women walk alone at night in your home city?"

I find that statistics provide perspective. Considering the worst — murder — a recent year's figures showed eight murder victims per 100,000 in the United States and .02 per 100,000 in all of Israel, including deaths caused by terrorism.

In 1986, Jerusalem had a total of 16 murders in a population of more than 400,000 Arabs and Jews who often are angry with each other. Four of those deaths were from terrorism. Add to the resident population, the hundreds of thousands of tourists and temporary residents who swell Jerusalem's population, but aren't included in a census, and the number of terrorism victims becomes even smaller.

The thing that is out of proportion is the headlines a terrorist murder in Israel makes worldwide. The same applies to disturbances on the West Bank. These distort our perspective on Israel. Israelis complain over and over: "Americans, especially, don't realize what a peaceful country this is."

But what about a man or a woman alone? How safe is that person? Infinitely safer than in the United States. I can walk alone at night in West Jerusalem with considerable confidence —- but I always stay alert to my surroundings. Purse snatchers are notorious around the King David and Sheraton Jerusalem Plaza hotels.

Arab East Jerusalem is another story. As early as 9 p.m., I feel uncomfortable there. In contrast to Jewish West Jerusalem, practically no one is on the streets after dark. The same is true of the Old City. I try to leave the Moslem Quarter before the shops close. Even the Jewish Quarter becomes spooky to me at night.

Day or night, it is risky for a woman to go with anyone who presents himself as a guide and offers to take her sightseeing. Rapes have resulted from these offers. *Bona fide* guides have official credentials, and they don't materialize out of nowhere.

Hitchhiking (called here *tremping*) is a common form of transportation throughout Israel. (*Tremping* technique is explained in Chapter 4, "Getting Around.") *Tremping* isn't considered as safe as it used to be. *Trempers* have been raped and murdered. But there are times, such as when buses have stopped running, when *tremping* is the only way of reaching your destination. Try to avoid getting into that situation, but if *tremp* you must, be cautious. Women shouldn't *tremp* alone.

Despite these precautions, Israel, basically, is a peaceful country, just as the natives say. Absent is the general violence that has come to haunt women's lives in the United States. For that reason, being in Israel can be a glorious, liberating experience for a woman.

Jerusalem —
The Fashion Center of Nowhere

Not long ago, the *Jerusalem Post* carried an article quoting an Israeli businessman who was temporarily living in the United States. He complained that only a few of his countrymen who came to North America on business "know the rules of the game".

"These rules," he continued, "include dressing smartly, wearing shoes and socks — not open sandals, wearing a necktie with a jacket — not a short-sleeved open shirt, and so on."

That says a lot about the way Israelis dress. Tel Avivians may be a bit more stylish than other Israelis, but rest assured, Jerusalem decidedly isn't the town for fashion mavens. As an American doctor's wife from Albuquerque commented after living in the capital for a year while her husband worked at Hadassah Hospital, "You never can be too underdressed in Jerusalem."

But frankly, my dear, it's a relief. What to wear — except to meet a few religious requirements — isn't a question to take up much of anybody's time in Jerusalem.

As for those religious requirements, they are for men: a head covering in synagogues. And that's about it. What else a man wears there — shorts, jeans — doesn't matter.

For women: "modest" dress in ultra-Orthodox neighborhoods, which usually means upper arms covered and no slacks. Shorts? Don't dream of it. Pay attention to those signs that warn women about proper dress. The people who put them up mean it — and can get mean about it. In churches, women will be no more welcome — but with fewer spitballs — if they have bare shoulders or wear shorts.

Listen carefully to Liz' story about her walk that morning through ultra-Orthodox Mea She'arim which she enthusiastically reported to her Israeli friend, Batya.

"Everyone was getting ready for Shabbat," she said. "Everyone seemed excited. The food stalls had crowds of people around them. Dead chickens were piled on carts. A lot of men in black coats were pushing their children in strollers or carrying their babies in their arms. That was sweet.

"Some of the men already were dressed for Shabbat. They wore white knee socks. Some had black and gold striped robes and wide, black beaver hats. The little boys were looking spiffy in their best clothes. When they walked, their sidelocks bounced like corkscrews.

"I tell you, it was a colorful scene. I thought I was in a Russian village 100 years ago."

Batya smiled. "I'm glad you had a good visit. How were you dressed?"

Liz looked at her wide-eyed. "The way I am now — pants and a T-shirt."

Batya looked stricken. "Don't you know you shouldn't go into that neighborhood like that? That you should wear a skirt and have your elbows covered? That something could have happened?"

Liz laughed. "That's a lot of nonsense. I had no problem with the way I dressed. No problem whatsoever. The only thing that was unusual was funny. As I walked along, a housewife upstairs dumped her bucket of scrub water onto the street, and it landed on me. But nothing happened otherwise."

"I see," Batya responded, knowingly.

Outside of the dress requirements in ultra-Orthodox neighborhoods, anything goes — within common standards of propriety, of course. The basic informality of the country and high clothing costs keep people from getting gussied up. So when choosing clothes to bring to Jerusalem, keep them simple, sturdy and washable. Dry cleaning is enormously expensive.

All this isn't to say that Jerusalemites don't have their own style. Among men, influences of country of origin are strong. If he's Israeli and wearing a suit and tie (something of an oddity here), you almost can bet that he comes from a German or English-speaking country (but not North America). You aren't likely to see a young male sabra dressed like that, unless he's at his own wedding, and probably not even then.

Tie manufacturers love Israel about as much as bathing suit makers love Siberia. A man may go anywhere in Israel without a tie. Even Hasidic men, who wear long black coats whether the temperature is 45 or 95 degrees Fahrenheit, leave their shirt collars open. If the foremost Jerusalemite, perpetual Mayor Teddy Kollek, doesn't deign to wrap a tie around his bull neck, why should anyone else? True, recent prime ministers and presidents have been seen in public dressed like members of the international diplomatic fraternity, but they probably adopted the uniform because the foreign press was going to take their picture.

The moment the weather warms, men are in their beloved sandals, short-sleeved shirts and shorts. Even businessmen, lugging their briefcase to the office, dress like that.

As for blue jeans, they are ubiquitous most of the year, except when the temperature gets very hot.

Women in Jerusalem's informal life dress with improvised verve. The variety of what you see is endless: ankle-length skirts, fluttery dresses of Indian cotton (great in hot weather), capes and big, colorful scarves draped in various ways around the neck. I know a young woman who wore to work a street-length black academic gown over a bright red skirt and blouse. This imaginative outfit looked great on her and was typical of Jerusalem women's ingenuity.

Most women are as liberated as the men when warm weather arrives. At the earliest possibility, off come the panty hose — even among the varicose-veins set. Bare legs are socially acceptable in the best (but not the most religious) circles. Women who are strictly observant wear hose, no matter how high the temperature.

Local women are at ease tottering on high heels across Jerusalem's bumpy sidewalks, but for a visitor with limited suitcase space, it's more important to have good walking shoes for city and country, than fancy footwear. It's easy to get along without the latter, but feet will revolt without the former.

Warning: as strange as it may seem, anyone expecting to be in Jerusalem in the winter should prepare for cold weather. When it rains, it rains icy torrents, and it can rain incessantly from November to April. Snow even descends occasionally, turning the Golden City white. And since central heating is rare and there are few places to get warm, you feel the cold deep in your bones.

So for winter, arm yourself with an umbrella, waterproof boots, a parka and/or a warm coat (an all-weather coat with a zip-in lining should get you by), heavy socks and sweaters, wool or corduroy slacks, gloves and a hat. (See "What to Bring" in the Appendix.)

The Dome of the Rock stands on Mount Moriah, The Temple Mount. Here Abraham had prepared to sacrifice Isaac, Solomon built his Temple and Jesus amazed the rabbis.

Chapter 3:
The Jerusalem Saga

History and the Bible are under your feet, in front of your eyes and even become part of your conversation in Jerusalem. You walk the route Jesus is said to have walked as he carried the cross to his death. You see the slopes of the city King David built. You talk about going to a *bar mitvah* at "the Wall" — the last remnant of the Second Temple.

Even the names of the streets evoke the mosaic of Jewish history — its tumultuous times (Rehov Hapalmach, Rehov Kaf Tet be-November), great leaders (Rehov Bar Kochba, Sderot Herzl), learned men (Rehov Harav Kook, Rehov Ibn Gabirol) and important women (Rehov Hannah, Rehov Rahel Immenu).

Jerusalem has been a city for 4000 years — maybe even longer than that. Archeology keeps surprising us with new information. Jerusalem already was 1000 years old by the time "upstart" Rome, which got the title "the Eternal City", was founded.

The first known residents of what was to become Jerusalem were Canaanites known as Jebusites. For 3000 years, since King David conquered the city from the Jebusites and bought a threshing floor from Araunah the Jebusite to use for an altar for the Holy Ark of the Covenant, Jerusalem has been not only a city, but a spiritual home. First for Jews, then Christians and Moslems.

Even an abbreviated account of Jerusalem history must be lengthy.

But you will hear the high points referred to repeatedly during your stay. You will need a handy reference. The following touches on landmark events:

First Temple Period

960 B.C.E. — After King David started Jerusalem on its path to its future worldwide status, his son, King Solomon, began an ambitious building program with the First Temple. But 38 years later, the Egyptians plundered the city.

922 B.C.E. to 586 B.C.E. — Invading Egyptians were followed by the Assyrians and their king, Sennacherib, who were followed in turn by the Babylonians and their king, Nebuchadnezzar. Nebuchadnezzar not only destroyed the city in 587 B.C.E., but the Temple, as well and carried away most of Jerusalem's inhabitants to captivity in Babylon.

Second Temple Period

515 B.C.E. — In the rising, sinking tide of rulers' fortunes, Cyrus of Persia rode the next wave. He conquered Babylon, sent the Jews home and allowed them to rebuild their Temple. It was completed in 515 B.C.E., but the land was a province of Persia.

332 B.C.E. — The benign Alexander the Great arrived on the scene. Those who succeeded him, Ptolemy of Egypt and Antiochus III of the Hellenist Syrian Seleucid dynasty, were far less tolerant.

170 B.C.E.—Antiochus IV Epiphanes entered the city. His desecration of the Temple and forced pagan ceremonies inspired a revolt led by the Maccabee family.

164 B.C.E.—Judah Maccabee took Jerusalem, cleansed the Temple (an event celebrated by Chanukah) and commenced a century in which Jews were sovereign again in their own country.

63 B.C.E.—With the Roman occupation, Jewish self-rule disappeared for almost 2000 years.

Pompey tore down the city's walls and fortifications. In the name of Rome, Herod the Great ruled. A big spender, he rebuilt Jerusalem entirely and turned it into the greatest city of the Middle East. He even refurbished the Temple.

33 C.E.—Jesus, who like all Jews made pilgrimages to Jerusalem, came to the city for the Passover pilgrimage. It was then that the Roman Procurator, Pontius Pilate, had Jesus crucified.

66 C.E.—Jews began a revolt against Roman rule.

70 C.E.—Titus crushed the revolt, destroyed the Second Temple, exiled Jews from Jerusalem and took many to Rome as captives.

Roman Period

132 C.E.—Bar Kochba, a Jew, led another revolt, but Hadrian, the Spanish-born Roman emperor, triumphed. He plowed the city over, turned it into a Roman garrison town and changed its name to Aelia Capitolina. On the Temple Mount, he erected a temple to Jupiter and a statue to himself. To further obliterate Jewish history, Hadrian renamed the land, "Syria Palestina", or "Palestine" for the Philistines, a non-indigenous Mediterranean people who have faded into history. Hadrian forbade Jews to live in the city on penalty of death. For the next 2000 years, Jews were allowed back in, banished again, over and over according to the whims of foreign rulers.

The Roman conquerors laid out their new Aelia Capitolina like a Roman colonial city with two main streets at right angles to each other. The *Cardo Maximus* (north-south) began at what today is Damascus Gate; the *Decumanus* (east-west) from Jaffa Gate. Both can be seen today.

240 C.E.—The Roman Tenth Legion, which had been stationed in Jerusalem since the year 70, was replaced by Moors loyal to Rome.

Byzantine Period

324 C.E.—Jerusalem had become the focal point of the ever-expanding Christian faith, and in that year, Queen Helena, the mother of the Byzantine emperor Constantine the Great, traveled to the city. She identified what she believed to be holy sites, determined the place of the crucifixion and ordered churches built over them.

614 C.E.—The Persians destroyed many lives and churches when they reconquered Jerusalem.

Moslem Period

638 C.E.—Arabs, belonging to the new Islamic religion and led by the Caliph Omar, became the newest rulers.

The Dome of the Rock was completed in 697 to commemorate the spot from which Islamic legend says the Prophet Mohammed was carried on his winged horse to visit Allah in heaven. Some Jews maintain that the Dome of the Rock is on the location of the Temple. The nearby Mosque of Al-Aqsa was built at the beginning of the 8th century for prayer. Both were intended to keep Moslems loyal to the Umayyads based in Damascus from being lured to Mecca and falling under the sway of opposing Moslem sects.

During the next 400 years, Jerusalem went from the jurisdiction of the Damascus-based Umayyad Caliphate to the Baghdad-based Abbasids, to the Fatimids of Egypt and to the Seljuk Turks.

1071 C.E.—The Turks banned Christian pilgrims, thus setting the stage for the Crusades.

Crusader Period

1099 C.E.—Europeans rallied to recapture Jerusalem and the Holy Land from the Moslems and sent military expeditions on a religious crusade to the Middle East. Carrying the standard for Christianity, Godfrey de Bouillon captured Jerusalem, slaughtered Jews and Moslems alike and forbade their settlement in the city.

1187 C.E.—Under Sultan Saladin, the Moslems recaptured the city, allowing Jews back in.

Mameluke Period

1250 C.E.to 1517 C.E.—Jerusalem was ruled by the Egyptian Mamelukes, slaves who became kings. They, in turn, were replaced by the Turks of the Ottoman Empire.

A colorful mosaic landing on the stairway of a house in the Talbia neighborhood.

Ottoman Period

1537 C.E.—Sultan Suleiman the Magnificent rebuilt the walls and gates of Jerusalem. Except for a short time in the 1830s, when Mohammed Ali of Egypt ruled, the Ottoman Empire remained in power until 1917.

1850 C.E. to 1900 C.E.—In the last half of the 19th century, the Ottoman Turks allowed Christian churches to be built in and around the Old City.

1860 C.E.—During this same period in which the Turks cautiously opened doors to Jerusalem, Sir Moses Montefiore administered the construction of Mishkenot Sha'ananim, which he hoped would be the first Jewish settlement outside the city's walls. It didn't take. The first successful neighborhood outside the walls was Mahane Yisrael, on Rehov Hess off Rehov King David, near Rehov Agron. It was built in 1868 for immigrants from North Africa.

A year later, Nahalat Shiva was established off Rehov Yafo, guided by the driving spirit of Yosef Rivlin. This was the first new neighborhood built outside the walls for and by Jerusalemites themselves, and often is counted as the first neighborhood, period.

British Mandate Period

1917—The Ottoman Turks, having made the mistake of being on the losing side—the German side— in the First World War, were replaced by the British. British General Edmund Allenby led his triumphant troops into Jerusalem on behalf of his country. The period of the British mandate began.

The British brought stability that hadn't existed during the last years of the crumbling Turkish empire, a period made even worse by terrible hardships for the people during World War I. Also improving things after 1917, Jewish efforts in farming and commerce brought prosperity that had been absent for thousands of years.

The combination attracted immigrants — not only Jews, but Arabs as well. While Jews had been the majority in Jerusalem since 1864, British census figures show that between 1922 and 1931 the city's population grew by more than 20,000 Jews and 21,000 Christian and Moslem Arabs, most coming from abroad.

1931 to 1939—Jerusalem's population increased by 26,000 Jews, most of them refugees from Germany and Poland, and 15,000 Arabs, primarily from Syria and Jordan.

But the influx of Jews sparked a series of Arab riots in 1920, 1929, 1936, 1938 and 1939. While heavier casualties were inflicted elsewhere, Jerusalem didn't escape. Forty-four Jews were killed during the riots and 4000 had to leave their homes in 1929 alone. In 1937 and 1938, Jewish extremists retaliated and killed 25 Arabs.

May 1939—Despite the approach of World War II and the rise of Naziism, the British restricted Jewish immigration to a maximum of 75,000 annually and gave the Arabs a veto on all Jewish immigration after 1945.

With World War II and the Holocaust against the Jewish people ended, underground Jewish armies, with much of their leadership in Jerusalem, carried out armed resistance to British rule and Britain's continued limitation of Jewish immigration.

1947—The United Nations voted to partition Palestine into Jewish and Arab sectors and place Jerusalem under international administration for ten years.

Independence

1948—The British Mandate ended May 14. On May 15 (the fifth of Iyar in the year of 5708, according to the Jewish calendar) Jews declared their portion of the partitioned land to be the independent nation of Israel. Immediately, five Arab countries invaded. Jerusalem was under siege. Battles took place in the city and when they ended, Jerusalem was cut in two. The Old City—the Western Wall, itself—and eastern neighborhoods were occupied by Jordan and forbidden to Jews. The western and some southern areas went to Israel.

1949—Despite the city's split, Prime Minister David Ben-Gurion declared it the Israeli capital.

Living in the city during those years was risky business. Jordanian soldiers took potshots across the valleys and streets. The lives of West Jerusalemites who lived close to the dividing line were in constant danger.

June 1967—In the lightning Six-Day War, which began June 5 (26th of Iyar), Israel, after bloody battles, captured the Old City and the rest of Jerusalem. With peace, one of the world's great traffic jams occurred in the city as old-time Jewish West Jerusalemites and old-time Arab East Jerusalemites headed out to visit each other after so many years of being kept apart.

Under Israeli rule, Jerusalem's religious sites were opened to all. Later, the areas previously occupied by Jordan were annexed formally to make one unified city. For the first time since 63 B.C.E., all of Jerusalem was under Jewish jurisdiction.

The city blossomed. No longer was it a dead end for Jews and Arabs alike. New residents were attracted to it and the city grew with an unprecedented building boom. As of the mid-'80s, it is Israel's largest city.

No more a sleepy town in which the only things to do after 9 p.m. were to sit at a sidewalk cafe or go to a movie, Jerusalem is becoming a major cultural center. Renowned artists of the world appear here.

To balance that aspect, the city has developed a viable commercial life. Factories and businesses have become part of the economy.

Jerusalem may never again resemble the city of Herod with its grandeur and magnificent buildings. But its glory doesn't depend on architecture. Under foreign armies, the city's past has been bloody. Now, for the first time in thousands of years, Jerusalem's future depends on Jerusalem people themselves. If the city's patchwork-quilt population can hang together, Jerusalem will have a future in which its name, as the City of Peace, will be a reality. No building could rival that in glory.

Chapter 4:
Getting Around
(Public Transportation)

To get around town—and in and out of town—the bus system, named "Egged", works beautifully. It's inexpensive and buses run frequently. But before learning bus routes or schedules, every bus rider in Israel needs to know how to holler, "*RAY-guh!*" That's the Hebrew equivalent of "Hold it" or "Wait a second". Israelis shout "*Rayguh*" as they run down the street to catch a bus, as they board a bus, as they get off a bus and probably in their sleep.

With "*Rayguh*" ingrained on the subconscious, anyone who frequently travels the city on the Egged bus system would do well to buy a *cartesia*, a card that allows 25 rides for the cost of 20.

In exchange for your fare, the driver gives you a receipt, which you probably will shove into a pocket to join the stash of bus receipts already there. Annoying as it is, hang onto that little piece of paper so long as you are on that bus. Every so often, an inspector boards and goes down the aisle asking everyone to produce that shred. If you don't have yours, you may have to pay again.

In Israel, people still give up their bus seat to the elderly. And children tend to slide out of theirs for any grown-up. If you travel during going-to or coming-from school time, you may feel as if you have fallen into the proverbial can of worms when you see the bus packed with wriggling children. The kids, besides being adorable and speaking Hebrew better than you or I, appear to be harmless.

In reality, they can be lethal. Strapped to their backs are book bags. When the youngsters turn away from you, guard your eyes or ribs, whichever is closer to their portable People Whammer.

I may be the only person who couldn't figure out how to get off certain Jerusalem buses after I got on. But if there is someone else as easily baffled as I, the following should help: even I could spot the pull cords on older buses, but on new ones, I could find none. Still, I'd hear a ring and the bus would come to a halt. Luckily for me in my ignorance, there always was someone else getting off at my stop. I'm embarrassed to admit how many times I rode the bus before I realized that the black knobs on the vertical poles encase buttons to ring the bell.

The tourist publication "Your Jerusalem" carries a map of bus routes, which is fairly accurate. The publication is slow to catch up on route changes. "Your Jerusalem" may be found in hotels and the Government Tourist Information Office. The Egged numbers for route information are 523-456, 528-213, 528-232.

Remember, all Egged buses—interurban, too—stop running close to midnight daily and 4 p.m. on Fridays. They don't resume until Shabbat ends on Saturday. East Jerusalem buses are an exception to the hiatus.

Getting Around on Shabbat

If you must travel in Jerusalem on Shabbat, even without a car, it isn't impossible. **Rehavia Taxi**, Tel. 224-444, operates around the clock seven days a week. Call or hike to the nearest main street and flag down a taxi. They aren't infrequent, but they are up to 25 percent more expensive at this time.

City Taxis

Taxis in town are plentiful and not exorbitant. Call on the phone and they come to your door. Some company names and numbers: **David Hamelech**, 222-510; **Hapsigah**, 421-111; **Rehavia**, 224-444. Make sure the driver turns on the meter—it's a legal requirement. You can get a printed-out receipt if you ask.

Taxis go into their "Tariff 2" rate schedule after 9 p.m. and may be as much as 25 percent more than during the day. Watch for the number that appears on the meter.

No tip is expected, but it is customary for a single passenger to sit in the seat next to the driver. As Israelis love to tell you, "This is a democracy." But if you are a woman taking a taxi alone at night, you may want to reconsider your own democratic convictions. In early evening, I take the front seat. Later, I go by my instincts, as should you.

Interurban Transportation

To get to Ben-Gurion Airport at those awful pre-dawn hours at which travelers often are expected to check in, **Nesher**, Tel. 633-333, is the taxi company to call. It is the only one approved by the Airports Authority to operate the Jerusalem-Ben-Gurion run, and its fares (about $10 one way) are set by the Transport Ministry. A lot of things in Israel don't work efficiently, but Nesher does. To make an appointment to be picked up, call or stop by the office at Rehov King George 21.

Egged's interurban buses, too, are an excellent way of getting from here to there. They also run frequently to Ben-Gurion Airport. Tel Aviv buses leave the Central Bus Station on Rehov Yafo constantly. The No. 405 is express. As soon as one 405 fills up and pulls out, another takes its place. Returning to Jerusalem at night, the bus swings down Rehov Yafo, up Rehov Agron and through Rehavia. So if you live near that route, the bus from Tel Aviv could take you almost to your door. Egged's interurban buses, like their city buses in Jerusalem, don't run on Shabbat.

Egged Tours, Rehov Yafo 44a, Tel. 223-454, sells an "Israbus" pass available for seven, 14, 21 or 30 days, which allows unlimited travel during that time and offers discounts on Egged tours, restaurants and other enticements. Passes may be purchased at any Egged Tour office throughout the country.

Besides riding a bus between cities, you can take a *sherut*—a taxi shared by seven passengers. *Sheruts* run seven days a week. Usually, you can find one to your destination—assuming it is relatively major—near Kikar Yafo on Rehov Lunz or Rehov Harav Kook. Ask around. A *sherut* doesn't leave until it is full. Then it will travel as if the driver is trying to break the sound barrier. A *sherut* is more expensive than a bus, but your heart will ride in your mouth at no extra charge.

One of two East Jerusalem bus stations in the city is on Sultan Suleiman St., between Herod and Damascus Gates. From here, buses leaven for Hebron, Bethlehem, Mount of Olives, Jericho, Bethany and other Arab communities south and west of Jerusalem.

The other is on Nablus Road, about a block from the Old City, with service north to such places as Ramallah, the Jerusalem Airport at Atarot and Mount Scopus.

Then there is a train line from Jerusalem to Tel Aviv (actually Holon) and up to Haifa. A southern spur goes to Beersheba. While the train operated, it was a leisurely trip on dreadfully uncomfortable seats, but with spectacular views between Jerusalem and Tel Aviv. It was a ride anyone in Israel for any length of time should have made at least once, one way.

But the train has closed down for economic reasons. There is talk of reviving it and even speeding it up. If it is running, grab it. The railway station is at Kokar Remez in Abu Tor. Tel. 717-764. The first-choice means of travel by members of the military is hitchhiking, called in Israel, *"tremping"*. Other people do it, too, and occasionally it simply is the only way of getting around in the hinterlands. To *tremp*, the thumb stays out of it. The *tremping* position is with the right arm down and away from the body at about a 45-degree angle and the index finger extended, but relaxed, pointing more or less down.

Certain marked places on highways in the countryside are official pick-up places for *trempers*. Women should remember my earlier advice and not *tremp* alone.

Missile Toes:
Private Transportation

There is one feature of the Golden City about which I can offer little advice: that is how to walk on a Jerusalem sidewalk.

The fact is, it's easier to walk along Fifth Avenue in Manhattan during rush hour than it is to walk on a Jerusalem sidewalk with only yourself and one other person approaching you from the opposite direction. In Jerusalem, getting from one block to another requires complete concentration. Jerusalemites walk as if they are heat-guided missiles. Wherever you are, they find you. In the neighborhoods, it's tough enough to walk on the narrow sidewalks, since three-quarters of their width is taken up by garbage containers and cars. Out of necessity, people often walk in the streets, which can be so peaceful, dogs snooze in them.

But when there is heavy traffic and you have to be on the sidewalk, these human juggernauts roll. Inevitably, a pedestrian comes to a place wide enough for only one person. With somebody heading toward you, somebody is going to have to step aside. Invariably, when I am in that situation, that somebody is me. I have found myself leaping out of the way for men, women, children, dogs. I am the gentleman of Jerusalem—never mind my gender.

My backing down causes me plenty of head scratching. Is it me because I blink first?

Something even more baffling occurs on wide sidewalks devoid of garbage cans and cars. There, I often find that a pedestrian approaching from the opposite direction shifts his path and heads straight for me. It's as if I were a target.

Occasionally, I've firmly made up my mind not to be the one to give way. Then I've walked with my head down, one eye on the sidewalk, the other (because I'm a pessimist) checking the advancing troops. Do you think the sight of me with my head aimed at the pavement is any deterrent to human javelins? Not on your life. I've walked with my elbows stuck out like battering rams. But they are as intimidating to Jerusalemites as cooked noodles. The only thing that comes of that is sore elbows.

It's exhausting to have to concentrate intently on the process of walking while walking. I resigned myself to being Jerusalem's sidewalk *shlemiel*, when one evening, I managed to stop a human missile in mid-flight. And I may have inadvertently hit on a solution.

It was almost 7 p.m. Stores were closing and Jerusalemites were rushing home with the determination of a wolf pack on a rabbit. I was on my way to a meeting, and being hungry and having no time to stop and eat, I did what Israelis constantly do—ate on the run.

I bought a large, juicy slice of pizza topped with mushrooms. Holding the slice horizontally so the mushrooms wouldn't tumble onto the pavement and with cheese stringing between the crust and my teeth, I joined the uphill stream of people battling the downhill stream of people.

Sure enough, out of the crowd, heading straight for me, came a human heat-seeking missile. Closer and closer he hurtled. Pressed by the rush-hour mob, I couldn't jump out of the way. But suddenly, the man saw my sloppy feast, high enough and almost close enough to land on his white shirt. He halted, laughed—and then he moved out of my way.

So maybe that's the answer. The secret of keeping people from crashing into you on Jerusalem sidewalks: anti-ballistic pizza.

The meandering alleys and streets of the Old City of Jerusalem are in sharp contrast with the broad avenues of the New City.

Chapter 5:
A Place to Lay Your Head

For a temporary stay in the Golden City, no one needs this book to get the names of the big Jerusalem hotels. What major city almost anywhere in the world doesn't have a Hilton, Sheraton, Intercontinental and an imaginative Hyatt? And your travel agent can tell you about four-star hotels like Kings, Ariel and Moriah (pronounced here, "Mo-ree-AH"), and even good carriers of three stars like the Windmill and the Jerusalem Tower. For stays of a week or more, excellent rates may be nabbed before or after the summer at all the above hotels.

But anyone willing to step farther afield can practice greater frugality by searching out less pricey alternatives. Among them are Arab-owned hotels in East Jerusalem, which are almost always less expensive than their West Jerusalem equivalents in stars. But it can be lonely walking to and from them at night.

You can be assured of reasonable comfort at any East or West Jerusalem three-star hotel. But those with fewer than three stars should be checked out beforehand with your own eyes (and nose and ears, I might add). You can never be certain what you'll find.

Here are some places to consider:

The YMCA in West Jerusalem at Rehov King David 26, Tel. 223-433, is a safe bet. The "Y" and most hotels include breakfast in their price. East Jerusalem has its YMCA, too, at Nablus Road 29, Tel. 282-375, and a YWCA in Wadi el Joz, Tel. 282-593, but they are not as conveniently located as most West Jerusalem hotels. For that matter, however, the West Jerusalem "Y" is in the heart of the city's purse-snatching area.

Apartotel, Rehov Yafo 214, Tel. 531-221, and **Homotel** (office is at Rehov Ben Sira 3, Tel. 225-062) combine the convenience of apartments and hotels. Both have kitchens. Several Homotel establishments are sprinkled throughout Jerusalem. Among its services, the manager will locate a baby sitter if needed. Homotel has an American office at 1170 Broadway, Suite 612, New York, N.Y., 10001, Tel. (212) 686-9344.

Israel Bed and Breakfast LTD., Tel. 817-001, guarantees you breakfast and the chance to meet the locals. The price of rooms can vary considerably, depending on their elegance. They start at $22 for a single with a 20 percent discount for stays of more than two weeks. Write well in advance to Judy Goldman, who heads the company, at P.O.B. 24119, Jerusalem 91-240.

Christian hospices are among the least expensive places to stay. The Ministry of Tourism, Tel. 240-141, has a list. Facilities can be spartan, but pristine dormitories or rooms large enough for families. Prices run from $8 for breakfast and a bed in what is described as "a cubicle" at the Ecce Homo Convent in the Old City, to $42 for full room and board at the Notre Dame of Jerusalem Center opposite the New Gate.

West Jerusalem has its share of **youth hostels** where prices go from $2.50 for a bed in a dorm (Amsterdam Hostel) to $12 for a single room (Geffen Hostel). Their names and addresses are **Amsterdam Hostel**, Rehov Metudela 4, Tel. 639-604; **Bernstein Youth Hostel**, Rehov Karen Hayesod 1, Tel. 228-286; **Edison Youth Hostel**, opposite the Edison Cinema, Tel. 232-133; **Geffen Hostel**, Rehov Havatzelet 4, Tel. 224-075; **King George Youth Hostel**, Rehov King George 15, Tel. 223-498. The **International Youth Hostel** at Rehov Ussishkin 35 has no phone. The newest in town is the 250-bed hostel at the **World Education Center for Progressive** (Reform) **Judaism** at Hebrew Union College on Rehov King David 13, Tel. 232-444. The hostels usually are packed in the summer.

Rooms for rent, usually let by widows in their apartments (called "flats" here), exist throughout West Jerusalem. They could offer the best price and the most personal treatment (possibly more personal treatment than you have in mind, since you could discover the quintessential Jewish mother). Often, these rooms are located through the grapevine. Plant its seeds early by telling everyone you know and meet in Jerusalem that you want to rent a room. It's surprising how many people will have heard of something that is available. A few rooms for rent are listed with the rental agency, **She'al**, Rehov King George 21.

Fresh produce arrives at a Rehov Agrippas falafel stand near Mahane Yehuda.

Chapter 6:
Travelers do not Live by Cordon Bleu Alone

What most people think of when they think of Jewish food is Eastern European food. Jewish food in Israel is Israeli Jewish food. The difference is as great as between a *matzo* ball and a *falafel* ball.

Cuisine

Israeli cuisine has gotten a bum rap. Tourists seem to expect gefilte fish and cheeseburgers here, and when they can't find them, they complain bitterly. Say, even a bagel as we know it is hard to come by in Israel. The average native knows nothing from corned beef and rye. This is the Middle East, not Lublin or Los Angeles.

Israeli cuisine still is evolving. It's like nothing back home, and yet a little bit of the whole world goes into the recipe.

Basically, this is the land of *houmus, tehina, pita, falafel, me'moola'im, shishlik, shwarma, kebabs, bourekas, hareef,* spicy peppers and a seemingly endless variety of olives. These are some of the elements of "*Mizrachi*" (Eastern) food indigenous to the Levant and its neighbors. It can be eaten in the local equivalent of a greasy spoon and in some of the finest restaurants.

Let's run past those foods again:

Houmus—chickpea sauce.

Tehina—sesame seed sauce

Pita (a Hebrew word) — round, flat bread often cut in half and stuffed with different kinds of food, especially falafel.

Falafel — round balls of fried ground chickpeas, also the name of a "sandwich" composed of layers of **falafel**, chopped raw vegetables, **houmus** and a dash of **hareef** (hot sauce) stuffed into a **pita** (another inexpensive meal in itself and eaten on the run).

Me'moola'ima—generic term for stuffed vegetables such as grape leaves, bell peppers, eggplant, *courgettes* (also called, "marrow"— a kind of squash), onion and so on filled with meat and/or rice and a myriad of spices.

Shishlik—barbecued meats.

Shwarma—meat thinly sliced off lamb barbecued on an upright spit.

Kebabs—ground, spicy meat shaped like fat sausages.

Bourekas — flaky pastry with a cheese or spinach filling.

Indeed, the stars of culinary glories shine in Jerusalem restaurants from the east and the countries Jews lived in from Morocco to Iraq. *Mizrachi* cuisine is only one mouth-watering example from that range.

Moroccan cuisine usually is considered the finest, because the French touch has given it delicacy. To be found in Moroccan restaurants are "cigars"—spiced meat, nuts, raisins and cinnamon in a thin crust and resembling its namesake, and *couscous*, a tasty stew with a semolina base.

Yemenite cooking includes a four-alarm soup heated up by *schug*, a sauce composed of hot peppers, garlic, cumin and coriander; *cubana*—a special Shabbat cake and that great delicacy, ram's penis (not to worry—not frequently found on restaurant menus).

Kurdis and Iraqis vie with each other for the reputation of making the tastiest *kubbeh* — meat encased in bulgar wheat and either boiled or fried.

Restaurants

Even as relatively small a city as Jerusalem has a variety of restaurants from which to choose. Food from around the world is available here. Yes, the gefilte-fish crowd who pine for the kind of food Grandma used to make—lungs, stuffed spleen (*miltz*) and jellied calf's feet (*pitchas*), not to mention goulash and chopped liver — can find what they are looking for. And so can corned-beef-on-rye and bagel lovers. But the taste won't necessarily be like back home. What are called "bagels" and sold at street stands are skinny and hard, resembling nothing with that name at Bagel Nosh.

Diners can choose from Indian, Iranian, Indonesian, Japanese, French, Italian, Argentine, American Southwestern and some ten Chinese restaurants. Then there are restaurants that feature natural foods, vegetarian dishes, soufflés or various kinds of pies.

Kubbeh, omelettes and falafel are the fare at this food stand.

Most of these places are kosher. Because of the dietary requirements of *kashrut*, sometimes a great deal of imagination has to go into preparing a particular dish at an international restaurant in order not to mix meat and dairy products. Out of this emerges a uniquely Israeli flavor. And out of this, also, vegetarians never had it so good eating out.

The biggest drawback to Jerusalem restaurants is the price. Eating out except for buying fast foods like *falafel* or pizza (improved considerably in Israel over the past few years) can set you back a chunk.

Breaking the piggy bank for a meal at Mishkenot Sha'ananim Restaurant near Yemin Moshe with its glorious view of the Old City (try it on a night with a full moon), as well as its food (a debatable subject in Jerusalem), is worth it at least once.

But with a broken piggybank, how do you afford lunch or dinner out? Ways of eating well and on the cheap do exist in Jerusalem. Almost any little *Mizrachi* restaurant has good food at reasonable prices. Don't be afraid to check them out. The following are some good, inexpensive (entrees around $5 or less, unless otherwise noted) restaurants that have, as a further distinction, little or no following among tourists. Remember, almost all West Jerusalem restaurants are closed on Shabbat. Among alternatives for people not concerned with *kashrut* are restaurants at the YWCA on Rehov King David and in East Jerusalem. Persons who adhere to Jewish dietary laws should inquire about paying in advance for Shabbat meals at hotels or check out **Me & Mi**, City Tower; **Jozi's Courtyard**, Rehov Emek Refaim 38, or the **Garden Restaurant**, Rehov King David 28.

Few Jerusalem restaurants require or even take reservations. But reservations are advised at the two most expensive restaurants in town, **Mishkenot Sha'ananim**, Tel. 221-042, and the **Cow on the Roof** in the Sheraton Jerusalem Plaza Hotel, Tel. 228-133.

Sima, Rehov Agrippas 82. A *Mizrachi* restaurant with one wall wide open to the elements even on the coldest day. You may have to stand in line, then climb over soldiers' Uzis, to reach an empty seat and be waited on by a wildly busy waiter who knows not one word of English, but is an expert on delivering grudging service. *Shishlik* with salad and chips (French fries) is superb. Mixed grill is the house specialty. The trick to keeping costs down here is to order half a portion of the meat dishes. Also on the menu (but somehow rarely available) is *shakshuka* (fried tomatoes, hot peppers and eggs). Also served are especially tasty *houmus* and *tehina*. Israelis come to Sima from far and wide.

Ima (Mother), where Rehov Agrippas meets Sderot Ben-Tzvi. The fare here is Kurdi, and the fried *kubbehs* are heavenly. Top them with a dollop of *houmus* or *tehina*. Other Ima lovers are equally devoted to the soft *kubbeh* cooked in sauce. The stuffed vegetables are to rave over, and so is the eggplant in *tehina* salad. When you sit down, the waiter will put bowls of pickled cabbage and carrots, green pickles and pita on your table. Ima has been enlarged since I first got to know it. It no longer is the simple place it once was. May its food, however, never change.

Rama, Rehov Agrippas 34 (are you getting the idea that you can't starve on Rehov Agrippas?). Another *Mizrachi* place, and one that, like Sima, has become an institution to the faithful for its grilled meats. Its own variation of *Mizrachi* fare is its stuffed potatoes and okra in spicy tomato sauce. Rama also has a take-out (called in Jerusalem, "take away") counter.

Bavli, Rehov Hanevi'im 54. Only vegetarian and fish dishes here. You can point to your choices on the buffet line, and the waiter will bring you your order. You can sit inside in what resembles a train station or outside on the large terrace. You won't escape tourists here, for Bavli is located near the Maskit store and some tourist attractions. Blintzes can be exotic with nut and mushroom filling, instead of cheese in the usual Ashkenazi style. Among the stuffed vegetables may be artichoke hearts. Other items may be fish cakes, *baba ganouj* (eggplant and tehina) and apple salad. A drawback to Bavli is that the food can develop a tired taste from sitting on the steam table too long.

Pinat Hahoumus, Rehov King George and Rehov Hahistadrut.

You can't eat for much less in Jerusalem and be able to sit down, too, than at Pinat Hahoumus. With only four tables, the place usually is jammed and the service fast. Climb over diners and grab the first available chair. Cut tomatoes, hunks of onion and hot peppers along with two pitas are set in front of you as soon as you sit down. A pot of *schug* is on the table. For about $1, you can eat *houmus* with *ful* (a flat bean) and one *pita*. You'll feel satisfied and, pardon the pun, pleasantly full.

The following are a bit more expensive:

Poondak Hehalav, Rehov Bezalel 17. A dairy restaurant with a variety of crepes that are baked in a sauce. Ice cream desserts are touted here. This place has a terrace for outdoor dining.

Hatzarif, Rehov Horkenos 5. In English, Hatzarif often is called, "The Pie House" (not to be confused with "The Pie Shop", a very different establishment). Hatzarif not only isn't kosher, one of its offerings is ham pie. Almost all the dishes are some sort of pie—veal, prunes and nuts or chicken, almonds, raisins and cauliflower in a bechamel sauce, among them. For dessert: sweet pies. The ambience includes the sound of James Galway over the loud speaker, a fire on a cold night, a wall of glass that makes you feel you're sitting in a tree house and a balcony for eating outside.

Steakiat Hehatzer, Rehov Yafo 27. The stylishness of Hatzarif isn't to be found here, but a certificate of *kashrut* is. Besides steak, the *shishlik* is a great favorite. *Kebabs* are patty-shaped here, instead of the traditional sausage configuration, but the taste is the same.

Marvad Haksamin, Rehov King George 12, and **Ruchama**, Rehov Yavetz 3, off Rehov Yafo 49. Two Yemenite restaurants that feature traditional favorites—calf-foot and oxtail soup. Ruchama also specializes in a variety of dishes made with *melawach*, the Yemenite pancake.

Zionist Confederation House, Rehov Emile Botta. At the end of the street behind the King David Hotel, to the right and down some stairs, you find a restaurant that offers the same view of the Old City walls as Mishkenot Sha'ananim—at least at the small tables by the three windows—at a fraction of the price. At a fraction of the elegant atmosphere, too, but the place is pleasant and easygoing. The cuisine is dairy and fish, but the dishes have a sense of adventure, such as plum or carrot soup, asparagus quiche, fresh pears with goat cheese, and mango tarts.

Mamma Mia, Rehov Rabbi Akiva 18. This is a place to warm your heart and feet on a cold night. (But don't ignore it when the weather is warm and you can eat outdoors.) Rustic furniture, a roaring fire and piping hot dairy and vegetarian Italian dishes are among the attractions. And not only does the menu include canneloni, ravioli, gnocchi, lasagna and spaghetti, but cappuccino.

Poire Et Pomme, Khan Theater, Kikar Remez 2. Located upstairs, overlooking the courtyard in what once was a Turkish hostel, Poire et Pomme has a balcony for dining outside and a fireplace when cold weather determines dining should be inside. Served here is what locally is called "crepe", but for which you will have to forget everything you ever learned about French cooking. Israeli crepes are another breed. Smothered in cheese sauce, they are hearty and delicious. With a helping from the salad bar and bread basket, you've got a meal, but the owners are expanding the menu to include Italian dishes.

Arab restaurants of East Jerusalem can be a good buy and are open Fridays and Saturdays. Order the mezze and you will get a little bit of a lot of things, ordinarily as many as 10 hot and cold dishes. They are meant to be appetizers, but they do well for an entire meal. Some of the better-known Arab restaurants are the ones on the rooftop of the **National Palace Hotel** and the **Philadelphia**, both on Rehov Az-Zahara.

But let's face it, every so often a person does get hungry for the familiar foods from home. And it is nice to be able to appease those yearnings once in a while. **Yossel's**, two levels up at Rehov King George 16 (on the ground floor when entering from the street behind), has a decent hot dog, which is served in a bun harder than Wonder Bread Bakery makes. The hot dog may be buried under sauerkraut for those who want it "New York style". Yossel Rosenzweig, a Canadian from Windsor, Ontario, makes his restaurant's corned beef, but buys pastrami and salami from B'nei Brak. At about 9 p.m., he calls it quits from culinary matters and serenades his customers on the guitar with his original compositions. If he has nothing else to do, he reads Elmore Leonard mysteries.

For others, **MacDavid's** at Rehov King George 16 may be a kosher substitute for McDonald's.

My personal yearning in Jerusalem is for a bubbling-hot cheese enchilada, a good Margarita and blueberries. Only one "Mexican" (by which I mean, of course, Tex-Mex) restaurant exists in town.

Cactus, Rehov Keren Hayesod 36, isn't kosher, nor could it, when last visited, satisfy my yearning for a cheese enchilada. No such thing was on the menu. But the beef enchilada, while not totally authentic and a bit greasy, is acceptable. The price, however, is astronomical. The Israeli owner, who lived in California, said, "But you should know what they charge in New York." He should know how little they charge in Santa Fe. But the Margarita at Cactus is excellent. Cactus is open Friday nights.

As for blueberries, **Off The Square**, a dairy restaurant at Rehov

Yoel Solomon 6, has blueberry pie. But putting blueberries into pie is a great way to ruin them. A blueberry crisp would be far better or, talk of heaven, blueberries and sour cream. Also on the menu at Off the Square is pecan pie.

Everyone has his or her favorite place for *falafel*. And of course, I have mine, which I will share if you promise not to crowd me out of line. My favorite *falafel* is from **Falafel Shalom**, a genuine hole in the wall, slightly below sidewalk level next to the Urfali Synagogue on the corner of Rehov Bezalel and Rehov Evan Sappir.

The above is not a comprehensive restaurant list; only a mention of those that are easy on the budget or have other redeeming qualities. Give your check a hard look before you pay: service often is included.

As a word of caution, please remember that a restaurant's longevity is harder to predict than the weather. If you find that any of these places are eating dust instead of still serving food, let us know.

To track down those Indonesian, soufflé, Eastern European and other restaurants with tantalizing menus, pick up a copy of "This Week in Jerusalem" or "Your Jerusalem" in hotel lobbies or the Government Tourist Information Office. Most of them advertise there.

A last word: there is one Jerusalem dish which is named for the city, but which you are unlikely to find in any restaurant. It is Jerusalem kugel—a baked noodle pudding made with sugar and a lot of pepper and that has been cooked so long, it is almost black. It is served in some synagogues after Saturday morning services. Yeshivat Torah Chaim on El Wad in the Moslem Quarter of the Old City and Rananim next door to Hechal Shlomo are two likely synagogues in which to taste Jerusalem kugel. It's worth going to great lengths to taste the dish to which the city has given its name. After all, Proust had his *madeleines*; you could have your Jerusalem kugel.

But whatever or wherever you eat, as Israelis say before the first bite at a meal, "B'tayavon"—"Good appetite."

Garinim: Seeds of Israeli Culture

And wherever you go, there is one more food item of which you'll need to be in the know.

In 1930, the Ashkenazi writer Ya'acov Rabinowitz complained in "The Wanderings of Amasai" that every Shabbat, Sephardic Jews and Arabs come together "and fill their balconies with nutshells. They crack and crack. It is nauseating."

What Rabinowitz probably was referring to weren't nuts that were being cracked, but seeds—especially sunflower seeds. In Hebrew, sunflower seeds are called *garinim cham* or, usually, just plain *garinim.*

Time brings changes, and these days Arabs and Jews aren't getting together on Shabbat as much as they used to—much less to "crack nuts". But another such change time has brought is that, among present Israeli Jews, you don't have to be Sephardic to love sunflower seeds. Along with soccer, *garinim* chomping is a national mania.

Look on the pavement around a bus stop. You'll probably find it speckled with *garinim* shells. Walk into a movie theater and a sign in Hebrew will urge: "Please don't leave *garinim* shells on the floor."

It isn't the sound of the turtle dove one hears in the land of milk and honey, but the incessant chomping of *garinim.*

I know a young Israeli man who went to study in chilly, orderly Denmark. While an American away from home may pine for a good, greasy hamburger, Yuval was going out of his mind missing *garinim.* Then he made an exciting discovery: pet stores carry sunflower seeds for birds.

He rushed to satisfy his yearning, but when he saw the sunflower seeds in a store, he sadly shook his head. "They're so small," he exclaimed to the clerk.

"The birds don't mind," she blithely said.

Yuval agonized over whether or not to confess his mission, that he wanted larger sunflower seeds not for any bird, but for himself. Finally, he did. He was desperate. The Danish woman was astounded

David gives a lesson in how to eat garinim.

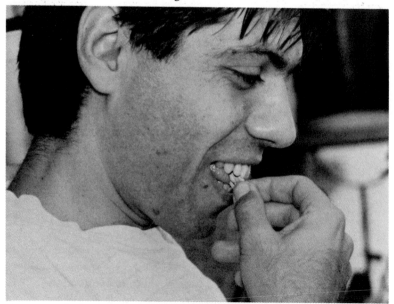

to encounter such bizarre tastes.

Sooner or later, a visitor to Israel will find himself in an Israeli home with everyone gathered around a bowl of *garinim*. Besides sunflower seeds, the bowl may contain pumpkin seeds and, if somebody splurged, pistachios, cashews, almonds (a fertility symbol), peanuts, hazel nuts, pecans and even Brazil nuts.

Everyone will be talking and digging non-stop into the bowl. Another bowl will be close by to catch the shells, but more shells may be on the rug and stuck to clothing than in the bowl.

With everyone lustily reaching for *garinim*, eventually, you'll do the same—and not be able to stop after you've had just one or even a dozen.

But you could be frustrated by the way the veteran *garinim* crackers around you go about their business. They are fast and efficient. You don't see them pulling shredded shells from their mouth and wondering where the seed went. You don't see them struggling to push smashed sunflower shells that stick like molasses off their wet fingers.

With these experts, you hear a neat crack or two of the shell between their teeth. Then you see them draw from between their lips a cleanly split shell. Their fingers aren't even damp.

How do they do it? I asked some experts. David, a sabra with Ashkenazi roots from Poland, told me his secret one Shabbat. ("That's the only day I have time for this," he said. And that may be the main difference between Ashkenazim and Sephardim: Sephardim always have time for *garinim*.)

David's method is to put the narrow end of the sunflower seed between his teeth, crack it gently—just so the shell separates, but not so it's been broken to shreds—and then, with his tongue, flip the seed into his mouth.

Shaya, whose grandparents came from Yemen and who can't watch his 21-inch color, remote-control TV without chomping *garinim*, insists one crack on the shell isn't enough. He says, "make two."

Whatever works.

A shopping lane in the Moslem Quarter of the Old City.

Chapter 7:
Shopping

Shop Warn

No word exists in Hebrew that is equivalent to the English word "shopping", which connotes a leisurely venture. Israelis go to "buy". They don't have time to "shop". For them, shopping is a serious business.

To meet your shopping and commercial needs in Jerusalem, all you have to remember is:

- Hairdressers and barbers are closed Monday afternoons.
- Grocery stores, pharmacies, hardware stores, laundries and dry cleaners are closed Tuesday afternoons.
- Some branch post offices and travel agencies are closed Wednesday afternoons.
- Banks are closed Monday, Wednesday and Friday afternoons.
- Just about every place except the big supermarkets and stores in self-contained shopping centers like Centre 1 is closed every day between 1 p.m. and 4 p.m. One supermarket, Super-Sol on Rehov Agron, has taken a big break from tradition and now is open until midnight Sundays through Thursdays.
- And almost everything in West Jerusalem closes by 3 p.m. Fridays and stays closed through Shabbat. That includes restaurants.

Got that schedule? In the Jewish Quarter of the Old City, the same schedule as in West Jerusalem is followed. In the Arab portion of the

Old City and in East Jerusalem, Moslem-owned shops are closed Fridays, and Christian-owned shops are closed Sundays.

With schedules like these, it may seem, on one hand, as if business places are always closed when you need them. On the other hand, it may seem as if it always is possible to go shopping somewhere.

Wherever you shop, whatever you buy, remember this basic rule: shop prudently. In general, the local law of return is that no refunds are given. The best you can expect is to make an exchange. The big department store, Hamashbir Lazarchan, is an exception, but here a customer has only seven days in which to make a return.

One final warning, as the following story so clearly shows, what you see is not necessarily what you get.

"Ah, just what I was looking for," Wolff said to himself when he spotted a tiny shop that had watches and clocks jampacked in its window.

Wolff, an American from New Mexico, was in Jerusalem and on the staff at Hadassah Medical Center for a year. His watch needed fixing, and he finally had found, he thought, a watch repair shop.

He entered the shop which was no bigger than a closet.

"I'd like to have my watch fixed," he told an elderly man who appeared to be the proprietor.

"I don't fix watches," the man said.

"You don't fix watches?" Wolff asked, surprised. "What do you do?"

"I am a *mohel*," the man answered. He performed Jewish ritual circumcisions.

Wolff chuckled over his mistake, but he asked, "Then why do you have all those watches in the window?"

With a slight smile and a shrug, the man said, "What else should I put in the window?"

Bargaining Daze in the Amazing Maze

By now, you realize that shopping in Jerusalem takes more than money. It takes time. And nowhere is this as true as in the Old City, specifically the shopping area, the *souk*, in the jumbled, dimly lit maze of the Christian and Moslem Quarters.

There, the entire process of shopping and concluding a sale is as labyrinthian as the Old City itself.

Items on sale by any one store may be so numerous and varied, a novice shopper's natural tendency simply is to gawk at them. Displayed pell-mell inside and outside the shops are Bedouin dresses, sheepskin jackets, camel saddlebags, rugs, brass and copper items, jewelry, Hebron glass, baskets, pottery, T-shirts, Indian scarves and sheer junk.

And while your eyes have lost control, your ears are beset by hawking store keepers calling out their standard lines: "Come into my shop. I have something wonderful for you. Come into my shop. I can tell you are good luck for me today. Come into my shop—just to look—nothing else—just to look." You may practically be pulled bodily inside a shop. Once you are inside, the merchant's talk never ends. And for women shoppers, the pinching may begin.

Now you must have a will of iron to be able to walk out empty-handed. If you happen to be made of such stern stuff, know also that the merchant may shout epithets after you.

I try to be that firm. It doesn't always work. One Christmas morning, an Arab friend who owns a jewelry store saw me passing by and invited me in to drink tea with him and his red-haired cousin. Or so the invitation went. We compared our experiences in Bethlehem the night before, and the two young men complained of having hangovers. But the red-haired cousin wasn't so hungover he didn't have the presence of mind to show me a board on which several necklaces were displayed and to ask the leading question, "Which do you like?" Because of my personal connection with the store owner, I lost my nerve.

Instead of insisting I wasn't buying anything and heading for the door—and risking the cousin's claim that I had wounded his very soul—I babbled, "Oh, that one's nice—and so's that one, but I don't need another necklace and I can't afford to buy anything right now and I don't know anyone in the world I could give...." Never mind. The red-haired cousin added a pair of matching earrings to the first necklace I had pointed to, had them wrapped up and in my lap and his hand out for payment, while I still was insisting I wasn't buying anything that morning.

So be tough. Do you think Old City merchants aren't? They share a major characteristic with diamonds (and I don't mean sparkle). No matter how soft these merchants appear to be, no matter how much poetry they may recite to you, nothing scratches them.

If you are looking for a specific item, go comparison shopping. Prices vary from one establishment to the next. I carry pencil and paper to jot down the asking price of what I see and where it is located, so I can remember and find my way back.

And when you determine what you want, a new game begins: Middle-East bargaining. It's said that the best price in the *souk* is for Arabs; the worst for American tourists. A variation has it that the worst price is for Israelis. That may be, but Israelis aren't timid about getting that price where it belongs.

The rule of the game is to never, never, accept the first price the merchant gives you. Nor the second. Nor even the third, unless it is considerably lower than the first. Your line, in response to the

*Baskets,
buckets and
maybe a bathtub
outside a household
goods store on
Rehov Agrippas.*

merchant's line is, "It's lovely, but I simply can't afford it." Do not insult his merchandize. He may ask, "What can you afford to pay?" You then come up with a figure well below what you are willing to pay. He will groan and say, "Impossible." You will groan and raise your offer a tiny bit. He will groan and bring his down. Eventually, you should meet. Remember, it *is* a game.

If you shop for Bedouin dresses or jackets, look them over carefully. Most are second-hand. They are desirable because they are old. But check that color discrepancies from one section of the dress to another are acceptable to you.

Don't let pickpockets ruin your shopping trip. All that jostling and bumping against you in crowded lanes won't be accidental.

If you need a respite from the hard-sell *souk*, find an Arab bakery on Khan Ez-Zeit Street. The honeyed pastries will soothe your nerves and sweeten your excursion.

The Better Things in Life Aren't Free

The most enjoyable things to shop for, let's face it, are those special gifts for yourself or others. And Jerusalem abounds with tempting, unusual items for sale.

You may find that eventually you will ask to be led through the Old City *souk* blindfolded to avoid squandering any more money.

That part of Jerusalem is one concentrated temptation.

West Jerusalem's lures are more spread out and offer a shopper a chance to catch his breath. I will mention some of them, but only those that sell Israeli-made products.

One of the most tantalizing, as well as pricey, is **Maskit** at Rehov Harav Kook 12. This establishment (which Ruth Dayan founded to preserve Israeli ethnic arts) carries just about everything from jewelry to linens to children's clothes to ladies' dresses with gorgeous Yemenite embroidery. Everything is handcrafted. To visit the first floor is like wandering through a gallery of modern art. Elizabeth Taylor shops here. She can afford it.

More accessible financially is the **WIZO Shop**, operated by the Women's International Zionist Organization, at Rehov Yafo 34. All proceeds for arts, crafts and clothing go to WIZO projects, which include day-care centers and care of disadvantaged children.

Another place where proceeds go to a worthy cause is **Lifeline for the Ages** showroom on Rehov Shivtei Yisrael. Murals, batiks and hand-crocheted items are among the stock.

Nearby is the newest center for Judaica art in Jerusalem on **Rehov Yohanan Migush Halav**, which runs from Kikar Zahal along the back of City Hall to the gates of the Russian compound. Woodwork, metal work, illuminated calligraphy and jewelry can be found here in combination studio-shops.

A similar but more upscale arrangement combining artists' studios and shops exists on **Khutzot Hayotzer**, a lane outside the Old City, below Jaffa Gate and at the base of Yemin Moshe. Several internationally known artists and crafts people are located here.

One of Jerusalem's newer establishments for the benefit of craft workers, is the **Alix de Rothschild Crafts Center** on Rehov Or Hahaim, next to the Old Yishuv Court Museum in the Jewish Quarter of the Old City. The center provides a place for craftspeople to display their wares and for the public to purchase them without a middleman. It is open afternoons.

Friday mornings, **City Cellar** in the basement of City Tower is full of craftspeople selling their work. Among them is Reuven Prager, who has designed what he calls "Israeli garments for the modern Israeli man." They are hip-length tunics, inspired by Biblical clothes. Prager says they conform to all religious clothing requirements, so they make being observant a cool matter for men during the summer. Prager, an enterprising American, also rents wedding gear such as a crown for the bride to wear and a litter upon which she may be carried to the *chupah* (canopy), both according to Biblical specifications.

Some specialty shops not to be missed are:

Kuzari, in a wonderful old house, the Davidoff mansion, at Rehov David 10 (also called Rehov Habucharim) in the Bucharan Quarter. This is an embroidery workshop. Stitchery includes exact replicas and stylized versions of work done by Jews from Morocco to Buchara in Asian Russia. On sale are wall hangings, purses, ritual items such as *challah* covers and *tallit* bags and those wonderful high-rimmed embroidered caps that are identified with Bucharan men.

Modern and traditional side-by-side on Rehov Yafo.

Chen Jewelry, near Kuzari at Rehov Habucharim 9. Here silver "thread" has been worked into jewelry and religious objects by three generations of one family. It all began with the grandfather when he he came to Jerusalem from Kurdistan.

Jerusalem Pottery, 14 Via Dolorosa in the Old City, and **Palestinian Pottery,** 14 Nablus Road, across from the United States Consulate in East Jerusalem. These shops long have been the places to buy Armenian ceramic work. The owners used to be partners. Armenian ceramic tiles have special significance to Jerusalem, for street signs are made by Armenian craftsmen. The colors on these tiles give them their robust character, but it is the strong presence of cobalt blue in the design that declares the tiles' identity. Not only can decorative tiles of a variety of designs be bought, but also dishes, mugs, vases, ashtrays and nameplates for the door.

A recent addition to the Armenian pottery scene is **Hagop's Studio,** inside the Old City Armenian Quarter. Hagop Antreassian is trying to go back to basics and eliminate Arab, Turkish and Persian influences on Armenian art. As a result, he uses smaller, repeated patterns, and his work has a classic and, at the same time, more modern look.

JERUSALEM SCENE:

The scene was the ladies' room at Hamashbir Lazarchan, Jerusalem's largest department store, on a busy afternoon.

It was a full house. Three giggling girls, about nine or ten years old, came in and waited in line. Soon, an older American woman entered and got in line behind them.

In a New York accent, she asked the girls if all the stalls were occupied. They looked up at her with expressions mixing puzzlement and embarrassment.

"Don't you girls speak English?" the woman asked.

In response, she got a chorus of giggles as the girls exchanged looks that asked each other, what is she saying?

"What do you speak?" the woman persisted. "Yiddish?" She sounded hopeful. "Do you speak Yiddish?"

Silence. The giggles were absent as the girls tried to figure out how they could be polite to their elder when they hadn't the faintest idea what she was saying.

"No? Well, what language do you speak?" The tone of her voice was beginning to evince exasperation. "What about Spanish? Do you speak Spanish?"

The girls began to confer with each other.

"Oh," the woman exclaimed in amazement, as if she had discovered an oil gusher. "You're Israelis! You must speak Hebrew!"

Chapter 8:
Is There Life After Dark in Jerusalem?

You bet there is. Plenty goes on in Jerusalem at night, and I don't mean plenty of lectures on religion (though admittedly there are lots of those) or shopping at Super-Sol until midnight.

Reputations have a way of sticking like Velcro, even when they have been outlived. Tel Avivians, for example, still say they wouldn't dream of being trapped in Jerusalem at night. They are convinced, as one critic put it, that Jerusalem's night scene is "half the size of the New York City cemetery and twice as dead." But that was years ago. The unified city is learning to stay up at night and go out on the town. Since 1967, more and more events lure Jerusalemites out of their homes.

To relax after a hard day's walk, you can choose from a variety of events.

Classical Music

The Israel Philharmonic Orchestra, with world-famous conductors, performs ten times a season, approximately from October to May, in Jerusalem's Binyenei Ha'uma across the street from the Central Bus Station. Although tickets are hard to come by, you can almost always find people outside the theater just before a performance trying to sell tickets they can't use. It's worthwhile taking a chance on landing one or two.

Concerts by the **Jerusalem Symphony Orchestra** shouldn't be overlooked. Even without the allure of Zubin Mehta, some magnificent music can come from this smaller orchestra. It is gaining even greater stature now that it has its own home in Henry Crown Symphony Hall at the Jerusalem (Sherover) Theater at Rehov Marcus 20 in Talbia.

Chamber music exists in Jerusalem in abundance. Performances take place in several locations such as the Church of the Redeemer in the Old City and the Dormition Abbey on Mount Zion.

Dance

Dance concerts by the major Israeli dance companies, such as Bat-Dor and Inbal, usually are performed at the Jerusalem Theater.

Pop Concerts

Don't fail to attend Israeli pop concerts. You'll sink in amidst sabras and feel surrounded by Israeli life. The Israelis here are out to have a good time, and they do. When a song touches them, a surge of emotion sweeps through the crowd. You can feel it and be carried along on its wave, too. Listeners freely clap their hands with the music, one, two, three, four, clump, clump, clump, clump. Whether the attraction is Yehoram Gaon, Ophra Hazza, Jo Amir or the Hasidic Song Festival (where you aren't likely to find a genuine Hasid either among the spectators or performers), the audience is half the show.

Theater

While dance and music need no translation, going to the theater can seem forbidding to anyone less than fluent in Hebrew. Help exists. **The Jerusalem Theater** offers simultaneous English translations through headsets. Rental is about $2. Before curtain time, check to make sure your set works. Usually, one female and one male translator are on hand for a performance. They divide all the roles, and not necessarily according to sex.

Not all seats in the theater are equipped with headsets, so persons who understand some Hebrew may have to decide if they want to sit closer to the stage, where they can see the fine points in the action and perhaps not understand all the dialogue, or sit at the rear, where they will understand what's going on, but may miss dramatic subtleties.

Israeli theater companies tour the country, so Jerusalem, sooner or later, gets to see plays of Tel Aviv's **Habima** and **Cameri**, the **Beersheva Municipal Theater** and the **Haifa Municipal Theater**. Surprisingly, the theater company of stodgy Haifa often presents the most original, inventive and, occasionally, scandalous work. From

Habima often come Greek and Shakespearean classics. Anyone familiar with them should find the Israeli versions fascinating.

Major theater companies appear at the Jerusalem Theater. Less
affluently produced, but every bit as interesting, are plays at **Tzavta**,
Rehov King George 38; **Pargod**, Rehov Bezalel 94, and the **Khan**
(pronounced with a guttural "h"), at Kikar Remez 2.

East Jerusalem has its **El Hakawati**, an Arab theater and arts
complex in the former Nuzha Cinema behind the Tomb of the Kings.
While theatrical productions are in Arabic, English summaries are
available. The theater company is developing a broad range of presentations.

Folk Dance

For persons who want to kick up their heels, folk dancing is a
great way to do it. Camaraderie is instant when people join together
in one big circle for Israeli dancing. And the joy of it can't be matched.

Some places for dancing are **Liberty Bell Park** on Saturday nights
(free), the YMCA on Mondays and the **International Cultural Center
for Youth** (ICCY) where you only have to be young in heart, nobody
checks your birth certificate on Sundays and Wednesdays.

Melave Malka

Melave Malka is the festive weekly leave-taking of Shabbat always
celebrated at the **Israeli Center**, Rehov Strauss 10, and the **Mount
Zion Center of the Diaspora Yeshiva** with performances by pop
musicians. The musicians often are Orthodox *ba'alei teshuva* (returnees
to Judaism), and their music reflects secular influences on their lives
from American rock and country to the diversities of Israel music.
But the words are religious.

At the Mount Zion Center, the usual attraction is the Diaspora
Yeshiva Band. Different headliners appear at the Israel Center. Sometimes melodies are lifted from other sources. One familiar song
emerged at the Israel Center: "This land is your land, this land is
my land/from the Negev Desert to the Heights of Golan/From the
port of Haifa, to the Sea of Galilee/this land was made for you and
me."

At the Israel Center, the price of admission includes free cakes and
beverages, so, God forbid, you shouldn't go home hungry.

Night Clubs and Pubs

Night life to some people is synonymous with night clubs or, as
is often said in Jerusalem, pubs. Jerusalem has a few. Lounges and
pubs exist in all the major hotels and sometimes even independently.

They are patronized more by tourists than Israelis. Closing time is 2 a.m. The legal drinking age in Israel is 18. The following are places Israelis frequent:

The Red Brick House, in a former brick factory near the suburb of Motza. This place is typical of what night life means to Israelis. It is informal, serves traditional Israeli food, and features public sing-alongs on Wednesdays and Thursdays. Israeli singers, many of them well-known, perform on weekends. The cover charge is less than $4 and includes the first drink.

Penny Lane at Rehov Hanevi'im 29. This cafe also features local talent, but the sounds range from Baroque music to Flamenco guitar to jazz. There is no cover charge.

Scandals, Rehov Dorot Rishonim 8. Here the music usually is rock. One popular rock duo heard here is composed of two Scottish men who have lived in Israel for several years. Scandals tries to mimic an English pub in decor.

Ety's Piano Bar, at the train station, Kikar Remez. It has no piano bar, but it has Ety's belly dancing. The place doesn't wake up until after 2 a.m.

Jazz

A surprising amount of jazz is heard regularly in Jerusalem. The center of the Jerusalem jazz world is **Pargod**, with Wednesday night performances and jam sessions most Friday afternoons in its tunnel-like Quonset hut. While listeners nurse Kinley orange pop, tea, coffee or a Maccabee beer, rather than hard liquor, the smoke gets as thick as in a Chicago jazz joint.

The American Colony Hotel in East Jerusalem is fine for jazz on Thursdays. Performers tend to be Americans semipermanently in Jerusalem, while the clientele is composed primarily of hotel guests from northern Europe and a sprinkling of Jewish and Arab Jerusalemites. Even though the service is solicitous, feel free to nurse a Maccabee (or Tuborg or Lowenbrau, if you prefer) for the entire set.

You reach the subterranean jazz room at the American Colony via several colorfully tiled rooms. On your way out, you probably will wish you had dropped pebbles along the circuitous route when you came in.

Hatayelet, on the Haas Promenade, East Talpiot, usually has one or two jazz nights a week. The promenade, built on a ridge, and Hatayelet are newer Jerusalem additions. Jerusalemites in droves walk the promenade for its views. For the splendid sight of Abu Tor, the Old City and the Judean Desert, alone, Hatayelet is worth a visit.

Folklore Night Clubs

The ultimate in kitsch, sentiment and boisterousness in Jerusalem's night life is its "folklore night clubs". **The Khan** (adjacent to the theater mentioned above) is the best-known. Sure, the show is designed for tourists, and a night at the Khan isn't cheap. But it offers irresistible corn.

The club is part of a complex that was a Turkish hostel for travelers and camel caravans dating back to the early 19th century (the date is disputed). The show room is like a stone cavern. Ceilings are arched, seats are low and the room is quite small. Mosquitoes love the place during warm weather for all the bare legs and sandaled feet gathered in one place for them.

The waiters' forte is to rush about their business carrying a tower of glasses reaching almost to the (low) ceiling. With a sleight-of-hand trick, they plop glasses and bottles of *mitz* (juice-flavored soft drink) and Israeli wine in front of you. From then on, you help yourself. No matter how much or little you drink, the price is included in the cost of admission.

Entertainment begins with a small troupe of nubile young women and handsome, dark young men presenting Israeli ethnic dancing, usually including a Yemenite work dance and wedding dance. Also to be counted on is an "un-Kosher" Hasidic dance in which men and women dance in a circle together — not an acceptable practice among the Orthodox.

Afterwards, the featured singer appears. It could be Yafa Yarkoni or red-haired Dahlia Cohen, who sings "Zippity-Doo-Da" in Hebrew. But the title gets no translation.

Chances are, Yarkoni and Cohen will be wearing the style of dress many women singers wear here—flowing long sleeves and soft, ballooning harem pants. The look is exotic and distinctly Israeli.

Following the performances, the audience has a chance to get up on that little stone stage and dance—to the latest English and American hits. One night, I saw a group of paraplegic and quadriplegic tourists hoisted onto the stage, where they danced in their wheel chairs as heartily as everyone else.

Another folklore night club is called, **Jerusalem of Gold**. To find it, look for its blindingly bright, golden sign at the bend of Rehov Ein Rogel in Abu Tor. The club's most dazzling feature is its view of the Old City and the Hinnom Valley.

Here, the format is much the same as at the Khan, except that the building is newer and has a bona fide bar and lounge. And at Jerusalem of Gold, during the Yemenite wedding dance, two people from the audience are pulled onto the stage to be part of the show. So break a leg!

Festivals

Jerusalem bursts with activity during the annual **Israel Festival**, which more and more is concentrated in the Golden City (take that, Tel Aviv!). Some 50 different theater, dance and music productions take place in the space of about three weeks in late spring, with performers coming from around the world. One recent year included theater from Poland, music from Argentina and ballet from England.

It's seventh heaven for jazz lovers when the **International Jerusalem Jazz Festival** takes place in August with such performers as Al di Meola, Manhattan Transfer, Joe Farrell, Airto and Flora Purim.

Tickets and Schedules

To know what performances are taking place in town, keep an eye on posters affixed to billboards, get the weekly schedule published by the Government Tourist Information Office and read the Jerusalem Post and "This Week in Jerusalem".

Posters tell at which outlet tickets are sold. Jerusalem's ticket agencies are **Ben-Naim**, Rehov Yafo 38, Tel. 224-008; **Cahana-On**, Rehov Dorot Rishonim 1, Tel. 222-831; **Kla'im**, Rehov Shammai 8, Tel. 240-896, 230-461; **Kahane**, Rehov Shammai 12, Tel. 244-577; **B'nei Kadoori**, Clal Building 204, Rehov Yafo, Tel.241-979, or inquire at that source of endless information, the Government Tourist Information Office.

Tickets for performances at places such as the Jerusalem Theater or the Israel Museum may be purchased at their respective box offices in advance. Museum members get ticket discounts.

If you are a student anywhere in Jerusalem — *ulpan*, Beit Ha'am, *yeshivot*, etc. — bring your student card when making a purchase. You may get a discount.

Forget about tickets summer nights when the **Watermelon Bazaar** takes place across from Damascus Gate. Just wander over. An otherwise vacant lot is bedecked with lights, tables are covered with plastic and, besides watermelon, there is grilled fish to eat, and beer and *mitz* to drink. Nobody planned the Watermelon Bazaar. It materialized when some men who had watermelons to sell saw an empty lot where they decided to sell them. It is Jerusalem's night life event that stretches almost to the day. The city is trying to get rid of this spontaneous outdoor restaurant and gathering, insisting that it is a public nuisance. But watermelon vendors and Jerusalemites would be happy to see it take place every year.

Now, if you still are at a loss for something to do at night, there is **Super-Sol**. You can cruise the aisles and nibble olives in the Rehov Agron supermarket until midnight Sunday through Thursday.

Part Two:
Celebrate the City
(Tours and Holidays)

Chapter 9:
To Begin the Feast

Jerusalem is a million-calorie, endless serving of sights and sites. It is easy to be intimidated by so many choices all at once. If you feel daunted, just remember, even an elephant can be eaten one bite at a time.

Use the Government Tourist Information Offices at Rehov King George 24 and Jaffa Gate and the Municipal Tourist Information Office, Rehov Yafo 17, to get your bearings. They provide free maps, listings of events and advice. The Christian Information Center near the Jaffa Gate post office has lists of church services and hospices.

For the feast that Jerusalem is, there's nothing like a good guide to help digest it. You may look on it as spoon-feeding, but I look on it as being educated properly. Jerusalem may be the most complex city in the world.

Beware of individuals who approach you on the street and offer to show you around for a price. It's illegal for non-licensed guides to accept money. Licensed guides have had 18 months of intensive training by the Ministry of Tourism, wear a distinctive pin and don't do business by cornering wide-eyed tourists.

You can hire your own licensed tour guide, but some excellent group tours exist. Schedules for the following and other group tours are available from "This Week in Jerusalem" or "Your

Jerusalem", free in hotels and at the tourist offices mentioned above.

Archeological Seminars, Rehov Habad 34, Jewish Quarter of the Old City (above the Cardo) has seminars and tours usually lasting two hours. They cost $4.50 and are prefaced by a talk on the area to be visited. (Archeological Seminars also publishes an excellent, brief review of Jerusalem's archeological history: *Getting Jerusalem Together* by Fran Alpert.)

Walking Tours, Ltd., which meets at the Citadel courtyard near Jaffa Gate, specializes in various aspects of the Old City and nearby areas. Tours average three hours and cost $7 ($5 for students).

The municipality has a free walking tour to a different site each week leaving from the city's tourist office, Rehov Yafo 17, at 10 a.m Saturdays.

The Sheraton Jerusalem Plaza Hotel, corner of Rehov King George and Rehov Agron, has excellent free tours, not only to the Old City and adjacent excavations, but to such places as Mea She'arim and the Bucharan Quarter. Participants share taxi costs from the hotel to the tour site. A $2 tip should go to the guide. Get the schedule at the hotel's front desk.

Reservations aren't required for any of the above tours. Just show up. All are conducted in English.

The Society for the Protection of Nature has a few Jerusalem tours in English. "Your Jerusalem" prints that schedule, too. For these, reservations are required. Call the SPNI, Rehov Helena Hamalka 13, Tel. 222-357.

Dress modestly on tours or while sightseeing on your own, since you are likely to visit religious sites or pass through some very conservative neighborhoods. Men need head coverings at synagogues. Indeed, head coverings for anyone sightseeing is a good idea in any event, for the sun can be fierce. Respect it.

The heart of Jerusalem is small enough to walk from place to place and explore neighborhoods. Some of your most memorable moments will come from spontaneous excursions.

So you won't miss the choice delicacies of Jerusalem, the "absolutely must-see" sites, I have put together itineraries for one- and two-week visits and a third for those who have visited the city before or are staying put here for weeks or months. Following these is an invitation to join in the myriad of secular and religious celebrations, private and public, that take place throughout the year.

There's nothing sacrosanct about the itineraries. I know my favor-

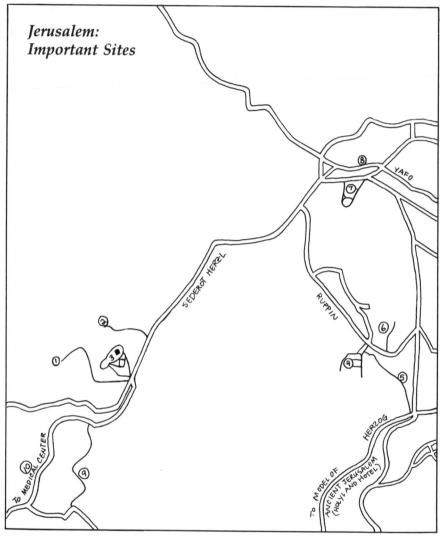

Jerusalem:
Important Sites

1. Yad VaShem (Holocaust Memorial)
2. Military Cemetery
3. Tomb of Herzl
4. Shrine of the Book (Israel Museum)
5. Monastery of the Cross (Greek)
6. Knesset
7. Binyenei Ha'uma
8. Central Bus Station
9. Koryat Haove'l Swimming Pool
10. Hadassa Medical Center
11. Biblical Zoo
12. Mahane Yehuda Market
13. Urfali Synagogue
14. Bat Ha'm
15. Rehov King Goerge 24
16. Jewish Agency and JNF
17. Hechal Shlomo
18. Tomb of Jason
19. L.A. Mayer Institute for Islamic Art
20. Presidential Residence
21. Jerusalem Theater
22. International Cultural Center for Youth
23. Jerusalem Swimming Pool
24. P.M.'s House
25. Jerusalem Sheraton Plaza Hotel
26. Baba Tama (Bucharan)
27. Mea She'arim Quarter
28. Ethiopian Church
29. Municipality Information Office
30. Central Post Office
31. Conservative Synagogue
32. YMCA
33. Hebrew Union College (Reform)
34. King David Hotel

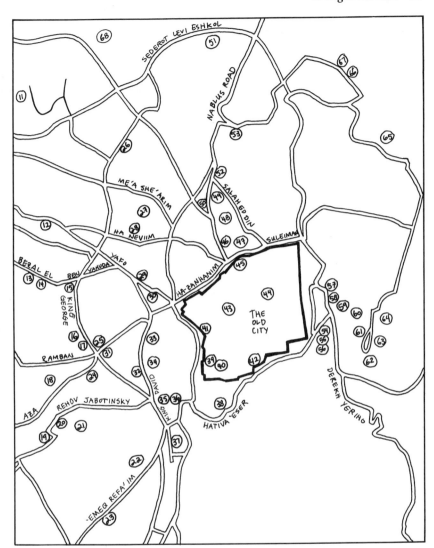

35. Montefiore Windmill
36. Jerusalem Music Center
37. Khan Theater
38. David Palombo Museum
39. St. James Cathedral (Armenian)
40. Mardigan Museum
41. Jaffa Gate
42. Bate Mahse
43. Church of the Holy Sepulchre
44. Antonia's Fortress
45. Cave of Zedekiah (Solomon's Quarries)
46. Garden Tomb
47. East Jerusalem Central Bus Station
48. Church of St. Stephen (Dominican)
49. Church of St. George (Anglican Cathedral)
50. YMCA (East)
51. Giv'at Hatahmoshet (Ammunition Hill)

52. American Colony Hotel
53. Tomb of Shimon Hatzadik (Simon the Just)
54. Absalom's Pillar
55. Tombs of Sons of Hezir
56. Tomb of Zechariah
57. Tomb of Mary (Church of the Assumption)
58. Church of All Nations (Church of the Agony)
59. Church of Mary Magdalene (Russian)
60. Church of Dominus Flevit
61. Tombs of the Prophets
62. Jewish Cemetery (Mount of Olives)
63. Intercontinental Hotel
64. Church of Pater Noster
65. Hebrew University (Mount Scopus)
66. Hadassah Hospital (Mount Scopus)
67. World War One Cemetery (Mount Scopus)
68. Tombs of the Sanhedrin (Sanhedriyya)

ite ways of showing Jerusalem to newcomers, but you know your own interests.

But the first two itineraries offer a way of becoming "grounded" in what Jerusalem is about. As I see them, they form a basis for everything else.

Beyond these, if it suits you better, each day's suggestion can be swapped for another and parts may be interchanged. And if a day as outlined seems too strenuous, you might want to substitute part of it for a visit to a museum described in Chapter 12, "Linger Awhile: Substitutions and Extenders, More Museums." Or you may want simply to pass the time watching little children swinging in a park. After all, it's your visit.

Feel free to visit a synagogue on Shabbat, Friday nights or Saturday mornings, or a church on Sunday mornings or for Vespers in the early evening. There, you can see in action what inspires Jerusalem.

During your evenings, take advantage of Jerusalem's night life, even if it is only to rest your feet at a Ben-Yehuda Mall cafe. But my hope is that the city will energize you to do more than that, and you will rub elbows with Israelis at the places where they spend their evenings.

Don't feel discouraged by the enormous number of places to visit in the Golden City. Even lifetime residents complain that they haven't been able to get to them all. What's more, it seems as if anytime anyone digs up so much as a teaspoon of Jerusalem's earth, another archeological site has been uncovered. But that's one of the reasons to return again and again.

Chapter 10:
In the Beginning

You may be feeling an irresistible urge to embrace as much of Jerusalem as you can, as soon as you can. You may even have looked at the itinerary I recommend for your first day here, and be thinking that it will hold you back from the thick of Jerusalem, the Old City, particularly, and its sites, shops, aromas, crowds and excitement.

You're right. That's exactly what I want to do. "A" comes before "B", and today's tour is "A". It is the prerequisite for everything else you will see in Jerusalem. Besides, there is plenty of excitement on this tour—but without the crowds and strong aromas.

Today you can become oriented to the Golden City, through Egged's bus No. 99, be introduced to the country's vast culture, and ancient heritage as presented in the Israel Museum and, most importantly, touch Israel's soul at Yad Vashem. Physically, this isn't a lot for one day of sightseeing. Emotionally—well, that's another matter.

First Day

To get "the lay of the land" and learn what's where outside the walled Old City, ride the Egged Bus Company's bus No. 99. Designed for tourists, it zigzags through the city to reach 34 major attractions, including the **Israel Museum** and **Yad Vashem**. Tickets may be bought on the bus for a single tour without on and off privileges or for one or two days of unlimited travel. The trip starts at Jaffa Gate where the bus leaves every hour on the hour from 9 a.m. to 5 p.m. Sunday through Thursday, to 2 p.m. Friday and holiday eves, but you can board any place bus No. 99 stops. Further information is available from 248-144 (the Jaffa Gate Egged terminal) or any Egged number. Steve Zerobnick's book, the *Round Jerusalem Guide*, describes what you see from bus windows and the attraction at each site and also gives the bus departure times. It is available in local bookstores and hotel newspaper stands.

If you ride the No. 99, stop at the Israel Museum first.

Israel Museum

The Israel Museum is spread out atop a hill off Rehov Ruppin in West Jerusalem. It actually is a collection of museums: the Samuel Bronfman Museum of Biblical Archeology, the Bezalel National Museum, the Children's Museum, the Billy Rose Sculpture Garden and the Shrine of the Book. Yet another, the Nathan Cummings Pavilion for 20th-Century Art, is under construction.

The main building, which houses the first three museums, is up the stairs from the entrance gate. A shuttle will take you there, if you wish. Inside is a sumptuous collection of archeological and ethnographical artifacts, ceremonial art, paintings by Cézanne, Chagall, Van Gogh and Picasso — and perhaps a janitor or two dancing. One of the prize exhibits is of traditional Jewish dress from several different countries.

In the **Billy Rose Sculpture Garden**, designed by Isamu Noguchi, you will see sculptures by Rodin, Picasso, Lipchitz, Maillol, Henry Moore and others.

The unusual shape of the **Shrine of the Book** has become a much photographed Jerusalem image. The exterior of this spectacular building that houses the Dead Sea Scrolls is built in the shape of the lids of the jars that contained the scrolls. But locals often describe the building as looking like a breast.

Entering the shrine is like stepping into the cave at Qumran, where some of the scrolls were discovered. Inside are originals and copies of the Dead Sea Scrolls, religious writings from between 100 B.C.E. and 68 C.E. The first was found in 1947 by Bedouin youths in a Judean Desert cave near the Dead Sea. Also on exhibit are the oldest-known version of the Book of Isaiah, portions of Genesis and the Book of Psalms. The Book of Isaiah is on a drum that turns, so all of it can be read. I have seen young Israelis going through it word by word. Later writings include letters written by Bar Kochba, whose disastrous revolt against the Romans was put down in 135 C.E.

You may have lunch in the Israel Museum's moderately priced cafeteria. If you want a change of scenery, take a taxi to Ima's or bus

No. 9 or 24 to the Central Bus Station and walk from there. You can pick up bus No. 99 again at the Central Bus Station.

> **Hours: 10 a.m. to 5 p.m. Sunday, Monday, Wednesday and Thursday; 4 p.m. to 10 p.m. Tuesday; 10 a.m. to 2 p.m. Friday and Saturday. Free guided tours in English are offered at 11 a.m. Sunday and Wednesday and 4:30 p.m. Tuesday. Entrance fee. Separate ticket required for Shrine of the Book. Buy Saturday tickets in advance. Annual membership is one of the best deals in town for anyone who is going to be around awhile. It allows unlimited entrance not only to the Israel Museum, but to the Rockefeller, Tel Aviv and Haifa Museums and discounts at museum programs and in the gift shops. Tel. 698-211.**

Yad Vashem

For a fundamental understanding of Israel, **Yad Vashem** must be visited. Almost everything and everyone in Israel has some sort of relationship, some link to the Holocaust in which six million Jews were killed by the Nazis and their sympathizers. In ways, the very existence of modern Israel is an outcome of the Holocaust. But no thinking person would consider it a *quid pro quo*.

Yad Vashem is on Har Hazikaron (Mount of Remembrance) near Mount Herzl on Sderot Herzl in West Jerusalem. Its name means "a monument and a name", from Isaiah 56:5: "I will give them in my house and within my walls a monument and a name better than sons and daughters; I will give them an everlasting name which shall not perish."

Sometimes, I detect impatience in the non-Jewish world over Jews' ever-lasting memory of the Holocaust. It always is one of life's challenges for a person to understand someone else's pain. And in this case, those affected, Jews, are a people with a memory. The lessons of the past are a constant in their lives. Reminding the world of the Holocaust is seen by Jews and others as a way of preventing anything like it from happening again to any people. The tragedy of the Holocaust, however, has been compounded, for it seems as if the world doesn't want to learn the lesson.

The "monument and name", Yad Vashem, stands as witness. It is composed of several parts, each with its own purpose and theme. One of them is a research center which holds the largest Holocaust archival collection in the world. Many items in the archives are kept in the low-lying buildings to the right, up the hill from the street. Much of Yad Vashem's research is conducted here. These buildings aren't open to the general public.

You will see a tree-lined walk up the hill. It is the **Avenue of the Righteous Gentiles**. Before each tree is a plaque honoring a non-Jew who risked his or her life to save Jews.

Exhibitions in the main museum trace the rise of Hitler in 1933, his destruction of Jews in Europe and the death camp liberations in 1945. Most of the photographs were taken by the German military. Alongside are literature and other art produced by death-camp inmates. Included is a section on Jewish resistance, focusing on the Warsaw Ghetto uprising. Also in the building is the **Hall of Names**, which has gathered biographical information on about half of the Holocaust victims.

Across from the museum is the **Hall of Remembrance**, the focal point of the memorial. It is a somber structure of black basalt and concrete and invites reflection. Inside, heavy silence fills the dimly lit, crypt-like room. The focus of the room is an eternal flame burning from a low platform on the floor in memory of the murdered. It is a symbol of the unquenchable human spirit and will to live. Chiseled into the dark, uneven paving stones which surround the flame are the names of 21 Nazi death camps.

A park on the grounds is named for Janusz Korczak, who headed a Warsaw Jewish orphanage. By choice, he died with his 200 children in the Treblinka gas chambers, rather than abandon them.

New to Yad Vashem are the **Hall of Mirrors** memorializing the one million Jewish children killed in the Holocaust and the **Valley of the Destroyed Communities** with its colossal wall the shape of Europe bearing names of 5000 Jewish communities that were obliterated.

A visit to Yad Vashem is harrowing, saddening beyond words. But Yad Vashem must be experienced in order to understand much that you will encounter in Israel. After I leave the grounds of Yad Vashem and feel the burst of Jerusalem's vitality around me, it is as if I have stepped from one world to another, from death to life. Surrounded by Jerusalem's exuberance, I am in the midst of an affirmation of life. To miss Yad Vashem is not to touch Israel's heart, beating against all odds.

Hours: 9 a.m. to 4:45 p.m. Sunday through Thursday, to 12:45 p.m. Friday. Closed Saturday. Free. Tel. 531-202.

After a strongly emotional day such as this, you may be ready for a stiff dose of the positive. Perhaps there is a concert tonight by an Israeli pop singer like Yehoram Gaon or Naomi Shemer. Or perhaps this is sing-along night at the Red Brick House. At either place, you will be in the midst of an enthusiastic, warm, boisterous crowd whose existence collectively communicates the words to a famous Israeli song, *"Am Yisrael Chai"* (The People of Israel Live).

Second Day
The First Half of the Old City

Now comes tour "B", which yesterday has led up to. Today's tour is for an understanding of the depth of Jewish history in Jerusalem. But a walk on another day will take you hundreds of years even further back in time. This day's journey through the ages is within the physical distance of about one kilometer. It starts beside the Western Wall that supported the Second Temple, then leads through the Jewish Quarter, most of it recreated from ashes. Later the journey introduces another of Jerusalem's fabled mosaic pieces — the Armenian community — and continues to Mount Zion.

Start early and wear your most comfortable shoes. You can prepare yourself for the Old City's confusing lanes by bringing along Aharon Bier's clearly marked Old City map. It is available in bookstores. Allow three hours for the Western Wall and the Jewish Quarter; two-and-a-half for the Armenian Quarter and Mount Zion, if a tour of the Mardigian Museum is included.

Eight Gates to the City
(The Many Ways into the Old City)

It is in the Old City that the elements that give Jerusalem its name, "the navel of the world", come together. Here, side by side and often built on top of each other over the centuries, are some of the holiest sites of Judaism, Christianity and Islam.

These, along with living quarters, schools, museums, bazaars, bakeries, restaurants, synagogues, churches, mosques, post offices and parking lots are squeezed into an area of only one square kilometer and wrapped in Suleiman the Magnificent's wall built in 1543. Like virtually every other structure in Jerusalem, Suleiman's wall had its predecessors, for it rests on walls built by the Crusaders and the Romans.

Suleiman's powerful wall, reflecting golden sunshine by day, golden lights by night, has at least eight gates. The ones commonly referred to are **Jaffa Gate** on the western wall facing West Jerusalem's **New Gate** on the northern wall and, continuing east around the Old City, **Damascus Gate, Herod's Gate, Lion's (St. Stephen's) Gate, Golden Gate, Dung Gate** and **Zion Gate**.

For a rundown on them by way of orientation: **Jaffa Gate** is named for the road that began here to the city of Jaffa on the Mediterranean Sea. It is the western end of the Roman's east-west main road and the busiest entrance into the Old City, for it is one of the few through which cars may enter (a matter currently debated hotly by the municipal government). The moat between it and the Citadel was filled in

Damascus Gate.

to make an appropriately grand reception area for Kaiser Wilhelm II of Germany's celebrated entrance on horseback in 1898. In contrast, when the British took control of Palestine in 1917, General Allenby got down from his horse and walked through the gate as an expression of his humility on entering the Holy City.

New Gate was built in 1889 to make an easier connection between the Christian Quarter and Christian properties across the road, outside of the Old City.

Damascus Gate in East Jerusalem is the largest and most impressive of the eight. It faces toward Damascus and was the northern end of the Romans' Cardo, their north-south road following the Tyropoeon Valley through the city renamed by them Aelia Capitolina. In Hebrew, Damascus Gate is called Sha'ar Shchem, because it opened onto the road to the city of Shchem. When the Romans, under Vespasian, built a city, Neopolis, near Shchem (the name evolved into the Arabic, Nablus), they also constructed two arched gates of classic design. These have been excavated and can be seen on either side of Damascus Gate.

Herod's Gate is past Damascus Gate to the east. It got its name from Christian pilgrims in the Middle Ages who thought Herod's palace was nearby. In both Arabic and Hebrew, it is known as the Gate of Flowers.

It was through **Lion's** or **St. Stephen's Gate** that the Israeli army entered the Old City in the Six-Day War. The gate has one of its names because of lions carved on both sides of it, and the other because it is believed that St. Stephen was martyred nearby. The Via Dolorosa, Jesus' path to crucifixion and burial (also known as the Way of the Cross), begins inside this gate.

Golden Gate (Gate of Mercy in Hebrew and Gate of Repentance in Arabic), near the middle of the wall's eastern side, was built by the Byzantines in the 5th century. It is said that Jesus rode on an ass into Jerusalem from the Mount of Olives through a predecessor of the gate standing today. The most beautiful of the gates with its two arches, it is the gate through which the Messiah will enter Jerusalem, according to Jewish tradition. Jews believe Moslems blocked it in 1530 to prevent the Messiah's entrance. Israelis, even after winning control of the Old City in 1967, have let the gate remain blocked.

Dung Gate is the gate closest to the Western Wall. It acquired its lowly name after the area around it became the city's dumping ground for refuse in the second century C.E. It often is said that garbage was dumped so close to the Western Wall by Moslems in order to humiliate the Jews.

Zion Gate (the Prophet David Gate in Arabic) connects the Armenian Quarter with Mount Zion. Mount Zion is on the same plateau as the Old City and used to be an integral part of it. When Hadrian built his Roman city on Jerusalem, his walls excluded Mount Zion.

The Western Wall

Rabbi Abraham Isaac Kook, a Chief Rabbi of Israel who is remembered for his erudition and compassion, wrote of the **Western Wall**, "There are men with hearts of stone and stones with hearts of flesh."

The Western Wall, the only remaining part of the Second Temple, is considered the holiest site in Judaism because of its closeness to the location of the Temple and because Orthodox Jews maintain that the Divine Spirit forever abides in the Wall. The Wall isn't only used as an outdoor synagogue, it also serves as a national gathering place.

It is part of a supporting wall for the landfill that created the Temple Mount. It is the largest section of the Temple area left standing after the Roman destruction of Jerusalem in 70 C.E. In Hebrew, its name is Hakotel Hama'aravi, the Western Wall, or, simply, "Hakotel". It is not — I repeat, NOT, the "Wailing Wall". (*New York Times* and Associated Press, please take note.) That title, a misnomer, was given to this stretch of wall by the British, because Jews who prayed there lamented the destruction of the Temple as well as the pain of not having their own country.

Several ways to reach the Western Wall exist. One is through Dung Gate. That is the most convenient entrance because the No. 1 bus stops outside, but I'd rather leave than arrive from that direction. Another entrance is via the Arab *souk* from Jaffa Gate, David Street to Bab el-Silsileh Street (Street of the Chain) and right on Western Wall Road. My objection to that route is that it makes too tumultuous a preface into the Wall area.

My preferred route for sheer aesthetic reasons is through the Jewish Quarter and down the Stairs of Rabbi Judah Halevi past Yeshiva Hakotel and Yeshiv Porat. The most dramatic first view of the Wall is from the stairs, and we all know there's nothing like a smashing first impression.

The way to get there is into the Old City through Jaffa Gate (reached by several buses from West Jerusalem), right on Armenian Orthodox Patriarchate Road and left on St. James Road, which leads into Rehov Or Hahayim. That lane leads, with some slight jogs, into Rehov Hakaraim, and that in turn ends at the stairs.

From the stairs, the Wall is below to the left across the plaza. You can see the gleaming Dome of the Rock above it on the Temple Mount and ahead to the Mount of Olives and the village of Silwan across the Kidron Valley. Beyond are the Judean Desert and, if the day is clear, the shimmer of the Dead Sea.

If it is a Monday or Thursday morning, 13-year-old boys will be

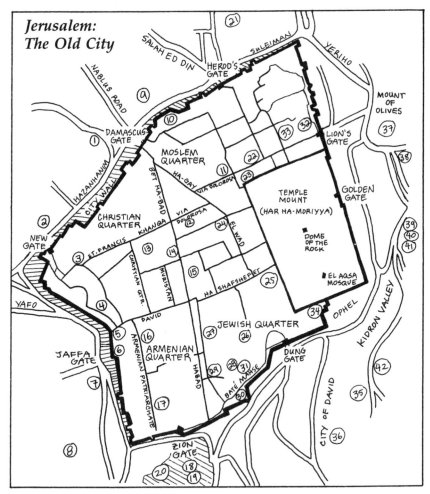

Jerusalem: The Old City

1. Armenian Mosaic Memorial
2. Notre Dame de France
3. Greek Orthodox Patriarchate
4. Latin Patriarchate
5. Information Office
6. The Citadel (David's Tower)
7. Kbutzot Hayotzer (center of arts & crafts)
8. Yemin Moshe
9. East Jerusalem Bus Station
10. Zedekiah's Cave
11. Ecce Homo Arch & Hospice
12. Armenian Catholic Church
13. Church of the Holy Sepulchre
14. Church of Alexander
15. Church of the Redeemer
16. Anglican Church
17. Armenian Patriarchate
18. Coenaculum
19. Tomb of David
20. Church of the Dormition
21. Rockefeller Museum

22. Church of Flagellations
23. Antonia Fortress
24. Mameluke Madrasa
25. Western Wall (Hakotel HaMa aravi)
26. Tiferet Yisrael
27. Hurva
28. Ben Zakkai
29. Ramban Synagogue
30. Old City Wall Promenade
31. Baté Mahse
32. Church of St. Anne
33. Bethesda Pool
34. Southern Wall
35. Hezekiah's Tunnel
36. Pool of Shiloah
37. Tomb of Mary
38. Church of All Nations
39. Tomb of Jehoshafat
40. Absalom's Pillar
41. Tomb of Zechariah
42. Oihon Spring

assuming the religious obligations of an adult male in their bar mitzvah ceremonies in front of the Wall. Singing, ululating (the high-pitched cry of joy made by Sephardi women), drumming, clapping, and chanting will waft across the plaza and up the stairs. On Friday nights and Saturday mornings, the hum of people praying and the buzz of spectators rise. Yeshiva (Jewish religious school) students put their hands on each other's shoulders and come singing down the stairs in a line on Friday nights. At the Wall, they form a circle and perform a simple swaying, shuffling dance as they sing. When soldiers take their oath of service at Wall, the young men's firm voices resonate. But during the heat of a summer afternoon, barely a murmur can be heard.

The vast plaza from the bottom of the stairs to the Wall wasn't there before the Six-Day War. For centuries, only a narrow lane existed between the Wall and a mass of shacks for Moslem North African immigrants. To the scene the Jordanians added the rubble left from their house-to-house battle to oust the Jews. During the 19 years of Jordanian occupation, Jews weren't allowed access to the Wall. During the preceding British Mandate, Jews could go to the Wall, but they weren't allowed to blow the shofar (ram's horn) or to bring the Holy Ark containing the Torah (the first five books of the Bible) or even chairs so they could sit.

Now, the part of the plaza that is closest to the Wall, with a fence between it and the rest of the plaza, is reserved for religious observance. Men and women have separate areas for worship. On Shabbat, even observers outside of the prayer area are forbidden to take pictures or to smoke.

What can be seen of the Wall reveals seven rows (the bottom two uncovered after 1967) of Herodian Stone from the Second Temple period and, above them, four rows probably from the early Arab period and then late Ottoman. The rows differ greatly in style.

The remaining Second Temple Western Wall begins at the bottom with massive, but elegant, Herodian stones with their distinctive narrow frames and smooth centers. The layers of stone above them are less refined in style as later builders took fewer aesthetic pains when they reconstructed the wall. Another 17 rows of stone exist below the Herodian stone. As archeological excavations proceed, more and more history is being revealed.

An entrance in a wall perpendicular to the Western Wall at the men's side leads to one of these excavations. Inside is **Wilson's Arch**, named for the man who found it. The arch is part of a bridge that spanned the Tyropoeon Valley to connect the Temple with residential areas in the Upper City. Digging to the base of the Wall is underway here. Women can reach the excavation by going through an entrance just before the men's prayer section in front of the Wall.

> Hours: 8:30 a.m. to 3 p.m. Sunday, Tuesday and Wednesday; 12:30 p.m. to 3 p.m. Monday and Thursday; 8:30 a.m. to noon Friday. Closed Saturday. Entrance fee.

The Jewish Quarter

The southeast quadrant of the Old City became the Jewish Quarter in 1267. Today, it is bounded by Ararat Street on the west, Rehov Hashalshelet (Street of the Chain) on the north to the Temple Mount, the Western Wall plaza on the east, and Rehov Batei Mahse to Dung Gate on the south.

The present Jewish Quarter only slightly resembles the Jewish Quarter that existed before the Jordanian occupation (1948-1967). During that time, most of the Jewish Quarter was destroyed and all Jews were banished. After 1967, some of the buildings were restored, but many more of them are new (none even hinting at the hovels that used to be here).

The new buildings were designed to fit in with the old, architecturally. It has taken several years for the new ones to begin to weather and blend with their surroundings. Happily, the Jewish Quarter is losing its just-built appearance and is settling in as an authentic community, despite the hordes of tourists who fill its narrow, twisting lanes and peek into its enticing courtyards.

In the process of digging foundations, numerable archeological sites were uncovered. The discoveries haven't stopped. They exist side-by-side with, and even as part of, today's buildings.

Begin the ascent from the Western Wall Plaza to the Jewish Quarter by returning to the Stairs of Rabbi Judah Halevi. The new buildings on the left are Yeshiva Porat Yosef, designed by the famed Israeli architect Moshe Safdie of Montreal's Habitat fame, and, above it, Yeshivat Hakotel.

Through openings on the left of the stairs is one of the latest Jewish Quarter archeological finds — a late Second Temple Period palatial mansion with mosaic floors and walls with frescoes. It is scheduled to open to the public soon.

To the right of the stairs are ruins of a Crusader period church destroyed by Saladin in 1187. A rose garden now grows in one of the courtyards.

At the top of the stairs, on Rehov Tiferet Yisrael and opposite several refreshment stands, is the **Burnt House**. This home, owned by a well-to-do priestly family, was among those destroyed when Romans burned Jerusalem and killed its inhabitants in 70 C.E. One of the poignant finds inside was the remains of a young woman's arm reaching for the stairs. An excellent audiovisual show recreates the events. It can be seen in English every two hours between 9:30 a.m. and 3:30 p.m.

> Hours: 9 a.m. to 5 p.m. Sunday through Thursday, to noon Friday. Tel. 287-211. Entrance fee.

The snack stands opposite the Burnt House make this a good place for a rest stop. Public lavatories are in an alcove around the corner from the snack stands.

Left on Rehov Misgav Ladach and right on Rehov Hakaraim, to the right are the ruins of **Tiferet Yisrael**, a synagogue built by Hasidic Jews in 1867 and one of the largest and most famous in Jerusalem. Its dome could be seen from every part of the Old City. The synagogue was destroyed in 1948 during the War of Independence.

A few steps farther up Rehov Hakaraim is the **Karaite Synagogue**. A visit at this time is optional. It is described in detail in "Linger Awhile, Substitutions and Extenders, More Museums", Chapter 12.

A narrow lane to the left, Rehov Hamekubalim, after a jog, becomes Rehov Galeed. That brings you to the back of the large and grand **Beit Rothschild** with two floors of arches, built by the Austrian branch of the famous family as residences for the poor. It now houses the offices of the Jewish Quarter Restoration Company. If you want to go around to the front, you will see how Beit Rothschild faces the attractive **Batei Mahse Square** with buildings financed by German and Dutch Jews.

Rehov Galeed continues to the **Sephardic Educational Center** at Rehov Beit Mahse 1, in a building that dates from 1874. Inside its courtyard is a little bit of Spain. The center is engaged in outreach work with young Jews in such far-flung countries as India and Mexico. Open also to Ashkenazim, the center works as a bridge between Jews regardless of political or religious ideology.

Perhaps the most famous Old City synagogues are the **Four Sephardic Synagogues**, founded in the 16th century by Spanish Jews or Jews of Spanish descent. They are reached by going out the front of the Sephardic Center and right on Rehov Mishmerot Hakehuna. The entrance to the inter-connected synagogues is down a stairway. During the centuries of Moslem rule, synagogues and churches often were built below street level, because of a decree that they must be lower than mosques. These synagogues were the community center for Old City Jews. After a six-month siege during the War of Independence, they gathered here to surrender to Jordan. During the next 19 years, contents of synagogues were stolen and the buildings were turned into warehouses.

The first synagogue entered is named for **Rabbi Yohanan Ben Zakkai**, who taught his pupils on this site in the first century C.E. Its unusual twin arks and the blue and gold mural above them give a hint of the opulence that once existed here.

A door at the rear of Ben-Zakkai Synagogue leads to the **Eliyahu Hanavi Synagogue**. This is the oldest of the four and has a chair near the door reserved for the Prophet Elijah. A traditional story is that Elijah was the 10th man at this synagogue to form a *minyan* (the required number of men to participate) for prayers on one Yom Kippur eve.

In Ben-Zakkai Synagogue again and toward its front is the door to the **Emtza'i (Middle or Central) Synagogue**. This is the smallest of the synagogues and used to be the women's section for Ben-Zakkai; the plaster art work on the ceiling is original.

From the Emtza'i, you can enter the **Istanbuli Synagogue**, founded by Turkish Jews in 1764. Its ark and its *bima*, on which persons leading prayers stand, were brought from Italy.

> All the synagogues are open for prayers early in the morn-
> ing and late in the afternoon. Sightseeing hours are 9 a.m.
> to 4 p.m. Sunday through Thursday; to 1 p.m. Friday.
> Entrance fee.

Out on the street again and to the right, close to a minaret, is the **Ramban Synagogue** named for Rabbi Moshe Ben-Nahman. Great rabbis are known by several names, one usually being an acronym. "Ramban" is Nahman's acronym. He also is known as "Nachmanides". The synagogue has a letter the Ramban wrote in 1267, the year he arrived from Spain, in which he describes the pitiful condition of Jerusalem Jewry. The Ramban has become a popular prayer center for today's Jewish Quarter residents. It is open for morning and evening prayers and other unpredictable times.

To the left of the synagogue and right on Rehov Hayehudim are a single, sweeping arch and four broken walls that are all that is left of the **Hurva Synagogue**. Built in 1700, it was destroyed by Moslems twice. It was rebuilt after the first time. What exists now remained after the 1948 destruction.

Both on nearby Rehov Plugat Hakotelat and at a place in the Cardo ahead can be seen remains of the **Broad Wall** from the First Temple Period. King Hezekiah had the Broad Wall constructed around what then was the northern boundary of Jerusalem at approximately 701 B.C.E.

Close by, running below and parallel to Rehov Hayehudim, is the **Cardo**, a Byzantine extension of Hadrian's main north-south street. Because of the historical importance of the Cardo as a Jerusalem landmark, it was a particularly exciting archeological find when it was uncovered a few years ago during excavation for new construction.

Reconstructed with some original pavement, columns and arches, it now houses some elegant shops and singing idol Yehoram Gaon's music establishment (but he doesn't watch the store). Shopping hours on the Cardo are until 7 p.m.

Up a flight of stairs, at the corner of Rehov Habad and Rehov Or Hahayim, is the **Habad Synagogue**. It is one of the few in the Jewish Quarter that survived the 1948 war and Jordanian occupation.

At Rehov Or Hahayim 6 is the **Museum of the Old Yishuv** (old settlement), a restoration of one of the oldest houses in the quarter. It provides a rare picture of Jewish life during the last years of Turkish rule.

> Hours: 9 a.m. to 4 p.m. Sunday through Thursday. Closed
> Friday and Saturday. Entrance fee. Tel. 284-636.

Rehov Or Hahayim, to St. James Street in the Armenian Quarter, brings you out at the Armenian Orthodox Patriarchate Road. To the right, the road leads to Jaffa Gate and out of the Old City, to the left to the Cathedral of St. James and the entrance to Mount Zion.

The Armenian Quarter and Mount Zion

The Armenian Quarter, reached most easily through Jaffa Gate and down the Armenian Orthodox Patriarchate Road past St. James Road, is a walled enclave within walls in the southwestern corner of the Old City. It is bounded by city walls to the west and south, David Street on the north and Rehov Habad on the east.

Before entering the Armenian compound, turn left off Armenian Orthodox Patriarchate Road onto St. James Street and left again on Ararat Street, named for Armenians' holy mountain as well as the place where Noah's Ark is believed to have come to rest. On the right, where Ararat makes a jog, is the Syrian Orthodox Monastery with its **St. Mark's Church**. Here, Syriac, a language close to ancient Aramaic, still is spoken.

Syrians believe that this location, not the Coenaculum on Mount Zion, is the site of St. Mark's house and where the Last Supper also took place (the church is described in Chapter 13, "Discover Heavenly Jerusalem Churches, Synagogues, Family Ties".

> Hours: 9 a.m. to noon in the summer. At irregular times
> in the winter.

Continuing on Armenian Patriarchate Road, the new (1975) Armenian Seminary is on the right. The entrance to the Armenian Quarter is on the left. Some 2000 people live in this walled "town" with its own language, schools, churches, social life and soccer field. It is a tight enclave, made all the tighter because its gates are locked from 10 p.m. until 6 the next morning. Sightseers aren't encouraged to wander beyond the quarter's major attractions, but they aren't actively discouraged. And during the average day, few residents are out and about. The quarter can appear to be deserted.

In 303, Armenians were the first people to convert as a nation to Christianity. The quarter focuses on the **Cathedral of St. James**, said to be built on the place where Herod Agrippa I decapitated the Apostle James the Greater in 44 C.E. A head, thought to be that of James, is entombed in the chapel to the left inside the cathedral. The cathedral also is named for St. James the Lesser, Jesus' brother and the first bishop of Jerusalem, according to Armenians. He is reputed to be buried under the altar.

Crusaders helped Armenians erect the present cathedral in the 12th century on the ruins of two other churches. A wooden clapper, instead of bells, still is used to announce services. Bells were forbidden by the Moslems until after 1840. *Khachkars*, stone crosses, are inlaid in the walls around the cathedral courtyard. They are memorials for people and events, and each of the 22 is unique.

Inside are altars to St. James the Lesser, the Virgin Mary and St. John the Baptist. The church is startlingly beautiful in a fairy tale way with blue tiles, carvings and dozens of hanging lanterns.

Hours: 3 p.m. to 3:30 p.m. Monday through Friday; 2:30 p.m. to 3:15 p.m. Saturday and Sunday.

Outside, a stone-covered walkway leads to the main compound and courtyard. In it are the **Armenian Press** (established in 1833, it was Jerusalem's first printing press), the **Gulbenkian Library** and, facing a landscaped courtyard, the **Mardigian Museum of Armenian Art and History**, located in the old seminary. The small museum gives a powerful view into the world of this little-known people. I highly recommend visiting the museum at this time, if endurance allows. It is described in detail in Chapter 12, "Linger Awhile, Substitutions and Extenders, More Museums".

Hours: 10 a.m. to 5 p.m. daily, except Sunday.

Outside, down a few stairs to the right, under an archway and to the right again is the **House of Annas** (Convent of the Olive Tree). Annas was the father-in-law of Caiaphas, the high priest. It is said that Annas had Jesus bound and tied overnight to the nearby olive tree before he delivered Jesus to Caiaphas.

Back on Armenian Orthodox Patriarchate Road and left (watch out for cars from behind you) is Zion Gate on the other side of the road and outside the Old City walls. Through it is **Mount Zion**.

A quiet afternoon in the Armenian Quarter.

Mount Zion has been enclosed by the Old City walls at various times. An Arab tradition says that after Suleiman the Magnificent had the walls reconstructed, he ordered the two engineers who neglected to include Mount Zion and its Tomb of King David within the walls executed. Their graves are reputed to be near Jaffa Gate. If the story is true, the deaths were in vain, for modern archeologists deny that King David is buried here.

The road to the right leads to the black-topped, Romanesque **Church of the Dormition**. It was built by German Catholics in 1910 and badly damaged during the fierce fighting in the War of Independence. It was constructed over a series of ruined predecessors marking the spot where, according to tradition, Mary died. The interior is impressive for its many mosaic designs. The one on the floor is of three interlocking circles and the words in Latin, ''Holy, holy, holy''.

Hours are 7 a.m. to 12:30 p.m., 2 p.m. to 7 p.m. daily.

To the left is a building complex whose various parts reflect Jewish, Christian and Moslem religions, although neither Jews nor Christians were allowed inside for centuries until the Israelis won control of Mount Zion in 1949. Through the first gate to the left and upstairs is the **Coenaculum**. Christians (except the Syrian Orthodox) believe it to be the site of Jesus' Last Supper and the Holy Ghost's appearance to the Apostles. The classic Crusader room of the Coenaculum includes two Crusader coats of arms.

Hours: 8:30 a.m. to sundown daily.

Outside, opposite the entrance to the Chamber of the Holocaust and downstairs into a dark, narrow room is what is believed by some to be **King David's Tomb**. The stone coffin, covered by a synagogue altar cover, dates from Crusader times, but the room may have been a post-Second Temple synagogue. Men will need a head covering.

Hours: 8 a.m. to 6 p.m. (5 p.m. in winter) Sunday through Thursday, to 2 p.m. (1 p.m. in winter) Friday. Closed Saturday.

This complex also houses the Diaspora Yeshiva. Its famous (at least in Jerusalem) Yeshiva Diaspora Band or a reasonable substitute present a lively performance here at a *Melava Malka* every Saturday night, 9 p.m. in summer, 8:30 p.m. in winter. Entrance fee. Tel. 722-339. Expect spontaneous dancing with yeshiva students' *payot* (sidelocks) flying.

Across a path is the **Chamber of the Holocaust** (Martef Hasho'ah in Hebrew), a candle-lit memorial to Hitler's Jewish victims. White stone tablets are on the walls, each carrying the name of a destroyed Jewish community. Blue and white urns in one of the rooms contain ashes of death camp victims.

Hours: 9 a.m. to 5 p.m. Sunday through Thursday, to 2 p.m. Friday. Entrance fee.

Close by is the **King David Museum**, which shows King David's life through art.

Hours: 8 a.m. to 6 p.m. Sunday through Thursday, to 2 p.m. Friday. Entrance fee.

Turn left and you will come to the **David Palombo Museum**. Palombo was an outstanding sculptor, whose impressive career was cut short by his accidental death in 1966. He designed the gates to Yad Vashem and the Knesset (Parliament Building). The museum is open at irregular hours, but most often in the morning.

Palombo virtually risked his life daily by living on Mount Zion before 1967. He was literally under Jordanian guns. The Mount was in Israeli hands, while the Old City and East Jerusalem were under Jordanian occupation. Part of Abu Tor, across the Hinnom Valley, also was under the Israeli flag. Israeli soldiers rigged up a cable across the valley that rested on the ground during the day and was put into action at night. It transported supplies and messages between the two sides. Sometimes, it even carried wounded soldiers. You still can see the cable from the southern end of Mount Zion.

From Zion Gate you can follow the road left back to Jaffa Gate for a bus or take the road to the right and to the Jewish Quarter parking lot to catch bus No. 38 to West Jerusalem.

After this day, with its visits to ancient sites that go back 2500 years, the juxtaposition of buildings from different centuries and the exposure to the complex Jewish and Armenian cultures, you may feel as if you have been bludgeoned by history. History does come at you from all sides in Jerusalem. And there is another half of the Old City to be explored, yet. But the order of the first two tours are the ones I feel strongly about. The arrangement of the remaining tours is a suggestion based on a logical sequence.

Third Day
The Other Half

The two other parts of the Old City, the **Christian and the Moslem Quarters** are the setting for a walk that is traditionally looked on as following Jesus' footsteps as he labored to carry the cross to his crucifixion. The backdrop is the sights, sounds and smells of the ancient city's crowded, narrow lanes. The last part of the walk will take you to important examples of Islamic architecture, their beauty almost obscured by the darkness of the streets.

Bring a flashlight to discern the treasures in the Church of the Holy Sepulchre. Allow three hours for the Christian Quarter, about two for the Moslem Quarter, depending on how many shops entice you.

The Christian Quarter and the Via Dolorosa

The Christian Quarter of the Old City first was established when the Church of the Holy Sepulchre was built in the 5th century. In the northwestern section, it is bound on the north by the Old City wall to Damascus Gate, on a short southwestern side by the wall south to Jaffa Gate, on the south by David Street and on the east by the three market streets, Souq el-Lahhamin, Souq el-Attarin and Souq el-Khawajat. But since little is neatly arranged in Jerusalem, a visit to major Christian sites takes one through the Moslem Quarter in the northeast quadrant, as well.

Bus No. 23 or 23a goes to Herod's Gate. Through it and to the left, take El Qadisieh Road, which becomes Aqabat Darwish to Al Mujahideen Road. A left turn here leads directly to Lion's (St. Stephen's) Gate. Just before the gate, on the left, through its own gate, is a peaceful enclave presided over by the Crusader-built **St. Anne's Church**, believed to be located where the house of Anne, mother of Mary, once stood. The building was destroyed and rebuilt many times. The present church dates from 1192 and is regarded as an example of the transition between Roman and Gothic architecture. It was preserved because Sulieman the Magnificent used it as a Moslem school. The church is famous for its excellent acoustics. Stand quietly at the back and pilgrims may give you a demonstration by singing a hymn.

Beyond the church doors is the **Pool of Bethesda**, in a cool, tranquil spot surrounded by greenery, where Jesus is said to have healed the sick. Excavations have uncovered the original structure with its steps leading down into the water.

> Hours: 8 a.m. to noon, 2 p.m. to 6 p.m. Monday through Saturday. In winter, from 2 p.m. to 5 p.m. only.

A few blocks west on Al Mujahideen Road, the **Via Dolorosa** (Path of Sorrow) begins. It is both the name of the route held to be that which Jesus took to his crucifixion and a street in the Christian Quarter. Actually, they aren't one and the same. The street of that name first was constructed during Crusader times and has deviated since then. Archeological findings have changed Jesus' route and even increased the number of Stations of the Cross. The number of places along the route at which there were significant occurrences have increased from seven to 14. But for pilgrims who follow the 14 stations, the spiritual and emotional factors of the journey far outweigh the historical. What may come as a shock is that until the stations fall within the Church of the Holy Sepulchre, they are found in the midst of vivid, ongoing life, often in the heart of a market place. What you see and feel may seem like a paradox, but Jesus had to pass through a similar scene almost 2000 years ago.

At 3 p.m. every Friday, Franciscan priests lead a procession along the route. It begins at Station I and is open to everyone. Perhaps, once in a while, pilgrims will send grateful thoughts toward Israel, for before Israel gained the Old City in the Six-Day War, the Via Dolorosa storm drains ran with sewage and the walkway itself often was littered with garbage. The Israelis dug up the route, laid sewage pipes and utility conduits underground and repaved the streets with new cobblestones. Whenever they uncovered the original massive Roman paving stones, they inserted them into the walk. The effort enabled pilgrims to think about their mission, instead of what they were smelling and where they were stepping.

The courtyard of the El-Omariyah School on Al Mujahideen Road is **Station I** of the Cross. Only few remains exist of the colossal

Antonia Fortress, which stood here. It was built by Herod the Great on an existing Hasmonean fortress and named for his friend, Mark Antony. After Herod's death, Roman governors used it during local festival days, such as Passover. Pontius Pilate was based here (some scholars say he was located in the Herodian Palace near today's Jaffa Gate) when Jesus was brought before him for a private trial in the courtyard.

For a wonderful view of the Temple Mount, walk up the stairs of the boys school and look through the barred windows.

Station II, opposite the school, is where Jesus took up the cross. Inside the Franciscan monastery, on the left is the **Chapel of Judgment,** with flagstones from the Antonia Fortress. On the right is the **Chapel of the Flagellation,** where Jesus was scourged.

> Hours: 6 a.m. to noon, 2 p.m. to 6 p.m. Monday through Saturday. In winter, from 2 p.m. to 5 p.m. only.

Ahead on the Via Dolorosa, the **Ecce Homo Arch** spans the street. The way begins to be more crowded with tourists, local residents and merchants at this point. Rather than think of the increasing commotion that will be going on around you as a distraction, you can think of it as help in simulating the events Jesus endured.

Tradition has it that at the Ecce Homo Arch, Pontius Pilate looked down on Jesus while he was being presented to the waiting crowds and declared, "Ecce homo! (Behold the man!)" However, in fact, the arch is part of a gate constructed by Roman Emperor Hadrian in the second century C.E. to commemorate his victory over the Jewish revolt led by Bar Kochba.

Inside the adjacent **Ecce Homo Convent** can be seen the arch's continuation and pavement stones that were considered to be from the Antonia Fortress until a Dominican scholar proved in 1972 that this area lay outside of the fortress. The stones were grooved to allow water to run to a cistern, which still exists below the paving, and scratched into squares and triangles by Roman legionnaires who passed the time playing games.

> Hours: 8:30 a.m. to 1:30 p.m., 2:30 p.m. to 5:30 p.m. Monday through Saturday. In winter, 8:30 a.m. to 4 p.m.

At the next right turn, the Via Dolorosa leads into El-Wad Road. Narrow as it is, it's a main, commercial artery of the Old City. Left, and almost immediately left again, where a Roman period column lies on the ground, is **Station III.** This is where Jesus fell from exhaustion the first time. Look for large Roman pave stones in the street. Above the door of the small Polish chapel here is a relief showing Jesus fallen under the weight of the cross.

A short distance ahead, past a vegetable market and a cafe and up a few stairs in the street, a relief on the arch over the entrance to the Armenian Church of Our Lady of the Spasm marks this as **Station IV**, where Jesus met his mother. Two sandal prints inside represent where Mary stood as she watched her son go by.

After passing Barquq Road on the left, Hebrew signs appear over a door also on the left. This is the **Yeshivat Torat Chaim**. The Arab family that looked after it during the Jordanian occupation protected it from looters. Religious services resumed here after the city was reunited. At the *kiddush* following Saturday morning services, Jerusalem kugel often is served, a treat not to be missed.

Around the corner to the right into the Via Dolorosa is **Station V**, where Simon of Cyrene, a passerby, was recruited by Roman soldiers to help Jesus carry the cross — probably so Jesus could survive this difficult journey long enough to be crucified.

Just before an arch ahead is **Station VI**. Here Veronica wiped Jesus' face with her handkerchief. Whether or not Veronica knew Jesus before this moment is debated by historians.

At the junction with the bustling Khan ez-Zeit Street, the marker for **Station VII** is above the entrance to a Franciscan chapel facing you. This marks where Jesus fell a second time. It is believed that a gate out of Jerusalem for those condemned to death stood here during Jesus' time. It is possible he saw his own execution notice on the gate.

Across the street and up the slope of Aqabat el-Khanqa, on the left is a cross on the wall of the Greek Monastery of St. Charalambos marks **Station VIII**. This is where Jesus consoled the women of Jerusalem and warned them of catastrophes ahead.

Back to the corner and right into the Khan ez-Zeit Street, there is a stairway on the right. Up the stairs and right is the Coptic Orthodox Queen Helena Church. Ahead is the Coptic Orthodox Patriarchate, **Station IX**, where Jesus fell a third time.

The Coptic community has been on this site since 1219. Beyond the steps to the left is the Ethiopian Compound. It is a terrace on the roof of the Chapel of St. Helena, which is within the Church of the Holy Sepulchre below. Ethiopian monks live in these huts. They say that the olive tree enclosed by a wall is the bush where Abraham found the ram caught in a thicket.

Down to Khan ez-Zeit Street and right, right again into Souq ed-Dabbagha is the Russian Orthodox **St. Alexander's Church** on the right. It has yet to be determined if an ancient wall uncovered on its premises is a remnant from the Second Temple period, the Roman forum or of Emperor Constantine's Church of the Holy Sepulchre.

Hours: 9 a.m. to 1 p.m., 3 p.m. to 5 p.m. Ring the bell.

At the intersection, to the left, is the entrance to the **Lutheran Church of the Redeemer**. Prussia built the church in the last half of the 19th century in 12th-century architectural style on the site of the original church. It was destroyed by Moslems in 1009 along with the rest of this area, known as the Muristan District. The church has a historical link to Jaffa Gate, for it was consecrated by Kaiser Wilhelm II on his 1898 visit. For a great bird's eye view of the Old City and beyond, climb the church tower.

> Hours are 8 a.m. to 1 p.m. Monday, 9 a.m. to 1 p.m. and
> 2 p.m. to 5:30 p.m. daily except Sunday. Entrance fee. Tel.
> 262-543.

Angling off from Souq ed-Dabbagha, close to the entrance to the church, is the area called the **Muristan** (a corruption of the Persian word for "hospital"), where the Crusader Order of the Hospitallers, the Knights of St. John, had its hospital and headquarters. The area now is a Greek bazaar, named Souq Aftimos. The ornamental fountain in the middle of the Muristan was built by the Greek Orthodox Church in the 19th century.

Back to the intersection and left is the **Church of the Holy Sepulchre**, which houses the remaining five Stations of the Cross and the site many Christians believe to be of the crucifixion, entombment and resurrection.

> Hours: 4:30 a.m. to 8 p.m. Modest dress required.

This holiest shrine to much of the Christian world is a dark, confusing warren with a jumble of chapels. It stands over what the Byzantine Queen Helena was convinced was the hill of Golgotha. The name is derived from the Hebrew word for "skull". Perhaps the hill was given that name because that was what the treeless height resembled centuries ago or because of legend that Adam's skull was buried here.

Apparently, this actually was a burial ground at the time of the crucifixion. Later, Hadrian erected a Temple of Venus here. The Byzantine Emperor Constantine had the temple destroyed, so his mother, Helena, could have the first church built on this spot in 335 C.E.

The church was destroyed by the Persians in 614, restored and alternately destroyed and rebuilt several more times. Fire severely damaged the structure in the 19th century and an earthquake in 1927 left its mark. Today, it seems to be constantly under repair.

Still, what is seen now closely resembles the Crusader building of 1149. Only the rotunda above what is held to be Jesus' tomb resembles Queen Helena's 4th century church.

Six Christian communities, none of them Protestant, share responsibility for the church. Each is wildly jealous of the other and each fiercely guards its own turf and rights. They even battle over the prize of which community gets to clean the church. But it is the powerful Greek Orthodox Church that won almost two-thirds of control, so the Greeks tend to sit by serenely while the five other churches fight over what is left. The crumbs have gone to the Ethiopians, whose rooftop monastery you saw earlier in this walk. Because they have the least, they fight most often with the Copts, who have the next least and also a rooftop monastery. For the sake of peace, church doorkeepers are Moslem.

Inside the church entrance is a slab of red stone on the floor. It is the **Stone of the Unction**, which dates from 1810 and covers the spot where it is said Jesus body was anointed after being taken down from the cross.

The Greek Orthodox **Chapel of Adam** is to the right, before the stone. The cleft in the rock here is held to have split apart during an earthquake at the time Jesus died.

The steep stairs on the right lead up to **Calvary**. This is where your flashlight will be a great advantage in getting a better view of the icons and other objects in the next three stations. The Chapel of the Sorrows has two naves. The one on the right is **Station X**, where Jesus was stripped of his garments. Close by is **Station XI**, where he was nailed to the cross.

On the far left is the Greek Orthodox chapel that is **Station XII**. This is believed to be the place of the crucifixion and is richly decorated with precious metals, icons, statues and suspended lamps. Tradition says the cross stood in the silver-inlaid hole in the rock.

Jesus' body was taken off the cross at **Station XIII**, marked by the small Roman Catholic Stabat Mater Dolorosa Altar between the 11th and 12th stations. The wooden statue was made and sent from Lisbon in the late 17th century.

On ground level, to the right, a curved passageway leads to the left. Just past a flight of stairs and directly opposite the entrance to the edicule under the rotunda is the Armenian **Chapel of the Division** of the Raiment on your right, where soldiers distributed Jesus' clothing.

Right and curving to the left, seven arches can be found, each with a different column. These are remains of a Byzantine Church called, **Archway of the Virgin**. A left turn leads to **Station XIV**, the Holy Sepulchre in the center of the rotunda.

The rococo 19th-century edicule, with its onion-shaped cupola, is the focal point of the church. Inside are two tiny rooms. The **Chapel of the Angel** is first. This is where an angel is said to have sat on a stone and proclaimed the resurrection. The sepulchre, the tomb, is next and reached through a low, arched doorway. This is **Station**

XIV. A marble chest in the tiny chamber is considered by many to be Jesus' grave. A priest in these tight confines will offer to burn a candle for you.

Around to the rear of the tomb is the **Chapel of the Copts**. A Copt monk sitting at the entrance will invite you to put your hand through a small hole and feel the rock that was Jesus' tomb. At the opposite side of the church down 13 steps, past crosses scratched on the walls by Christian pilgrims, is the **Chapel of the Discovery of the Cross**, reputed to be the place where Queen Helena found the original cross during her stay in Jerusalem.

Throughout this walk, various sites and the Church of the Holy Sepulchre, especially, indicate the importance of the Greek Orthodox Church in Jerusalem. It is the strongest Christian presence here. If you would like to get a fuller picture of the church, visit the **Greek Patriarchate Museum**, appropriately on Greek Orthodox Patriarchate Road. The priest-curator encountered during a recent visit was from Prospect Park in Brooklyn. Pilgrims' gifts, various patriarchate acquisitions and writings are on view in its Crusader building.

> **Hours: 9 a.m. to 1 p.m., 3 p.m. to 5 p.m. Tuesday through Friday, 9 a.m. to 1 p.m. Saturday. Tel. 284-006.**

For a lunch break outside of the Old City (which will refresh your memory as to what sunshine is), it will be necessary to exit from Damascus Gate. The route takes you left from Greek Orthodox Patriarchate Road onto Christian Quarter Road, right a short distance later at Aqabat el-Khanqa, and then left on Souq Khan ez-Zeit. The last street leads directly to Damascus Gate. The moderately priced Al-Umayyah Restaurant is across the street, between Damascus and Herod Gates.

If you wish to remain within the Old City walls, in the Moslem Quarter, Abu Shukri on El-Wad is among Jerusalem restaurants known for having "the best houmus in town." If that popular place is too crowded, Linda's, another restaurant with "the best houmus in town," is around the corner on the Via Dolorosa.

Jerusalem Syndrome

Now that you have rested your feet and your spirits and, I hope, regained your sense of humor, you may be interested in learning how some other tourists fare when they become immersed in the Holy City's sites, particularly the Christian sites.

Every so often, a tourist who is on pilgrimage comes down with an ailment peculiar to the Holy City. It is called "Jerusalem Syndrome".

Bradley Wilson's experience is typical. Bradley (the name is completely fictitious) manages a supermarket in his hometown in Missouri. He has had excellent relations with his employees and customers, been a loving family man and a devout churchgoer. While he enjoys a good joke, no one has ever held the slightest suspicion that there was anything the least bit eccentric about Bradley.

After many years of dreaming and saving, he and his wife made a pilgrimage to the Holy Land with a church group. The preparations to go were fraught with excitement. From anticipation, Bradley couldn't sleep for days beforehand. When he stepped from the plane at Ben-Gurion Airport, he resisted an urge to get down on his knees and kiss the ground.

His elevated state remained unabated while the group toured Nazareth, Capernaum and other places important in Jesus' life. And then, with his spirits soaring, Bradley and the group journeyed to Jerusalem. Coming on top of everything else he had seen, Jerusalem overwhelmed him.

His second day here, he disappeared from his wife and the rest of the group. Something told him he was John the Baptist.

With his face glowing with a beatific expression and his eyes glazed as they focused on a distant sight only he could see, he stood at a busy Jerusalem intersection and began preaching — not to anyone in particular, but the whole world, in general. He aimed his words over the heads of the crowds that passed him, and when he started to declare his faith in a loud exultant voice, Jerusalemites paid him scant, but sometimes bemused attention.

He was John the Baptist, he shouted, baptizer of Jesus Christ. He had walked the streets of Jerusalem in an earlier time, he insisted, and now he was home once again, ready to baptize one and all. Plainly ecstatic, he preached on and on.

Then he started taking off his clothes.

At that point, a Jerusalem policeman appeared and gently ushered this latter-day John the Baptist away and to a police station. People shouting their messages on Jerusalem street corners is one thing, but getting undressed is another.

It was plain to the authorities that Bradley was another victim of the ailment local physicians and psychiatrists call the Jerusalem Syndrome. The doctors say that when some tourists finally realize their dream of being in Jerusalem, they are shocked by reality. They are carried away emotionally and, like Bradley, take on behavior they never demonstrated before.

The authorities have developed a method of treatment. With Bradley's drivers' license as identification, one person called all over Jerusalem to find out if he was attached to a tour group and another person called Bradley's home telephone in Missouri. It was 5 a.m.

there, and Bradley's teenage son sounded sleepy when he first spoke. Bradley was given the phone and heard his son say, "Hi, Dad, how's the trip? Did ya find me a Coke bottle in Hebrew?" It didn't take long for the victim of Jerusalem Syndrome to realize that instead of John the Baptist, he was Bradley Wilson and had to track down a Coca-Cola bottle for his son.

That's the treatment Jerusalem authorities practice. They have learned that victims of their city's peculiar ailment quickly get in touch with their "other", everyday selves by talking with their family. And that's all it takes: recovery is a phone call away.

But these persons don't come back to reality with a thud when they step out of their temporary St. John the Baptist persona. Even if they went so far as to strip naked in the heart of town, they may be embarrassed, but they aren't sorry. Bradley's feelings were typical. He said that the time when he was being carried along by the Jerusalem Syndrome, "was just about the happiest I've ever known."

And now it's back to the narrow lanes of the Old City. From the more familiar Christian sites, this walk goes to the more remote Moslem world.

The Moslem Quarter

The **Moslem Quarter** of the Old City used to be considered the "mixed" quarter, because Jews as well as Moslems used to live there. But Jews were killed in Arab riots, particularly those in 1929 and 1936, and many fled. Finally, after the Jordanian occupation of the Old City, no Jews remained anywhere in the Old City. In 1948, women and children were sent to West Jerusalem; the men were taken to Jordan.

Since the city's reunification in 1967, Jews have returned to what now is known as the Moslem Quarter. Although not in great numbers, they are back to pray in their synagogues, study in *yeshivot* and even to live. A Jewish dentist, born in Morocco, has opened her office in this part of the Old City. In any walk through the Moslem Quarter, it is intriguing to look for signs of the Jewish presence, past and present. It's like uncovering a secret.

The largest quarter, the Moslem Quarter is in the northeast part of the Old City. Roughly, the quarter is bounded by the Old City's external walls on the north from Damascus Gate east and from the northeast corner of the wall south to the Temple Mount. Internally, the quarter, generally, is east of Souq Khan ez-Zeit from Damascus Gate south and its extensions to David Street, and north of Bab el-Silsileh St (Street of the Chain).

Entrance through Damascus Gate isn't direct. You have to make two turns to get inside. The better to stymie invaders with their long lances.

Inside is a jumble of stores, street vendors, sights, smells and a few stairs to negotiate. On the left, almost immediately is a home that belonged to a Jewish doctor in the 19th century. Now under restoration, it is one of the clearest examples of the Jewish presence in the Moslem Quarter years ago.

Ahead, angling off to the right is Khan es-Zeit Street (with its tempting pastry shops), which was the beginning of the Romans' Cardo, following the natural descent of the Tyropoeon (Cheese-maker's) Valley. The street straight ahead is El-Wad. Following it in the midst of this heavily Moslem atmosphere you find the Christian Stations of the Cross III, IV and V, which you saw this morning. Jewish institutions are another non-Moslem presence here. After Barquq Road, **Yeshivat Torah Chaim** is on the left and just past the Via Dolorosa farther down on El-Wad, the **Synagogue of the Georgian Congregation** is on the right. Both are in active use today.

Turn right at Aqabat et-Takiya Street. On the left side is a building now used as a school, **Madrasah** (theological seminary) **Resaiya**. It is distinguished by its striped facade of black basalt, pink marble and white limestone, blending both Mameluke and Ottoman features. Up the stairs to the left is a Moslem orphanage built in 1398 as a palace.

The Mamelukes, slaves who became kings, are remembered for their architecture with rows of alternating colored stone, an arch like a clam shell or the roof of a stalactite cave over entrances and projections on either side of these entrances for guards.

In the reverse direction, the street on the other side of El-Wad, is Ala Uddin (Aladdin). This street is the **African Quarter**. It is quiet here after El-Wad and the quarter seems isolated and poor. The quarter is said to be named for Africans who came here in the 1930s from Chad, Senegal, Nigeria and the Sudan and now number 200 families. Others maintain the Africans came with the Mamelukes. The buildings in which they live are 13th century. On the left is the oldest Mameluke doorway in Jerusalem.

At the end of the street, leading to the Temple Mount, **is Bab el-Nadir** Prison Gate — named for the prison that one of the nearby buildings used to be. Back to El-Wad and left at Bab el-Hadid Street, you will pass the 15th century **Madrasah Muziriya** on the right. The street forks. The left fork, at the end, is a short stretch of the Western Wall, a continuation of the same Wall seen at the plaza. This stretch, called **Hakotel Hakatan** (The Small Wall), is closer than the famous portion of the Wall to what is considered the location of the Second Temple. Shabbat services take place here.

Back at the fork, the side that wasn't taken before, which now is on the left, leads through a dark tunnel. Pay attention to the stairs.

You will come out at the **Souq el-Qattanin** (Cotton Market). A flourishing cotton market after it was built in 1329, it is only partially used and forlorn now. But you still can find some fabric on sale in the Mameluke-period stores on both sides of the market.

A right turn into the souk and there is El-Wad yet again. Across it and into Aqabat el-Khalidieh, you may notice, here and on other streets in the quarter, paintings on walls and doors of Jerusalem's Dome of the Rock and Mecca's Qa'ba, Islam's most sacred shrine. These paintings announce that a resident within has completed pilgrimages to Islam's three holy cities, Mecca, Medina and Jerusalem.

Another item of interest to watch for is a place on the right of doorposts that looks as if the stone has been gouged. The damage is the result of efforts by non-Jews to remove a *mezzuzah* (a rectangular-shaped object containing a Biblical verse) which previous Jewish occupants had affixed to the doorpost according to religious law.

This area, around Aqabat el-Khalidieh especially, was the location of synagogues, *yeshivot* and other Jewish institutions. One of the most intriguing Jewish institutions that has made its home in this quarter is housed in a three-story building on the right that belonged to a charities trust for North African Jews. Today it is known as **Yeshivat Torah Hakohanim.** The men studying here are learning the religious responsibility of the Jewish priestly class, the *Kohanim*, so they will be ready when, as they believe, the Messiah will come and the Temple will be restored.

The route returns to El Wad and left at Bab el-Silsileh (Street of the Chain). On the right, just past Rehov Ladach is the **Tashtamuriya Building,** the first of several examples on this street of outstanding architecture. This one goes back to the 13th century. Left, opposite the beginning of Rehov Hakotel leading to the Western Wall Plaza, is the **Jaliqya Building**. Opposite it is el-Khaldiya, a library now closed. Before the Gate of the Chain is the **Madrasah et-Tankiziya,** a lovely Mameluke building built in 1329 and now a Moslem college.

Rehov Hakotel will take you to the Western Wall Plaza. Dung Gate is at its opposite side. There you can find taxis and bus No. 1 to West Jerusalem.

A tour of the Christian and Moslem Quarters can be a turbulent experience for the emotions it raises about Jesus and the impact of his life. Although, Jesus, too, was surrounded by a crush of humanity as he made his way up "the Street of Sorrows", you may have found yourself squelching introspective emotions as you dodged donkeys and slid through crowded, narrow lanes. And despite the time spent in the Moslem Quarter and seeing its graceful, imaginative architecture, this culture remains behind closed doors.

Perhaps this is the time to find a quiet place to sit and reflect. Some

A view of the "Christian Quarter" of the Old City of Jerusalem.

options are Independence or Liberty Bell Parks or the top of the Eilon Tower Hotel (City Tower) at Rehov Ben-Yehuda and Rehov King George where there is a restaurant and a magnificent view of the Holy City and the setting sun changing the color of its stone.

Fourth Day
From the Mountain to the Valley

For a change of pace from sunless, narrow lanes and crowds of people, this walk goes to a part of Jerusalem that is like the countryside. This tour starts at the top of the **Mount of Olives** (Olivet), where Jews believe the Messiah will announce his arrival by blowing a *shofar* (ram's horn). The descent includes visits to some of the loveliest churches in Jerusalem and to one of the oldest cemeteries on earth. From there, the tour continues into the **Kidron Valley** with its ancient tombs and examples of burial customs from thousands of years ago.

The longer you are in Jerusalem, in all likelihood, the more tombs you may visit. This may seem macabre, but in Jerusalem, tombs have historical as well as religious significance. The ways in which they were used, their architecture and their artwork speak about the people who were buried there.

In the afternoon, I recommend a visit to **Bethlehem**, a short (five miles—eight kilometers), inexpensive bus ride south of Jerusalem.

Be sure to protect yourself from the sun on this walk. Refreshment stands are scarce, so you might want to bring along a beverage and a snack. Bring a flashlight for viewing the tombs. It's best to avoid this walk on a Sunday, when church services will limit sightseeing. On Saturday, a Jewish burial site on the Mount of Olives is closed. But the tombs in the Kidron Valley will be open. Keep in mind that Christian sites close from noon until 2 p.m. or 3 p.m. To reach the Mount of Olives by public transportation, flag down East Jerusalem bus No. 75 (these buses are green) at Damascus Gate. Allow two-and-a-half hours for the descent and at least that much time for Bethlehem.

The Mount of Olives

From the **Mount of Olives**, you can see, if not forever, at least Jerusalem's yesterday and today. The view carries the eye into the Kidron Valley and its tombs, across to the ruins below Dung Gate of the Jerusalem that was King David's, to Mount Zion, to the walled Old City, to the towers of new Jerusalem beyond, even to Nebi Samuel, where the Prophet Samuel is said to be buried.

Try to see this view at night also, when Jerusalem is golden not from its stones, but from its lights.

The Mount of Olives, 2600 feet high, once was thickly covered by the trees that gave it its name. Now it is covered with graves, shrines, churches and monasteries and topped by a hotel.

To most Jews, the Intercontinental Hotel, built near the Mount of Olives' highest point during the Jordanian occupation, is a jarring presence. The original road to the hotel was laid over Jewish graves. Arab builders even incorporated headstones into the road. The Israelis installed a new road and reconstructed the graves.

The Mount of Olives is Judaism's most holy place of burial. The belief is that when the Messiah blows his shofar from the top of the Mount of Olives, the dead will awaken. Those buried here will be awakened first. Those buried elsewhere will get here by rolling underground.

It was on this mountain that King David is said to have cried over Absalom, the son who betrayed him, and it was from this mountain that rabbis waited for the sight of the new moon to indicate the start of a new month. With its appearance, they built a huge bonfire. At the sight, watchers on other hills built their signaling bonfires, and so the word was spread.

For Christians, churches on the mount commemorate events in Jesus' final entry into Jerusalem. But to make things confusing, there are at least two Gethsemanes and two places credited as the location

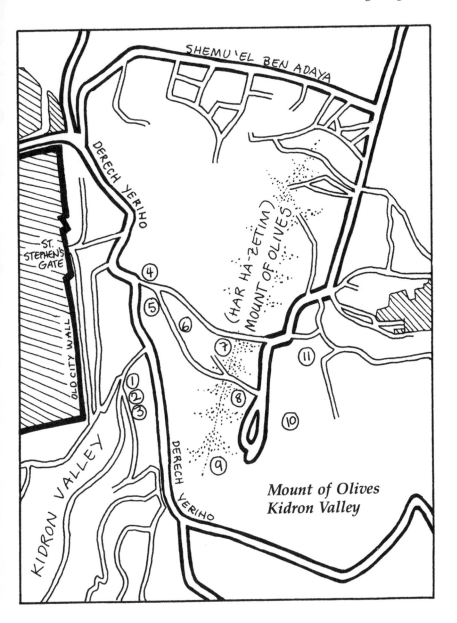

Mount of Olives
Kidron Valley

1. Absalom's Pillar
2. Tombs of the Sons of Hezir
3. Tomb of Zechariah
4. Tomb of Mary (Church of the Assumption)
5. Church of All Nations (Church of the Agony)
6. Church of Mary Magdalene (Russian)
7. Church of Dominus Flevit
8. Tombs of the Prophets
9. Jewish Cemeteries
10. Intercontinental Hotel
11. Church of Pater Noster

for Jesus' ascension to heaven. One of the latter is at the Russian Orthodox Monastery, behind and to the right of the Intercontinental, where the six-story bell tower was constructed on the spot from which the Russians believe Jesus rose. The monastery is closed to the public.

The main road from the Intercontinental leads to a string of churches, Christian religious sites and, by a bit of a detour, to the Jewish cemetery on the mount. Keep in mind that in Jerusalem's typically "layered" architecture, almost all the churches of today were built on what were mosques, which in turn were built on what were churches.

The first church reached is the **Church of Eleona** and the **Church of the Pater Noster** to the right from the hotel and through a gate. Churches have been built and destroyed on this spot since the 4th century C.E. The present Pater Noster, where Jesus is believed to have taught the Lord's Prayer, was built in 1874 and financed by a French princess. Inside, the Lord's Prayer is commemorated on plaques in more than 40 languages. At the end of the church courtyard is a reconstruction of the Byzantine Church of Eleona, where Jesus is said to have revealed the Second Coming.

> **Hours: 8:30 a.m. to noon, 3 p.m. to 4:30 p.m. daily except Sunday.**

The Church of the Ascension, opposite the Pater Noster. With its dome and minaret, it is on the highest point of the Mount of Olives and is one of the claimed location of Jesus' ascension to heaven.

The octagonal Church of the Ascension, located on an earlier church, was built by the Crusaders in the 12th century. A rock inside shows the imprint of what is said to have been Jesus' foot. This church is a focal point of the celebration of the Feast of the Ascension.

An Arab family living next door are caretakers. Apply to them for entry into the church, if it is closed.

The route back in the direction of the Intercontinental will bring you to a sign giving the direction of the Common Grave of the Fallen of the Old City. A stairway here leads down the mountain and along the edge of the Jewish cemetery. **The Tombs of the Prophets** is a cave with a fence around it back in the Jewish cemetery. Haggai, Malachi and Zecharia are said to be buried here.

> **Hours 8 a.m. to 3 p.m. except Saturday. Free.**

A Common Grave for 48 who fell in the battle for the Jewish Quarter in the War of Independence is farther down the slope, also on the left. Their bodies were found after the Six-Day War reunited the city, and they were reburied here. If you check the ages on the stones, you will see how young some of the fighters were.

Feel free to walk through the cemetery. It is covered, mostly, by flat headstones. The pebbles on top of the slabs were left by mourners.

The **Basilica of Dominus Flevit**, off the road continuing down. With a tear-shaped cupola, it was built in 1955 to mark the spot where Jesus wept. Architect Antonio Barluzzi preserved a Byzantine mosaic floor, left from the original Crusader church that was here, in the apse.

> Hours: 8 a.m. to noon, 3 p.m.to 6 p.m. summers, to 5 p.m. winter, daily.

The **Russian Church of Mary Magdelene**, farther down to the right. Its seven golden onion domes make it the most distinctive sight on the Mount of Olives. It was built in the 16th-century Russian style by Czar Alexander III to honor his mother. Consecration was in 1888. The church claims Gethsemane on its grounds.

> Hours: 9 a.m. to noon 2 p.m. to 5 p.m. Thursday and Saturday, 10 a.m. to noon Sunday. Tel. 282-897. Entrance fee.

Church of All Nations (Basilica of the Agony), just below. Contributions from 12 nations paid for the building. It was designed in 1924 by architect Antonio Barluzzi, who also designed Dominus Flevit. Many domed, Byzantine in design, its colorful mosaic facade shines brilliantly as it reflects the sunset.

The **Grotto of Gethsemane** is reached through a door next to the church. With its grotto of olive trees, this makes a peaceful rest stop. The Franciscans have owned this place since 1392.

> Hours: 8:30 a.m. to noon, 3 p.m. to 6 p.m. summer, to 5 p.m. winter.

Follow the sign on Jericho Road that points to the Kidron Valley.

The Kidron Valley Tombs

The **Kidron Valley** at the foot of the Mount of Olives was once far deeper than it is now. It probably was more like a canyon. Accumulations over the centuries of ruins, garbage and silt have changed the configuration. In it are examples of Second Temple period memorials and tombs. Like sentinels themselves, they stand unguarded: there is no fence to protect them and no ticket taker to sit before them. They simply are open to all who want to explore. But visitors need necessary tools of exploration: a flashlight to see and a body that can fold up like a pretzel in order to climb in and out of the small tomb openings.

During the Second Temple Period (536 B.C.E. to 70 C.E.) and after, well-to-do families buried their dead in natural or quarried caves that belonged to the family. Inside, ledges were cut and the dead laid on them. Then the entrance was closed until nothing was left of the body but bones. The bones later were gathered and interred in stone containers called ossuaries, which were placed farther back in the cave. A cave could hold generations of bones. Thus a dead person's bones almost literally were gathered unto his father's.

The ossuaries and the caves weren't bare, but had floral and geometric decorations carved into them. Humans and animals weren't included, because of the rabbinic interpretation that the Second Commandment forbids their reproduction.

South on Derech Hashiloah, off Jericho Road, are four tombs or memorials carved out of bedrock. The first one reached and the last one built is **Absalom's Memorial Pillar**. It dates from some nine centuries after Absalom lived. Absalom, said to have been King David's favorite son, turned on his father and led a revolt against him. The structure acquired that name, for some inexplicable reason, during Crusader times. Freestanding, the memorial shows an amalgam of Egyptian, early and later Greek influences.

Close by is the **Tomb of Jehoshaphat**. It was uncovered only in 1924. Jews of Jerusalem used the tomb to bury their worn-out holy books. Since the books carried the name of God, they couldn't be destroyed. As it turned out, this practice has led to some major historical finds in our day.

A few steps south is the **Tomb of the Sons of Hezir**, an artificial cave with pillars in front. The priestly Hezir family is mentioned in the Book of Nehemiah. The tomb has several rooms and is a classical example of Second Temple Period burial practices.

Next is the **Tomb of Zechariah**, carved out of rock and topped by a pyramid. This tomb had several names over the centuries, but finally its present name stuck. Like the Hezir Tomb, it probably was cut during Hasmonean times, between 129 B.C.E. to 63 B.C.E.

Why tombs for Zechariah both on the Mount of Olives and in the Kidron Valley? Some rabbis point out that because he told the king and people what they didn't want to hear, the prophet was stoned to death. That was an unforgivable act against a prophet, so the construction of two tombs for him was a way of making amends.

Be sure to look up at the view from here of the sun-bleached tombstones climbing the Mount of Olives and of the Arab (and formerly also Yemenite Jewish) village of **Silwan** clinging to its hillside. This sight inspired Saul Bellow to write in *To Jerusalem and Back* that the city reminded him of sun-bleached bones. Closer to you may be some silvery olive trees and shiny, ample-leafed fig trees.

Arab buses back to the city may be found back on Jericho Road or by continuing along the Kidron Valley to the Gihon Spring, about half a kilometer south. The energetic can hike up the slope to Dung Gate, but to go on to Bethlehem, it is most convenient to return to East Jerusalem, via a bus on Jericho Road, and then to take Arab bus No. 22 at Damascus Gate or a *sherut* at the stands across the street.

If you wish to have lunch in Bethlehem, the Granada Grill Bar and El Andalus Restaurants (both of which serve Arab food, despite their names) are in Manger Square and the St. George Restaurant is in the Municipality Building.

Bethlemen

About one-and-a-half miles before Bethlehem is **Rachel's Tomb**. According to the Book of Genesis, Rachel, Jacob's wife, was buried "on the road" to Ephrat (Bethlehem). The hard-working Englishman, Sir Moses Montefiore, won Jewish ownership for the tomb. In one of its two rooms (the other is for men) is a large tomb, which usually is encircled by red twine and surrounded by fervently praying women.

> **Hours: 8 a.m. to 6 p.m. Sunday through Thursday, to 1 p.m. Friday. Free.**

The name, Bethlehem, translates in Hebrew as "House of Bread"; in Arabic as "House of Meat." It has been significant to both Jews and Christians. Besides being near the place where it is believed Rachel died some 1600 years ago, it is known in Judaism as the city in which Ruth, that loyal convert to Judaism ("Whither thou goest, I shall go"), met and married Boaz. From their line, David was born, the shepherd who became king.

But Bethlehem is most famous for being known as Jesus' birthplace. The Church of the Nativity, commanding Manger Square, marks the place where it is believed He was born. It is one of the few Christian buildings remaining intact from the early Christian period. The Samaritans destroyed the first church built here in 326, but Emperor Justinian erected the present church in the 6th century. Persians invading in 614 spared it. Its physical changes have been minimal.

Similarly to the Church of the Holy Sepulchre in Jerusalem, ownership of the Church of the Nativity is shared. Here, there are fewer denominations involved. Still, the Greek Orthodox, Armenians and Latins (Roman Catholics) must adhere strictly to schedules.

To enter the gloomy church through the Door of Humility, it is necessary to bend (or bow, according to one's interpretation). Stairs on either side of the altar in the nave lead to the Grotto of the Nativity, dimly lit and its air heavy with incense.

> **Hours: 6 a.m. to 6 p.m. Men must wear long pants. And obviously shorts also are out for women.**

Part of the complex of chapels and grottos attached to the Church of the Nativity is the Latin **Church of St. Catherine**, reached through a door in the apse of the older building. It's in this bright church that midnight mass at Christmas is televised to the world. Not all those persons packed into the church that night are Christians. Jewish Israelis love to attend for the pageantry. It is exotic to them.

Hours: 8 a.m. to noon, 2:30 p.m. to 6 p.m. Tel. 742-425.

The Milk Grotto is on Milk Grotto Street, southwest of the Church of the Nativity. The Franciscans built a church over the place where Mary was believed to have spilled milk while nursing Jesus.

Hours: 8 to 11:45 a.m., 2 p.m. to 5 p.m.

Aside from its religious significance, Bethlehem is a charming town with its winding streets, white buildings and views out to the desert. It also has a souk, beginning off Manger Square, which some avid shoppers prefer to the one in Jerusalem's Old City.

Except for Rachel's Tomb, outside of the city, Bethlehem's place in both Jewish and Christian history, isn't obvious. You have to carry its importance to Judaism in your memory of Bible stories. In its Christian aspect, Bethlehem is the reversal of the Church of the Holy Sepulchre where Jesus died. Bethlehem celebrates life.

The Kidron Valley tombs aren't the last that should be seen during a visit to Jerusalem. The tombs of the Kings, the Sanhedrin, Jason and Simon the Just are others. It isn't only their art work that makes them intriguing. The bones may have been removed, but the spirit of the dead rattle around inside. You can feel it, without its being either spooky or mystical. It's almost as if you can touch their laughter, ambitions and tears. And this feeling, too, is characteristic of Jerusalem. The way Jerusalem entwines past and present is among its magical aspects.

JERUSALEM SCENE:

On the road south of Bethlehem, Morty, who is driving his battered car to Tekoa, sees a truck facing the opposite direction stopped at the edge of the road. A man sits at the wheel and several others stand around it. They are Arabs.

Morty stops his car and asks in Hebrew if they need some help. The man sitting at the wheel responds in English, "Speak English." In the identical tone of voice in which he asked the question in Hebrew, Morty asks in English, "Do you need some help?"

Now he gets an answer. In English, the man says, "No." Still with the same tone of equanimity he had used before, Morty says, again in English, "I just wanted to know if I could be of help," and he drives on.

The Fifth Day
Further into the Past

The further reaches of Jerusalem's history, bit of adventure and some delicate beauty are part of this walk. This walk goes deeper into Jerusalem's history than previous ones by a millennium and more. It begins in the morning at the **City of David** — the Jerusalem that King David built on the slopes of the Kidron Valley. Close to it, you may travel through the tunnel where King Hezekiah's men worked desperately to outwit invaders. These places have dramatic stories to tell. In contrast, the afternoon offers the tranquil beauty of the Temple Mount. Keep in mind that the sites on the Temple Mount are closed Fridays.

The area of the City of David that is open so far can be reached by descending the slope to the right of Dung Gate (Bus No. 1 will drop you there), as you face it. A right turn below the parking lot brings you to the road to Siloam Pool, which leads to the southern entrance to the City of David. If, instead of making that right turn, but continue on the road, you will reach the northern entrance. A right turn there puts you on Observation Point Path to the City of David. Allow two-and-a-half hours for the City of David and the tunnel walk; two hours for visiting the Temple Mount.

Don't forget your hat. Also, bring a flashlight and wear sneakers and clothes that can get wet.

Despite this information on how to find the City of David and Hezekiah's Tunnel, I highly recommend joining an organized tour for visiting them. It isn't easy for persons on their own to find their way around at these places. Besides, wading through the narrow, unlit tunnel is more comforting when done in the company of others.

The City of David and Hezekiah's Tunnel

The oldest part of Jerusalem is outside of the walls of the Old City. The original Jerusalem, which is called the **City of David**, wasn't on the heights by the Temple Mount, but on the slopes of Ophel, south of it.

Excavations, conducted systematically only since 1978, have uncovered 25 strata going back to the Chalcolithic Period in the fourth millennium B.C.E. Later findings are of the Canaanite period in the second millennium B.C.E., as well as of King David's and King Solomon's reigns and even after the Jews' return from Babylon. Jerusalem's oldest houses — 5000-year-old, early-Canaanite one-room structures — have been uncovered on bedrock. Among items found were two stone toilet seats from the 8th-century B.C.E., which Israelis love to note are in sharp contrast to the Turkish holes in the floor that were standard in Jerusalem even in modern times.

Cities preceded David's here by 2000 years, because this place was both high enough to be defended and close to a stream in the valley. The Jebusites, a Canaanite people, built a shaft to obtain water from the Gihon Spring without leaving city walls. One story about David's conquest of the city tells of one of David's men who discovered and scaled the shaft. David's army then took control of the water supply, so the Jebusites were forced to surrender.

Named for the man who found the opening in 1867, **Warren's Shaft** is open to the public. With your flashlight, you can look up its height. It is located about 110 yards below the entrance to the City of David on the south side.

> **Open from 9 a.m. to 5 p.m. Sunday through Thursday, to 1 p.m. Friday. Entrance fee. Tel. 224-404.**

The entrance to **Hezekiah's Tunnel** is below Warren's Shaft. The profound Jewish memory of the past saved the day, when in 700 B.C.E. another Jewish king, Hezekiah, remembered the story of how David couquered the Jebusites. Chronicles II: 32, tells how the Assyrian Sennacherib and his army descended on Jerusalem "like wolves on the fold." King Hezekiah took action to keep them from controlling the city's water supply. First, he stopped the waters of Gihon. Then he had a tunnel dug that brought water from outside the city walls into the city. Afterwards, he blocked the tunnel entrance from outside the walls.

You can walk ("slosh" is more accurate) the 570 yards through Hezekiah's Tunnel in your "may-get-wet" clothes. Water height varies, but averages thigh level. This is an experience not to be missed. On the one hand, you can feel as adventurous as a kid. On the other, you can feel the anxiety of the men who hastily labored to achieve this startling engineering feat to save Jerusalem from Sennacherib. The water flow, which used to rise and fall unexpectedly, is mechanically controlled, so there is no danger of suddenly finding yourself swimming. The tunnel was dug with great urgency from both ends at once. Tool marks on the walls tell the story of which direction the excavators were coming from.

The tunnel barely was finished when King Sennacherib's army arrived. But the invaders mysteriously succumbed to disease, beat a quiet retreat and left the Jews victorious and with a remarkable and handy water tunnel.

You exit at the **Pool of Siloam** (Shiloah) and a huge Coca-Cola sign. Jews come to the pool during Rosh Hashana to cast their sins into the water symbolically. Christians believe this is where Jesus told a blind man to wash and he would see, and the man did. Because of this, some people consider the pool to have healing powers.

The tunnel is open from 9 a.m. to 3 p.m. Sunday through Thursday, to 1 p.m. Friday. Closed Saturday. Entrance fee. The pool is open from 8:30 a.m. to 4 p.m. Sunday through Thursday, to 3 p.m. Friday. Closed Saturday. Free.

An Arab bus, which stops on the road near the Pool of Siloam, goes up the valley to the East Jerusalem side of the Old City. From there, the entrance to the Temple Mount from the ramp at the Western Wall Plaza can be reached through Damascus Gate. An alternative way of getting there is by hiking back up the slope to Dung Gate, a moderately strenuous walk of about half an hour.

If you are energetic enough to hike back up to the Old City, you can have lunch in the Jewish Quarter at Hahoma, Rehov Hayehudim 128, near the Cardo, which serves kosher Moroccan fare, or the Quarter Cafe, upstairs near the Burnt House, which is the more informal and the less expensive of the two.

The Temple Mount

The Temple Mount, Mount Moriah (pronounced Mor-ee-AH), (also known as Haram esh-Sharif by Moslems) is considered by the Jewish mystical writings, the Zohar, as the center of the world. Its history offers quintessential evidence that because of continuous religious wars, harmony was absent for centuries from the center of the world's City of Peace.

This is where Abraham is said to have followed God's orders and offered his beloved son, Isaac, as a sacrifice. King David put an altar here, and his son, Solomon, built the First Temple on this rise in the 10th century B.C.E.

Nebuchadnezzar destroyed the First Temple in 587 B.C.E. Some 70 years later, after the Jews returned from exile in Babylonia, the Temple was rebuilt.

Then the Second Temple on the Temple Mount, which Herod had raised to become an elevated plateau, was destroyed by the Romans.

The site became a shrine to Jupiter which, in turn, was transformed into a Christian church. With the Moslem conquest, evidence of Christianity was wiped from the Mount, and the **Dome of the Rock** was erected in 691 over the very rock on which Abraham was said to have offered his son. The Crusaders turned the building into a church, but it was restored to its original purpose when Moslems regained Jerusalem. Although Israel was the most recent conqueror of the Temple Mount, it has made no move to alter the status quo.

The Dome of the Rock isn't a mosque. It enshrines the rock from which Moslems believe Mohammed made his Night Journey astride his horse to visit Allah in heaven. But there also was a strong political reason for the Dome of the Rock's existence. The Moslem world at

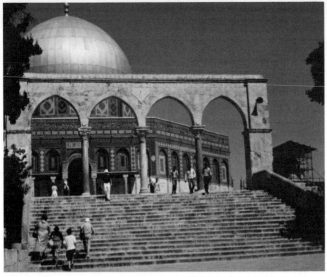

The always impressive approach to the Dome of the Rock.

the time was torn by conflict over which faction could claim to be Mohammed's heir. Khalif Abd el-Malik, an Umayyad whose seat of power was Damascus, wanted to discourage his followers from making pilgrimage to Mecca and possibly falling under the influence of his rivals. Therefore, he had the Dome of the Rock constructed in hopes of establishing Jerusalem as the major Moslem pilgrimage destination. His effort didn't achieve that objective, but it left a magnificent legacy.

Guides will point to an indentation in the rock as the hoofprint of Mohammed's horse. There is no evidence that Mohammed ever actually was in Jerusalem.

The eight-sided building, blue and golden, is one of the loveliest and most graceful to be seen anywhere. Many of its 45,000 exterior tiles were installed under Suleiman the Magnificent in the 1500s. Its golden dome, which provides the signature view of Jerusalem, was real gold at one time. Today its gleam is from gilded aluminum. There is a plan to cover the dome with gold leaf, eventually.

Inside, mosaics cover the walls. The mystical, mythical rock under the dome is surrounded by a wooden fence. A structure nearby contains three hairs from Mohammed's beard. They were sent to Jerusalem by a Turkish sultan in 1609.

Opposite the entrance to the Dome of the Rock is **al-Aqsa Mosque**, built on the site of previous churches and mosques destroyed by war, earthquakes and fire. Al-Aqsa means "the farthermost point" and refers to the farthermost point the Prophet reached from Medina in his flight on his miraculous horse. That point was construed by Moslems as meaning Jerusalem. Little remains of the original mosque built in 670.

The spacious, rectangular building, with its 12 white Carrara marble pillars, can hold 5000 worshipers. Much to be seen inside is the result of extensive restoration in the 1930s and '40s. Outside, its silver dome contrasts to the golden dome opposite it like the moon and the sun. It was at al-Aqsa's entrance that King Abdullah of Jordan, grandfather of King Hussein, was murdered in 1951 by an Arab.

The trapezoid that forms the Mount is a pleasant, park-like space with fountains and other, smaller buildings. To the right of the ramp from the Western Wall plaza is the **Islamic Museum**, which houses a rich display of items from the Temple Mount. The Islamic Museum shouldn't be confused with the Museum of Islamic Art in West Jerusalem.

> Hours for the Dome of the Rock, al-Aqsa and the Islamic Museum are 8 a.m. to 12:30 p.m., 1:30 p.m. to 4 p.m. Saturday through Thursday. Closed Friday. Hours differ during Ramadan and some other Islamic holidays. Entrance fee.

One of the most overpowering aspects of this walk and those through the Old City is the layering of cultures and religions that is right before your eyes. Whoever is the most powerful at the moment gets to knock down what existed before. Even in mid-20th century, Arabs destroyed Jewish houses of worship, as well as almost everything else in the Jewish Quarter in Jerusalem. Yet the current "rulers" of all of Jerusalem, the Israelis, have let Islamic and Christian religious sites be. They improved some of them (the Via Dolorosa), opened them to all and turned their administration over to their respective parent religions. Does this mean the world improved between 1948 and 1967? or, are Israelis more sensitive, less cruel — or just smarter as to the repercussions?

Sixth Day
A Great Leap Forward

The locations of this day's walk take you centuries forward from the previous ones. In this, your surroundings will be little more than 100 years old. After the previous walks, that should seem scarcely a hiccup in time. This walk is through some of the most picturesque and religiously orthodox neighborhoods in West Jerusalem. Be sure to dress modestly. If you go on a Friday, **Mea She'arim** should be full of hustle and bustle while its residents prepare for Shabbat, but time yourself to get to the **Bucharan Quarter** before its shops — Kuzari Kuzari and Chen Jewelry — close at 12:30 p.m. The second half of the day goes to old neighborhoods that have been reconstructed: **Mishkenot Sha'ananim, Yemin Moshe** and an artisans' quarter, **Khut-**

sot Hayotzer. Plan on two-and-a-half hours for the morning walk, two hours for the afternoon's.

Nahalat Shiva, Mea She'arim and the Bucharan Quarter

Enter **Nahalat Shiva** (Estates of the Seven) by turning down Rehov Ma'alot off Rehov Yafo, below Kikar Zion (Zion Square). It was the third neighborhood founded outside the wall, the second that was permanent and the first by and for people who already lived in Jerusalem. The seven men who established it in 1869 were led by the dedicated (some said, "crazy") Yosef Rivlin.

The neighborhood may appear to be falling apart, but it now costs a pretty penny to buy into it.

Notice the way the houses are arranged around courtyards. All the cooking was done in courtyards where rainfall was collected in the cisterns and provided the only water supply.

The route to Mea She'arim goes across Rehov Yafo and up Rehov Harav Kook (named for the same Rav Kook quoted earlier in the section on the Western Wall). On the left will be the **Ticho House.** Now a museum and vegetarian restaurant, it was the home of artist Anna Ticho and her ophthalmologist husband. Inside the thick-walled Arab-style house are the Ticho's extensive *chanukia* (Chanukah candelabras) collection and Anna's splendid paintings of the desert around Jerusalem.

> **Hours: 10 a.m. to 5 p.m. Sunday, Monday, Wednesday and Thursday; to 10 p.m. Tuesday; to 2 p.m. Friday. Closed Saturday. Entrance fee. Tel. 698-243.**

Across Rehov Hanevi'im is Rehov Hahabbashim, probably more famous as **Ethiopian Street.** On it, you'll see some of the loveliest houses in the city. Every other one is set back on its lot, so every house has four exposures. With houses not lined up in a straight line, as they usually are, the street was given greater interest than it otherwise would have had (what a pity that idea has been lost). On the right is the **Ethiopian Church,** described in Chapter 13, "Discover Heavenly Jerusalem: Churches, Synagogues, Family Ties." Across the street, marked by a plaque (unless it's been removed by Jews who don't recognize the state of Israel) was the home of Eliezer Ben-Yehuda, the dedicated man who revived Hebrew as a living language at the end of the 19th century.

Ethiopian Street jogs after a cross street and becomes Rehov Shlomo Zalman Bahran, named for Mea She'arim's founder. Rehov Mislonim on the right and the gate at No. 34 on the left leads into **Mea She'arim** (Hundred Fold, named for a line in Genesis). The community of ultra-Orthodox Jews was founded for ultra-Orthodox Jews. It is important to remember that these people were there from the neighborhood's beginning.

Mea She'arim is a series of row houses in an almost fortress-like setting. When initial construction was completed in 1875, it was situated in a wilderness. The need to provide protection for the population from marauders was paramount.

If you are there on Friday, the bearded men of the neighborhood may already be in their various styles of holiday dress.

The flavor of Mea She'arim, with men in black frock coats, women with scarves covering their hair and the frequent sound of the Yiddish language instead of Hebrew, is old-world Ashkenazi. It is almost as if the clock has been set back a few hundred years. Don't be surprised by the posters and graffiti that heap epithets on the State of Israel. Many people here refuse to recognize the legitimacy of the nation's existence. Their position is that only God can create the Jewish nation. The Zionist position is that only God could have created the miracle that allowed the nation to be born and survive an invasion of five Arab nations' armies.

An exit at the far side of Mea She'arim will put you on Rehov Mea She'arim. A left turn will bring you to Rehov Yehezkel. To the right, six blocks later, is Rehov Habucharim (Rehov David), the center of the **Bucharan Quarter**.

The neighborhood was built in 1893 by wealthy Jews who came from the Asiatic-Russian province of Buchara. Today, Buchara is part of the Soviet Republic of Uzbekistan. A community of Persian Jews also has been part of the neighborhood from its early years.

After Mea She'arim, this neighborhood has a spacious feel to it. Some of the homes are palatial. But now they are sadly in need of repair. One of the homes, now a school, is adorned with a sweeping exterior staircase facing the Temple Mount. It was built in anticipation of the Messiah's arrival. The expectation was that he would climb these stairs when he came to visit the owners.

The Russian Revolution brought about a drastic change to these Bucharans' lives. They and their elegant homes sank into poverty. The quarter now is mixed ultra-Orthodox.

One of these lovely homes is at Rehov Habucharim 10, east of Rehov Yehezkel, is getting a new lease on life, as Kuzari, where North African and Middle Eastern folk embroidery is made and sold. (See Chapter 7, "Shopping", for a fuller description.)

> Hours: 9 a.m. to 7 p.m. Sunday through Thursday; to 12:30
> p.m. Friday. Tel. 826-632.

On the same street, on the other side of Rehov Yehezkel, are **Chen**

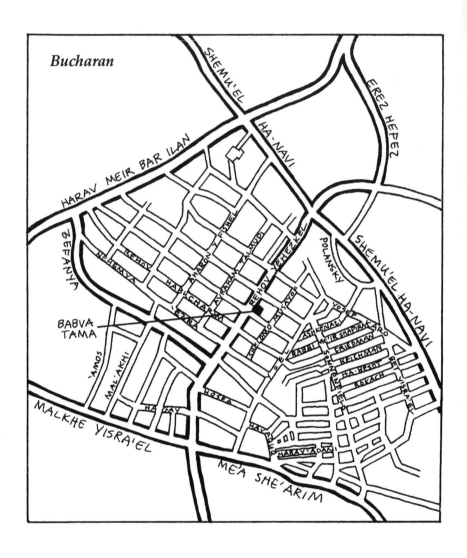

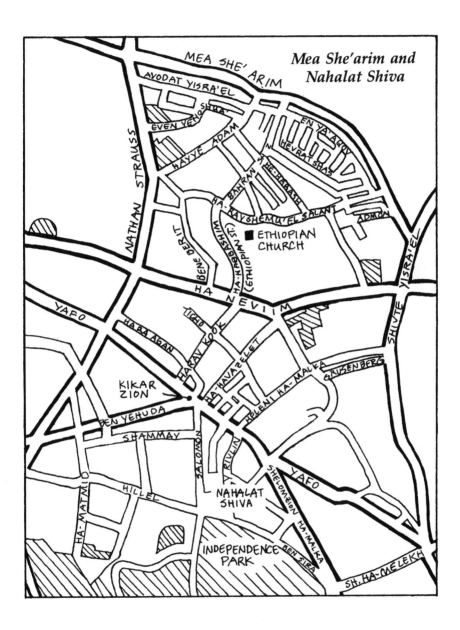

Mea She'arim and Nahalat Shiva

Jewelry, where Kurdistani Jews carry on a tradition of silver filigree work, and, opposite it on Rehov Habucharim, two old synagogues.

For a snack, continue on Rehov Habucharim two blocks to Rehov Yoel. Close by on that street is Eliahu Cohen's bakery that specializes in *eshtanur*, a thin, round, flat Iraqu bread. But the place closes at 1:30 p.m. and reopens for an hour at 6 p.m.

Several bus lines on Rehov Yehezkel will return you to the center of town where you can have lunch. Some recommendations are Beit Ticho at Rehov Harav Kook 7, where you can dine in its lovely courtyard; Bavli, nearby at Rehov Hanevi'im 54; Shemesh, Rehov Ben-Yehuda 21, where you can eat delicious stuffed vegetables; or Pinat Hahoumus, Rehov King George and Rehov Hahistadrut, where you can have a genuine Mizrahi meal.

After lunch, several bus lines on Rehov King George will drop you where that street meets Rehov King David, close to your next walk.

Mishkenot Sha'ananim, Yemin Moshe and Khutsot Hayotzer

The adjacent neighborhoods known as **Mishkenot Sha'ananim** and **Yemin Moshe** are on a mountain slope with a breathtaking view of the Old City, Mount Zion and the Judean Desert. The top of the slope is at the intersection of Rehov King David and Rehov Keren Hayesod and through the Bloomfield Garden to the east. The blades of the Montefiore Windmill (described in Chapter 12, "Linger Awhile: Substitutions and Extenders, More Museums") make a good landmark to aim for.

Open from 9 a.m. to 4 p.m. Sunday through Thursday, to 1 p.m. Friday. There is no admission charge.

Rehov Yemin Moshe is the dividing walkway between Mishkenot Sha'ananim on the right and Yemin Moshe on the left.

Mishkenot Sha'ananim was Moses Montefiore's attempt in 1860 to lure Jerusalemites out of their hovels in the Old City and live in fresh air. Even though he built a wall around the buildings and paid the residents to come out to what was a dangerous wilderness, his effort failed. Every night, the residents would scurry to the higher, sturdier, walled safety of their former homes.

Mishkenot Sha'ananim (Tabernacles of Tranquility) consists of two long, low buildings. The top one now is the **Jerusalem Music Center**, established with the help of American violinist Isaac Stern. The lower, longer building, the first of the two built, now provides quarters for visiting artists of all kinds who are guests of the municipality. From their apartments, they have box seats to view the changing shades of gold of the Old City.

Because of its propinquity to Mishkenot Sha'ananim, **Yemin Moshe**, named for Montefiore, often is assumed to have been the next Jewish settlement built outside of the walls. Not so. Yemin Moshe came 30 years and several other settlements later.

In the 1950s, Jerusalem's poor lived here and had to put up with dodging potshots from the Arab Legionnaires across the valley. With post-1967 redevelopment, the entire neighborhood got a dramatic face lift. Property values soared, and the poor and the artists who lived here took the money and moved elsewhere.

Two beautiful synagogues are on this slope. The one closest to the stairs leading from the park is Sephardi. The other, in a more austere building near the center of the neighborhood, is Ashkenazi.

A staircase at the far side of the neighborhood will take you down to **Khutsot Hayotzer**, another redeveloped area which consists of two rows of artisans and craftsmen's shops displaying excellent quality.

From the shops, the Jaffa Gate bus stops are to the left, up Rehov Hativat Yerushalayim.

It comes as a surprise to Jerusalem visitors that as old as Jerusalem's older, distinctive neighborhoods are, they are newer than most American cities. Outside of the Old City, pent-up energy once confined to those ancient narrow lanes was able to explode and express itself in new ways. Perhaps that is one of the explanations for the electricity in the air in West Jerusalem. After all, it still is a young city.

If you haven't done so before, tonight might be ideal for lingering over the nighttime, stage-set view of the Old City from either Mishkenot Sha'ananim or the Zionist Confederate House restaurants.

Seventh Day
To the Desert

The Lord may rest on the seventh day, but a tourist? Rarely. No visitor should miss a day at Herod's desert fortress-palace, **Massada**, and a float in the salt-thick **Dead Sea**. Bring your bathing suit and a towel.

The Egged Bus Company has service from Jerusalem to both, but excellent tours that combine the two are available through the Society for the Protection of Nature, Egged Tours, United Tours and Galilee Tours. Tours with these last three companies may be arranged at their local offices or through major hotels.

The Dead Sea

Oh, to be lazy and simply float in the **Dead Sea** (Yam Hamelah-Salt Sea). And that's all one can do or dares to do in that extremely saline body of water. Its salt content is almost nine times that of the Mediterranean Sea. And getting the salt, magnesium, bromide and iodine that is concentrated in this water into your eyes, or on an open wound, hurts a lot.

The Dead Sea, at 1069 feet below sea level, is the lowest spot on the face of earth. It also is in an incredibly bleak area. Still, there are plenty of luxury seaside hotels for the many people who come from far and wide, attracted by the Dead Sea's reputed therapeutic properties.

Visitors for the day should make sure they take their Dead Sea dip in an area where they can shower with fresh water afterwards. It isn't a good idea to leave all those chemicals on your body for a lengthy time.

The Sodom and Gomorrah story from the Bible took place on these shores. Geologists maintain that the shallow southern tip of the Dead Sea was formed by an earthquake at a time that is close to the time of the Biblical account. It could be that this explains the speedy destruction of Sodom and Gomorrah.

Other visible Biblical connections are on the opposite (Jordanian) side of the sea. Moses was said to have been buried in the Moab Mountains, on the left. The Hebrew tribes of Reuben and Gad and

The pillars of salt and chemicals in the Dead Sea make ideal platforms for sun worshippers.

half of Manesseh chose to settle in that area when the Hebrews came
to the Promised Land.

If you are traveling with a tour group, a lunch stop will be part of
your day. If you are on your own, snacks are available at beach areas
along the Dead Sea. A better choice is the cafeteria at the base of
Massada.

Massada

About two and-a-half miles west of the Dead Sea, a boat-shaped
mountain rises 1300 feet from the flat plain. It is **Massada** (MatzaDAH
in Hebrew), where one of the most dramatic events in Israeli history
took place almost 2000 years ago. Its impact resonates through the
subconscious of Israelis even today.

Herod the Great built a palace, a beautiful marvel, atop the mountain and then surrounded it with a 13-foot thick wall with 35 towers
more than 80 feet high.

About 100 years later, the Jewish rebellion burst forth in 66 C.E.
A group of Zealots struck out for the desert and captured Massada
from the Romans. With giant cisterns on the grounds with capacity
for holding eight years' worth of water, conceivably, they could remain
indefinitely.

Five years later, after the fall of Jerusalem, the Zealots were joined
by other refugees from the Romans. The number of people in the
mountain-top fortress grew to 960 men, women and children.

The Jewish historian, Flavius Josephus, told the story of how the
Romans returned to Massada in 72 C.E. with the Tenth Legion and
thousands of Jewish slaves to lay siege to the fortress. The siege
lasted three years. With construction of a huge ramp up to the top
of the mountain and a battering ram rolled up to that height, eventually, the Romans broke through the walls and entered the fortress
Massada.

Inside, they discovered silence. They found an ample amount of
provisions, which proved starvation hadn't been a threat, but the
men, women and children were dead. The Jews had decided they
never would become slaves or be abused by the Romans, so they
committed suicide.

Two women and five children survived by hiding in caves. They
told the details of the suicide and reported how the Zealot leader,
Eleazar Ben Ya'ir, exhorted the men not to be taken alive or to allow
their families to be taken alive by the Romans. His speech has come
down through history.

To reach the heights of Massada, you can hike up the winding
Snake Path, which takes about an hour; take the Roman Ramp on
the west side of Massada, which takes half-an-hour; or be carried up

on the cable car in a few breathtaking minutes. Don't hike when the sun is high.

The view of the Dead Sea, Jordan beyond it and the desert all around are spectacular from this height. From various places on Massada, it is possible to look down and see, even these many centuries later, the outlines of the eight Roman camps at the base of the mountain.

Yigal Yadin, probably Israel's most famous archeologist, led a team uncovering Massada in 1963. Digs and reconstruction still are underway. A black line distinguishes what is original from reconstructions.

Herod's private palace for his leisure is at the northern end of the mountain. In it are original frescos and columns, as well as a bath-house where Yadin uncovered skeletons, probably of a Zealot family, and arrows, potsherds and parts of a Jewish prayer shawl.

On the summit is the Zealot's synagogue, overlooking the Roman camps. To date, it is the oldest synagogue found in Israel. Parchment scrolls discovered here contained portions from the books of Deuteronomy and Ezekiel.

Like the synagogue, the mosaics in the Western Palace are the oldest to be seen in Israel. The only colored Herodian mosaics are on the entrance hall to the throne room. But the finest Massada mosaics, of oranges, grapes, figs and pomegranates, are on the floor of the Byzantine Chapel. They were left by Christian monks who were ensconced in this secluded spot for a short while during the 5th century C.E.

The desert ride back to Jerusalem after the impact of Massada can be a welcome time to reflect on how the past informs the present in this part of the world. Some Israeli observers say the country has a "Massada complex". Standing on Massada where the tragedy happened, hearing its history and the moving story of the Zealots, it's possible to understand this expression. Between Jews' 20th-century history and their ancestral memory, Israelis know what it is to be cornered. The expression means that Israelis have made a promise to themselves and to Israelis of generations to come that it shall never happen again.

Chapter 11:
A Second Week in Jerusalem

With a second week in Jerusalem, the pressure is off — a bit. The city's pell-mell impact may communicate to you by now its own Levantine sense of order. A second week in the Golden City offers a chance to absorb what you already learned and experienced; to expand that into finer detail; and to continue learning and experiencing, but at a less hectic pace.

With the itineraries in this section, you may use this second week for additional archeological exploring in the Old City area to become more familiar with West Jerusalem and to discover East Jerusalem. Another suggestion is that during this time, you delve into some of the small, specialized museums scattered throughout the city or even take a break from history, but not the Bible, at the Jerusalem Biblical Zoo. The zoo and many of these museums are described ahead and in Chapter 12, "Linger Awhile, Substitutions and Extenders, More Museums". Or, this week may include the opportunity to return to the museums on the one-week itinerary which you only could skim or, perhaps, even had to skip.

The following chapters have itineraries for six days of your second week in Jerusalem. Keep in mind that closing hours make some of the itineraries impossible on certain days. When this occurs, the introductions make note of that. Since the trips are arranged as if they were started on a Sunday, if followed in sequence, closing hours shouldn't present a problem.

On the seventh day, if you haven't had a chance to do so before, spend the morning at a Jewish or Christian house of worship. I guarantee the experience will be different from that at any of its counterparts back home.

However you choose to juggle your sightseeing this week, keep walking. At every opportunity, keep exploring neighborhoods. Jerusalem is one of the world's great cities for walking. Distances are small. But a mere turn around a corner can lead you into a totally different way of life from the one behind you. Adventure awaits you.

First Tour
Back to the Old City

A visit to a fascinating new archeological park at the **Southern Wall** abutting the Temple Mount and, if not a bird's-eye view, at least an elevated view of the Old City are on the agenda. Topping things off, literally, will be a walk on **Soleiman's Wall**, and the **Tower of David** (the Citadel) with its exhibits and sight of Jerusalem spread out below you.

A visit to the excavations can be mercilessly hot, so be sure to protect yourself from the sun. Plan on one-and-a-half hours for the Southern Wall, three hours for the Ramparts and the Tower of David.

The Southern Wall

Bus No. 1 will take you to Dung Gate. Just inside it is the entrance to the **Southern Wall** of the Temple Mount archeological park. Excavations here keep uncovering surprises. The site includes the remains of an Arab palace complex (the existence of which even Arab scholars hadn't been aware), a Byzantine house with a well-preserved mosaic floor, some 60 ritual baths used by priests and pilgrims before entering the Second Temple and two stairways leading to double and triple gates into the Temple area. A gateway tentatively has been identified as being of the First Temple Period. If so, it is the first structure from that period to be uncovered.

Pilgrims at the time of the Second Temple approached the Temple Mount up the restored, grand stairway. And it is grand. They were continuing the First Temple tradition of entering the Temple Mount from the south.

> Hours are 9 a.m. to 5 p.m. Sunday through Thursday, to
> 1 p.m. Friday. Closed Saturday. Entrance fee.

For lunch, if you so far have missed dining at either the Moroccan-French restaurant Hahoma, Rehov Hayehudim 128, or the Quarter Cafe with its gorgeous view upstairs near the Burnt House, this would be the time to make up the omission.

The Ramparts Walk
and the Tower of David (The Citadel)

The **ramparts** of Suleiman's magnificent wall are a walking trip in themselves. The entire circuit is about two-and-a-half miles. From the ramparts' height, you see the slope of the Tyropoeon Valley and into residents' backyards. You can check out families' laundry and their chickens, as well as count the number of TV antennas versus minarets. Your view from on high will allow you to study a classic example of local architecture: the dome-roofed house. Builders piled up sand within the structure's four walls until they achieved the shape of their desired dome. Then they lay stone in mortar on the sand. When the stone and mortar were firm enough, the house had its roof. The sand was scooped out, and the residents moved in.

Entrances to the ramparts are at Jaffa Gate, the Citadel, Zion Gate, Lion's Gate and Damascus Gate. At Damascus Gate, entry is through the elaborate, 2nd-century Roman Gate which stands beside Damascus Gate. The walk can be prefaced by a visit at that spot to Roman Square, a small museum of the Roman garrison.

> Hours: 9 a.m. to 5 p.m. daily. Entrance fee. Tel. 231-221. Gates to the ramparts are open from 9 a.m. to 3 p.m. Friday. The stretch between New Gate and the Citadel at Jaffa Gate is open until 9:30 p.m. Sunday through Thursday. There is an entrance fee. Buy tickets for Saturday in advance. Hang onto your ticket: it is good for two days. Tel. 224-403.

The Citadel or **Tower of David** next to Jaffa Gate is a good place for an overview of the Old City, and new Jerusalem, as well. The Citadel was built by Herod in 24 B.C.E. When the Romans demolished Jerusalem, they left one of Herod's three towers, because it could serve as a good watchtower.

Herod's structure now is a melange of overlays of construction and handiwork by Romans, Moslems, Crusaders, Mamelukes (to whom the tower's minaret is owed) and Suleiman the Magnificent. Sultan Suleiman was responsible for most of the Citadel's current appearance.

Inside is the city's historical museum and a charming Museum of Modern Religious Dress with clothing styles worn by thick-ankled dolls that look as if they shared ancestry with Cabbage Patch Dolls. A slide show of Jerusalem is on view at ground level. Climb to the top of the tower for a great sight of the Old City and much more.

A model of 19th-century Jerusalem, now exhibited here, has had something of an odyssey. It was built in Jerusalem in mid-century, displayed for the first time in Vienna in 1873 and then ended up in storage in Geneva. It was rediscovered in 1984 and brought to Jerusalem a year later. You will recognize the places you have visited and see how some sites that are in ruins today, such as the Hurva Synagogue, appeared originally. A model of Jerusalem 2000 years earlier is on the fifth tour's agenda.

A multimedia Sound and Light Show (Son et Lumière) in English, French, German and Hebrew on Jerusalem's history, particularly in Biblical times, is presented outdoors every evening except Friday and holiday eves from April through November.

> Hours: 8:30 a.m. to 4:30 p.m. Sunday through Thursday,
> to 2 p.m. Friday. Entrance fee. Tel. 286-511. English shows
> are at 9:15 p.m. Entrance fee. Tel. 286-511. Dress warmly.

By now, you probably have learned your way through Old City streets. Its host of first impressions are becoming familiar. What surely is emerging this second week are details, even in the manner of dress you see around you. For example: the variety of ways Orthodox women tie a scarf to cover their hair from everyone except their husband; how the way they tie their scarves differs from the way Moslem women tie theirs; or the many different skull caps worn by men, Jewish and, sometimes Moslem, which communicate religious and political positions. People's clothes send messages in Jerusalem.

Do you get the feeling that if you close your eyes for a moment in Jerusalem, stop to relax and turn the rest of the world off, you'll miss something?

Second Tour
Go East

Jerusalem's other side, its predominantly Arab side, is to the east. Governments may draw their boundary lines between people, but people always have had a way of living their lives to reveal how artificial these lines are. And so East Jerusalem may be looked on as Arab, but Jews, Armenians and Protestants, also, have claim to parts of this area.

East Jerusalem close to the Old City is a lively, commercial area in which, during the day, enthusiastically played Arab music emanates from stores and restaurants, and sidewalks are crowded with food vendors and residents leisurely chatting. But a few blocks away, East Jerusalem is peaceful and like a mixture of small town and countryside.

For a walk through East Jerusalem, allow all day, with a stop for lunch. Because you will be so close to West Jerusalem, there is no strategic problem in your calling it quits any time your feet tell you

to. Bring your flashlight for more tomb exploring and a sweater for the cool of Zedekiah's Cave.

East Jerusalem

You can start a visit to East Jerusalem with an example of its cultural mix: the **Mosaic of the Birds**, north side of Rehov Hanevi'im, east of the intersection with Rehov Hel Hahandasa. Bus No. 1 stops close by. The entrance is between two buildings. You have to look sharp to find it. Inside is a 5th-century, 26-by-14-feet Armenain mosaic that may be the first memorial to an unknown soldier. It probably was part of a chapel honoring Armenian soldiers who died fighting the Persians in 451 C.E. The lovely mosaic shows a variety of birds perched on grapevines.

Hours: 8 a.m. to 5:30 p.m. daily except Sunday. Entrance fee.

At the corner of Rehov Hanevi'im and Rehov Hazanhanim, you may see that public Arab typists have set up shop on the sidewalk, and customers are standing by to have their official business communications typed.

On the side of the street at the Old City, between Damascus and Herod Gates, is **Zedekiah's Cave** (also known as Solomon's Quarries, Suleiman's Cave and a few other names), thought to have been the source of white "*Melekeh*" limestone for the First Temple.

It is believed that Judean King Zedekiah tried to flee from the conquering Nebuchadnezzar in 587 B.C.E. through these quarries via a passageway connecting with his palace. The caves are important to Freemasons who claim that their group descends from Solomon's masons.

This five-acre underground expanse has paths that lead to separate rooms, nooks and crannies. It is lighted the entire way, so the claustrophobic need not be intimidated. But visitors should bring a sweater. It is cool and damp in the cave.

Hours: 9 a.m. to 5 p.m. daily. Entrance fee. Tel. 231-221.

Farther east, across the street and almost opposite the corner of the walled Old City, is the **Rockefeller Museum**, one of the most important in Israel. It was planned and built during the late 1920s under the British Mandate. John D. Rockefeller's gift of $2 million insured that the museum would carry his name.

The oldest item in its collection is the remains of a 10,000 year-old man found on Mount Carmel. Notable are flint utensils from Stone Age cave dwellers, Roman sarcophagi and sculptures and stone tablets from the Egyptian Pharaohs Seti I (1313 B.C.E.) and Ramses III

(1198-67 B.C.E.), which were found at Bet She'an, near Tiveria. From the entrance, the best route to the exhibits is to the left.

> Hours are 10 a.m. to 5 p.m. Sunday through Thursday; 10 a.m. to 2 p.m. Friday and Saturday. Entrance fee. Buy Saturday tickets in advance. Entrance is free to Israel Museum members.

Around the northeast corner of the Old City is a Moslem cemetery. In it is a monument to Arabs who died in the Six-Day War.

The Garden Tomb, off Nablus Road (Derech Shchem), above the East Jerusalem Central Bus Station, is a quiet sanctuary of Aleppo pines and almond trees amidst the hurly-burly of this part of East Jerusalem. Signs on the street give directions. General Charles Gordon of Khartoum fame popularized this, not the Holy Sepulchre, as the true grave of Jesus. It is a two-chambered tomb carved out of rock on a hill that appeared to him like Golgotha, the skull-like rise where Jesus was crucified. Anglicans and other Protestants hold to that belief.

> Hours 8 a.m. to 12:30 p.m., 2:30 p.m. to 4 p.m. daily except Sunday. Free tours in summer.

If you are ready for lunch, you can get a light snack at the Pâtisserie Suisse at 18 Salah ed-Din St., which you passed walking from the Rockefeller Museum to the Garden Tomb, or superb *mezze*, that array of salads and appetizers, at the Philadelphia Restaurant, downstairs at 9 Az-Zahra St., off Salah ed-Din St. An alternative is to wait until you reach the American Colony Hotel.

Farther up Nablus Road is the Dominican monastery of **St. Stephen** (St. Etienne). Within this complex of buildings, is a church, a monastery, tombs hewn out of rock and the French Institute for Biblical Archeology. The present church was built in the late 1800s on the ruins of a 5th-century basilica said to house the bones of St. Stephen, the first Christian martyr.

Still farther up Nablus Road, surrounded by an iron fence across the street from the American Consulate, is a remnant of **"the third wall"** around the city during the Second Temple. Opposite the **American Consulate**, which is located in a beautiful former private home, is **Palestinian Pottery**, where lovely blue Armenian pottery is made and sold. Closed Sunday.

Continuing up Nablus Road, **St. George's Cathedral** can be found to the right. It is distinguished by its tower named for King Edward VII of England. The cathedral has a lovely garden with lush citron trees. Citrons look like grapefruit-sized lemons. Reportedly, they make good marmalade.

At the intersection of Nablus Road and Rehov Salah ed-Din, above

George's, a sign points to **Tombs of the Kings**. It was long thought that this impressive necropolis 28 feet below street level was the burial site of Jewish kings, hence the name. But its story is more interesting even than that. The tombs were cut about 45 C.E. by Queen Helena (as she was called by the Greeks) of Adiabene in Mesopotamia for herself and her sons. They settled in Jerusalem and all converted to Judaism.

These are truly grand tombs. The edifice, cut out of rock, even includes *mikvot* (traditional Jewish ritual baths). The richly decorated sarcophagus of the queen is in the Louvre, for these tombs are the property of the French government. Other sarcophagi have disappeared. A sequence of rooms and elegant stone carvings may be seen by stepping through the small tomb opening. Here you will need your flashlight.

Hours: 8:30 a.m. to 5 p.m. daily. Entrance fee.

The American Colony Hotel is even farther up Nablus Road. The hotel was once the home of a wealthy sheikh. Its lovely courtyard makes for an ideal pause for refreshment. The hotel is named for Americans who bought these buildings from the sheikh in 1881. They came for spiritual reasons, but a group of 19th-century equivalents of hippies gathered around them. Eventually, the American Colony was considered scandalous, but all that was long ago. Today, the hotel, still owned by descendants of the Americans who established the colony, is a favorite of United Nations personnel. Because the United Nations has been looked on with disfavor by Israelis since at least 1967, (the withdrawal of United Nations forces from the Sinai opened the path for Nasser's Egyptian army to swoop toward Israel), UN people undoubtedly get a warmer welcome at the American Colony in Arab Jerusalem than at hotels in Jewish Jerusalem.

Just beyond the hotel is the tomb of the Moslem saint, **Sheikh Jarrah**, from whom this Arab neighborhood got its name.

Ahead on Nablus Road, the next road to the right takes a left fork that leads through a field and to a burial cave attributed to being that of **Shimon Hatzadik** (Simon the Just). It is surrounded by other burial caves. This is where the Jewish festival of Lag Ba'Omer is celebrated in the spring with crowds of Orthodox Jews gathering to give three-year-old boys their first haircuts (details about Lag Ba'Omer can be found in Chapter 14, "The Cycle of Celebrations: Happy Holidays".)

The Sheikh Jarrah neighborhood extends as Nablus Road climbs the slope. This neighborhood has many luxurious homes. Its residents include some of the most illustrious Arab families. The streets invite exploration. To get back where you started, all you have to do is go downhill.

East Jerusalem's open spaces are one of its greatest charms. Even in the city, you can expect a young boy to lead a herd of sheep past you.

But plotting this walk has incited me to climb on a soapbox. If Jerusalem truly is a unified city, then why don't the street maps include as many street names of East Jerusalem as they do of West Jerusalem? Tell me that, Survey of Israel, which prints maps, and Israel Ministry of Tourism, which distributes them.

Third Tour

Get Out of Town

Jerusalem may be on a mountain, but it isn't on an island. Bethlehem and Massada are the big out-of-town attractions, not to be missed, but here are five other places to choose from that are worth a visit and that will get you out of town: **Ein Kerem**, the **Soreq Stalagmite and Stalactite Cave**, **Bethany**, **Wadi Qelt**, and **Jericho**. Because distances within Israel are so small, these places only *seem* far away. The first three can be half-day trips. The last two can take up to an entire day.

Ein Kerem

True, **Ein Kerem** is within Jerusalem's city limits. But it is a big enough change from the center of the city, you will feel as if you have made a huge trip. Actually, it won't be huge, but as bus No. 17 takes you over hills and into valleys, it will be slow, perhaps 45 minutes.

Ein Kerem remains bucolic, has many fine, old Arab houses and, as the traditional birthplace of John the Baptist, contains several Christian sites of note.

These include, the Franciscan **Church of St. John the Baptist** with its Grotto of the Nativity; the **Spring of the Virgin**, next to an abandoned mosque; and the **Church of the Visitation**, which commemorates Mary's visit to Elizabeth, John's mother. Nearby is a Russian convent, **Mar Zakariya**.

The notable restaurants in Ein Kerem are Michael's at the Ein Kerem Inn, which serves continental dishes at an expensive price, and The Barn, also at the Inn, which has considerable charm and lower prices.

Soreq Stalagmite and Stalactite Cave

The **Soreq Stalagmite and Stalactite cave** in the Avshalom Shoham Nature Reserve is about 12 miles (19 kilometers) southwest of Jerusalem, near the village of Nes Harim. The cave, an awesome 5000 square meters, was discovered only in 1968 and was opened to the public in 1977. Lighting highlights the colors in the stalagmites and stalactites which continuously, but minutely, grow.

Egged and United Tours provide the only direct route to the cave. The alternative is to take a bus from the Central Station to Nes Harim and then walk less than one-and-a-half miles (two kilometers).

> Hours are 8 a.m. to 4 p.m. Sunday through Thursday and Saturday, to 1 p.m. Friday. Admission fee includes a slide show and guided tour. Tel. 011-117.

Bethany

Bethany, on the Jericho Road and about two-and-a-half miles (four kilometers) from Jerusalem, is the village in which Christians believe Jesus raised its most famous resident, Lazarus, from the dead. Jesus is said to have visited Bethany on the eve of his fateful Passover on the invitation of Lazarus and his sisters, Mary and Martha. According to the Gospel of John, Jesus raised Lazarus after Lazarus had been dead four days. Another well-known Bethany resident was Simon the Leper, whom Jesus cured.

Bethany was the name of the village in Jesus' time and the name by which it is known today to Christians. In the 4th century, it was a Christian settlement, called Lazareion. Now an Arab village, it is known as el-Azariye, a variation of its previous name.

The Franciscan Church of St. Lazarus, built in 1954, has mosaics that depict Lazarus' resurrection. Antonio Barluzzi, the man responsible for Dominus Flevit and the Church of All Nations on the Mount of Olives, designed this church as well. **Lazarus' Tomb**, down a flight of stairs, is looked after by Moslems who may deliver a dramatic account of his resurrection.

> Hours are from 8 a.m. to noon and 2 p.m. to 6 p.m. daily. Entrance fee.

Bethany can be reached by taking Egged bus No. 42 or 43 (except on Saturday) from the bus station on Nablus Road (Derech Shchem), or East Jerusalem bus No. 36 from the East Jerusalem Central Bus Station on Sultan Suleiman St.

Wadi Qelt

The gorge of **Wadi Qelt**, a spring east of Jerusalem, makes for an adventurous, dramatic day-long hike. Bring your lunch and beverage on this trip. The best way to make the hike is with the Society for the Protection of Nature in Israel, which takes groups through weekly. Besides walking the aqueducts (not for the fainthearted or anyone who fears heights), a hiker stops at the Greek Orthodox Monastery of St. George, which has clung to its cliff side since the 6th century.

According to legend, a cave within the monastery was where the Prophet Elijah lived after he fled Samaria. Only eight monks live in this huge edifice.

Hours are 8 a.m. to 4 p.m. daily. Entrance fee.

Jericho

Jericho, a below-sea-level oasis 17 miles (28 kilometers) east of Jerusalem, is known as the oldest city in the world. It was founded approximately 11,000 years ago. It is remembered as the city whose walls Joshua's priestly trumpeters "blew down", and as being close to the banks of the Jordan River where John baptized Jesus.

Jericho can be reached on Egged buses from the Central Bus Station and East Jerusalem buses from the station near Dasmascus Gate. On the return to Jerusalem, East Jerusalem buses stop running close to 5 p.m. Egged buses run until 7 p.m.

Tel es Sultan (also known as Tel Jericho), a partially artificial mound northwest of the city, may be the location of the city walls the Bible says were destroyed when Joshua's men marched around them seven times. This is the site that substantiates Jericho's longevity claim. Archeological findings go as far back as 8000 B.C.E.

Hours are 7a.m. to 6 p.m. daily. Entrance fee.

North of the tel are the remains of a **5th-century synagogue** with outstanding mosaics and an Aramaic inscription that says, "Peace unto Israel."

Hours are 7 a.m. to 6 p.m daily. Entrance fee.

The major attraction is **Hisham's Palace** (Khirbet al-Mafjar in Arabic). These are ruins of an 8th-century palace built for Caliph Hisham, the Umayyad ruler who found Jericho a lot more pleasant than Damascus in winter. Rubble from an earthquake shortly after the palace was built protected its magnificent mosaic floors for centuries.

Hours are 8 a.m. to 5 p.m. Saturday through Thursday, to 4 p.m. Friday from April through September. From October through March, the palace closes one hour earlier each day. Entrance fee.

The Mount of Temptation, where Jesus was said to have been tempted by the devil for 40 days and 40 nights, is on the western edge of Jericho. A half-hour walk takes you to the summit with its excellent views of the Mount of Olives and the Dead Sea.

Jericho abounds with cafes and food stands. Finding a place to eat presents no problem.

Jericho is strikingly lovely in May when it is ablaze with its brilliant,

Yes, he has some bananas in this Mahane Yehuda stall.

red poincianas.

Whichever way you travel, east or west, north or south, it always helps to get out of the city to fit Jerusalem into its environment. And afterwards, there is a quiver of excitement, a quickening of the heart beat, to be felt on returning.

Fourth Tour
From "Judah's Camp" to Italian Beauty

Arabs have their "souk", and Jews have their "shuk", (pronounced "shook"), which usually refers to the open-air market at Mahane Yehuda. This day includes a stroll through **Mahane Yehuda** and its aging neighborhoods and a visit to the **Museum of Italian Jewish Art**, which is open Sunday mornings and Wednesday afternoons.

Mahane Yehuda, Mazkeret Moshe, Ohel Moshe

There is a combative atmosphere in the **Mahane Yehuda** ("Camp of Judah") market, especially that major part of it that sells fresh produce. Located between Rehov Agrippas and one of the more dingy portions of Rehov Yafo, the market's narrow aisles are crowded with shoppers making their way between stalls whose owners are trying to outshout each other over the price of their produce. But instead of offering a shopper efficient, kindly service, the stall owner usually acts as if he has better things to do than wait on her, like shouting the price of his produce. This off-hand treatment is part of the Mahane Yehuda tradition. The challenge for the shopper is to appear to be unintimidated. Never mind how she really feels: she must show a tough exterior.

The market is noisy, but rich with color in the produce section, which is most of it. Ripe red watermelon halves cover a table. Yellow, plucked, fresh chickens with a rainbow of other colors on their shiny skin lie limp on top of each other on a counter. Green peppers that reflect the light are stacked in a gravity-defying tower. These and many more sights of the fruit of the earth and a few slaughtered barnyard creatures are repeated stall after stall.

In an adjacent section of the market, on sale are kitchenwares, linens, clothing and pop music tapes (some of which are pirated).

Actually, Mahane Yehuda has become less and less of an open-air market over recent years. The aisles have been covered so shoppers and sellers can laugh at the weather. What's more, the shuk is about to get a face lift. Sentimentalists may decry any effort to make Mahane Yehuda look like just another place to shop. But it is doubtful that whatever happens to it physically will alter the traditional disposition of its stall owners.

Outside of Mahane Yehuda, across Rehov Agrippas and in the

direction of Rehov King George, there is a small, open archway along the sidewalk. Through it are twin neighborhoods, **Mazkeret Moshe** and **Ohel Moshe**. They were built in 1883 by the Moses Montefiore Foundation and are another example of the dedicated Englishman's influence. The twin neighborhoods were planned to be fraternal, not identical. Mazkeret Moshe ("Remembrance of Moses") was constructed for Ashkenazim and Ohel Moshe ("Tent of Moses") for Sephardim. But both were for low-income families.

It is easy to stroll about here, for the small homes, some now a jumble of additions over the years, were constructed around a courtyard; in the middle is a small park. Both neighborhoods still are poor, but colorful, and with an indication here and there of renewal. A building close to the Rehov Agrippas entrance is a community center. The women from the neighborhood gather here to sing together.

Narrow lanes at the far end of the neighborhoods and to the left lead to Rehov Mesillat Yeshar. This street will bring you close to the rear of the department store, **Hamashbir.**

If you haven't yet explored Hamashbir Lazarchan (called by everyone, simply, Hamashbir), this would be a good time. It is Jerusalem's largest and finest department store, no matter how you or I perceive it.

A great advantage to Hamashbir was, because of its central location, its handy rest rooms. They still are handy, but management caught on to non-shoppers like me, who came in only to use the facilities. Now a man sits outside the lavatory entrances and collects a fee for use. (By the way, women may have noticed by now that men usually clean the women's lavatories. I was disconcerted at first to find a man in the ladies' room, but then I concluded, ah ha, another local custom: if it doesn't bother him, it shouldn't bother me.)

The front of Hamashbir faces Rehov King George. One block to the right, below Rehov Ben-Yehuda, is Rehov Hillel on the left. Down the slope, you will find the Museum of Jewish Italian Art at Rehov Hillel 27.

If you are ready for lunch, Mamma Mia's at Rehov Harav Akiva 18, a right turn off Rehov Hillel, will put you in the mood for the museum. Besides its heartening Italian food, Mamma Mia's is one of Jerusalem's most charming places to dine.

Museum of Italian Jewish Art

The Museum of Italian Jewish Art is reached through a courtyard and up to the second floor at the end of a building on the left. On the landing, a short corridor has entrances opposite each other to both the museum and the Italian Synagogue. The synagogue, open for viewing during museum hours, is described in Chapter 13, "Discover Heavenly Jerusalem: Churches, Synagogues, and Family Ties", on worship in Jerusalem. Here, only the four-room museum will be discussed.

At the entrance to the Italian Synagogue are Hebrew words that read: "Do not leave this place in haste." Indeed. The words apply spiritually to the synagogue, but because of its arts collection, the museum, too, is a place to tarry.

While the Jewish community in Italy goes back some 2500 years, probably the oldest object in the museum is a plaque that advises: "Know before whom you stand." It dates back to the end of the 15th century and is decorated with neo-classical, Renaissance designs. The plaque originally was above the Holy Ark in the great synagogue of Padua. Although the great synagogue was badly damaged by bombs during World War II, the ark and plaque escaped harm.

In the museum's third room are the Holy Ark of Mantua and a pair of chairs beside it. The chairs are a beehive of carved wood. An inscription on the ark states that it dates from 1543, which makes it the oldest dated Holy Ark in Israel.

A *maftir* book from Urbino stems from a lovely, unusual tradition. In that city, each boy who reached *bar mitzvah* age received a book with the portion of the Haftorah (selected writings from the Prophets) that was his to read during his first time participating as an adult in a worship service. This particular book was written and illustrated by hand in 1704 by the *bar-mitzvah* boy's grandfather.

Lacy embroidered clothes for the baby boy during his circumcision ceremony are astoundingly luxurious. Time has taken little toll: those shining threads aren't Lurex.

In the last room is a machine for making *matzo*, the flat, brittle, unleavened bread eaten during Passover. You may find examples of the machine's end product on the table. Perhaps some scholar will research the variety of *matzos* Jews in different parts of the world produce. Italian *matzo* is white, round and shot with pencil-size holes. It looks like a clumsily crocheted doily (a Jewish-Italian woman in Jerusalem confided to me that she punches the holes in her *matzos* with her fingers).

The examples in the Museum of Italian Jewish Art reflect a rich and exuberant lifestyle. The museum has identified and explained the displays well and also provides a four-page free guide in English that takes a viewer through the museum virtually step by step. *Fa bene, Museo di arte Ebraica Italiana!*

Hours are 10 a.m. to 1 p.m. Sunday; 4 to 7 p.m. Wednesday. Entrance fee. Tel. 241-610.

Note: I have planned this trip so you can follow it on a Wednesday and walk downhill. If you prefer to walk in the opposite direction, starting with the museum, take the trip on a Sunday.

This walk is one of my favorites in Jerusalem for its wide view of Jerusalem's multi-cultural life. Try to visit the Italian Synagogue during a service, especially on Shabbat. If you love opera, you will love the Italian Synagogue. Tonight, you can maintain the Italian mood by having dinner at Pomme et Poire at the Khan, Kikar Remez 2. Despite its French name, its Italian owners are adding Italian dishes. If the weather is suitable for dining outdoors, this is the proper dramatic setting for ending the day.

Fifth Tour
From Hadassah to Hadassah
with Several Places in Between

How about a break today and a chance to rest your feet during long bus rides? This trip literally will take you from one end of Jerusalem to the other. But the **Knesset** (Parliament), one of the places included today, is open for tours only on Sunday and Thursday.

Your old friend, bus No. 99, will chauffeur you. The link between visits to the **Sanhedrin, Mount Scopus Hadassah Hospital** and **Hebrew University,** the **Knesset** and the **Holyland Hotel** is (besides bus No. 99) art and architecture of Jewish masters, ancient and modern. Another destination today is the **Hadassah Medical Center at Ein Kerem.** Bus No. 99, alas, doesn't go there. To reach it, if you board the No. 99 after you leave the Holyland Hotel, you can ride it to Mount Herzl where you can take bus No. 27. An alternative is to ride No. 99 until it reaches a place on Derech Manahat where you can take bus No. 19. Ask the No. 99 driver which would be more efficient.

Before setting out, decide if you want to tour the Knesset Building or see the Israeli parliament in action. Scheduling problems make it difficult to do both. Read the details in the section below on the Knesset. To be admitted to either event, bring your passport.

With a decision to visit the Knesset for the tour, it should take three hours from the time you leave Jaffa Gate until you arrive at the Holyland Hotel. Visiting the Hadassah Medical Center in the Ein Kerem spur should take two hours, a lot of that time spent sitting on the bus and enjoying the view.

Tombs of the Sanhedrin

The **Tombs of the Sanhedrin**, in northern Jerusalem, have some of the finest stone carvings in the city. The Sanhedrin was the highest Second Temple religious court until it was disbanded under the Romans in 70 C.E. Its members were given a special burial site. The tombs are in an attractive park in a neighborhood called Sanhedria, near the junction of Rehov Hativat Harel and Rehov Shmuel Hanavi. When you enter the park, you see many burial tombs cut out of rock. The 71 crypts of the judges are at the end of the park, carved out of the hillside. The tomb is recognizable by the courtyard in front and the largest, most graceful lintel gable of any Jerusalem tomb.

Hours are from 9 a.m. to sunset, Sunday through Friday. The park is open daily.

Mount Scopus:
Hadassah Hospital, Hebrew University

Hadassah Hospital on Mount Scopus (Har Hatzofim) is in the northeastern reaches of the city between the British War Cemetery for those who died in World War I and the campus of Hebrew University. During the 19 years of Jordanian occupation, Mount Scopus was an Israeli island surrounded by warring Arabs. Every two weeks, the United Nations supervised a convoy of people and supplies to the embattled outpost. UN supervision came about, partly, because of the murder by ambush of 78 doctors, nurses and university personnel traveling to Mount Scopus in a convoy during the War of Independence. Out of necessity, Hadassah Medical Center in Ein Kerem and the Hebrew University campus at Givat Ram were built during the years Jerusalem was a divided city.

Buildings and a Jacques Lipschitz sculpture aside, the best things about wandering on Mount Scopus are the views of the city, the Judean Desert, the Dead Sea and the Moab Mountains.

Hospital tours in English, which include seeing Jacques Lipschitz' "Tree of Life", are at 9 a.m., 10 a.m. and 11 a.m. and noon Sunday through Friday. Tours in English of the university are at 11:30 a.m. Sunday through Friday starting from the Beit Sherman. The university tour is free.

If hunger pangs are consuming you before the Knesset, the next stop on this tour, you can get off at the City Tower Hotel, stop number 15, in the Jerusalem centre and have lunch nearby at Poondak Hehalav, Rehov Bezalel 17; or Zeh Zeh, a cafe-style dairy and fish restaurant in the Gerard Behar Centre, Rehov Bezalel 11. For alternatives, you can dine at the Holyland Hotel after the Knesset visit or take No. 99 from the Holyland to the Shalom Hotel in Beit Hakerem.

Knesset

The Hebrew word, *knesset*, means in English "assembly". Israel's **Knesset** building is off Rehov Eliezer Kaplan in roughly the same neighborhood as the Israel Museum. This modern building is the

Knesset's third home in Jerusalem since 1948. Earlier, it was located in the Jewish Agency Building and then in a building that now houses the Government Tourist Information Office, with which you probably are well familiar by now. Both are on Rehov King George.

Across from the entrance stands a large, bronze *menorah*, the seven-branched candelabra that symbolizes Israel. It is the work of Benno Elkan. The iron gate at the entrance to the Knesset Plaza is by David Palombo, whose memorial studio was included on the first week's Mount Zion walk.

Colorful and large examples of Russian-born Marc Chagall's work can be seen on the upper foyer in his tapestries, wall paintings and floor mosaics. The huge tapestries show moments in Jewish history.

To see the Knesset in action, visit between 4 p.m. and 9 p.m. Monday or Tuesday. It can be quite a show, but it is in Hebrew, occasionally Arabic. No subtitles provided. Note the informal style of dress and manner by these legislators.

> Free guided tours in English run from 8:30 a.m. to 2:30
> p.m. Sunday and Thursday only. For tours in other lan-
> guages, call 554-111. Passports are required.

Model of Ancient Jerusalem

The Holyland Hotel's **model of ancient Jerusalem** gives an image of what Jerusalem was like in its Second Temple heyday. This model depicts the Jerusalem built by Herod. The model is as accurate as possible, with changes constantly being made to keep up with latest archeological discoveries. Recorded explanations of the model can be heard from various locations around it.

This Holyland Hotel is in southwest Jerusalem in Beit Vegan. Another Holyland Hotel, not to be confused, is in East Jerusalem. Whether their name appears as one word or two varies with both of them.

> Hours are 8:30 a.m. to 5 p.m in summer, to 4 p.m. winter,
> daily. Entrance fee. Saturday tickets must be purchased in
> advance from a ticket agency. Tel. 630-201.

Hadassah Medical Center

The bus ride west to **Hadassah Medical Center** in Ein Kerem is a leisurely, picturesque trip. At the western edge of Jerusalem, Hadassah has as its non-medical attraction, 12 stained glass windows by Marc Chagall. Chagall, who had been living in France for many years before his death, made a gift of the windows, depicting the 12 Tribes of Israel, in 1962. They are in Hadassah's synagogue. The famed painter of a fiddler on a roof later replaced four windows that were shattered during the Six-Day War.

Because these stained glass windows were made for a synagogue

— and a Jerusalem synagogue at that — Chagall followed the Biblical injunction that has been interpreted as a prohibition against representation of the human figure. He looked on this as a challenge and took such imaginative flights as transferring human characteristics to animals.

> Medical Center tours in English at 8:30 a.m., 9:30 a.m., 10:30 a.m., and 11:30 a.m., 12:30, Sunday through Thursday. The Friday tour at 9:30 a.m. is by appointment only. Meet at the Kennedy Building. Entrance fee. For a visit to the Chagall Windows only, visit between 2 p.m. and 3:45 p.m. Monday through Thursday. Entrance fee. Tel. 416-333.

Note: I urge you to verify the synagogue's afternoon hours. If these hours no longer are available, begin the day here. Afterwards, take bus No. 19 to its stop closest to Hechal Shlomo on Rehov King George and then take No. 99 to the Knesset. After that, continue riding No. 99 to the other stops on this itinerary, but you will forgo formal tours on Mount Scopus.

A wide range of artistic expression was included on this tour. The Second Commandment says, "You shall not make a graven image or any likeness of anything that is in heaven, in the earth below or that is in the water." From this, both Jews and Moslems, traditionally, forbid the representation of the human form in art work.

But Jews always have drawn from cultures around them. Paintings made as long ago as those in the 4th century C.E. Dura-Europos Synagogue in Mesopotamia include one of Moses reading the Torah. He is shown as a tall, slender, pleasant-faced young man who wears a trimmed beard and a Greco-Roman toga. He isn't at all the stormy Moses we picture descending from Mount Sinai.

Still, Jews didn't severely challenge the Second Commandment until they began leaving their shtetls and ghettoes in the late 19th and early 20th centuries. Then, many took the drastic step of choosing to become artists. Several, such as Pissarro and Modigliani, became integral to any account of modern art history.

One can't help wondering about the wrench someone like Chagall felt when he left behind a small, conservative Jewish village in Russia to go to the cosmopolitan capitals of Europe to fulfill a dream. His work makes it plain that he never left that village behind in his artistic imagination. Perhaps he reflected on the Second Commandment which goes on to say, in Exodus, 20.4, "You shall not bow down to them (graven images) or serve them," and decided he wasn't making idols to be worshipped, he only was putting his dreams on canvas.

Sixth Tour
"God's Expanse"
and Its Neighbors

This outing takes you through a neighborhood that was and still is one of the most famous in Jerusalem. It was where the makers and shakers of modern Israel and its founding fathers and mothers lived — and some still do. Also on the agenda are views of the prime minister's and president's official residences and a visit to an exquisite medium-sized museum, the **Museum of Islamic Art**. This is an easy day. The walk and visit to the museum should take about three hours. You could preface it with a tour of the **Wolfson Museum** in Hechal Shlomo, around the corner from the walk's starting point. Or you could return to it, afterwards.

Rehavia, Homes of Famous People

Modern Jerusalem began in **Rehavia**, the pie-shaped area wedged east of the juncture of Rehov King George and Rehov Keren Hayesod, south of Rehov Ramban and north (more-or-less) of Derech Aza to the ridge of the Vale of Rehavia (Valley of the Cross).

When it was founded in 1921 by middle-class Ashkenazim, Rehavia ("God's Expanse") was to be one of several new "garden" communities. That it certainly became. From barren rock, it now is packed with bougainvilleas, eucalyptuses, cypresses, palms, cacti and roses. People from new neighborhoods complain that Rahavia is "too dark — you don't see the sun."

The British introduced 20th-century architecture to Jerusalem when they took over Palestine from the Turks in 1917. They also made it a law that buildings had to be faced with Jerusalem stone. In Rehavia, you can see how the old stone and the then-new architecture first came together. The buildings usually have flat roofs, square windows and, often, curved art deco lines on the balconies.

During the later Mandate years, the neighborhood bristled with illegal planning for independence. Building after building was a site of secret activity.

With Israeli independence, Jerusalemites asserted their independence from the past by rescinding the British law requiring use of the city's characteristic stone. Fortunately, that didn't last too long. Considered observation of the results led to that law's reinstatement. You can see a few buildings in Rehavia from that brief time.

After visiting the old, poor neighborhoods of Mazkeret Moshe and Ohel Moshe, Rehavia's well-being and cosmopolitanism are strikingly apparent. For years, Rehavia smacked of snobism. However, recently, the community has declined because of the intrusion of offices into

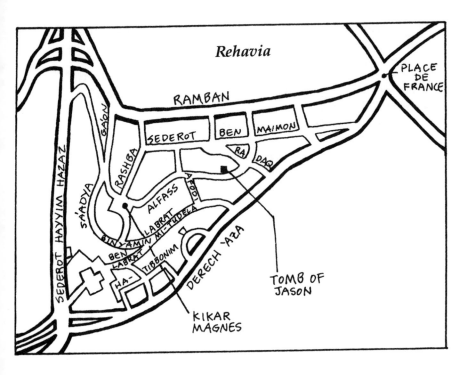

apartment buildings (a situation that a new law limits), and its population has become more ethnically mixed. It remains a pleasant, convenient and expensive place to live.

Starting at Kings Hotel at the corner of Rehov King George and Rehov Ramban, its next-door neighbor on Rehov Ramban is a new shopping center built around Jerusalem's second famous windmill (the first being the one seen your first week, the windmill that Moses Montefiore built). This newer one was built by the Greek Orthodox Church in 1875. At that time, what was to become West Jerusalem was dotted by windmills to grind local flour.

At the entrance to **The Mill**, as this shopping center is called, there is a permanent exhibit of the history of the mill and Rehavia.

Continuing on Rehov Ramban away from Kings Hotel and right at Rehov Alharizi, the narrow street leads to the back of the **Jewish Agency**. From its balcony at the front facing Rehov King George, such people as David Ben-Gurion and Golda Meir gave speeches about independence to tumultuous crowds.

Left on Rehov Keren Hakayemet and ahead is the **Hebrew Gymnasia**, founded in 1909 as the first high school in Palestine in which all subjects were taught in Hebrew. It is part of the public school system. The Haganah, while still an illegal army, gathered in its basement during the Mandate.

Across the street, between No. 19 and 21, a walkway goes down some stairs to another segment of Rehov Alharizi, a quiet enclave with graceful houses.

From the middle of the block, around a green metal wall is a narrow path that zigs and zags, cross Rehov Abravanel (another attractive, secluded street) and continues through a tunnel of trees back to Rehov Ramban. Ramban, to the right, past a variety of architecturally interesting houses, goes to Rehov Sa'adya Gaon, which curves to the left.

Sa'adya Gaon overlooks the **Vale of Rehavia** (the Valley of the Cross). It offers one of Jerusalem's grandest views, including, from left to right, the community of Gilo, the brooding Monastery of the Cross in the valley, the Israel Museum, the Knesset and (alack and alas, but they are there for good) those prodding fingers in the skyline, Wolfson Towers.

Sa'adya Gaon connects with Rehov Alfassi, which climbs a hill. Rehov Alfassi 25 had one of Menachem Begin's many secret residences during the Mandate period. The British tried to arrest him at this address, but as he was returning home, a colleague gave him the high sign. Begin turned around and never came back again.

Little can bring home the amount of history hidden under Jerusalem more than a stroll along the crooked bends of Rehov Alfassi. There is no question but that you are surrounded by the 20th century, albeit the look of the first half of the 20th century. Then you reach Rehov Alfassi 10 and 12 and a gap on the street between those numbers. What you find here carries you back in time more than 2000 years

Jason's Tomb

Where you would have expected another building on Rehov Alfassi, there is a wall and what looks like a park behind it.

It is a park in a way, but the greenery is a carpet leading to the small, graceful **Jason's Tomb** constructed toward the end of the second century B.C.E. in the Hasmonean Period, apparently by a well-to-do family. Much less grand than the tombs in the Kidron Valley, its pyramidal roof and arched gateway and especially its stillness are in striking isolation from the modern life around it.

The tomb is named for the unknown Jason who is referred to in one of several inscriptions written in Hebrew, Aramaic and Greek in the burial chamber. Beside the words about him on the wall are charcoal drawings of boats, a crouching deer and some of the earliest

The quiet neighbor in Rehavia — Jason's Tomb.

representations of the seven-branch *menorah*.

The tomb was built far from the Jerusalem of that day, for burial within the city was forbidden under ancient Jewish law. An earthquake in approximately 30 B.C.E damaged the structure, but it was used at least once again as a tomb after that. Then the burial chambers were sealed. Entrances were blocked and the courtyard filled with stones. As the centuries went by, debris piled up, grass grew and eventually the tomb, itself, was buried.

Then, in 1956, during excavation for a new building, workers discovered masonry blocks. With more digging, Jason's Tomb emerged. Archeological sites are protected in Israel, and the discovery ended the future of any new construction on this spot. The tomb was cleaned, restored and turned into yet another Jerusalem archeological site. This one, however, is enveloped by one of the choicest residential neighborhoods in the city.

So who was this Jason? Could he have been a seaman? Is that the significance of the ships? Or, since according to the Bible, Simon Maccabee of the Hasmonean dynasty used boat drawings to decorate his father's tomb, were ships simply a motif of the period? Another curiosity is that Jason is a Greek, not a Hebrew, name. But was it fashionable among upper-crust Jews of the time to adopt Greek names? Probably as fashionable as it is today for Jewish boys to be named Scott, Brandon or Bruce.

The words in Jason's tomb that refer to him say only that his friends promised to grieve and mourn for him. So far, and maybe for always, Jason's identity remains a mystery.

The people who live on Rehov Alfassi know one thing about Jason for sure: he makes for a quiet neighbor.

> Hours are supposed to be 10 a.m. to 1 p.m. Monday and
> Thursday. (But don't count on it.) Free.

The prime minister's residence is nearby. Continue up the hill, right at Rehov Radaq, left at Derech Aza and right at Rehov Balfour. The house on the left side after Rehov Smolenskin is the prime minister's official residence, usually recognizable by the presence of a collection of protesters. The protesters maintain their vigil in hopes the prime minister, the press — somebody — will notice them.

A few men in uniform near the house and a small guard's tower along the fence are the tipoff that this is an official residence of some kind. Other than that, it could be any well-to-do person's home in this neighborhood. Speaking of which, although Rehov Balfour is south of the officially designated Rehavia boundary, this area often is called Rehavia by its residents.

If you want to rest or eat lunch at this point, Savion is close by at the point formed by the junction of Rehov Aza and Rehov Ben Maimon. Savion, which has a fish and dairy menu, is like an island in a sea of traffic. It's a place where journalists, waiting for news from the prime minister's home, often wait it out over coffee.

Rehov Balfour continues to Kikar Wingate. Across the street and to the right on Rehov Jabotinsky (the "J" is pronounced by Hebrew speakers) is the much more sumptuous **residence of Israel's president** (after all, prime ministers come and go).

Neither residence has visiting hours. The best most of us can do is just to look. But on the holiday, Succot, in the fall, the president usually has open house to anyone who wants to show up in his garden or official reception room indoors.

Past the president's home, Rehov Jabotinsky becomes Rehov Haqeshet, and where that street twists and becomes Rehov Hapalmach, at No. 1, you can find a public building of pink stone.

Museum of Islamic Art

Not to be confused with the Rockefeller Museum in East Jerusalem or the Islamic Museum on the Temple Mount, the **Museum of Islamic Art** is formally known as the L.A. Mayer Memorial Institute of Islamic Art.

And how does it come to be that this excellent and instructive museum of the art that developed out of daily life in the Moslem world is located in the heart of a Jewish, middle-class, West Jerusalem neighborhood?

This is the story: Vera Frances Bryce Salomons, daughter of Sir David Salomons, the first Jewish mayor of London, was a long-time Jerusalem resident. Unhappy over the squalor around the Western Wall where Jews prayed, she tried, unsuccessfully, to buy the Wall from the Turkish rulers. When the British took over from the Turks, she tried again, but with no greater luck. After Jerusalem was divided in 1948 and the Western Wall fell under Jordanian control, her goal seemed hopeless.

Meanwhile, Ms. Salomons developed an interest in Islam out of her close friendship of many years with Leon Arie Mayer, a Hebrew University professor of Islamic studies. Finally, with the same amount of money she would have spent to buy the Wall, she established the Museum of Islamic Art, as well as setting up a retirement home next door to it for academics. Mayer was to be museum director, but he died in 1959, before it opened.

Exhibits are clearly laid out and displayed. They draw from the entire range of the Islamic world, from the Atlantic coast of Africa to East Asia. The more than two floors of exhibitions are awesome for their breadth, depth and beauty of Islamic art. In most cases, museum information on the exhibits is extensive and detailed.

A particular display — on pottery, for instance — not only points out variations in artistry from community to community, but gives a historical background and tells how outside influences impinged on the art. The glass-blowing exhibit explains the process step by step and how different effects, such as the creation of luminous colors, were achieved. A huge amount of information is packed into each room.

But, alas, the Islamic Art Museum isn't what it used to be. One of its greatest attractions — which had nothing to do with Islam — has been reduced to a smidgen of its former self. A multi-million dollar collection of antique timepieces that had belonged to Ms. Salomons' father, the London Lord Mayor, occupied the museum's ground level. Some of the pieces dated as far back as the early 17th century. Marie Antoinette owned one of the watches.

But in 1983, in the largest such loss in Israel's history, burglars hauled away an estimated $7.5 million worth of the horology collection.

> Hours are 10 a.m. to 1 p.m.; 3:30 p.m. to 6 p.m. Sunday
> through Thursday, 10 a.m. to 1 p.m. Saturday. Closed Fri-
> day. Entrance fee. Buy tickets for Saturday in advance at
> the museum or major hotels. Tel. 661-291.

Like other Israeli museums, the Islamic Art Museum offers more than insight into art. It also offers insight into Israel itself.

One day, among museum visitors was a class of Jewish school children escorted by their teacher, also a group of teenaged Arab boys on their own and a large group of Israel Defense Forces soldiers on a lecture-tour. The diversity of viewers that day was typical, but it was startling to realize that not only were soldiers being taken to an art museum, but that they were learning about the art of a people who, largely, refuse to recognize the existence of the soldier's country, and an art which, at the same time, is the heritage of some of their fellow citizens. This paradox of military tension combined with mutual cultural admiration is part of Jerusalem's mystery.

Chapter 12:
Linger Awhile

Substitutions and Extenders: More Museums

The preceding itineraries are not at all exhaustive of what Jerusalem has to offer sightseers. The total amount is enormous and ever increasing, as archeologists uncover more, and sites once closed are reopened.

Every new find is news. Jerusalemites, perhaps the most history-hungry people in the world, flock to new discoveries and discuss them incessantly. Every Jerusalemite (newly arrived or with roots reaching back over centuries) seems to be an authority on the archeology and history of his beloved city and loves to talk about it.

If you are staying on in Jerusalem, or returning for a repeat visit, how lucky you are! You can get to know the city beyond its major tourist attractions. I had that opportunity. During my year living in Jerusalem, I went sightseeing with persistence, curiosity and a sense of amazement (I haven't stopped). Often, I went about it on my own. But many times, I was guided by professionals, especially by three Jerusalem *mavens*, three authorities on the city *par excellence*, whose names should be singled out for their help and knowledge: Jeff Halper, the urban anthropologist, and Muriel Isaacs and Jonah Wahrman, whose love and knowledge of Jerusalem make their work as professional guides far more than just a job for them.

Besides trying to learn everything I could about Jerusalem life, neighborhoods and world-famous sites, I also made a point of visiting the not-so-famous museums that tourists might miss. They offer broader insights, and a more intimate picture of Jerusalem. At some, you might find yourself the only non-Israeli. At others, you could be one of only a few adults. Descriptions of them follow.

The view from the Mount of Olives looking down over the Jewish cemetery toward the Old City.

Ammunition Hill

With its solid, newer buildings and colorful playgrounds, the neighborhood of Ramat Eshkol is settled, comfy, middle-class and monotonous.

It's hard to imagine what this part of formerly divided Jerusalem was like before the 1967 Six-Day War. Then, there was no Ramot Eshkol and this area was in Jordanian hands. Harder still is to contemplate the bloody battle that took place here while the Israelis forced the Jordanians out.

But the museum on Ammunition Hill (Givat Hatachmoshet), in Ramat Eshkol, helps give a picture of what happened during that brief, tumultuous upheaval.

The museum, off Sderot Eshkol, west of Nablus Road, is in a now idyllic setting at the top of a hill covered by a pine grove. Children play and birds sing, while the elderly rest on benches. Only the sight of deep trenches sliced into the hill hint at the history of this lovely place.

For 19 years, this was Jordan's most fortified and heavily guarded position in East Jerusalem.

The museum is, in part, the reconstruction of the Jordanian bunker and mess hall that existed here. The rest is new construction with arches, rough stone walls and soaring ceilings.

Inside, maps and aerial photos show the area before the war and during battle. Huge photos capture the perspective of Israeli soldiers as they fought their way up the hill.

It was the capture of Ammunition Hill from the Jordanians that made it possible for Israeli forces to enter the Old City, reach the Western Wall and bring about reunification.

A rotating exhibit near the front of the museum gives a glimpse into the short lives of the 183 Israeli soldiers who died in that battle.

Hebrew documents are translated into English in this well-displayed museum. That includes soldiers' letters, poems and essays. One of the items that remains on display is an excerpt from Ofer Feniger's book, *The World Lives Within Me*. In "Letter from Ofer", he writes to a friend about the emotional impact he felt after reading, for the first time, a book about the Holocaust. The letter is read aloud every year at Remembrance Day assemblies for Holocaust victims. Feniger was killed in hand-to-hand fighting on Ammunition Hill. He was 24 years old.

The soldiers' writings are astoundingly eloquent, as is their art work and photography. These were young men with the emotional freedom to look inward and a wealth of artistic talent to express outwardly what they found within themselves. Reading their biographies stirs the feeling of frustration over the wasted promise in these outstanding lives that were so short.

> **Hours are 9 a.m. to 5 p.m. (until 7 p.m. in July and August) Sunday through Thursday, 9 a.m. to 1 p.m. Friday. Entrance fee. Tel. 284-442.**

Hall of Heroism

Jerusalem is a haunted city and one that doesn't forget its ghosts. Among the city's hovering spirits, those at the Hall of Heroism, dedicated primarily to the fight for a Jewish homeland and against the British Mandate rulers' severe limitation of Jewish immigration, are among the most poignant. The men memorialized here appeared to be reckless for challenging the British Empire. Few contests could have been as lopsided. Yet these men did so with complete dedication to a seemingly impossible dream — a home for the homeless Jews in their own ancestral land.

The museum is tucked away behind a parking lot in the Russian Compound. Inside, against stone walls in a small room, is a photo exhibit of Jewish men, some scarcely old enough to be called "men", who were put to death by the Turks in 1917, in Syria in 1965, or by the British and Egyptians during intervening years.

Past the portrait gallery, you enter what was Jerusalem's Central Prison during the Mandate Period (1917 to 1948). Inside the prison is a long, shabby corridor hung with impressive and intriguing maps, documents and large photos relating to the prisoners and their resistance of the Mandate. But alas, as at many Israel museums that aren't top tourist attractions, English translations are frustratingly rare.

When I walked through the exhibit, no one else was visiting the echoing prison. My footsteps were frighteningly loud. Creaking sounds added to the eeriness and seemed ghostlike in this forsaken place, as if all its terrible memories were stirring.

As it turned out, the sounds came from an open window moving in the breeze, but such is the atmosphere of this prison. The ordinary assumes unreal proportions.

Display cases exhibit the inmates' craftwork while they waited for their fate. A neatly woven, tiny container for cigarettes looks like a gift for Dad that a youngster made during summer camp. Also on display are **tzitzit** — the fringed undergarment worn by religiously observant Jewish men — woven by a prisoner, perhaps for himself.

Thirty to forty men at a time were jammed into the small cells here. Some of the men were locked up for overt acts against the Mandate forces. Others were there for a "crime" such as blowing the *shofar* during High Holiday prayers at the Western Wall, an act banned by the British even though it is an integral part of Rosh Hashana and Yom Kippur, the most important Jewish religious observances.

In one of the death cells, a mat and a pair of shoes seem as if they had been left there only moments earlier. Around a corner, almost hidden, is the gallows with the hangman's noose and pulley at the ready.

Actually, the British, for fear of sparking an uprising, didn't execute Jews in Jerusalem. Instead, on execution day, they spirited the prisoners far away to Acco, a largely Arab city close to Lebanon, and hung them.

A plaque in the corridor relates that two prisoners condemned to death refused to let the British get their way with them. Two hours before their scheduled execution, they pressed smuggled grenades against their hearts and blew themselves up. One was 17 years old.

Sunshine in the courtyard, where prisoners were allowed for one half hour a day, seems to mock the dark history of the Hall of Heroism.

Hours are 9 a.m. to 4 p.m. Sunday through Thursday, 10 a.m. to 1 p.m. Friday. Entrance fee. Tel. 223-209.

Herzl Museum

When Capt. Alfred Dreyfus of the French Army was convicted of treason in 1885, journalist Theodor Herzl covered the Jewish officer's trial for a Viennese newspaper.

While years later, it was proved the case was tried on false documents, the blatantly anti-Semitic treatment of Dreyfus made such an impact on the 35-year-old Herzl that it changed the course of his life. Remembering the prejudice he had endured as a child in Budapest, he concluded that Jews never would be freely accepted in any country, no matter how long their families had lived there or what patriotic contributions they had made to it. The only solution for them, he decided, was their own homeland. And so it was that Herzl, virtually alone, started the modern Zionist movement.

More than half a century later, Herzl's bold campaign came to fruition with the re-establishment of the State of Israel.

The small museum on Mount Herzl off Sderot Herzl is dedicated to telling Herzl's life story. It is tucked at the bottom of a slope between the entrance to Yad Vashem and the Military Cemetery on Mount Herzl.

Included are Herzl's handwritten letters and a re-creation of his study. The Hebrew and English comments beside each display provide a continuous, if sometimes abbreviated, glimpse into Herzl's life.

It may come as a surprise to learn that this intense man with an all-consuming mission, had a less serious side to his personality and professional life. He was the author of 20 plays, most of them comedies.

In 1887, Herzl called together the first Zionist Convention. The exhibit includes a collection of oval photos of the delegates who came to Basel, Switzerland, for that fateful event. The men and women appear spruced up as if for a school yearbook. They seem to be comfortable, middle-class Ashkenazim — not world shakers.

The exhibit points out the little known, bizarre historical fact that in the early 1900s, the British first tried to establish a Jewish home in the northern Sinai. Failing that, they offered Eastern European Jews a portion of Kenya that later became modern Uganda.

A copy of Herzl's will states his request for "a poor man's funeral". He asked that his body be re-interred in Palestine. He died on July 3, 1904. The anniversary of his death is a national memorial day in Israel.

His body was indeed re-interred in the land he sought for the Jewish homeland. It rests at the top of the Jerusalem mountain named for him. His grave is marked by a simple black slab of stone on which one word is engraved: Herzl.

Hours are 9 a.m. to 5 p.m. Sunday through Thursday; 9 a.m. to 1 p.m. Friday. Free. Tel. 531-108.

Jerusalem Biblical Zoo

What could be more earthly than a zoo? But in the heavenly city of Jerusalem, religion even finds a place here.

The Jerusalem Biblical Zoo off Rehov Brandeis in Romema not only has the same features as its counterpart in, say, Grand Rapids, but has, in addition, its own specialty. Within its space (pocket-sized compared to the great zoos of the world) is a gathering of animals, birds, snakes, insects and plants mentioned in the Bible.

By each zoo creature is a plaque with an appropriate Biblical verse printed in Hebrew and English, such as, "My beloved is like a roe or a young hart," from the Song of Solomon, next to the deer enclosure; or "Behold, he shall fly as an eagle," from Jeremiah, beside the eagles' cage.

The Koran gets a plaque, too. At a monkey cage are words from the Islamic holy book that warn in fractured English: "Those who transgressed the Shabbat were turned into driven-away monkeys." What? These simians cheerfully swinging on the bars?

The hippopotamus is in a unique position in an Israeli zoo, for the Hebrew name for that hulking animal is *"behemoth"*, which means in English, something enormous. The Biblical words beside the hippopotamus are from the Book of Job: "Behold now, behemoth."

The Jerusalem Biblical Zoo, founded in 1939, originally was located on Mount Scopus, which fell to the Jordanians in the War of Independence. In 1950, the 18 animals that remained from the 122 that had been in the zoo before the war were moved by armored convoy to this site in Romema's Schneller Woods. From those 18, the new zoo was born. But in 1967, the redeveloped zoo was hit by a Jordanian shell and 110 animals were killed.

Few people could have expected the financially strapped institution to survive this second blow. The zoo already was so impoverished that a few years before the bomb hit, its main keeper was arrested for "stealing" vegetables from the municipal dump. He did so to feed the animals.

But miracles tend to happen in Israel. Greatly recovered now, the Biblical zoo has just about everything, Biblical and non-Biblical tigers, panthers, flamingos, black swans and those creatures that particularly evoke this country, graceful, gentle gazelles.

Families, Arab and Jewish alike, come to visit the animals, picnic under the shade trees or boat on the tiny lake.

The zoo is scheduled for expansion. A "Noah's Ark" will be built in accordance with specifications given in the Book of Genesis. Along with it will be progenitors of modern domestic animals, such as local wolves, wild goats and wild cats.

Visitors have the choice of two self-guided tours. Blue arrows are for the condensed tour of about two hours; red arrows direct the way to the complete tour, which could take four.

> **Hours: 8 a.m. to sunset daily except Rosh Hashana and Yom Kippur. Vivarium open 10 a.m. to noon. Entrance fee. Purchase tickets in advance of Shabbat. Tel. 811-334.**

Karaite Museum And Synagogue

Among the mosaic of people that make up Jerusalem are the Karaites — members of a Jewish sect founded by Anan Ben-David in Persia in the 8th century. It is said that Ben-David emigrated to Jerusalem and built the Karaite Synagogue. It is in use today at Rehov Hakaraim 3, Jewish Quarter, Old City.

Karaites accept only Tanach, an acronym for Torah (the Five Books of Moses), Nevi'im (Prophets) and Ketuvim (Writings, such as the Books of Daniel and Ruth and the Proverbs). They believe Tanach is binding and to be interpreted literally. Out of this, they have developed traditions that vary from those of mainstream Jews.

Among their practices, during Shabbat, Karaites don't eat cooked food or leave lights burning as mainstream Jews do. They have no light at all throughout that time. Nor do they leave their homes on Shabbat, except to go to the synagogue and pray.

According to the museum caretaker's wife, who speaks French and Hebrew, but no English, some 50 Karaite families live in Jerusalem and about 20,000 individuals in all Israel. Karaite communities exist, or have existed, in Turkey, the Crimea, Poland, Lithuania, Egypt and, in the United States, in Chicago, San Francisco and Los Angeles. For centuries, the center for Karaites was Egypt. The establishment of an independent Israel inspired some to move here from Egypt. But most arrived after they were forced out, after Israel briefly won control of the Sinai in 1956.

The museum is in a tiny room a few steps below street level and holds mementos of this small, dispersed community. The most beautiful, surely, is a delicate, white, 100-year-old bridal gown from Egypt with a pair of pearl-covered slippers beside it.

Photos of Karaite rabbis from another era line the walls. Many of the religious leaders wear white-topped black turbans.

At the far end of the museum, a visitor may look into the synagogue below. The synagogue originally was completely underground, built that way both because it could be a handy shelter when needed, and because the ruling Moslems required synagogues and churches to be inconspicuous. Improvements after the Six-Day War raised the synagogue floor, which added natural light.

Still, this house of worship remains quite dark inside. Much of what is in the room emerges only slowly from the shadows. Its Torah Scroll is in a cabinet in the corner to the right. There is a small *bima* (platform on which services are conducted) by the ark, and a screen at the rear reserves a tiny portion of the room for women. Richly colored carpets cover the stone floor. The room has no furniture because worshipers, who must leave their shoes outside, often prostrate themselves during prayer.

> To visit, call 280-657 for an appointment, or go around the corner and enter a courtyard opposite the arch of the ruined Tiferet Israel Synagogue. Then knock on the caretaker's door (but not during nap time, please). There is no charge to visit the museum, but contributions may be placed in a box near the synagogue entrance.

Mardigian Museum

"Who remembers the Armenians?" That was the rhetorical question the Nazis are said to have asked before they embarked on the slaughter of 6 million Jews. The Nazis learned well the lesson of history and concluded it would be as safe for them as it was for the Turks, who set out in 1915 to annihilate a people, while the rest of the world paid scant attention and, afterwards, quickly forgot.

Wars and politics unfortunately had put the largest chunk of the ancient Christian land of Armenia within the borders of Moslem Turkey. Under the cover of World War I (as the Germans later used World War II), the Turks destroyed 1.5 million Armenians.

But survivors and their descendants aren't about to let the Turks forget. They want the Turks to acknowledge what happened to their people in the early years of the 20th century. And they have hopes that even at this belated date, the rest of the world will learn from it.

That is one of the purposes of the Helen and Edward Mardigian Museum near the Armenian Cathedral of St. James in the Armenian Quarter of the Old City. Edward Mardigian, a Detroit industrialist and active worker on behalf of Armenian causes, endowed the museum with $250,000 in the 1970s.

Also important is the museum's exhibition of Armenian art, especially as it praised God and expressed devotion to the Church over the course of centuries.

Entrance to the museum is from Jaffa Gate, along the Armenian Orthodox Patriarchate Road to the right and then, after the second archway, through a modest doorway on the left, and then through a courtyard.

Three thousand years of Armenian history are surveyed in a series of ground-floor rooms in a two-story 19th century building that used to house seminarians. Through maps, audio-visual presentations and pictures, the vivid story is told. The Armenians' expertise with metal turned them into chariot drivers in 2000 B.C.E. Between 70 and 50 B.C.E., they briefly became conquerors, spreading their territory from between the Black and Caspian Seas to an area that included Syria and northern Israel.

In a stunning photo, Mount Ararat, spiritual symbol of the Armenian people, rises out of a rocky wasteland. The mountain is echoed in the pointed headdresses of Armenian Orthodox priests and in the pointed, conical towers of their churches.

Photos of these churches line the walls in a first-floor room. The churches are significant as the link between Byzantine and Islamic architecture. The ones on view are those that, at least until the time of the photos, survived both their lack of care against the region's bitter winters and what Armenians allege is deliberate Turkish destruction.

Samaritan men gather to sacrifice lambs during their Passover on Mount Gerezim. Women watch from bleachers.

On the second floor, photographs recount Turkish genocide. In one, a group of Turkish men proudly stand beside a pile of severed Armenian heads. In another, orphans who managed to escape the Turkish storm gaze forlornly at the camera.

A room of Armenian glory, instead of defeat, shows examples of Armenian art, such as a 1685 world map drawn by an expatriate residing in Amsterdam. His map includes a vast area called "America". Next to "America" is a large island called "California". On seeing this, some Americans today might say that the artist was prophetic, for surely some day California will float out to sea.

Added to the museum not long ago are examples of the rich collection of religious art belonging to Jerusalem's Armenian Orthodox Patriarchate. In 301 C.E., Armenia was the first nation to adopt Christianity as its state religion. Pilgrims from that country have been coming to Jerusalem ever since, always bringing the best they could as a gift to the Patriarchate. Gifts range from copper pots, to illuminated manuscripts, intricately patterned carpets and altar curtains emblazoned with gold thread.

The exhibit of religious art changes about every six months. Bit by bit, the Jerusalem Armenian Patriarchate's immense collection will see the light. Perhaps someday, the exhibit will satisfy rumors that the Patriarchate owns what is purported to be the world's largest pearl (an inch wide) and the longest piece of amber (4 feet 8 inches).

Meanwhile, art exhibited at any given time is awesomely rich: vestments of such fine gold and silver thread that the designs are as smooth as paintings, chalices of gold filigree inlaid with pearls and gemstones. The never-repeated designs of the crosses, alone, are bedazzling.

The cross of the Armenian Church is distinctive for usually being equilateral, and having four open, split branches. It is said that each cross is different. But rarely is there a crucifix. Museum curator Kevork (George) Hintlian explained this absence by saying, "The cross should represent victory — not pain."

Hours are 10 a.m. to 5 p.m. daily except Sunday. Entrance fee. Tel. 282-331.

Montefiore Windmill

Funny that a windmill would be one of the most famous landmarks in Middle-Eastern Jerusalem.

More than a hundred years ago, this windmill of Northern-European design built by Sir Moses Montefiore was one of many that dotted the uninhabited, rocky countryside outside the Old City.

Almost all have disappeared. This one is near the top of a hill looking across a valley to Mount Zion and adjacent to the neighborhood, Yemin Moshe. It now stands as a museum commemorating Montefiore's incredibly long life and astounding impact on the development of Jerusalem.

Today, the windmill, even to its huge blades, is beautifully restored. Next to it is a small building that houses the carriage Montefiore used in Europe and in some of his journeys to the Holy Land. His family crest on the door had a lion and buck holding up banners of Jerusalem. Beneath them was the family slogan: "Think and Thank."

The display within the windmill is excellent for its clarity and breadth. Eight well-lit panels have photos and reproductions of documents, paintings and drawings pertaining to Montefiore's life. Beside each panel is an explanation in Hebrew and English, and above each one is a blown-up photo of old Jerusalem. The photos go as far back as the 1840s.

In late 1986, in an act of utter stupidity, arsonists destroyed the carriage. A replica is planned.

From the terrace in front of the windmill, you can see some of the more spectacular views in Jerusalem of the Old City, the Hinnom Valley and the Judean Desert.

Montefiore was born in Livorno, Italy, in 1784 into a family that already had settled in England. He died in England at the age of 101 and was buried there. Because of his steadfast devotion to Jerusalem, a stone from the city was placed beneath his head before he was buried.

A wealthy man, he retired at 40 to devote himself completely to Jewish causes. He was blessed with a lot of time and a lot of money — his own and access to other people's — to dedicate to his efforts.

Montefiore and his wife, Judith, visited Palestine seven times. The history of Jerusalem probably would have been far different without this man. He recognized that the Jerusalem of his day, totally within walls, was impoverished and pestilence-ridden. Montefiore believed that for their health and welfare, Jews had to move outside the walls. If they were afraid — for it was a dangerous wilderness — he would offer them inducements such as employment and a stipend.

First, the three-story windmill went up in 1855 both to provide flour at a reduced price and work for poor Jews. Then in 1860, Mishkenot Sha'ananim, elongated structures of tiny apartments where the mill workers and their families from the Old City were to live, was built just below the windmill. But even being paid to live in Mishkenot Sha'ananim wasn't enough for these Jerusalemites. Because of marauders, they insisted on creeping back to the safety of their old homes every evening.

Both the windmill and Mishkenot Sha'ananim were failures. The mill wasn't designed for the tough demands of grinding Middle-Eastern wheat and Jerusalemites weren't ready yet to be pioneers. But Montefiore wasn't discouraged. The exhibit in the windmill chronicles the many neighborhoods where Montefiore and the foundation that continued after his death had success creating a new Jerusalem.

One of these neighborhoods was Yemin Moshe ("the righteous Moses"), named for the English philanthropist. Located next to Mishkenot Sha'ananim and the windmill, it often is credited for being the first permanent neighborhood outside the walls. Not true. It wasn't even the second neighborhood outside the walls.

Yemin Moshe was begun in 1891, after Montefiore's death, on land he had purchased. After the Six-Day War, it went from being a jumble of hovels for the poor to an artist colony to a high-priced neighborhood largely inhabited by "Anglo-Saxon" Jews.

Montefiore, himself, didn't finance the projects he pursued in Jerusalem. He was an expert fund raiser. The money for Mishkenot Sha'ananim, for example, came from the will of Judah Touro, the first American Jew to make a large contribution to the Land of Israel. A hard-to-find plaque in Mishkenot Sha'ananim's facade credits both Touro and Montefiore for construction.

The windmill, in ways a monument to Montefiore's failed early efforts in Jerusalem, almost didn't survive the British Mandate. Before the British left Palestine in 1948, they blew off the windmill's top, reportedly to make it more difficult for the Jews to defend the soon-be-leaguered city from Arab attack. Jews dubbed the British act, "Operation Don Quixote." Ironically, when Montefiore built the windmill almost a hundred years earlier, it could have been called the same thing.

> Hours are 9 a.m. to 4 p.m. Sunday through Thursday; 9 a.m. to 1 p.m. Friday. Free.

Tax Museum

The Tax Museum at Rehov Agron 32 is said to be one of only two such museums in the world. It is on the ground floor of the Israeli Tax Building, which is distinctive for its ornate grillwork at its windows, its neat, new sidewalk in front and the modernistic iron fence on the traffic island on Agron. Israelis, with rue in their voice, insist that these elaborate touches are sure signs that the government collects more tax money than it knows what to do with.

A museum on how a government collects taxes may seem merely to offer a good way to duck out of the rain or sun. The reality comes as a surprise: this place is amusingly quirky and has items any sightseer will enjoy.

Inside is a single large room that looks as if it contains the discards of several Israeli equivalents to attics. In the midst of the clutter, uniformed officials stand at attention and a young woman sits at a table near the door. While all may share a similarly blank expression, only the woman is real, a fact that may be detected by her clicking knitting needles.

The sight of the uniforms and all those documents hanging edge to edge along the wall may produce angst in a beholder, as if yesterday were the deadline for filing tax returns and nothing had been done about it.

In a tiny section on taxation in ancient times is a clay slab with a painted line of awkward, young women dancing. The slab dates from 4th century B.C.E. Persia. An explanation printed in English states that by dancing in a Persian temple, the women could square their "labor tribute" — whatever that was.

In an ominous vein, the Taxation in the Diaspora section has an 18th century notice from London that warns Jews that if they don't want to be stoned on the street, they had better promptly pay the special tax levied on them.

Nearby, a neat parchment printed in Hebrew from 17th century Mantua, Italy, reminds Jews that their taxes to the Jewish community are due and advises that they should be paid in "moral and strict righteousness."

One part of the museum shows the many clever ways people tried to smuggle items into Israel and thereby avoid import taxes. Of course, those ways weren't that clever. Otherwise the shabby coat that had 97 silk scarves sewn into its lining or the cute baby doll that now is without the load of jewelry that had been stuffed into its body wouldn't have been confiscated and put on display. A note: There may be some meaning in the fact that a museum dedicated to taxation, an activity that runs counter to every natural inclination on the part of those taxed, is open in the afternoon when almost everything else in Jerusalem is closed.

> Hours are 1 p.m. to 4 p.m. Sun., Tues. and Thurs, 10 a.m.
> to noon Mon., Wed. and Fri. Entrance fee.

Tourjeman Post Museum

Within its beautiful, battered house, the Tourjeman Post tells the story of Jerusalem's division in 1948 to its reunification during the 1967 Six-Day War.

The splendid four-family, partially shattered house at Rehov Hel Hahandassa 1 was built in the mid-1930s. The Arab Baramki family constructed it on land bought from Ahmed Bey Tourjeman. Curiously, the pink and white stone house, with Crusader arches and Corinthian columns, retained the name of the former landowner, instead of taking on the name of the builder.

After the Arab residents fled in 1948 during the War of Independence, Israeli forces turned the house into a fortified blockhouse at the edge of "no-man's land".

For 19 years, the Tourjeman House overlooked the Mandelbaum Gate, that makeshift border between Israel and what the Jordanians and British called "Jordan" which split the heart of Jerusalem from 1948 to 1967.

With the city's reunification, it was decided that the house would become a museum. The building's shell-blasted balcony was left as it was when the fighting ended. The poignant sight makes the events described within seem as if they happened yesterday.

Inside are maps, documents, audiovisual presentations (the voice of David Ben-Gurion announcing Israel's independence is one) and dramatic photographs.

A series of photos follows the little drama that occurred when a nun in the Notre Dame Hospice on the Israeli side leaned too far from a window and her false teeth tumbled to the ground. They landed on a strip of no-man's land between the warring forces. With white flags to signal their peaceful mission, United Nations personnel are seen hunting for the lost teeth. Finally, there is a photo of the triumphant nun happily showing off her dentures, which are once again in her smiling mouth.

Here, too, is a blowup of the famous David Rubinger photo of Israeli paratroopers' first, emotional encounter with the Western Wall of the Temple Mount, which they regained during the Six-Day War. That was the single most stirring event of the brief war.

The exhibit ends with a look at the Jerusalem of the future. The prediction will cause any lover of the city to have severe indigestion. In a model, the entire Jerusalem of the future looks like the intrusive Wolfson Towers and the fortress-like Gilo. Historical and charming neighborhoods have fallen to the wreckers' ball. This display sent me out of the enchanting Tourjeman House with a feeling of despair and the wish that tomorrow never come.

Hours are 9 a.m. to 3 p.m. Sun. through Thurs. Closed Fri. and Sat. Entrance fee. Tel. 281-278.

Natural History Museum

There is no chance for weary feet or boggled minds in the Natural History Museum located at the north edge of the German Colony at Rehov Mohliver 6. It is a small, succinct and inviting place.

A huge, red model of a heart, perhaps 4-feet high (not counting the arteries hanging off the top), begins to beat at the push of a button.

For a nominal fee, you may thrust your arm into an opening of a machine nearby and get a report on your blood pressure. Instructions on this particular machine are in English — a rare occurrence here. The paucity of English explanations is frustrating, but not a hindrance to appreciating this otherwise well-exhibited museum.

Elsewhere are skulls, a skeleton and a picture of Darwin looking down on the exhibits as if with fatherly approval.

In a room showing insects, an enormous black model of a fly caught in a spider web and of the spider, itself, hang from the ceiling.

Particularly colorful and informative are the rooms of birds and animals of Israel.

But perhaps the most attractive thing about the museum is the building in which it is located and its surrounding grounds. It used to be a private mansion. Historians think the house may have been designed by Conrad Schick, the former Christian missionary who became early Jerusalem-beyond-the-walls' pre-eminent architect. The house, which dates from the late 1800's, probably was built for a wealthy German or Arab. For its large size and graceful design, it is distinctive amidst the foursquare lines of the other houses in this village which German farmers established. There are three lovely arches over the entrance. Their echoes on the second floor have been filled in, thus muting the architectural poetry.

The house is set a distance from the street, facing a large garden and a view of the Judean Hills beyond a surrounding wall.

During a visit, you can find the garden an idyllic spot. Other times, it is filled with chatter of school children — Jewish children fanning out to explore the pathways or young, sedate Arab girls in their smocks and long pants walking sedately with their teacher.

> Hours are 9 a.m. to 1 p.m. Sunday through Thursday, 4 p.m. to 6 p.m. Monday and Wednesday. Closed Friday and Saturday. Entrance fee. Tel. 631-116.

Wolfson Museum

Directly across the street from the Sheraton Jerusalem Plaza, rises Hechal Shlomo at Rehov King George 58. It isn't named for King Solomon, but for the father of Sir Isaac Wolfson, the English millionaire. Sir Isaac built it out of filial respect.

The tall, domed building houses the headquarters of the Ashkenazi and Sephardi Chief Rabbinates; the huge Great Synagogue, and a reconstruction of a small Italian synagogue. It also houses, on the fourth floor, the Wolfson Museum of Jewish religious art and an adjacent collection of three-dimensional scenes from Jewish history.

The museum is just right for an hour or so of museum-going. It has drawn from countries as disparate as Yemen and Holland to display a rich variety of religious objects used at home and in the synagogue.

The permanent collection contains arks, jewelry, amulets, Passover Seder plates, and even such humble objects as charity boxes and circumcision clamps that, through embellishment, have become works of art. Rotating exhibits focus on different themes.

Among the treasures are a pair of rare Persian rugs more than 100 years old that together portray Moses, Aaron and the sacrifice of Isaac. They contrast in style with a 17th-century Florentine tapestry showing Moses receiving the Ten Commandments from a shadowy representation of a white-bearded God.

While the Persian weaver's Biblical characters wear the clothing and have the stylized faces seen in classic Persian miniatures, the Italian Moses wears red leggings and a jaunty cape as would any Florentine blade of the day. Framing the Italian scene are four chubby cherubs holding up towering piles of fruit.

The walls of one small room are lined with marriage contracts, which became (and still are) vehicles of artistic fancy, despite their legal purpose. Those from mid-19th century Jerusalem have an improvised air and are charmingly askew. Those from Persia and Afghanistan are more formal.

In the large back room, the tops of the lighted display cabinets contain works of art not to be missed. Up there, in semi-darkness, are Torah covers in colors from sky blue to wine and in various metals and wood. Their variety is striking.

One small room is devoted to photos of Sir and Lady Wolfson at the many places in Israel and England they have endowed, as well as standing side by side with the doers and movers of the world, including everybody's favorite figureheads, the British royal family.

The museum is skimpy on identifications. As an example, art by contemporary Israeli artist Michael Ende is exhibited side by side with historical items and could be assumed to be centuries old, also.

Across the hall from the Wolfson collection is a display of three-dimensional scenes from Jewish history. These are in miniature with the figures about one-inch high. The display begins with Abraham and his family leaving Ur and ends with Dr. Chaim Weizmann, Israel's first president, on the White House lawn presenting President Harry Truman with a Sefer Torah on May 25, 1948, shortly after the establishment of modern Israel.

Scenes include casts of thousands or, at least, they look that way. There is Pharaoh's army, about to be swept away by a huge wave of the Red Sea roaring in on it. There is Jerusalem, under siege by the Roman army swarming around its walls.

The artist not only shows the main characters of his scenes, but parallel lives around them: while Queen Esther begs her Persian husband to save her people's lives, three bare-breasted women do a wild dance out in the courtyard; while Philo pleads with Emperor Caligula to annul his anti-Jewish decree, far from that emotional scene, a slave serenely hauls water from a pool.

Downstairs is Rananim, the more endearing of two synagogues in the Hechal Shlomo complex. Its neighbor is the Great Synagogue, whose services are attractive to tourists and Israeli prime ministers. For the likes of the Great Synagogue, you don't have to leave Beverly Hills to see — but take a peek, anyway. The Rananim synagogue in the Hechal Shlomo south wing is quite small and infinitely more intimate than its grand neighbor. Within its gray-blue, unadorned walls is a Baroque brown and cream 18th-century *bima* and ark brought from Padua, Italy. In addition to its physical attractiveness, this synagogue can be recommended to women for services. From the women's section in the balcony, it affords one of the most unobstructed views of activities in the men's section than in almost any other Jerusalem Orthodox synagogue.

Hours are 9 a.m. to 1 p.m. Sun. through Thurs., 9 a.m. to noon Fri. Closed Saturday. Entrance fee.

The Church of the Holy Sepulchre is the most Christian site in the Holy Land. It marks the site of the crucifixion, burial and resurrection of Jesus.

Chapter 13:
Heavenly Jerusalem: Churches, Synagogues and Family Ties

The myriad of alluring paths in Jerusalem can turn you into an explorer. The paths can take you outward from yourself and into the Jerusalem around you. Or they can turn inward as Jerusalem leads you, eventually, back to yourself. This chapter is devoted to guiding you towards a discovery of yourself.

Jews can attempt a concrete search for their heritage by researching Jerusalem's archives. Although the material is meager, until you start your search you never can tell what might be there. (See Chapter 19: "Recreation in the Land of Creation", section on "Digging for Roots".)

But the greatest opportunity for discovery is in the spiritual realm. I have written much in this book about earthly Jerusalem — its movie theatres and its all-over-the-place pedestrians. Jerusalem is a real, down-to-earth city. But, there is a spiritual factor in Jerusalem that lifts it into a heightened sphere. A clerk is cranky, an ultra-Orthodox Jew and a more liberal Orthodox Jew carry on a shouting match, the trash is on the streets because of a strike: all this goes on. But still, it seems as if, no matter what else occurs, this is Jerusalem, after all, and somehow heavenly, no matter what. It may merely be a perception we bring to the city. Perhaps not. Whatever its origin, in Jerusalem, you do feel closer to God. If that is difficult to acknowledge, I'll put it this way: at least you feel closer to the divine spark within yourself.

Through its Jewish, Christian and Moslem houses of worship, alone, the spiritual avenues you can travel in eternal Jerusalem are many. Surprisingly, perhaps, the avenues lead you to yourself. Explore your inherited path, and the joy of discovery can give you pride, as well as knowledge. Explore the path others have cut, and you will be enriched.

But no matter how important these many, varied houses of worship are, Jerusalem's spirituality isn't confined within them. It flourishes in homes, hotel ballrooms and in front of ancient tombs whenever and wherever families and friends share life's milestones. And it floods the streets when the city celebrates religious festivals, as it seems to do incessantly, and even just as much when the city cries over the lost 6 million or its fallen defenders.

The paths have no end. The search is limitless. But along the way, by absorbing its spirituality, you will have found the key to discovering what Jerusalem is all about.

To pray in Jerusalem is the dream of people around the world. Jews, Christians and Moslems have given Jerusalem its reason for being.

King David made the city on the hill a holy site when he bought a threshing floor from a Jebusite some 3000 years ago. He turned it into an altar and a home for the Ark of the Covenant and thus laid the foundation for the Holy City.

From that time, through destruction, dispersal, reconstruction and in-gathering, Jerusalem has been the center of Jewish spiritual life. Their prayer, "Next year in Jerusalem", is like the main theme of a symphony.

A thousand years after David, like all Jews, Jesus was drawn to the Holy City. His last days and his death were in and around Jerusalem. After Christianity developed, its followers established magnificent churches here in Jesus' honor, and every place in the city that had a connection to him became revered.

More than 500 years later, Moslems swept in from the Arabian peninsula and conquered Jerusalem in 638. While it isn't named in the Koran, nor did Mohammed ever actually come here, Jerusalem became the third holy city in Islam, after Mecca and Medina. Islamic belief, held every bit as strongly as fact, is that Mohammed's winged horse carried him to heaven from the rock atop Mount Moriah. Jews believe that was the very location of the their First and Second Temples. Jesus may have prayed at the Second Temple.

And thus these three great religions intertwine in one small spot on the globe.

A babel of prayer resounds through Jerusalem, with Moslems claiming Friday as their sacred day of the week, Jews keeping Friday sunset to Saturday after sunset as their holy time, and Christians marking Sunday as their special day of the seven. Also, the followers of each religion have prayers the rest of the week with several times of the day designated for that purpose.

Guests are welcome in every synagogue and church, not only as sightseers, but also to be present during worship. On a visit, keep in mind the proprieties. Some synagogues have strict dress codes for women. (Detailed in Chapter One, "Getting There".) Churches expect a certain amount of decorum from women, such as no shorts or bare shoulders. Some require a woman to cover her head.

Visits to mosques are another matter. The religious leader of Moslem Jerusalem insisted to me that non-Moslems, women as well as men, are welcome to observe services. But my own experience contradicts that. I've been shooed from Islamic services like a chicken strayed from its coop. However, a non-Moslem man might have better luck.

Following are brief descriptions of three churches and three synagogues. Each has a flavor not duplicated anywhere else. To call these churches and synagogues representative would be like saying that if you have tasted an enchilada, you know what Mexican food is like.

After all, in Christianity alone, the differences in style and content between Protestant, Roman Catholic (Latin) the Eastern Orthodox denominations (Greek, Russian, etc.) and the monophysites or Oriental Orthodox, such as Armenian and Ethiopian, make an enormously wide range of atmosphere and ritual in Jerusalem's churches.

Similarly, each synagogue and mosque has its own individuality. Again, its own flavor or, as Jews would say, *"Ta'am"* (taste).

So go taste. Try a church here, a synagogue there. And do try to visit a mosque. Discoveries will occur, perhaps some of them wonderful, no matter what your state of religious observance.

For you to ignore the religious life of Jerusalem would mean dealing with the body, but not the soul of the city. Likewise, family life is part of its soul. So, following the descriptions of places of worship, I take you to the Jewish observance of two rites of passage: the bar mitzvah and the wedding. In Judaism, when you share in these events, you are sanctified.

Churches

St. Mark's Church

St. Mark's Church is the Jerusalem home of the Syrian Orthodox congregation, which is reputed to be the oldest Christian denomination. The church originated in the first century.

St. Mark's is located at a bend in the Assyrian Convent Road at the western edge of the Jewish Quarter. The 12-century building is true to Jerusalem's churchly tradition by being dark inside and far removed in spirit from the outside world.

Also typical for Jerusalem, is the layering of new houses of worship on this location. A church that existed here in the 7th century was demolished by the Moslems. One pillar of that church remained. A mosque and hospice occupied the site, until the Crusaders built the present church in the 12th century. This edifice and its monastery were restored in 1940.

St. Mark's is rich in tradition. It is said that here is where Peter was imprisoned, where he set up the first church, and where the Last Supper took place (not the Cenaculum on Mount Zion, as is generally held). The Syrian Orthodox maintain that Mary was baptized at the baptismal font in a small chapel in the church. Syrian tradition also has it that this is where the house stood that belonged to the other famous Mary, mother of John the Evangelist, known as John Mark.

Paintings of the Virgin Mary on the south wall are credited by the Syrian Orthodox as the work of Luke the Evangelist. Historians maintain they originated later in the Byzantine Period.

The Syrian Orthodox monks who serve a congregation of some 75 families, far less than the 1000 that were here before the Six-Day War of 1967, maintain that many of their rites resemble Jewish practices. They speak Syriac, a language that is close to Aramaic, which was the language of the Talmud.

Perhaps the Church of St. Mark's major contribution to the community as a whole is its youth marching band, which beats its drums and blows its horns through the lanes of the Old City at many festivals. The youngsters invariably appear at Christmas and during Easter Week. And this, the oldest Christian denomination, recently came up with a major innovation and accepted girls into its marching band.

Morning prayers and vespers take place daily, but liturgical services are scheduled in the church at 7:30 a.m., Fridays only. The rest of the time, the congregation attends services Sundays in the church's chapel in the Holy Sepulchre and on Wednesdays at the Tomb of the Virgin at the foot of the Mount of Olives, close to the Cave of Gethsemane.

**In summer, the church is open to the public from 9 a.m.
to noon. In winter, hours are unpredictable. Tel. 283-304.**

Christ Church

Most churches in Jerusalem are somber, but the Anglican Christ Church is one of the few that is bright and inviting. Located inside Jaffa Gate in Omar Ibn el-Khatab Square, it was the first "modern" building in the Old City when it was completed in 1846. It became the cultural center for Protestants in Jerusalem, especially British Protestants. These days, accents heard here, even of the preacher, tend to be more often American than British.

The church's white building stones are different from others in Jerusalem, because at the time of construction, there were no stone-cutters in the city. Stonecutters had to be imported from Malta, and they weren't familiar with the characteristics of Jerusalem stone. But they taught their skills to Arab apprentices from Bethlehem and left behind a legacy of stonecutters who are busier in today's Jerusalem than at any other time in their history.

Founders of Christ Church adopted the soft-sell approach toward Jews, whom they hoped to convert. Therefore, the interior didn't even contain a cross, originally, and a Hebrew prayer book was used.

There are crosses now, but they are small and made of wood so that they blend into their surroundings.

A 9:30 Sunday morning family service begins with a hymn or two. Then the children are led off to Sunday school.

Prayer is from the New International Version of the Bible. Its words are modern and now have a man "sleeping" with a woman, instead of "going in unto her."

The hymns and sermon move along speedily here, all in a very self-contained and subdued spirit. Clocks here apparently are synchronized, for the children troop back into the sanctuary just as the adult service ends.

> **Evening prayers are at 6 p.m. Monday through Saturday, Holy Communion is at 8 a.m., Family worship at 9:30 a.m. and Evening Prayer at 6:45 p.m. Sunday. The church is open from 8 a.m. to 6 p.m. weekdays during the summer. Tel. 282-082.**

Ethiopian Orthodox Church

Another church that seems disarmingly plain after the darkness and rich decor of so many others is the circular Ethiopian Church at Rehov Hahabashim 10 (Ethiopian Street). But this is only relative, for it actually contains a multitude of decorations. What makes the church seem so different is its brightness, for here, artwork can be seen in sunlight streaming from the many high windows.

Entry is under a stone lintel topped by two Lions of Judah, the symbol of Ethiopia. Ethiopian kings claimed descent from the Queen of Sheba and King Solomon.

The altar is in the center of the building, following the design of the Second Temple. Around it are salmon-colored pillars with bright blue trim. Walls are hues of blue and on the ceiling is a splash of gold stars. Painted flowers decorate the tops of the encircling pillars.

Many large icons hang from pillars and walls. When you remember how often European religious paintings in the Middle Ages and Renaissance reflected the society in which the artist lived, it comes as a surprise that these paintings don't reflect Ethiopia. The faces are pale.

The Ethiopian Church has a New Testament written by hand on parchment. A priest pointed out to me with pride that is how Jews make their Torah scrolls.

The church is divided into men's and women's sections, but not by partitions. Men and women simply congregate in separate areas during services. But wooden partitions designate a separate monks' area. In it, directly opposite an opening to the altar, is a throne-like chair for the bishop.

For a 4 p.m. vesper service, worshipers enter the church, fall on their knees and almost touch the floor with their forehead in a motion that is more Moslem than Christian.

The service begins in silent prayer. The bishop enters wearing a sumptuously embroidered red and gold gown with a green and gold cape over it. Then soft singing begins. The sound is repetitive and finally a drone is established. Eventually, the singing is like the wind or even an organ and becomes hypnotically enveloping. The vesper service becomes a sort of reverie. I have been told that at the church's Pascal services, in addition to the sounds of the distinct style of singing, drums are played.

The church maintains a gift shop in the courtyard, near the church entrance. Inside are Ethiopian-made baskets, embroidered items and horsetail fans.

> **Vespers are 4 p.m. weekdays, 3 p.m. Sunday. Liturgical services take place at 4 a.m. weekdays, 6 a.m. Sundays. Tel. 286-871.**

The Beit Knesset (Synagogues)

The word "synagogue" comes from Greek and has worked its way into the English language. The Hebrew name for what we call a synagogue is *beit knesset*, which has a simpler, more down-to-earth connotation. It means, "meeting house".

Each *beit knesset* is strikingly different from the next. It isn't simply a matter of Orthodox or non-Orthodox, at least 99 per cent of Israel's Jewish houses of worship are Orthodox. But each *beit knesset* reflects the distinctions between Ashkenazim and Sephardim. And within that division, each takes on the special character of the major ethnic background of its worshipers.

The Great Synagogue in Hechal Shlomo is the grandest and, to me, most pompous and least attractive of Jerusalem synagogues. Hechal Shlomo on Rehov King George is the seat of the Rabbinate. Israel's two head rabbis, one Ashkenazi, the other Sephardi, have their offices here, so the Great Synagogue has a quasi-official standing. When I think that perhaps this place is an indication of what a Third Temple would be like, I shudder. Stuffy. That's one way it would be. The greatest interest in this synagogue lies in the fact that whoever is prime minister usually can be seen in prayer here.

Soon, a *beit knesset* being built in another part of Jerusalem by a Hasidic sect will be even larger than the Great Synagogue. It may be enormous, but run by Hasids, it won't be stuffy.

I am happy to ignore the so-called grand and glorious for the grass-root, neighborhood houses of worship. These are the ones that are most enjoyable and informal. These aspects probably go together.

But while visitors are welcome, women entering a *beit knesset* may face a challenge. Since from puberty the sexes are strictly separated in synagogues, a woman visitor first must figure out where the women's section is located and how to get there. At some synagogues, men and women enter through the same main door and then they separate. At others, women must go around to a side of the building and climb stairs up to the women's section. It can be most confusing. If a woman blunders into the men's section, she causes a minor ruckus as the men turn (some smiling benignly) and wave her off in the proper direction.

The separation of men and women in synagogues can be disconcerting to a lot of Western Jews used to more liberal ways. Only a handful of Jewish houses of worship exist in Jerusalem where men and women sit together. Everywhere else, while services are under way, much of the time, women (if they can see them at all through curtains or lattice work) simply observe the men, who usually are downstairs in the synagogue's main room.

It can be immensely pleasurable to watch the warmth and camaraderie among the men, but watching isn't the same as doing. At festive times, women are free to dance with each other, but attention focuses on the men's dancing. It seems implicit that women are the act's "second banana".

Ultra-Orthodox synagogues are sticklers when it comes to women's dress (see Chapter 1, "Getting There", for details). Other synagogues are more *laissez-faire*, so long as good taste is used. Men need only be concerned that they wear a head covering.

The greatest difference between worship services in synagogues and churches is that in churches, the feeling is of reverence and restraint; in synagogues it is of reverence and exuberance. Added to these, synagogues often house a constant buzz, either from children running between their father's legs, their mothers in the women's section, or the fathers, themselves, greeting and chatting with old friends. Occasionally, there even can be a feeling of chaos.

While this might strike people not used to Orthodox services as undignified, I'm inclined to look on it the way composer John Cage looks on extraneous sounds during a concert. "It's all music," he once said as a fire engine went by during his performance. As Judaism is a celebration of life, perhaps children's voices and adults' communications, too, are a way of celebrating life.

Italian Synagogue

At the entrance to the Italian Synagogue at Rehov Hillel 27, these words are written: "Do not leave this place in haste."

A person wouldn't want to, especially if he is of the male species and may enjoy a clear, unobstructed view of the synagogue's glories during services.

The Italian Synagogue occupies the far corner of a large building that has a side on Rehov Hillel. The synagogue is at the other end of the courtyard and up a flight of stairs. Its entrance is directly across the hall from the Museum of Italian-Jewish Art.

The design of this *beit knesset* is authentically and lavishly Baroque. The interior belonged to a 1719 synagogue in Conegliano Veneto, some 60 kilometers from Venice. It was removed in its entirety after Jews no longer lived in that city and was installed in Jerusalem in 1952. Since the Jerusalem location has slightly different proportions than the original building, the layout isn't identical to what it once was.

Nevertheless, the Italian Synagogue is a brilliant sight with its shining silver chandeliers, gilt curlicues around its ark and stucco strings of grapevines along the walls.

Men and women enter together, but women immediately step into their section at the back of the main room. Men continue through the single aisle in the women's section to get to their place. Women remain and sit on risers behind an elaborately carved wooden screen. Not only can they barely see what is going on during the service, but they can't even appreciate the beauty of the screen hiding their view, for only the flat, unadorned side faces them.

Perhaps the display on the walls of the women's section of *katubot* (marriage contracts), some going back 200 years, is some comfort. But they hardly measure up to the sight of the Torah Scroll with its red cover and silver, tinkling finials as it is carried around the *bima*,

A graceful curved arch marks the site of the massive Hurva Synagogue, built in 1856 and destroyed during the Jordanian occupation from 1948-1967.

the raised platform from which services are conducted, before and after it is read.

The service is neither Sephardi or Ashkenazi. It goes back to ancient Roman traditions. And, you know it's Italian. The cantor delivers a lot of solos with many operatic flights. Only at the end of the service does the congregation join in with two rousing songs.

One Saturday morning, a young man was called to the *bima* to read as an honor before his forthcoming marriage. He took over the role of cantor. When he finished, his future in-laws, of Tunisian background, flung candies from the women's section over the wooden screen in their traditional North African way of wishing him a sweet marriage.

As the candies whacked the wooden floor, the Italians were shocked. Nothing so indecorous had happened in their synagogue, they grumbled. Clucking their tongues, they insisted, "That's not Italian."

Jews pray three times a day, morning, afternoon and evening, but usually afternoon prayers take place late enough to merge with evening prayers. Shabbat services are held Friday evenings, Saturday mornings and evenings (Havdalah). They begin at times determined by the occurrence of sunset. Event schedules from the *Jerusalem Post* and the Government Tourist Information Office provide these prayer times.

Urfali Synagogue

The *beit knesset* of the Urfalim — Kurds from the town of Urfa, politically in eastern Turkey, but culturally in Kurdistan — is at Rehov Bezalel 19.

Men go up the stairs from the sidewalk and enter directly into the sanctuary. Women must climb a flight of steep stairs that demand the agility of a cat. Then they find themselves in a balcony.

There, a virtually opaque white curtain blocks the view into the main room below. The curtain is parted briefly during services when the Torah Scroll is carried around the *bima*. At that time, some of the women blow kisses toward the Torah.

And if there is a special *simcha* — blessings for a happy occasion such as an impending marriage — the curtain is thrown back again, so the entire congregation may see and participate.

The Urfali Synagogue is in a poor neighborhood, and the women's dress reflects that. Many wear scarves tied under their chin, *babushka*-style. Others are bareheaded.

The building is freestanding, so windows on all four sides let in a flood of light. The walls are covered by peeling pale-yellow, floral wallpaper. Six chandeliers, most of them different from each other, hang from the ceiling. Two are light violet in color. The *bima* is of stone and has large, round glass decorations at each corner. Benches around the *bima* are covered by bright red Turkish rugs.

Two clocks sit high enough on the walls that a worshiper's glance at them could be interpreted as a yearning look toward heaven.

The most startling sight to a newcomer to Sephardi synagogues is that in many, fluorescent lights snake around the ark. Here, narrow blue and green fluorescent ribbons trace the blue, curtained ark and its reproduction of the Ten Commandments above it.

The Urfali worshipers are energetic participants during services. As the cantor sings, he pinches his notes and sends them skyward as he ends a phrase. Among closing songs, the congregation joins for a lusty rendition of Naomi Shemer's popular "Jerusalem of Gold", which praises the city of which these people are an integral part.

One Saturday morning, the *simcha* was special blessings for the father of a new baby boy who would have his *brit milah* (ritual circumcision) during the coming week. Upstairs, the baby's grandmother went from woman to woman in the balcony and poured cologne into her hands. Later, the baby's grandmother gave each woman a little sack of hard candy. When blessings for the father and his new baby were concluded, the women threw candies at the man while uttering ululating cries.

When services end at the Urfali Synagogue, women shake hands and take a heady whiff from a jar full of aromatic greenery, a reminder of sweet Shabbat, before they descend the steep stairs.

Mevakshei Derech

Mevakshei Derech, a congregation loosely related to the American Reconstruction movement, is one of the synagogues in which not only do men and women sit together, not only do girls become *bat mitzvah* and women go to the *bima*, but any woman who wants to can freely don a *tallith* and *kipah*.

The congregation owns one of the newer buildings in town. It is a striking, graceful structure on Sderot Shai Agnon, uphill and on the same side of the street as a shopping center and a Bank Leumi branch.

Because Mevakshei Derech isn't an Orthodox congregation, it gets no government financial assistance. The members' eagerness to take on the responsibility of its own sanctuary indicates their dedication.

Inside the white-walled building, the congregation sits on three sides of the *bima*. The Torah is kept in a niche carved in the wall behind the *bima* with a plain maroon velvet curtain. Above is a simple lamp for the eternal flame.

In contrast to so many synagogues in Jerusalem, fluorescent lights aren't in day-glo colors and wrapped around the ark. They are white and simply hang from the ceiling, doing their duty as lamps to illuminate the place.

For women, dress can be as formal or informal as they wish. The men's style, also, shows individuality. Some wear the colorfully embroidered, high-rimmed Bucharan *kipah* (skull cap).

On a Saturday morning, when I was at Mevakshei Derech, a brother and sister were marking their *bar* and *bat mitzvot*. Relatives and friends tossed candies at them and everyone sang the traditional congratulatory songs.

The congregation sings during the prayer service. Several melodies are *hasidic* (religious) songs that have become Israeli hits.

The bulk of the congregation is composed of "Anglo-Saxons" — Jews from English-speaking countries. The atmosphere, while friendly, plainly reflects Anglo-Saxon reserve.

Family Ties: Joys Be Shared

To partake of Israel means to partake of family life. From the *brit milah* (ritual circumcision) of the infant son, to his first haircut at age three, to his *bar mitzvah* when he is 13, to marriage and death, the family and the extended family gather.

It may come as a surprise that here, the extended family encompasses people that other societies regard as strangers. Israelis tell you that when you are in Israel, you are with family. Their behavior bears this out.

When they celebrate major events in their immediate lives or their cousin's or nephew's lives — it's all the same to them — they will invite you. "Invite" may be too formal a word in this country. They expect you to come to family events. And their invitations aren't for Jews only. Non-Jews, too, feel in Israel as if they suddenly discovered relatives they never knew they had.

The sharing of life's happy milestones is part of the Jewish religion, and in Israel that part truly is practiced.

You may be invited to a wedding or a *bar mitzvah* or a *brit milah*. It may be that you've never laid eyes on the bride or groom or any of the other major actors in these major life events. It may be that the person who invited you is an aunt or cousin of the hosts and not the person putting on the celebration. Because of that, you may hesitate to accept the invitation. You may feel it would be an imposition for you to show up; after all, you don't even know the host family.

You'd never dream of accepting such an invitation back home. But, my dear, this is Jerusalem. Go. In Israel, joy is to be shared. That's all there is to that. You will be welcomed. You will be fulfilling a a *mitzvah* be carried out. In Judaism, it is the host's *mitzvah* to welcome the stranger. It is the stranger's mitzvah to share the host's happiness.
a mitzvah be carried out. In Judaism, it is the host's *mitzvah* to welcome the stranger. It is the stranger's mitzvah to share the host's happiness.

And the heartfelt emotions of the occasion will warm you. These will be the times you will treasure.

Weddings: Oh, How We Danced!

In Israeli terms, the young couple's wedding was an intermarriage. The bride was an American from a Long Island family of Ashkenazi background. Her parents weren't Orthodox. The Sephardi groom was the son of strictly observant Iraqi immigrants. But Joanne and Avner had known each other for five years before they were married in Jerusalem in exuberant festivities replete with Jewish disarray. More and more such cultural mergers are taking place in Israel.

Guests were invited at 7 p.m. to a hotel in Romema that is among Jerusalem's popular wedding sites. One large, multi-purpose room would serve for the pre-nuptial reception, the wedding ceremony, the dinner and the festivities. Places were set at tables for a sit-down dinner for 150. Fewer than that number had been formally invited. Friends of relatives and friends of friends were expected to show up.

Joanne and Avner's families stood in a reception line at the entrance to the room greeting guests as they arrived. For the guests, the end of the reception line led to a table of appetizers — hot peppers, pickles, *houmous*, marinated beets, a creamed vegetable salad and huge twisted buns. Against one of the long walls, a band of young musicians was getting itself organized.

When Joanne and Avner walked into the room together, women emitted high-pitched ululating cries and the band burst into a song that inspired people to stop eating and start dancing — men and women separately, of course, for this was an Orthodox wedding. Men put their arms over each other's shoulders as they danced and shouted out the words to the song. Later, they formed two lines facing each other and moved toward each other and away, back and forth. Meanwhile, women had their own enthusiastic circle dance going.

At evening prayer time, the music stopped and the men went into a corner, slightly bowed their heads and let their bodies sway to the rhythm of their chanted prayers.

While this was going on, Joanne, in a white dress and with the veil behind her head, sat in the center of the room in an elaborate white chair, a sort of throne, and was greeted by guests.

After prayers ended, she remained there while the men gathered at a table and signed the *katubah* — the marriage contract. Presiding over things at this point was the nation's chief Sephardi rabbi, whose presence bestowed great honor on the marriage and the groom's family. He looked regal in a turban and black caftan with yellow embroidery outlining the front opening.

With the *katubah* signed, the wedding could begin. Avner approached his bride-to-be in her elaborate chair and, smiling at her tenderly, gently lifted her veil and allowed it to fall over her face.

Four men appeared, each holding a pole attached to a green, satin *chuppah* — the canopy under which the couple would stand during the ceremony. The men arranged themselves so the *chuppah* was upright in a clearing in front of the band. With Joanne, Avner and the rabbi now in their places under the canopy, guests and family crowded around them. The crush of people close to the young couple obstructed the view for most of the other guests. A voice over a microphone pleaded for everybody to take seats at the tables, so all could see. Some actually did, but most remained pressed in close. Only a few caught sight of the bride slowly walking seven times around her husband-to-be.

With a man now on either side of the couple pulling a *tallit* (prayer shawl) taut above the bride and groom's heads, Joanne and Avner took a sip of wine from a silver goblet. Avner placed a ring on Joanne's finger and said in Hebrew, "With this ring, you are consecrated unto me according to the law of Moses and Israel." The rabbi read the terms of the *katubah* and chanted seven time-honored blessings. The couple took another sip of wine, Avner stomped on a glass placed at his feet, the glass shattered with an explosive pop and the two were married. The ceremony lasted 15 minutes at most.

With a shout of joy from family and friends and ululations from the women, the dancing resumed. Avner was lifted high and carried by his male friends and relatives. He seemed to be ecstatic. His outstretched arms kept time to the surging music. Joanne was lifted up on a chair carried by her women friends and relatives. Above the crowd, Joanne and Avner's arms reached out to each other. Later, the men scooped up Avner's father and carried him, also, on their shoulders. Off their perches, Avner danced with the men and Joanne danced with the women. When Joanne stopped to rest, she took a seat in front of the men dancers, who seemed to be presenting their performance especially for her. Meanwhile, her American parents watched, as if in a daze, the abandonment of the dancers and the noisy celebration of the guests.

Between the athletic, energetic dances, the guests, if not the bride and groom, ate dinner. The first course was a pastry cup filled with meat. Heaping bowls of rice, corn and potatoes were set on each table, so guests could help themselves. Then, waiters went from person to person to serve chicken, beef and/or schnitzel. Dessert was cakes and the fresh fruit that was each table's centerpiece. Steaming Turkish coffee was the finishing touch. While each table had been laden from the start with *mitz*, brandy and *arak*, and the alcoholic beverages were imbibed freely, no one seemed to be drunk. Boisterously happy, yes; inebriated, no.

The dancing became more and more adventurous and flamboyant. Four men formed a circle with their arms on each other's shoulders. Faster and faster their circle turned, when suddenly two of the men's feet came off the floor and their bodies stretched away from the circle as if they were carried by the wind. In another demonstration of bravado, a young man put a bottle filled with water and flowers on his *kipah*-covered head and proceeded to dance. He held everyone's rapt attention and drew applause when he performed push-ups, still with that bottle perfectly balanced.

And the band played on. Israeli pop music is a mixture of secular and sacred. One song the band played that uses words of the Rebbe of Bratislav is an example. "Gesher Tzar Meod" says, "The world is a narrow bridge; the important thing is not to be afraid." One wouldn't assume that such advice would make for a hit song, but that is what the song became. Performed at this wedding, as the song, slow at first, but increasing in speed, reached its exultant climax, it made for yet another chance for family and friends to express wild jubilation.

Joanne and Avner's wedding was typical of Israeli weddings today. An atypical and colorful wedding event that may soon be exclusive to Israel is the Yemenite Jewish *henna* ceremony. Few Jews remained in Yemen (later divided into North and South) at the southern tip of the Arabian peninsula after "Operation Magic Carpet" flew the bulk of the population to Israel in 1948. Since then, the Yemenites have made major, positive cultural contributions to Israel.

But by now, weddings of Yemenite Jews more and more resemble typical Israeli weddings, except for the *henna* cermony that takes place the night before. It is strictly Yemenite and proceeds as follows.

In it, an esteemed, older female relative applies the red henna to the bride's palms and soles. In Yemen, designs in henna were drawn on the bride's face, but that part of the ceremony has been dropped here. Henna is applied to the hands of the groom and relatives, also.

The red dye is looked on as giving protection from the "evil eye". The idea is that bad spirits are fooled into thinking that this is the wedding, so then they won't be around at the real thing.

On this night, the bride and groom wear traditional Yemenite festive dress as if they were royalty. The bride is dressed in a silk caftan embroidered with gold thread and decorated with layers of ornaments from coins and trinkets to gold and silver filigree necklaces. Under the caftan, the bride has on "a thousand-and-one-nights" pants that hang loose, but are held tight to the ankles with embroidered leggings. Ornaments attached to her pants jingle with every step she takes.

And on her head is a magnificent, bejeweled, conical headdress, almost like a helmet, with part of it coming down under her chin. Often fresh flowers frame the tall headdress. Only the bride's face can be seen, and whoever she is, she always looks stunningly beautiful.

The groom, too, gets bedecked for the occasion in a silk caftan, necklaces and silk scarves.

Of course, singing, dancing to drums and cymbals and eating are part of the celebration.

The *henna* ceremony is so colorful and looked on in Israel as such a special part of the culture, that often in "mixed" marriages, if the bride is not Yemenite, but is marrying a man who is, she will go through the ritual.

One aspect of Israeli weddings I am unable to discuss is how long they last. All I know is that they inevitably outlast me, and no matter how late I leave, I'm on my way home while festivities still are in

With a rent-an-accordionist behind him, a 13-year-old celebrates his Bar Mitzvah at the Western Wall.

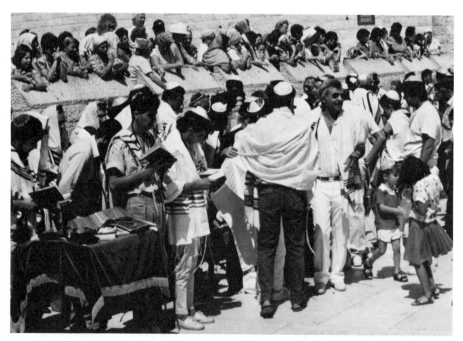

A Bar Mitzvah ceremony at the Western Wall. Female relatives watch from behind a fence.

full stride.

Bar Mitzvah: Rite of Passage

Monday and Thursday mornings are the times boys become *bar mitzvah* at the Western Wall. Twelve or 20 *bar mitzvah* ceremonies could be going on simultaneously.

The event marks a Jewish boy's coming of age religiously. From this point on, he assumes all the religious responsibilities of an adult male.

Having reached the age of thirteen, the bar mitzvah boy will read from the Torah while wearing for the first time (if the event isn't on a Saturday) a *tallit* and *tfillin* ("phylacteries"). The latter are two small leather boxes, each containing parchment inscribed with quotations from Hebrew Scripture. With leather cord, one box is strapped to the forehead, the other around the left arm to remind the wearer of the commandments.

One Thursday morning in March, it was Elon's day. Despite the auspiciousness of the occasion, he, like most 13-year-old boys, still looked like a gawky kid. He hadn't had much sleep the night before. His parents had an open house in his honor, and family, family friends and friends' friends showed up. They brought gifts and were served cakes, cookies, *bourekas* and other foods cooked in Elon's grandparents' native Iraqi style. Spurred on by wine, brandy and *arak*, the men, especially, sang loud and strong into the night. Afterwards, when he finally climbed into bed, Elon was too excited to sleep.

At 8:30 the next morning, under a gray sky, Elon's *bar mitzvah* began at the Western Wall. He and male relatives and male family friends gathered around a high metal table in the prayer area. They were only a few feet from a fence separating them from spectators. That way, women attending Elon's *bar mitzvah*, standing behind the fence because they weren't allowed in the men's prayer area, could be as close as possible.

With a video-cameraman recording the action, Elon, a slender boy with olive-skin and large, earnest, brown eyes, began reading the prayers. For the occasion, he wore a white long-sleeved shirt, white trousers and a white kipah. But a yellow T-shirt under his shirt showed at his neck.

At a certain point in the prayer service and ceremony, Elon's grandmother's brother, Mordechai, draped a white, linen *tallit* with black stripes at either end over the boy, covering his head for a moment. Elon lifted an edge of the prayer shawl to his lips and kissed it. This now was his very own *tallit*, an outward sign of his new responsibility. It may be that when the day comes, Elon will be buried with it wrapped around him.

Mordechai then rolled up Elon's left shirt sleeve, wrapped *tfillin* around the boy's thin arm and centered a small shiny black box anchored by a leather strap on Elon's forehead.

Prayers continued. Elon was escorted by the men to a corner at the Western Wall where they walked under an archway into a synagogue inside a tunnel. A few minutes later, they emerged. Elon proudly was carrying a Torah Scroll in a metal case with fluttering colorful scarves back to the table for the next stage in his *bar mitzvah*. When the men and Elon returned to their prayer stand near the fence, the women, as they did at every high point in the ceremony, burst forth in high-pitched ululations and pelted the *bar mitzvah* boy with hard, wrapped candies. Little children, both boys and girls, playing around the prayer stand during the service, scrambled to pick them up. Grown men, too, reached for some, whisked the hard candies out of their wrappers and popped them into their mouth.

With the resumption of the ceremony, the sun emerged, bright and warm. It would be a lovely day, after all.

The metal Torah case was opened and Elon read from the scroll with assurance. He looked pleased with himself (but what an advantage he had over the *bar mitzvah* boys and *bat mitzvah* girls around the world: after all, Hebrew is his native language).

Afterwards, he and the men returned the Torah to its place in the tunnel synagogue. When they emerged into the sunlight, this time, instead of Elon carrying the Torah, the men were carrying Elon. He was on their shoulders, and they were singing lustily.

The cameraman walked backward in front of them to preserve the precious scene. A rent-an-accordionist serenaded the happy group. Seeing the joyous procession, the women grew more fervent in their ululating and candy throwing.

When Elon was set down on his feet, a piece of candy still was lodged in the folds of his *tallit*. He was smiling broadly now — for the first time all morning, but more like a kid than a man.

This high point in a young man's life was being played out, with minor variations, all over the worship area beside the Wall. Songs by one group collided with songs from another group in the musical style of Charles Ives, while ululations rose and fell and candies glinted in the sun as they sailed through the air.

Time was, when the celebration after the *bar mitzvah* could take place right there in the huge plaza area in front of the Wall. But no more. What with all the elegant rebuilding in the area, that kind of Israeli-style down-homeyness has been banished.

So instead, Elon's parents led their guests away from the Wall, out of the plaza, across the street, down some stairs and into a parking lot. There, they hauled food out of their car. Cookies, *bourekas*, fruit, grapefruit *mitz* and brandy were consumed on the spot.

Should you be invited to a bar mitzvah, if you are a female and confined merely to watching, make the most of the situation. Arm yourself with a sack of wrapped candies for pelting. And if the woman beside you ululates, open your mouth, strike a high-pitch and let it rip.

Chapter 14:
The Cycle of Celebrations:
Happy Holidays

At any given moment, somebody is celebrating or commemorating something in Jerusalem, and a cacophony of ringing bells, *muezzin* calls and dancing in the streets fills the Holy City's sweet air.

As Moslem, Jewish and Christian sabbaths follow one after the other, week after week, so Moslem, Jewish and Christian holidays follow each other, one after the other, year after year.

In the "Navel of the World", time is measured in cycles of anticipation and experience. Members of each faith count their year by the events in their religion. For all, preparation feeds the excitement of the approach of a particular event and then the event, itself, be it joyous or solemn, blossoms forth and is savored. And so, yet another landmark in the year becomes shared communal history.

But six major cycles of anticipation and experience revolve simultaneously, each within its own time frame, so Jewish, Moslem, Roman Catholics, Protestant, Eastern Orthodox and Oriental Orthodox events often overlap.

With all this, Jerusalem is like a person who wears multiple wristwatches so he can contemplate several time zones at once.

Of course, the dominant time zone, the one with the most festivities that meet the eye and affect the course of the day, are Jewish. Jews who didn't grow up in Israel may be astounded when

Dressed for his Bar Mitzvah at the Western Wall, a boy of Bucharan descent wears a traditional Bucharan gold caftan and cap.

they experience religious holidays here. For a change, the world revolves around *them*. Here, Christmas and Easter are just ordinary days to most people; and it is the minority Christians in the community who are being deeply worshipful while everybody else goes shopping, or to the tennis courts or to work.

For Diaspora Jews who have grown up feeling that their religious life is a sort of underground subculture, being a member of the majority for a change can be amazing and invigorating.

The impact of the robust Jewish celebrations raises a question: how can a people with such a tragic history have such a joyous religion? Except during Yom Kippur, Tisha B'Av and a few minor occasions, Jews always seem to be feasting, tossing down drinks and kicking up their heels at religious holidays.

In contrast, when Christians observe their important religious events, pomp, ceremony and solemnity are the keynotes. Another thing Christians do that Jews don't, except at Purim, is offer more than one chance to experience a major festive occasion. Because of Christianity's schisms, there are three Christmases and two Easters in Jerusalem. If anyone misses out the first time around, or wants to go through it again, and again, he may have at it.

The Christian calendar is full of less-known holidays that pack the year. The Greek Orthodox, for instance, mark the beheading of John the Baptist with a special service on Sept. 11 at St. John's in the Old City; Roman Catholics have a procession in Jerusalem on Ascension Day.

Jerusalem's Moslems aren't out on the streets with their observances (other than protests) the way Christians and Jews are. Nor are their holidays generally publicized in advance. Keeping track of their important events requires close scrutiny. And since the Islamic calendar, even more so than the Jewish calendar, seemingly wanders in relation to the West's Gregorian calendar, it is harder to anticipate the dates. The best way to be informed is to inquire of a Moslem.

It isn't that Jewish and Moslem events occur according to some Oriental inscrutable mystery. They have definitely assigned times within their own year. The Jewish calendar is lunar-solar and adjusted by the addition of a 13th month at regular intervals, so a particular holiday occurs within a range of the same few weeks each year. Many Jewish holidays are timed to coincide with the full moon. The Moslem calendar is purely lunar, so over the years, Islamic holidays ease their way backwards from one season to another.

Not all celebrations and commemorations in Israel are religlious. Independence Day and Remembrance Day for those who "fell" (that's the term here) defending the country are secular. But their dates, too, are tied to the Jewish calendar.

Of course, any city where the residents insist with no trace of modesty that their hometown is the center of the world would have its own holiday. And so, every spring, Jerusalem has Jerusalem Day, celebrating its re-unification.

Some celebrations have no official standing and might be a legacy of the British or simply were carried into the local scene in immigrants' luggage. One is Sylvester's Day, which the Western world knows as the New Year's Day that occurs a week after Christmas — the first of the three Christmases, that is — and involves partying the night before. Another such event is April Fool's Day, which hardly seems an Israeli sort of thing at all, but is observed by the media.

Then there are festive events imported by specific national groups, simply out of sentiment for the Old Country, wherever that is. Americans have their Fourth of July and the Scottish have their Robert Burns Memorial Dinner.

With this abbreviated account of the numbers of holidays celebrated in Jerusalem, a person well may wonder, are businesses ever open? Does anyone every get any work done?

So let's follow the year chronologically in Jerusalem to find out who is celebrating what, when, where and how.

Shabbat: The Seventh Day

Shabbat is Jews' holiday every seventh day. It is more than simply "the Sabbath". To say only that it is a day of rest barely brushes Shabbat's meaning. Its importance can be recognized by the fact that it is the only religious observance included in the Ten Commandments and also the only one to have become personified in religious poetry.

From sunset Friday until three stars are visible in the sky on Saturday night, Jews are to obey the Fourth Commandment: "Six days you shall do your work. And the seventh day shall be a holy day, a Sabbath of rest." As the Book of Genesis says, "And God blessed the seventh day and made it holy."

Rabbi Abraham Joshua Heschel wrote of the revolutionary concept introduced by the ancient Hebrews, "Six days a week we seek to dominate the world, on the seventh day we try to dominate the self."

Shabbat is rife with symbolism, such as Shabbat as the bride, Shabbat as an honored guest, Shabbat commemorating the creation of the world, Shabbat remembering the Exodus from Egypt.

Jerusalem pursues its fast pace Sunday through Thursday. Friday morning, that pace picks up as people rush to finish what they have to do before Shabbat begins. Flower sellers are out in force, as custom is to buy flowers for one's own home or to give a friend.

Businesses begin to close at noon. By midafternoon, the Jewish parts of the city shut down. Traffic thins, buses stop running, traffic lights only blink instead of changing colors, sidewalks become empty and a hush descends on the city. When the weekly siren is heard, Shabbat officially begins.

Shabbat, "the bride", arrives and is welcomed and treated as such. Keep that image in mind, this seventh day. It helps to understand the specialness in which the day is held and the excited anticipation of its arrival.

I find an almost selfish pleasure in knowing that for some 25 hours, I can't possibly go on errands and that there are few people I can even telephone, for many don't answer the ring on Shabbat. I must stop my daily race with myself and simply let time be.

Observant Jews, in addition, won't ride in a car, light a fire or turn on an electric light or appliance. Certain lights are left on all night. Food is cooked in advance.

Before the siren has sounded, the dinner table has been set with the best dishes for Friday dinner, the most festive meal of the week, and the family has donned their nicest clothes. As the sky fades, the woman of the household lights candles and says a prayer thanking God for Shabbat.

Then, whole families can be seen heading for their synagogues. At the Western Wall, a colorful sight every Friday night is the procession of singing *yeshiva* (religious school) students descending the stairs from the Old City. They come down in a line, each man with his hand on the shoulders of the man ahead. When they reach the area in front of the Wall, they form a circle and to their joyous singing, dance a sort of two-step shuffle ("the Yeshiva Two-Step?").

After services, families return home to their welcoming dinner table. They say traditional prayers over a brimming cup of wine and *challah*, the special Shabbat braided bread, both of which everyone at the table tastes.

The food served varies according to the ethnic background of a particular family, but an important part of the meal is the singing of songs, some of which go back centuries.

In synagogues on Saturday morning, the Torah is removed from the Ark and a portion of it is read. After services, synagogues often have a *kiddush*, a serving of wine and cakes. The word, *kiddush*, means "to make holy". In Judaism, where every aspect of life is sanctified, partaking of wine and food after services is a holy act.

The afternoon meal almost always includes *cholent* (the "ch" is pronounced as in "choke", instead of with a guttural "h"). It is a dish of beans, vegetables and perhaps meat or chicken that has been cooking overnight.

A must afterwards is a nap. After eating a heavy meal of *cholent*, there really isn't anything else you can do.

Following evening services, with three stars in the sky, Shabbat, the bride, is ceremoniously ushered out with *Havdalah*. To separate Shabbat from the week, the sacred from the ordinary, a glass of wine is lifted, a candle is lit and a box of sweet smelling spices is passed from person to person to inhale and remember the sweetness of Shabbat.

Shabbat is with people. Jerusalemites — those in the Old City, particularly — open their homes to strangers who wish to share Shabbat with them. It is possible to make such a connection by chance. I was invited when I happened to ask a question of a couple at the Wall one Friday night. And it turned out, after their invitation, that they knew my family (yes, another example of the way things work in Jerusalem). Another, more dependable way of being invited to dinner and for the entire Shabbat, happens like this:

Often, men who may be active in certain synagogues or *yeshivot* spend time at the Western Wall Plaza, usually behind the men's side, looking for people to invite to spend Shabbat. They are especially interested in inviting Jews who never have participated in this kind of Shabbat observance, but they happily accommodate anyone who would like to do so again. Scruffy young men in blue jeans catch their eye the fastest, but if they don't find you, you should feel free to ask around to see if one of these emissaries is on the premises.

Other opportunities for Shabbat arrangements may exist through the Israel Center, the Center for Conservative Judaism or Hebrew Union College.

Everything will be arranged for you — a place to sleep and places to eat. Having a place to sleep is a must, if you will be in an Orthodox situation, especially in the Old City. No public transportation will exist to take you anywhere else, but, aside from that, spending the night ensures that you will partake of the experience to its fullest.

Where you sleep and eat may be in the same home, but usually you eat at several different places. Be sure to arrive with all your gear (and flowers for the family) at the place you will be sleeping, well before Shabbat begins.

Sleeping arrangements aren't likely to resemble the Ritz. It is possible that you will have to share a bed or sleep on a cot, so princes or princesses need not apply. At meals, you may be one of a few or of, literally, dozens of other guests.

Out of this may come an exhilarating experience with the high points the heady singing and intellectual discussions of the Torah around the dining table.

Then the *Havdalah* ceremony after sunset is a sweetly poignant way of saying goodbye to Shabbat.

With that, Jerusalem springs back to life. It seems as if the whole town then converges on the Ben-Yehuda Mall, and every teen-ager in the city is around the metal fence below the old clock in front of Hamashbir.

If you are reluctant to leave your retreat and face the now bustling world again, don't be surprised. You have experienced the peace of Shabbat. And next Friday, you will have the chance to do it all over again.

By the Silvery Moon (Moslem Holidays)

One of the many Jerusalem "time zones" is Islamic. Its workings are the hardest for a Westerner to understand. Indeed, the average Moslem doesn't waste energy trying to figure out precisely where he is in it, but instead leaves the matter to the *kadis* (religious judges) to announce about a week before, exactly when a holiday will take place.

It is the new moon that determines the Islamic calendar in a year of 354 days. Because of the 11 days difference between the Moslem and Gregorian year, the Moslem calendar retrogresses and holidays aren't anchored at any particular time in relation to the Gregorian calendar.

Instead of calculating days on the basis of sunset as the Jews do, Moslems (like Christians), figure the day from midnight to midnight.

Most Moslems in Jerusalem are Sunni Moslems and follow a certain amount of religious direction from Jordan.

The main Moslem holidays are Awwal Muharram (the First day of the New Year), the Prophet's Birthday, Ramadan and Id el-Adha. The word that Ramadan is going on gets around, but observance of the other holidays may escape non-Moslems' attention.

Moslem institutions are closed for the happy time of Awwal Muharram. A pastry called *mushabek* is eaten. It looks like a hardened, shiny yellow and pink glop of fat spaghetti and is incredibly sweet for a sweet new year.

In Jerusalem, the Prophet's Birthday is, as an East Jerusalem newspaper man noted, "becoming big". More and more, Moslem Boy Scouts can be seen marching through the streets to celebrate Mohammed's birthday. Afterwards, there are services at the mosques. Stores are open on this day.

The Moslem holiday best known to the rest of the world is Ramadan, which is the name of the ninth Moslem month. Like Jews during Yom Kippur, Moslems now contemplate atonement. The entire month is devoted to fasting during daylight hours. One of the purposes is to let everyone know what it is like to be poor. Besides food, beverage and smoking, the list of the forbidden includes sex — at least during daylight.

Work continues during the month of Ramadan, but only halfheartedly at best, especially in the afternoons. Ramadan is especially difficult when it occurs during the summer when the days seem, especially to Moslems, endless.

Most Arab restaurants are closed. Moslems, even those who don't observe the holiday, don't eat in the streets. I know Jews who have reason to visit Moslems during business hours while Ramadan is being observed, who pass up the customary offer of a cup of coffee from their hosts, so as not to make their hosts uncomfortable.

Before the fast ends for the day, customers line up at pastry shops. It is the custom to break the fast with something sweet. The favorite delicacy at this time is a special Ramadan pancake, *katayif*. Moslems take the pancakes home and fill them with almonds or fruit and honey and fry them.

A cannon blast signals the end of the day's fasting. Friends and family gather for a sumptuous meal or just to eat the cakes after sunset. This isn't a time for celebration, however.

Before dawn, drummers and muezzins' calls wake everyone to eat again.

After Ramadan, three days are given over to Id el-Fiter ("feeter"). This is a happy, social time and stores and businesses close down completely. Especially important during this holiday is for men to visit their sisters and bring them the unbeatable combination of money and chocolate.

Id el-Adha marks God's command to Ibrahim (Abraham) to sacrifice his son, who is, according to Moslem belief, Ishmael, not Isaac. The holiday lasts four days.

Mosques, especially Al-Aqsa, are full, but this is one of the pilgrimage festivals when many Moslems go to Mecca, as they are expected to do at least once in their lives. On this holiday, they are to go to Mount Arafat, near Mecca, to "stone the devil". After that, they are to travel to Islam's second holiest city, Medina.

To get ready for Id el-Adha, people go on a buying spree for presents, clothes and food. The observance includes the sacrifice of a lamb. Wealthy Moslems give lambs to the poor at this time. During Id el-Adha, businesses are open.

In 1987, a major religious-nationalist ritual, a large-scale pilgrimage to what Moslem's consider to be the tomb of Moses, was revived after a 50-year break. The tomb, Nebi Musa, lies in the hills between Jerusalem and Jericho.

In a holiday mood, some 50,000 pilgrims from Israel, Gaza and the West Bank rode in a convoy of buses and cars to the recently renovated Nebi Musa where they picnicked, made music, shopped at instant bazaars and listened to speeches.

The pilgrimages were stopped by the British Mandate in 1937 because they had become more political than religious. While Nebi Musa was under Jordanian control, officials of that country, aware of political potential of the pilgrimages, chose not to reinstate them.

It's ironic that this event should be reborn under Israeli administration. Whether or not it survives remains to be seen.

High on Holidays (Rosh Hashana/Yom Kippur)

The New Year most Israelis celebrate occurs in the fall on the first of the Jewish month of Tishrei. The precise date of Rosh Hashana ("head of the year") generally occurs in late September, occasionally in October.

Rosh Hashana, lasting two days, is a happy time, even though it marks the beginning of Ten Days of Repentance. During that period, Jews examine their thoughts and deeds, and, it is said, God evaluates their actions. It is believed that on Rosh Hashana, all the destinies of mankind are recorded in heaven for the New Year. The righteous are recorded in the Book of Life and the wicked are assigned to the Book of Death. But Judaism isn't a fire-and-brimstone religion, so people have 10 days in which to shape up and mend their ways.

Rosh Hashana ushers in three weeks of holidays. To assess the impact of the three weeks on Israeli life, multiply what happens in the Western World during the week between Christmas and New Year Year times three.

From Rosh Hashana to Yom Kippur (collectively called, "The High Holidays"), Jerusalem's streets are crowded with tourists. For many Jews, spending these days in Jerusalem is a spiritual pinnacle of their lives.

All activity in the city, for the month before, is directed toward the High Holidays. During that time, as you stroll about, you might hear the sound of the *shofar* wafting from synagogue windows. Huffing and puffing inside probably are young men hoping to master that ancient instrument. Not only is it tough to elicit a sound from the ram's horn in the first place, but it is murderously difficult to blow in the precise pattern required for the High Holidays.

Like Shabbat, Rosh Hashana begins at sunset. Stores close by 1 p.m. that afternoon before, and buses stop running at about 4 p.m. Candles are lit in homes so the New Year may begin in light. A siren sounds as the holiday starts, just as it does for Shabbat.

Then it seems as if Jerusalem *en masse* is off to the synagogues. The Government Tourist Information Office has a schedule of High Holiday services at synagogues throughout the city. Even though most synagogues sell tickets for High Holiday services, doors are open to all. Tickets only guarantee a seat. For a lot of people, participation in evening prayers at the Western Wall, where nearby *yeshiva* students arrive together singing, seems like the most inspiring way to start the New Year.

Afterwards, it is time for a holiday family feast. Tradition calls for apple slices to be dipped into honey to symbolize the wish for a sweet year ahead. And this is when round, instead of rectangular, sweeter *challah* is eaten.

The *shofar* with its fearsome bellow can be heard at morning services the next day. Also on that first day of Rosh Hashana, men carry out the ceremony of Tashlich, in which they are to cast out their sins. It is done symbolically by throwing bread crumbs on a moving body of water — an interesting requirement of a desert people. But Judaism has ways of working around obstacles. The ultra-Orthodox, especially, descend to the Pool of Shiloah below the Old City for this obligation.

As Rosh Hashana ends, buses begin to run again at about 6:30 p.m., and worldly life resumes. Until Yom Kippur, the following days ostensibly operate as normal, but the city really is in a holding pattern.

Yom Kippur carries the weight of being the most solemn day in the Jewish religion. It is called, "the Shabbat of Shabbats". For 25 hours, Jews partake of neither food nor drink and are to reflect on their lives and determine how to return to the "right path". They ask God's forgiveness for their transgressions. But before they do that, they must make amends with people they have wronged.

Dinner is served close to 4 on the afternoon before Yom Kippur begins. This is to ensure that the last bit of food is swallowed before the siren signals the start of this most holy day.

Of course, stores have closed and buses have stopped running, but on Yom Kippur, an awesome stillness grips the city like at no other time. After hearing Kol Nidre chanted in the synagogue, a person steps into darkened Jerusalem and finds the city transformed. Quietly, the people have taken over. Cars exist only as deserted hulks, occasionally resting over the curb as if they had been abandoned in a hurry. Jerusalem is enwrapped by stillness. The city belongs to the people who walk smack down the middle of what yesterday was busy Rehov King George. The only sound in the streets is the echoing clack of heels on the pavements and the hum of subdued conversation.

Even inside homes, there is a special quiet, for there are no radio or television broadcasts during this time, and people are solemn.

The next day, such simple things as birds twittering, leaves rustling and children laughing can be heard with startling clarity. And now, it's the children's turn to take to the streets. Even near pious Mea She'arim, a group of boys, their *payot* (side locks) flying, chase each other in the street. At the interseciton of Rehov King George and Rehov Yafo, children jump rope where at other times, traffic jams the street.

An incongruous sight in the ultra-Orthodox neighborhoods is of bearded men wearing their old-fashioned black coats and Beaver hats, but with running shoes on their feet. The running shoes aren't a sign of repressed athleticism, but of strict adherence to rules, for not wearing leather shoes is part of the observance of Yom Kippur.

Somehow, even hunger pangs are subdued during this completely peaceful, reflective time. Inevitably, seeing the city at a complete standstill, a person can't help but realize how vulnerable Israel is on such a day and remember with a chill that it was on Yom Kippur that war started in 1973.

As color begins to drain from the sky, there is added intensity in the air over the approaching end of this day. Yom Kippur, this deeply introspective period, goes out in a blaze of glory with triumphant blasts on the *shofar*.

Strange as it may seem after so many hours without food or drink, there may be a wish to slow the clock. The separation of this day from every other day, virtually, has been absolute. The peace the day

Children present songs and dances in the plaza before the Western Wall.

brought was fragile, precious and all too brief.

On leaving a synagogue at the end of the holiday, the sounds of car ignitions turning over, engines accelerating and a sudden quickening of the city's tempo brashly intrude on the night.

Breaking the fast usually occurs with family or friends partaking of a light meal. Another round of repentance can begin the next day for anyone who makes the mistake of stuffing himself now.

A growing tradition in Jerusalem after the fast is broken, is for people to gather at the Western Wall for singing and dancing.

Happy Name Day
(Armenian Patriarch's Name Day)

For pageantry, pomp and mystery, few religious events can match the observance by the Armenian Orthodox Church of the name day of its patriarch.

Taking place for the present patriarch on Oct. 10, it follows or sometimes coincides with the chaotic exuberance of the Jewish holidays that stretch from Rosh Hashana through Simchat Torah. Nothing could highlight better the difference in styles — indeed, in worlds — between Jews and Christians than the name-day mass.

Jews may have created Broadway and Hollywood, but for a show of sheer grandeur, one that is awesomely beautiful and dramatic, the Christians take the prize — Christians with popes and patriarchs and an elaborate hierarchy. They even get to start out with a wonderfully costumed cast of, if not thousands, at least a lot.

The Armenian celebration takes place in the morning in the Church of the Holy Sepulchre in the Old City. For the event, the denomination is given use of the rotunda, and mass is sung before the shrine that houses the tomb where it is said Jesus' body was laid.

Entering the gloomy church from the sunlit courtyard is akin to being pitched into a cave. It takes a moment for eyes to become accustomed to the dim light. But then, the gowns and capes of the various Armenian priests and, especially, the patriarch, dazzle the beholder with the glint of gold thread on shimmering fabric of brilliant colors.

Assisting the mass are altar attendants, young men and boys in red and tan gowns with delicately flowered yokes, who stand in lines on either side of the sepulchre. Occasionally, during the ceremony, the scene becomes cloudy with pungent smoke from swinging incense burners.

About midway through the celebration, school children troop in to witness the event and take their places behind the altar attendants. The girls in their green uniforms sit sedately on chairs behind one line, while the boys, with shushing from their teachers, plunk down on the stone floor behind the other line.

Twice during the mass, the patriarch, priests and altar attendants march in solemn procession around the sepulchre. As they make their way, they sing, and their voices fade and return, always resonating against the church's stone walls and hollows. The procession is led by two elders, not part of the clergy. The two men wear dark business suits and black shearling hats which are reminiscent of dress in their Armenian homeland. Each carries a tall, heavy wooden staff. With every other measured step, the men pound the stone floor with staffs — not simultaneously, but with a slowly tolling ker-plunk-pause-ker-plunk-pause. This creates an ominous sound.

With the backdrop of other-worldly music and pageantry, the impression is spine-tingling: an aura of doom hovers in the air.

The Armenian church music is melismatic, quasi-oriental and awesome. It is an integral part of the magnificence of the mass.

Then, as if arising from the depths of despair, the ceremony ends with the deafening but triumphant peal of bells from the tower above, followed by the clergy and congregation joining in joyous song.

If You Had a Hammer
(Succot/Simchat Torah)

After Yom Kippur, you will have four days to take a breather before the next holiday begins. Israelis will be moving ahead full blast, but ignore them. They like to travel without a speed limit.

Yom Kippur ends. People break their fast. And without a pause, they're off making preparations for Succot. Succot (beginning on the 15th of Tishrei and lasting eight days) is a combination harvest festival and commemoration of the time the Hebrews lived in the Sinai wilderness. As it says in Leviticus, "Ye shall dwell in booths (succot) seven days."

So up and down the streets of Jerusalem, the thwack of hammers can be heard as *succot* are built on balconies and in gardens.

Succot (the singular is "*succah*") are decorated with whatever one's imagination suggests and covered by palm branches, but open to the sky so the stars can be seen at night. Just before the holiday begins, the city of Jerusalem gives out free palm branches, but most people already have completed their booths by then.

In preparation for Succot, stands are set up on street corners to sell what is known as "the four species" or "symbols". A Jew is to have a palm branch, three myrtle twigs, two willows and an unblemished etrog (a sort of overgrown lemon). All these are to be held in both hands while a special blessing is said for them each day of the holiday (except Shabbat) in synagogue or at home. A Midrash

(Jewish commentary on Scriptures) says that each item's taste and aroma, or lack thereof, can be compared to the degree to which individual Jews keep the commandments, perform good deeds and study Torah. Therefore, bringing the four species together represents different kinds of Jews joining together. Since each item stands for a human quality or lack thereof, binding the four together represents a bringing together of all segments of Jewish people.

The plaza in front of Hamashbir is full of "four species" stands. Shoppers closely scrutinize each selection to make sure it is blemish-free. Also on sale are decorations for the *succot*: multi-colored streamers, paper pineapples, colored pinwheels, shiny paper cutouts and such. Someone from the West can't help but be reminded of Christmas by all this.

Indeed, inside Hamashbir, it seems even more Christmas-like, for the toy department is doing a booming business. Purchases are cheerfully gift-wrapped by a clerk in the drab maroon Hamashbir uniform. The clerk seems to be getting as much of a kick out of the gifts as she would if she were giving them away, herself.

When the holiday actually begins, the city's usual commercial hubbub is subdued for many offices and stores are open only half days; some are closed completely.

Succot has become a celebration for Christians, too. More than 5000 Christian visitors from such far-flung places as the Philippines, Costa Rica, India, Nigeria, Europe and the United States converge on the Golden City for "The Feast of the Tabernacles", which is sponsored by the International Christian Embassy in Jerusalem. The embassy schedules a full program of festivities, including marches with banners flying and a huge gathering in the auditorium at Binyenei Ha'uma.

As you walk down a residential street during Succot, the sounds you hear can seem like another Middle-Eastern version of a Charles Ives symphony. From time to time while families feast outdoors in their *succot*, they break into cheerful song. The song at one end of the block collides with the song in the middle of the block and they and any number of others heard on the street entwine abrasively. But the spontaneous joy of the music brings a sort of harmony, musical and otherwise, from dissonance.

Some people also sleep in their *succah*, just as Leviticus says to do. Most Jerusalemites, however, only take their meals there.

Among Succot events is the chance to get a good look at two of the most important people in the country — the president of Israel and the mayor of Jerusalem.

Each president has his own way of making himself available, but tradition requires him to be at his official residence in Talbia for one day to welcome anyone willing to leave his or her weapons at home (as requested on the invitation published in the newspapers) and then stand under a blazing sun in a line that moves forward by millimeters.

On this occasion, children are everywhere: scrunched down asleep in strollers, carried on their fathers' shoulders, swinging on railings. Meanwhile, the waiting crowd (being observed by sharpshooter soldiers on nearby rooftops) is entertained by an orchestra of teenage musicians playing tunes by Israel's composer laureate, Naomi Shemer, and from Broadway's "The Fiddler on the Roof".

One former president welcomed 350 people at a time. Each batch had burst out of a security bottleneck to flood the reception room in his modernistic residence.

There, the 350 were so crushed together, they fairly had to breathe simultaneously. At last, the president and his family appeared. The crowd cheered, threw flowers and candy while women ululated in the Afro-Asian sound that is the world's most vocal exclamation point.

The president welcomed the crowd, extended wishes for good holidays, advised Jews to stick together and then said goodbye. He was a big success, and the cheering resumed as he departed. He went through this perhaps 15 times day so all 5000 people were greeted.

The mayor holds his annual Succot reception at the Tower of David (Citadel) just inside Jaffa Gate. The *succah* here has pomegranates dangling from its beams and children's drawings pinned to its fabric walls.

Outside the *succah*, people sip *mitz*, chat with the mayor who casually wanders about, check out the dress of the various Christian priests, count the number of Arab dignitaries who show up and listen in awe to the Tennessee twang of an International Christian Embassy official.

Meanwhile, the mayor's reception is serenaded by the same teenage orchestra that played at the president's reception and with the same music.

At 9 a.m. on the third day of Succot, there is a special ceremony at the Western Wall for Jewish men who claim descent from the ancient priests — the *Kohanim*. The area before the men's side of the wall becomes a sea of white-shrouded heads as the men envelope themselves in their *tallitot*.

On the fifth day of Succot, the annual "Walk Around Jerusalem" begins at 6 a.m. north of the city. Walkers have their choice of 12, 22 or 25-kilometer routes. Afterwards, they gather for a parade early in the afternoon down Rehov yafo to the heart of West Jerusalem.

A less demanding Succot walk may be taken when artists and

artisans, who have their studios in Yemin Moshe and Khutzot Hayotzer, hold their semi-annual open house.

The Jewish Kurdish community has its own festival during this time — the Saharna, held in Sacher Park. It is an echo of how, back in Kurdistan — that area that includes portions of Iran, Iraq and Turkey — Jews would leave their homes during Succot and live in the wilderness, just as their ancestors did in Sinai. There usually isn't a lot of publicity about Saharna; the Kurds aren't interested in the public's participation. They are known as the "wild ones" of Jerusalem, and they prefer to be wild in private.

Simchat Torah

All this celebrating doesn't wind down at the end of the holiday. Instead, it explodes with Simchat Torah, immediately following Succot. On Simchat Torah ("Rejoicing of the Law"), the year-long cycle of synagogue Torah readings ends and immediately beings again. The men designated to read the last and the first of the Torah are called "bridegrooms of the Law". They have been greatly honored.

The Torah scrolls are carried around the interior of the synagogue seven times, each time accompanied by lusty singing and dancing. Men dance with their children on their shoulders or in their arms. In one synagogue, a sturdy young, bearded man stands amidst the crowd of men and holds the Bible in book form high in one hand. With his free hand, he conducts the men in singing. He belts a solo and the others answer as a group. Sometimes, he slows the tempo way down and then, with a flourish, leads an *accelerando* to a *vivace* while he dances about, putting everything he has into his song of reverence for The Law.

In another synagogue, a wizened old man hobbles on a cane into the middle of a circle of dancing men. He pulls his head into his shoulders like a turtle pulling into its shell, waves his cane in the air, grins from ear to ear and breaks into a wild dance that may have had its origin on the steppes of Russia.

But for women, who sit and dance separately from the men (or simply watch the men), and for men as well, the culminating expression of celebration is their descent from New Jerusalem to the Old City and the Western Wall. The descent takes place from synagogues all over the city.

The one from the Great Synagogue has its genesis when the men who had been dancing in the wide lobby of the building move outside into the blocked-off street. Two circles of dancers, one of men, the other of women, become even more animated than before. Finally, dancers and onlookers form a procession around the men carrying Torah scrolls. The Torah scroll carriers are treated in a way that again symbolizes a wedding. Little boys on men's shoulders hold the ends of a *tallit* so it forms a canopy — like a wedding *chuppa* — hover the heads of the scroll carriers.

Dancing young women lead the singing throng down Rehov Agron to the Old City. Men, too, dance, even as they and the accompanying crowd fight against gravity pulling them down the sloping street. More people than can find room in the street are on the sidewalk and skip along to keep up with the exuberant parade.

Onlookers in upstairs flats along the route toss candy onto the celebrating mass below. As the multitude approaches a government building, a tall, pot-bellied guard leaves his post, cuts into the line, kisses a Torah scroll and then takes it and protectively wraps his arms around it. With his treasured bundle, he dances down the street until he reaches the next intersection. He kisses the scroll again, carefully hands it back and returns to his post.

The jubilation continues as the procession moves on down the hill and through Jaffa Gate into the Old City. As the celebrants turn into the Armenian Patriarchate Road, a bent old woman with a scarf over her wispy gray hair looks up at the throng and ululates with a gloriously gutsy, abandoned sound. She slides like a piece of paper between the men and approaches a Torah scroll. The dancing men accommodate her by marking time in place and turning the front of a scroll toward her, so she can kiss it.

The parade takes the road that skirts the outside edge of the Old City. As celebrants, like a stream composed of countless rivulets, flow through the tunnels of the Armenian Quarter, the singing resonates with grandeur, as if from a mighty army of pilgrims, instead of a disorganized, spontaneous gang of disparate people bound by their commonality as Jews.

The road sweeps east and, suddenly, there is the enormous view of the Kidron Valley, the sun-bleached Arab village of Silwan beyond blending into the mountain to which it clings, the pink and purple Judean desert in the far distance, and straight ahead at the end of the road, the shimmering golden Dome of the Rock above the Western Wall.

The throng continues singing and dancing as the parade descends the steep road. As it nears the Wall, the people sing with even more exultation. Sweating after the strenuous trip, but too exhilarated to feel tired, they have brought the Law to the most meaningful symbol of Judaism that stands — and it is here in Jerusalem.

Simchat Torah ends that night, but without a sudden letting go. Partying continues with a free program in Liberty Bell Park. Dance performances on stage are presented by Hasidim, Yemenites and other Jewish ethnic groups. It often is the wild Kurds who steal the show.

Then, for days afterwards, huge palm branches — no longer needed to cover *succot* roofs — can be seen forlornly lying in the gutter, waiting to be collected by the trash men.

Solidarity (Sigd)

For thousands of years, the Jews of Ethiopia have made a pilgrimage every November to the mountain tops near their isolated villages.

During a day of fasting, they celebrate the giving of the Torah in Sinai, the return of exiled Jews to Zion from Babylonia in 538 B.C.E. and the rejuvenation of the Jewish spirit by Nehemia and Ezra. But perhaps most of all during that day, they pray to be returned to Israel.

The holiday is called Sigd. Since 1982, it has been replicated in November in Jerusalem by Jews who were able to escape from Ethiopia (where they are called *Falashas*, meaning "strangers") and come to live in their longed-for ancestral homeland. But these immigrants have added to Sigd thanks for their return and prayers for the release of their relatives and friends.

Said by some to be descendants of the Tribe of Dan, Ethiopian Jews may have numbered a million during their zenith when they controlled the northern part of that African country. Since their defeat by the Portuguese in the 16th century, they have been force-converted to Christianity, imprisoned, sold into slavery and terrorized in many other ways over the centuries.

During the height of the killer drought that gripped northern Ethiopia in the mid-1980s, hundreds of thousands of Ethiopians fled to the Sudan, where they were placed in refugee camps. For the Jews, who call themselves "Beta Israel", joining the flight was both a chance to escape hunger and the country which neither wanted them nor allowed them to leave. The disease-ridden camps, however, offered little respite. Death still stalked them.

Then, in what came to be known as "Operation Moses", the Israeli government surreptitiously and daringly airlifted thousands of Jews out of the Sudanese camps and brought them to Israel, where they joined a few hundred of their countrymen who preceded them here by a decade and longer.

The remnant of this once powerful people now totals approximately 24,000, with about 18,000 in Israel.

In Jerusalem, Sigd takes place outdoors on Mount Zion amidst a grove of pine trees. Not only do Ethiopian-born Jews and their Sabra children from all over Israel attend, but so do their paler-skinned co-religionists, who choose this time to demonstrate their solidarity with their fellow Jews.

Usually with the Israeli president participating, the ceremony is led by white-bearded *kessim* (the Ethiopian term for "high priests"), garbed in white from their turbans to their leggings. As do their counterparts in Ethiopia, they read the Ten Commandments, passages from the books of Nehemia and Ezra and prayers especially composed for this day. Readings are in Ge'ez, an ancient language, and the chanting is a virtual drone hovering around a single step in the Western scale. In the high priests' hands are horsetail switches, a classical African artifact.

Ethiopian women wear white, too, but with accents of bright colors in bands on their dresses and their scarfs wrapped like turbans around their heads. To the drone of the chanting, they add high-pitched ululation.

One of the loveliest aspects of Sigd is that it brings together Ethiopian friends and relatives who have been dispersed in Israel. There is much kissing, as many as six times from cheek to cheek, between men as well as between women. Happiness over these reunions spreads its warmth to the non-Ethiopians who are present.

Sigd culminates, after prayers and readings have ended, with the high priests leading a procession to the Western Wall.

Better to Light a Candle (Chanukah)

Sometime in December, occasionally as early as the end of November, Chanukah arrives on the 25th of the month of Kislev for eight increasingly colorful days.

Chanukah may be the first recorded celebration of religious freedom. It commemorates the victory of the Maccabee family and its followers over the Syrian king who attempted to destroy Judaism. The story goes that when the victorious Maccabees returned to the Temple in Jerusalem to cleanse it after it had been desecrated by the Syrians (acting on behalf of the Greek conquerors) there was only enough ritually pure oil to last a day. But through a miracle, the oil oil burned for eight days — enough time to prepare a new supply.

And so Jews all over the world light a "servant" candle (a *shammash*) and, with it in turn, light one candle the first night of Chanukah and an additional one each night that follows until all are burning on the eighth night.

In Israel, the candelabra is called a *chanukiah*, not a menorah, as in the Diaspora. And more and more in Israel, instead of lighting candles, people light oil as in ancient times.

Jerusalem during Chanukah truly is aglow. *Chanukiahs* are everywhere — in apartment windows, atop buildings, in public areas and at the Western Wall. Late every afternoon during the holiday, people gather at the Wall to watch enormous vats of oil set ablaze. That surely is the biggest *chanukiah* in town.

In the lobbies of the main hotels there are candle-lighting ceremonies each evening. Any visitor is welcome to attend and then
share in the entertainment, singing and refreshments that follow.

A major holiday sight takes place in the plaza in front of Hamashbir
where an enormous black metal *chanukiah* has been set up. There
you find Hasidic rabbis rising to greater heights aloft a "cherry picker"
to illuminate the *chanukiah* each night. When they finally are in position — which isn't achieved without the cherry-picker pilot having
to make a little adjustment here, a little adjustment there — the rabbis
say prayers, to which passersby join in and add their, "*Omayne*".
Afterwards, yeshiva students offer to any takers a shot of schnapps
and some cookies.

Of course, there is something special to eat during Chanukah. To
Ashkenazi Jews in the Diaspora, the special Chanukah food is potato
latkes (pancakes) under a dollop of sour cream or apple sauce. In
Jerusalem, potato *latkes* appear every day of the year on the menu
at the Sheraton Jerusalem Plaza Hotel, which makes them nothing
special. The truly special Israeli Chanukah treats are *sufganiot* —
small, delicious jelly doughnuts that bear little resemblance to the
clunky items Americans know as jelly doughnuts.

During these eight days, *sufganiot* are everywhere, not only in
pastry shops, but also such places as hotel *chanukiah* lightings, *ulpan*
(Hebrew class) parties and the annual Chanukah program at Hechal
Shlomo. Might as well dig in. *Sufganiot* disappear with the holiday.

Make sure to stroll through Jerusalem the last night of Chanukah
when every *chanukiah* is fully lit and yet another dimension of magic
is added to the already existing magic of the Golden City.

Silent Night? (Christmas)

To be a Christian in Israel during Christmas is to acquire an inkling
of what it is like being Jewish anywhere in the world other than
Israel or, perhaps, parts of Brooklyn.

Stores are open, the kids are in school, Christmas decorations are
absent. No repeated strains of "Hark the Herald Angels Sing" or
"Rudolph the Red-Nosed Reindeer" are heard on radio air waves.

All that may come as a surprise, compounded in Jerusalem, where
Bethlehem is something of a distant suburb, by the fact that three
Christmases are celebrated here — not just the one on December 25.

Christians with allegiance to the pope in Rome and Protestants
mark their holiday on December 25. Eastern and Oriental Orthodox
— including Romanian Orthodox, Russian Orthodox, Ethiopian Orthodox, Copts and, the biggest group, Greek Orthodox — follow the
Julian calender and celebrate Christmas Day on Jan. 6.

Bringing up the rear on Jan. 19 is the last Christmas, that of the

Armenians.

Celebration of the three Christmases follow similar patterns. Only faces, languages and religious dress are different.

To keep it all straight, the Government Tourist Information Office and the Christian Information Center have schedules of which church is having services when, where and in which language. You want Danish? You can get Danish. You want French? You can get French.

As the City of Jerusalem gives out palm fronds so Jews can build their booths at Succot, the municipality ecumenically gives away Christmas trees to its Christian residents for their celebration. The Jewish National Fund distributes cypress saplings to churches, diplomats, foreign correspondents and even sends them to United Nations headquarters in Damascus, Syria.

On Dec. 24, the Egged Bus Company runs a shuttle between Jaffa Gate in Jerusalem and Bethlehem from 8 a.m. until 3 the next morning for the thousands of tourists here for Christmas.

Festivities on Dec. 24 begin shortly after noon when the Latin patriarch begins his traditional procession from the Old City to Bethlehem's Manger Square. Modern times have made their inroads, for he rides in a limousine in a convoy which, at Mar Elias at the southern edge of Jerusalem, picks up an escort of mounted police and Christian Arab Boy and Girl Scouts beating drums, blowing trumpets and playing bagpipes.

In Manger Square, the patriarch is greeted by the mayors of Bethlehem and nearby Christian towns, as well as Israeli officials, perhaps even the prime minister. Then they all go to lunch.

As night falls, in Shepherds' Field close to the nearby village of Beit Sahur, Protestants enjoy a carol service and Bible reading in English, Arabic and Swedish on a rocky outcropping overlooking the Judean Desert.

From 7 p.m. until midnight mass begins in the Roman Catholic St. Catherine's Church, local and foreign choirs, some from as far away as Fiji, sing in Manger Square. Among them might be a Baptist church choir leader from Atlanta, Georgia, who invites the milling crowd to sing along with "Happy Birthday, Dear Jesus".

But it's when the Atlanta choir sings "O, Little Town of Bethlehem", with its line, "How still we see thee lie", that it is time for a look at modern Bethlehem. Quiet it isn't. At least not at Christmas.

Prosperous stores lining the square remain open at least until midnight mass begins. Business goes on at a fast clip. In a particularly elegant jewelry store, a clerk might ask a browser, "Wouldn't you like to buy yourself a diamond for Christmas?"

Outside the stores, the atmosphere is even less like Christmas Eve in the West. The square is full of people, most of them young, from various places in the world. And they are behaving just like young people in almost any small town. They're hanging out. Whether they are Arab, German, Scottish or American, they're hanging out in the square looking for action.

Most of the action consists of buying food from vendors and then dropping greasy paper wrappers on the pavement and kicking empty pop cans across the square. For many visitors and locals, alike, drinking excessive amounts of alcohol is a prime activity. The most interesting action to behold are the interchanges between young Arab men and young, blond foreign women. Their peers gather around to eavesdrop and check on the progress.

Finally, mass begins at the Church of St. Catherine. It is for this that churchgoers have gone through three body searches and the tumult in Manger Square. Admission is by ticket, available in advance at the Christian Information Center. Now the commercialism, hustle and high jinks in the square outside are forgotten. Inside the white-columned church is pageantry and joy.

Carrying a doll in his arms, the Latin patriarch leads a procession up the aisle. The doll is a replica of the Baby Jesus. The patriarch is surrounded by guards holding swords and silver staffs and is accompanied by prelates and officials. When he reaches the altar, the patriarch lays the doll on a cradle of straw.

For those who can't get inside the church, the mass is televised live on an enormous screen in the square.

Meanwhile, in Jerusalem, Christmas eve services have taken place in churches all over the city. Protestants usually have services early in the evening, 6:30 p.m. or 8 p.m. Other churches often begin mass at 10 p.m. so they end around midnight. While Jewish and Moslem Jerusalemites go about their routine lives, they are serenaded by a bell concert from the YMCA tower which spreads the sound of Christmas over the city.

Fewer tourists come to partake in the other two Christmases. But Orthodox Christmas offers even more color than does the Latin. For Orthodox Christmas, not one, not two, but three separate processions take place from Jerusalem to Bethlehem on the morning of Jan. 6. First, the Syrian Bishop makes his journey, then the Coptic bishop an hour later, followed an hour and a half later (the extra half hour is in deference to his greater influence) by the Greek Orthodox Patriarch. Their separate services in Bethlehem that night are staggered by the same intervals.

Egged offers no special shuttle for these celebrations, but buses to Bethlehem run frequently from the bus station near Damascus Gate.

On the morning of Jan. 6, the streets of Bethlehem are packed with people come to see the parades of Arab Boy and Girl Scouts.

Each troop has its own uniform. Even headdresses vary from tams with pompoms to red and white *keffiyahs* worn in the style of the Jordanian Legion. One of the most intriguing sights in the parade is of adolescent girls, insisting on marching in high heels for vanity's sake, struggling to keep up and not be undone by the bumpy streets.

After the parade, the Greek Orthodox Patriarch and other high churchmen majestically parade from one end of Manger Square to the other in their colorful vestments. Afterwards, they proceed to the Church of the Nativity, built over the Holy Grotto where tradition has it, Jesus was born.

The main religious ceremony is the midnight mass. It begins with a stately procession around the church and culminates in the Holy Grotto, itself.

On January 18, Armenian Christmas Eve begins with yet another procession from Jerusalem to Bethlehem. Like the previous ones, the mayors of Bethlehem and smaller Arab Christian villages, along with Israeli officials, greet the dignitaries. So long as it isn't Shabbat, some of the Israelis attend mass.

Usually the main service begins in the church at 10:30 p.m. and continues in the grotto at midnight. A second mass follows from 2 a.m to 5 a.m.

Not to be outdone by Latin Christmas, both the Greek and Armenian services are televised.

By the time this third Christmas is over, one wonders if the Atlanta Baptist choir leader had any idea that Happy Birthday to Jesus would be sung, in one fashion or another, again and again.

Sylvester's Here
(New Year's)

Depending on who your friends are in Jerusalem, you may barely notice when the Gregorian calendar flips to its new year.

The Gregorian New Year (as in "Happy New Year" and the popped champagne corks of the West), if referred to at all here, usually is called "Sylvester's Day".

Some "Anglo-Saxon" and Western European Jews have parties on the evening of December 31. The ultra-Orthodox are steamed about that. But unless December 31 falls on a Friday, the day Pope Gregory Gregory called "New Year's" is just another work day, except at banks. Banks get a holiday not because Sylvester's Day has any official recognition, but because banks in most of the rest of the world are closed. And that seems to be more important than whether or not Israelis need to transact business. So, if you go to a party on Sylvester's Eve, chances are it will end close to midnight, because tomorrow will be just another day.

Serious celebrators of New Year's would do well to trundle down to Tel Aviv where people party hard and nightclub revelries continue not until dawn, but until noon the next day. In hearth-loving Jerusalem, there may be one or two establishments that have a party. One Jerusalem restaurant advertised its attractions for the Sylvester's Eve celebration as including caviar, champagne, lobster thermidor, chocolate log and, lest anyone forget where in the world he is, belly dancing.

I Think That I Shall Never See...
(Tu B'Shvat)

Come to think of it, New Years outnumber Christmases in Israel better than two to one. In the Jewish calendar alone, there are six occasions on which a new year is celebrated. But granted, most of them don't get a lot of attention.

Of New Years, so far, we've had Rosh Hashana in the fall and Sylvester's Day on January 1.

Now, the end of January or the beginning of February brings another, Tu B'Shvat, the New Year of the Trees, on the 15th of the Jewish month of Shvat. It's the Jewish way of celebrating the coming of spring. The assumption is that most of the winter rains are over, the almond trees, the first ones to do so, have bloomed, the soil is ready for saplings and clear days are ahead. At least that's the assumption.

Rain or not, Tu B'Shvat is a festive time. The number one activity is planting seedlings. Planting trees in Israel long has been a big deal. Diaspora Jewish homes aren't complete without the blue and white *pushke* container into which coins are dropped and eventually sent to the Jewish National Fund primarily for reforestation.

These days, Israeli children go off with their classes to plant trees. Outings for tourists are arranged so they can go to one of the forests and, as publicity tells them, "plant a tree with your own hands."

But that's not all that takes place on Tu B'Shvat. Ben-Yehuda Mall is decorated, and Jerusalemites meet there for singing and dancing.

Are there special foods for Tu B'Shvat? Of course. According to tradition (how many times have you read that so far?) to mark the abundance that spring portends, on Tu B'Shvat, 15 different kinds of fresh fruit are to be tasted.

Off The Boat
(Vietnamese New Year)

Are you ready for one of the biggest surprises about Israel? It's the sight of a dragon-like creature, accompanied by a pot-bellied man in red, undulating its way through the streets to the staccato of exploding firecrackers.

But that's a scene from eastern Asia, not the Middle East, you say?

That's right. It is the celebration of Vietnamese New Year, which occurs sometime in February, according to the old Chinese lunar calendar adopted by the Vietnamese.

Woa! Is this yet another previously unknown Jewish ethnic group that has surfaced, like the Burmese Jews? No, these New Year's celebrants number about 330 "boat people", whom the Israeli navy rescued in 1977.

They celebrate together in a community center in Azor, near Tel Aviv. Israelis come from all over, too, to celebrate with the Vietnamese. So, you might also.

After the dancing dragon's show and inevitable speeches, there are gifts for the children. Then merrymakers move to the buffet table, which is a melange of Far Eastern and Middle Eastern food.

By the Bonnie Banks of the Mediterranean (Robert Burns Supper)

About the same time as the Vietnamese celebrate their New Year, the Scottish are remembering Robert Burns.

These tartan wearers and hearty singers of "Loch Lomond" and "Charlie is My Darling" aren't leftovers from Mandate days. They are Jewish Israelis from Scotland.

They have their sentimental fling over their country of origin at the annual kosher Robert Burns Supper, held in the middle of February in that partying town down the road, Tel Aviv, or its neighbor, Herzliya, and sponsored by the British Olim society.

What is a Scottish feast without *haggis*, sometimes considered the Scottish national dish? It is a dish that generates reverence or repugnance because of its contents of minced hearts, liver and lung of a sheep mixed with oatmeal, onions, suet and spices and boiled in the animal's stomach.

Well, Scottish Israelis believe it's the thought that counts, and they have learned to improvise and make a kosher *haggis*. It is eaten with as much gusto as the genuine article. After all, it is a culinary relation to the Jewish Eastern European dish, *derma*, cooked in a steer's intestines. The cockaleekie soup and *tatties*, also integral to the meal, are authentic.

For this party honoring poet Burns, who immortalized the main dish served this evening with "Ode to a Haggis", a piper's presence is a must. Whoever he is, he is a trouper, for not only does he play traditional Scottish songs, but he is expected to deliver a bagpipe rendition of "Hevenu Shalom Aleichem".

This being Israel, the biggest difference between this gathering and a genuine gathering of the clans is the absence of that most famous Scottish export, whisky. But there is plenty of mitz.

Having Scottish ancestry is no prerequisite in order to attend the Robert Burns Supper (but saying "Scottish" and not "Scotch" may be). Actually, all a person has to do to be accepted into the fold is to be able to sing "Auld Lang Syne" along with everyone else at the end of the evening.

Queen for a Day
(Purim)

Purim, in mid-Adar in late winter, offers the treats of Halloween without the tricks. And lots more, besides. It is costumes for adults, as well as children, special foods, a carnival spirit (dowdy Jerusalem style), silliness and too much wine.

Purim celebrates the deliverance of the Jews of ancient Persia from wicked Haman through the intercession of Queen Esther. Esther not only was beautiful, but secretly Jewish. Despite danger to her life, she dared to reveal that fact to her husband, King Ahasuerus, in hopes of saving her people. Her bravery succeeded.

On Purim, schools are closed, banks usually are closed and businesses may be open only half a day. The celebration lasts one day (Adar 14), but in cities that were walled at the time of Joshua, and that includes Jerusalem, the festival is celebrated on Adar 15, a day after it is marked elsewhere in Israel. This is because in the Purim story, the Jews of Shushan, a walled city, were saved a day later than the rest of the Persian Jews.

So someone who moves fast could run down to Tel Aviv and take part in Samba Purim (yes, Samba, as in Brazil) and then return to Jerusalem (or go to Safed or Tiveria) for what is called Shushan Purim the next day.

In synagogues on the evening Purim begins, the *megillah* (the Book of Esther) is read. Every time evil Haman's name is mentioned, children rattle noisemakers, blow horns or simply holler. Anything to drown out his name. It is perfectly acceptable for adults to join in.

At home, royal feasts are served, and a tradition is to send two ready-to-eat foods to two people. Since the tradition has kept up with the times, even popcorn qualifies as a ready-to-eat food. But the very special culinary treat of Purim is a triangular-shaped pastry filled with fruit or poppy seeds. Jews in the Diaspora call these cakes "Hamantaschen" — Haman's hats. But in Israel, they are "Oznei Haman" — Haman's ears. A difference for anthropologists to ponder.

As at other Jewish festivals, Purim also is a time to remember the needy with gifts.

Perhaps the most elegant Purim affair in Jerusalem is the grand costume ball for patrons of the Israel Museum.

But it's everybody's fete during the day. The main festivity, called "Purshalayim," takes place from 10 a.m. to 4 p.m. in front of the railroad station at Kikar Remez, which is closed to traffic.

Don't be surprised by some of the organized entertainment. It can be as disparate as a dog show and a demonstration of fire-fighting techniques. Don't ask what any of these have to do with the beloved Queen Esther.

The square is decorated with colorful, sausage-like balloons so big, they seem to stretch across the street. Hawkers sell candied apples and cotton candy, while each of the city's major hotels has a booth selling its own specialty cooked food. Band stands run continuous, diverse entertainment.

All Jerusalem gathers for the celebration. Costumed, gold or silver-crowned girls give the impression of a harem of little Queen Esthers. Teenagers show off their decorated faces and some adults wear funny hats.

Kikar Remez takes on as much of a carnival atmosphere as staid Jerusalem can muster. For floats, you have to go to Haifa. And for sheer craziness, like that Rio flavor, you have to repair to Tel Aviv.

But where else but in Jerusalem can you find a camel giving children a slightly seasick trip as it struggles to stand up on its Tinker-Toy legs and later kneels while the small passenger grips the saddle and bravely smiles?

The camel is the festival contribution of the Ram Hotel. Besides the camel, on a typical Purim, the Ram will have set up a Bedouin tent held together by large nails resembling enormous straight pins.

Inside, a four-piece band plays. The men wear, in Middle Eastern style, white coats like butchers. The man playing the *oud*, a member of the lute family, has a *kipah* on his head. It's impossible to tell if the other musicians are Jewish or Arab.

Out comes a belly dancer, aging and flabby, her body discreetly covered by black chiffon from neck to bare feet. But the moment she begins to dance, she is serenely beautiful with her eyes half shut and the light playing off her sculptured cheekbones. With her first step, spectators in the tent push forward and raise their hands over their heads to clap to the infectious rhythm. Some in the crowd pierce the music with ululations of approval.

The Ram also has a food stand. On sale are *Mizrachi* (Middle Eastern) dishes. A few dollars buy two stuffed grape leaves, one Moroccan "cigar" and two pastries filled with something that might be meat. Accompanying all this is a little plastic envelope, not with *hariff*, the traditional Israeli hot sauce, but, in a collision of cultures, ketchup.

Purim is a time for laughter. Pop music radio programs carry more laughter — in cackles, giggles, gales or torrents — than music. It's all part of the silliness that's Purim.

Even being tipsy is a Purim tradition. On Purim, it is considered a religious duty to drink a little too much wine — or *arak* or vodka.

But then comes the morning after. Perhaps men don't say much, but women complain that between all the baking they did, the company that came in and out of their home and all the parties they went to, they're exhausted. Despite its having been Purim, they never felt as if they were queen Esther or otherwise for the day.

Next Year in Jerusalem
(Passover)

"Next year in Jerusalem!" In the Diaspora, every Passover Seder concludes with these words. To be in Jerusalem at Passover is the dream Jews grow up with and harbor all their lives.

During the *Seder* (the order of things), the *Haggadah*, the story of the Hebrew people's escape from Egypt and slavery, some 3500 years ago is retold. Jews today not only have the responsibility to recite the story again, but each Jew is to feel as if he or she, personally, made that escape.

Passover begins on the 15th of Nisan in March or April. In the Diaspora, it lasts eight days and the Haggadah is read the first two nights, while family and friends are gathered around the dinner table laden with symbolic and delicious foods.

In Israel, Pesach, as Passover is called in Hebrew, lasts seven days and the *Haggadah* is read only the first night of the holiday. And no one has to say at the end, "Next year in Jerusalem!"

But no matter where they are, Jews don't eat leavened bread during this time. Instead, they eat *matzo*, a brittle, flat, quickly baked mixture of flour and water, in memory of the fleeing Hebrews who had no time to wait for their bread to rise. Ashkenazim also avoid certain legumes and rice during Pesach. But by some quirk of history, these foods are perfectly acceptable to Sephardim.

So what goes on during the week of this major, happy holiday in the magical Jerusalem Diaspora Jews dream of? Sorry to say, not a whole lot.

Despite its significance, Pesach is, primarily, a family event and, therefore, one of the most privately celebrated holidays in the Jewish calendar. Pesach doesn't announce itself outwardly.

Because school is closed during Pesach, a third of Jerusalem's population uses that time to head for Eilat or the Sinai, another third flies off to Majorca and the third remaining at home grumbles over not being able to get away.

Yet, streets are thronged, largely because of the influx of Diaspora Jews carried to Jerusalem on those words they first heard in childhood and by Israelis from other parts of the country who choose the capital for their vacation. Both groups create a vibrant mood in the city. Added to their numbers are Christians from around the world who come to Jerusalem to celebrate Easter. So the city is charged with an added abundance of energy in spite of the exodus of residents.

Jerusalem becomes one huge traffic jam, not only in the center — where certain streets are closed off to prevent cars getting stuck in their narrow lanes and not being extricated until the fall — but also on roads leading in and out of the city. The usual 25-minute drive from Jerusalem to the northern tip of the Dead Sea can take more than an hour, and cars are front to end, like joints of a some crawling monster.

But on the bright side (literally), the city is gloriously aflame with color, cherry trees are in bloom, and so are spring flowers growing in every possible space.

Before the holiday begins, because of the Pesach dietary prohibitions, every household must be cleaned from top to bottom to make sure no speck of *chametz* (leaven) remains. Look for small fires at curbsides in residential Jerusalem, the morning of Pesach. Going up in smoke is the household's gathering of crumbs.

At sundown, the siren sounds and the first day of Pesach settles on the city. As on Shabbat, businesses lock up and buses don't run.

While Jerusalemites get together in their homes for the *Seder* and its accompanying grand dinner, hotels have *Seders* for their guests and any visitors who wish to attend.

The nicest thing that could happen to you at Pesach is to be invited to an Israeli home for the *Seder*, especially (for an Anglo-Saxon) if the invitation comes from a Sephardi family. In the latter event, it could be the only time in your life you won't face a pale hunk of *gefilte fish* at the start of the meal. Food, music and ritual will be different from any other Pesach you might have enjoyed. Even the *matzo* that first night will seem strange.

At an Iraqi *Seder*, for instance, *matzo* will be bigger, browner and flatter than the kind bought in stores. And instead of being square, it will be round.

Several times during the *Haggadah*, everyone at the table will reach forward and grasp one *matzo* simultaneously as a prayer is being said. It is a pose that reminds a Westerner of the school football team with everyone touching the ball, just before charging forth to beat Central High.

Instead of hiding the *Afikomen*, that small piece of *matzo* for children to hunt down later, at an Iraqi home it is wrapped in a scarf and tied beneath the armpit of one of the women. At the end of the evening, everyone gets a piece of the *Afikomen*. You are expected to nibble it down to the size of a button and then put it in your pocket, where it is to remain until next Pesach.

For a Diaspora Jew, even though "next year in Jerusalem" is now, it may seem as if something is missing. There is. It's that second *Seder*. Eight days of Pesach exist in the Diaspora to insure that wherever they are in the world, Jews will share it together. But according to the rabbis, Diaspora Jews, even if in Israel at the time, are expected to observe Pesach for eight days as they would at home.

During the holiday week, businesses, if they open at all, are open only in the morning. Supermarkets and neighborhood food stores hang white sheets over shelves of the forbidden foods. Needless to say, bread bins are empty and every little crumb has been cleared out. While this is vacation time for most bakers, a few — at least one is in Mea She'arim — sell special Pesach cakes.

Pesach becomes a public event on the third day when the *Kohanim*, the descendants of Aaron, are blessed at the Western Wall, as they were during Succot.

A few secular activities have become traditional during this time, including a tour of the Temple Mount and a slide show and lecture on it sponsored by the Israel Center and free walking tours of the Old City sponsored by the municipality. Check the *Jerusalem Post* for the schedule.

Artists and artisans of Yemin Moshe and Khutzot Hayotzer, as they did during Succot, open their studios to the public.

The seventh day, Pesach is given a send-off for another year. With the siren ushering the last day in and businesses closed and buses not running, this last day of Pesach is treated like Shabbat.

After the holiday ends after dark, if you ache to sink your teeth into a fluffy hunk of bread after a week of crunching on *matzo*, take a walk through your neighborhood. Your nose will lead you to bakeries already turning out the leavened stuff.

And with Pesach ending, Mimouna begins.

May You Be Worthy
(Mimouna)

Since 1965, the celebration of Mimouna has been the Israeli way of culminating Passover.

Mimouna was brought to Israel by Moroccan and other North African Jews, but it is especially identified with the Moroccans.

The tradition was shared, with variations and called by other names, by most Jewish communities in Moslem lands. The common

Jews from Ethiopia celebrate Mimouna at a city-wide festival of Israel's varied ethnic groups.

feature is that the entire community would go into the countryside to celebrate for days at a time.

Since their homes usually were safeguarded by a local sheikh or khan while they were away, the Jews would begin their festival with tributes to their Moslem protector.

Having gone through that formality, they were on their own, out of sight of their Moslem neighbors, with whom, especially outside of Kurdistan, there weren't always cordial relations. Alone in the countryside, Jews could let loose. The subtle or not so subtle repression under which they lived as *dhimmies* — second-class citizens in Moslem regimes — could be overcome for a while.

They would feast, drink, generally whoop it up, visit back and forth, go courting — especially go courting — and revel in the freedom to behave in ways even their own society wouldn't allow back home. This outing acted as a sort of societal safety valve.

In Morocco, Jews ushered in the Mimouna the evening before setting out for the countryside by literally opening their doors to guests. There were no formal invitations. A house with its door standing wide open was invitation enough. The guest needed to bring no gift, only to be there and give the traditional greeting, *"Tirbachu V'tisadu,"* ("May you be worthy to succeed").

Today in Israel, both elements of Mimouna — the opening of doors to neighbors and friends and the expedition to the outdoors — have taken root, but in new forms.

As the head of Beyachad (Together), the sponsoring organization of this national celebration, has said, "You don't have to be Moroccan to enjoy Mimouna." An estimated two million Israelis participate in Mimouna either as hosts or guests. Moroccans are the largest ethnic group in Israel, but not that big!

Newspapers print lists of host families all over the country who open their doors to the general public (picture that in Los Angeles or London!).

Does the prospect of walking into a house where you don't know the hosts and probably won't know any of the other guests (and possibly may not even speak their language) seem intimidating? Take it from me, there's no need to be shy. This was my first Mimouna experience:

Out of the list in the *Jerusalem Post*, I chose to visit an official host family living in Jerusalem's Musrara neighborhood. While Musrara is known for its poverty and as birthplace of young political activists, it turned out that the Monsungo family lived in a middle-class enclave in the neighborhood.

My French-speaking hostess, dressed in a white, floor-length *jalabia*, welcomed me graciously. She found a seat for me between other guests, who were crowded around (but not quite at) the dining-room table which was weighted with varieties of Moroccan food. No one spoke English, other than myself, and my Hebrew was rudimentary. Body language was the common coin.

The food on the table was special for Mimouna. Nothing could be salty; only sweet. *Giveret* (Mrs.) Monsungo took a fork and twirled it in a large bowl of stiff, sugared egg whites dotted with nuts. With a flourish and a grand smile, she presented me with the fork and its sticky, sweet load. From then on, I was on my own.

Other elaborate dishes were passed. I tasted candied baby eggplants; candied pomelos (a cross between oranges and grapefruit); fried sultanas (raisins cooked with sugar and nuts and served cold); marzipan shaped like cherries; all kinds of nuts; and *moufletas* (hot, thin pancakes wrapped around butter and honey). Also on the table were freshly picked leaves, sheaths of wheat and a cooked fish — all for symbolic reasons.

When I left, my hostess beamed at me and said in Hebrew, "Again, next year."

The outdoor aspect of Mimouna begins the next morning with the big, central celebration in Jerusalem's Sacher Park. One part of the park is lined with tents and their displays. Adjoining are the picnic area and a wooden stage for entertainment that afternoon.

Families arrive early in the day to claim their turf. They spread blankets on the grass or set up tents as if to camp for a week. Nearly every group of at least two people has a brazier burning. Clearly, these people are comfortably ensconced for a long stay. By noon, the air is thick with the aroma of barbecued *shishlik, kebabs,* steak and chops.

Meanwhile, ice-cream and drink vendors — and even a digital watch salesman — make their rounds between the hot stoves as they sell their wares.

Over in the display area, Jewish ethnic groups (and even the non-Jewish American Black Hebrews) use the large tents to set up exhibitions of their cultures. Since 1983, the Beyahad organization has turned Mimouna into, not only a Moroccan festival, but a celebration of Israel's ethnic diversity.

In front of their display, Jews from Ethiopia wrap white scarves around their hips and then, with the flexibility of a contortionist, gyrate neck and shoulder muscles as they dance on the grass.

Yemenite women, wearing stacks of necklaces, sell from their tent, *yachnun*, a thick, flat bread spread with throat-burning *hariff* or refreshing *techina*.

Photos of Jews imprisoned in the Soviet Union are shown at one display. Yet another is devoted to Jews undergoing the same fate, but in Iraq.

Moroccans have the largest collection of handicrafts shown at the exhibition, but at various places, there also are scribes, a silversmith, an herbal healer, weavers and painters.

The formal part of Mimouna usually begins early in the afternoon when the president, prime minister, mayor of Jerusalem and other dignitaries join each other on the stage. Each, mercifully, pledges to speak no more than one minute.

Then, it's on with the show. Performers range from kibbutzniks singing contemporary songs to Moroccan Atlas Mountains musicians playing oriental melodies, to the Tats (a Jewish tribe from the Caucasus region of the Soviet Union) performing athletic dances. The audience loves them all.

Since few Israeli celebrations last only a day, Mimouna is no different. The evening after the second sunset is looked on as a coda in which to continue the good times. The night after festivities end in Sacher Park, the holiday usually culminates with a shift to a Tel Aviv theater for a performance of North African songs and dances.

As everyone is Irish on St. Patrick's Day in the United States, it may soon be that everyone is Moroccan on Mimouna in Israel. The spirit of Mimouna is one of mutual love. As Moroccan Jewry's gift to Israel, it is one of the richest, grandest gifts imaginable. One Israeli official of Moroccan background summed it up well, "Too often in the world there is hate with no reason; the Mimouna is love with no reason."

The biggest cook-out in Jerusalem takes place in Sacher Park during Mimouna.

Holy Week No. 1
(Roman Catholic and Protestant Easter)

While Jews from all over the world are in Jerusalem to celebrate their ancestors' escape from slavery, Roman Catholics and Protestants from all over the world are in Jerusalem to commemorate the crucifixion and resurrection of their savior, Jesus. During these simultaneous Jewish and Christian holy days with thousands of visiting worshipers, the city is akin to an over-ripe, juicy, bulging pomegranate, ready to burst and fling its seeds far and wide.

Some churches spread Easter events over an 11-day span from the Friday before Palm Sunday through the Monday after Easter with daily processions in and out of tortuous, narrow Old City lanes. This is the time to avoid visiting the *souk*. The Franciscans have such a heavy schedule of processions and masses, most of them in the Holy Sepulchre, observance can be a full-time, totally immersing activity.

On Palm Sunday, several thousand Christians, locals and pilgrims alike, form a double line for the 90-minute procession from the Franciscan monastery at Bethpage on the eastern side of the Mount of Olives, down the slope into the valley, up the other side and to St. Anne's Church, just inside the Old City at Lion's (St. Stephen's) Gate.

Elsewhere that day, the Lutheran Church of the Redeemer in the Old City has both an Arabic and an English service. The Baptist Chapel has a Palm Sunday walk beginning at 5:30 a.m.

The palm branches carried on this Sunday come from Jericho, as they did in ancient times.

The rites observed with the widest variation during Holy Week are the washing of the feet ceremony on Holy Thursday and the Blessing of the Fire on Holy Saturday.

In the first, Jesus' washing of his disciples' feet is symbolized by 12 people from the congregation who have their feet scrubbed by the most senior clergyman.

At St. George's Anglican Church, the ceremony takes place with a 6 p.m. communion and is followed by a vigil until midnight. In the Holy Sepulchre, the washing is at 2 p.m. with a Tenebrae Mass afterwards. But watch out: Holy Sepulchre doors are locked for a time on Holy Thursday, and no exit or entrance is allowed for many hours. Plan accordingly.

In Good Friday's main event, Franciscan friars repeat the walk they make throughout the year at 3 p.m. on Fridays. In their somber brown robes, they lead the people on the Way of the Cross Procession, inching along the Via Dolorosa. They follow the route Jesus is said to have taken from the place where he was condemned to Golgotha, the traditional site of the crucifixion, the place over which the Church of the Holy Sepulchre was built. As the large, international, solemn crowd makes its way from station to station, carrying an enormous wooden cross as Jesus did, the mood becomes increasingly tense and introspective.

Holy Saturday is the day of the Giving of the Fire, symbolizing the gift of new life. In the Holy Sepulchre, a Latin service at 6:30 a.m. includes the lighting of the Paschal candle and the Blessing of the fire. Other churches have their own elaborate ceremonies. At St. George's Cathedral in East Jerusalem, where the altar was stripped of its decorative objects on Maundy Thursday, a small taper is lit at the back of the darkened Anglican church. An enormous unlit Paschal candle is brought from the altar and lit by the taper. The large candle is then the only light in the church.

It is placed on a stand, and while the congregation sings Psalm 139, "Whither Shall I Go?," acolytes slowly spread light from the Paschal candle through the church by passing the flame to the unlit candle held by each of the worshipers. Gradually, the dark church is illuminated by brilliant light.

Late Saturday night, Roman Catholic churches begin their services to celebrate Easter. They hold regular masses on Easter day, itself.

Among Protestants, Easter Sunday may begin with a 5 a.m. sunrise service at St. Andrew's Church with its sweeping view of the Hinnom and Kidron Valleys. Another popular place for an early start is at the Garden Tomb, which Protestants consider to be Jesus' burial place. There, a series of services begins at 5 a.m. in German and continues at intervals in English, Danish, Finnish and Dutch.

All of these services are open to the public. The Christian Information Center and the Government Tourist Information Office have schedules for Easter events that take place during this Holy Week and the one that follows in about a month when Easter comes to the Orthodox churches.

Never Again
(Remembrance Day)

On the 27th of Sivan, less than a week after the tumult of Passover, Mimouna and Latin/Protestant Easter, comes Martyrs and Heroes Remembrance Day, when Israel, like a family, remembers the 6 million Jews murdered by the Nazis during World War II. It is a day that can tear your heart out.

Restaurants, movie theaters and other places of entertainment acknowledge the solemnity of the day by closing.

The central ceremonies in Israel take place at Yad Vashem in Jerusalem. In the evening, Holocaust survivors, soldiers, new immigrants, government officials and others gather at the Holocaust memorial for a quiet observance. Admission is by invitation, available from the Government Tourist Information Office.

At eight the next morning, sirens sound for two minutes. During that time, the country comes to a halt. Cars and buses pull to the side of the road. Some bus passengers slide out of their seats and stand. Jerusalemites in their flats step out onto their balconies as a way of sharing the memory with the community. The siren, its sound rising and falling, is an eerie cry.

Later in the day, there is another ceremony at Yad Vashem. Dozens of wreaths are laid, and non-Jews, given the title of "Righteous Gentiles", are honored for having risked their lives to aid Jewish victims of Naziism.

It's *possible* on Remembrance Day to avoid reading a description of how a man spent two years as a child squeezed between floorboards under a schoolroom floor. There, he could see outside through a crack in the wall and watch sheep — but not a Jewish child — wander freely. It's *possible* to turn off the radio and not hear a woman relate in a strained, choked voice how her terrified, screaming three-year-old daughter was pulled from her arms forever by German soldiers.

Even for those who never had to go through these experiences, to read and hear about them is shattering. But for those who were lucky enough not to be the wrong kind of person at the wrong place and time, not to share this day is to miss a major part of what Israel is about.

April Fool
(April Fool's Day)

Surprising as it may seem, April first, April Fool's Day, is a big deal in Israel.

Recognition of the day goes far beyond someone suddenly screaming, "There's a spider in your hair! Hee, hee. April Fool!"

No, nothing benign like that. Instead, you might pick up a newspaper and read that a new tax has been levied, which — Israelis know only too well — is within the realm of probability. Or you might turn on the radio and hear that henceforth, women must sit upstairs and men downstairs in the movie theaters.

So you might be sputtering, "Things have gone too far! This is too much!"

But no, don't blame the government or the ultra-Orthodox. It's the nation's news media gone a bit wacky. Let's hope nothing of genuine importance ever happens on April 1. No one in Israel would believe it!

Good Samaritans
(Samaritan Passover)

Among those myriad ethnic groups that add spice and surprise to Israel are the Samaritans. Yes, Samaritans, as in the Good Samaritans of Biblical fame.

Between the Samaritans who live amidst the Arabs of Nablus (Shchem) in the mountains of Samaria and those in the Jewish city of Holon, near Tel Aviv, the population numbers some 560 persons. Though they are called "the smallest ethnic minority in the modern world", their current number is a marked increase from the 135 that remained at the turn of the century after thousands of years of war, religious persecution, intermarriage and forced conversion to Islam.

This group may be enjoyed when Samaritans welcome guests to their celebration of Passover, which, according to their lunar calendar, can fall either before or after the normative Jewish Passover. At their Passover, the *Haggadah* is read, and they expand the observance by conducting a rite that mainstream Judaism abandoned long ago — the sacrificial slaughter of perfect lambs.

The sacrifice, which is the only part of Samaritan Passover guests are allowed to see, takes place on Mount Gerizim, near Nablus, 48 miles (75 kilometers) north of Jerusalem. Not exactly the suburbs, but since the Egged Bus Company and the Ministry of Tourism make it easy and inexpensive to take the trip, it shouldn't be missed.

The Samaritans' origins are lost in the haze of history. They claim descent from the tribes of Ephraim and Manesseh and say that when the Assyrians carried off the Ten Tribes of Israel, they were overlooked. On the other hand, some historians suggest that, instead, they are descendants of people imported by the Assyrians to fill the void left by deported Jews. Samaritans resemble pale Ashkenazi Jews more than the darker Sephardim. When they have intermarried with normative Jews, the Jew in the marriage has been required to convert to Samaritanism.

Their religion recognizes only the Five Books of Moses and the Book of Joshua. They diverge from normative Jews in other ways: Samaritans maintain that Mount Gerizim, not Mount Moriah in Jerusalem, is where Abraham brought Isaac for his intended sacrifice. The slab Abraham planned to use atop the mountain is pointed out to visitors. And to Samaritans, Mount Gerizim, not Jerusalem, is "the navel of the world". It is there the Samaritan Temple was built in the fourth century B.C.E. Some 200 years later, John Hyrcanus, the Hasmonean leader, destroyed it.

And it is to this Mount Gerizim that members of this group must make a pilgrimage every Passover or be excommunicated. Houses at the mountain top are open for the community's use only during the Passover celebration.

For the Samaritan Passover visit, the Egged bus leaves Jerusalem in mid-afternoon. The drive, over a narrow, winding road, offers views into green chasms and up cultivated terraces cut like steps into the slopes. Above the farmlands, the mountains rise rocky and treeless, rolling away to the horizon.

Arab villages here, unlike those in the desert below Jerusalem, have an ordered, prosperous appearance. Even in what still are called refugee camps, handsome, large new houses stand. The sight of these villages makes one wonder why Arabs construct stone buildings that are delicate and interesting, while Jews construct stone buildings — using stones cut by Arabs — and produce dull, ponderous edifices.

As the bus rolls along, there's always a good chance the driver will miss the turn off the main road to Mount Gerizim. In that case, there can be an unanticipated visit to Nablus. Despite its reputation as a hotbed of anti-Israel activity, it is an attractive, if sullen town sprawled over hills and valleys. Israelis call Nablus by its ancient name, Shchem, where, according to the Bible, Abraham built an altar after God promised the Holy Land to his descendants, where Jacob pitched his tent, where Joseph was buried, where Joshua assembled the tribes after they had conquered Canaan and where Abimelech was crowned King of Israel after the country split into two parts. The name, Nablus, is a corruption of the Roman name given a new city built here, Flavia Neapolis.

Up the Gerizim road, below the treeless mountain top, the bus passes the 1983 Jewish settlement of Bracha, a rugged, windswept, lonely looking place.

At the site of the Samaritan celebration on the top of the mountain, bleachers line either side of what looks like a small athletic field. It is here that the sacrifice will take place. Guests sit on bleachers on one side of the space and Samaritan women sit on the other. Between them, on the fence-enclosed field, men and boys wholeheartedly sing their traditional songs of narrow melodic range. The dusty scene is reminiscent of an American Indian pow-wow.

But the Samaritan head priest has a microphone to sing into, while around him, men and boys exultantly shout melodies in their ancient language. The musical lines run in parallel fifths and often scoop upward in pitch at the end.

The women, who don't take part in the sacrifice, wear their best Western clothes. The men dress in white. Their loose, cotton shirts flutter over billowing harem pants. Their headdresses tell a cultural story. Elderly priests wear white turbans. Others sport the *tarboosh* imported by the Turks. Younger men wear what has come to be the traditional Samaritan head covering, a white cap that looks like a navy gob's. Also seen are the knit caps with a pompon on top made in Czechoslovakia and favored by Arab workmen. Yet another sight is the number of men wearing a visor cap that seems to cry for the words "John Deere".

Protruding here and there out of the crowd of singing men are the woolly backsides of tightly held lambs, about to go to their death.

The mood of the music changes. Anticipation grows. With a shout from some of the Samaritans in the central area, men and women holler, laugh and clap their hands over their heads to the chanted words while some of the men do a simple dance.

And now the lambs, perhaps 26, usually one for each family, are sacrificially slaughtered according to the law set down in Exodus, Chapter 12.

With so many men and boys participating in the slaughter, it's unlikely that a visitor in the bleachers actually will see the killings through the crowd. But the bloody knives are raised high as each lamb is sacrificed.

The warm carcasses are laid on the benches directly in front of the bleachers where visitors sit. There, young boys energetically pull off the lambs' skins with their bare hands. The squeamish should be warned.

As part of the ritual, men dab blood on their foreheads. It recalls the story of Hebrews who put a mark on their doors in Egypt, so the Angel of Death would pass over them before the Exodus began.

The men who participated in the ceremony kiss each other on both cheeks, paying careful attention to keep their bloody hands off each other's white clothes.

The rite may be thousands of years old, but this is the electronic era and TV is here. Television cameramen aggressively jostle each other for position. And Samaritans, like people everywhere, bloom when those hot camera lights hit them. At one end of the sacrifice area, a group of Samaritan men, in a brilliantly lit space, lustily sing and clap on cue.

During all this, the near monotone chanting continues, led most strongly by a white-bearded, high priest holding a large, bright blue prayer book.

About this time, weather permitting, visitors can see, beyond the slaughter area, a glowing full moon rising.

Now the Samaritans prepare to roast the lambs. A long pole of green wood is run through each skinned lamb, which then is placed in a roaring fire pit to cook for three or four hours.

It won't be until about midnight that the lambs are ready to be eaten, but at this point, visitors are to leave. The festive meal is a private affair. All of the lamb must be consumed before night ends.

Riding back down Mount Gerizim, the bus again passes the settlement, Bracha, on its windswept perch. It sits under lights that turn night into day, as if perpetually under the eye of a TV camera.

As the bus cruises south to Jerusalem, the moon makes the rock-ribbed mountains and fertile farmlands dance under a silvery glow.

And after all that — the trip, the rite and the return — Jerusalem can be reached before 9 p.m.

Replay, or Holy Week No. 2
(Orthodox Easter)

The memory of Latin/Protestant Easter has faded away. Pilgrims have gone home. Jerusalem has done without a celebration or commemoration for, perhaps a week. Nervousness begins to pervade the air. Something seems to be missing. But before withdrawal symptoms set in, Eastern and Oriental Orthodox Easter arrives.

Fewer pilgrims descend on the city for Orthodox Easter, but more local residents participate. Greeks, Armenians, Syrians, Copts, Ethiopians and Russians who adhere to the Orthodox calendar, are integral to the Jerusalem community. So Orthodox Easter seems more like a hometown celebration than does its Latin/Protestant predecessor.

Of the pilgrims who do come from foreign countries, most are black-garbed Greeks or Cypriots, who walk the streets carrying olive branches.

Most of the Orthodox denominations have their assigned times and space in the Church of the Holy Sepulchre during holy week. The exceptions are the Russian, who conduct services in their church, St. Mary Magdelene on the Mount of Olives, and the Ethiopians who have their services in Dier es-Sultan, their religious warren constructed on the roof of the Holy Sepulchre.

Copts and Ethiopians still battle over their turf, and time was, Good Friday wasn't complete without priests of these two denominations stoning each other. Because each church jealously guards its rights in and on the Holy Sepulchre, a special unit of non-Christian guards stands by during Orthodox Easter to make sure that the celebration of the resurrection of the Prince of Peace remains peaceful.

Processions take place in the Holy Sepulchre every day between "Lazarus Saturday", the day before Palm Sunday, and Easter Sunday. But the Ethiopians conduct their processions on their rooftop space.

Of all the events this week, including the washing of feet on a raised platform outside the Sepulchre, the most spectacular and literally brilliant is the Ceremony of the Holy Fire (the Giving of the Fire) at 1 p.m. the day before Easter. All the Orthodox denominations — except the Ethiopians, who don't dare leave the roof for fear the Copts will take over — gather in the Sepulchre rotunda for this event.

Each denomination has a designated place to stand, but because the Greek Orthodox are the wealthiest and most numerous, they dominate the gathering.

Excited, expectant worshipers, carrying fagots of 32 skinny white, unlit candles, squeeze into the church and fill its many nooks as they face the edicule, the covering to what they believe was Jesus' tomb, the sepulchre, itself.

The church is so tightly packed, it is quite safe to faint — as is one's wont in the heat and crush — without the slightest possibility of hitting the floor.

Teen-aged boys climb the wooden edicule and stand on narrow ledges and hang onto any protrusion they can find. Their informality with the 19th-century, onion-domed structure comes as a surprise in view of the usual solemnity within this building.

Armenian orthodox priests lead the Easter procession service in a courtyard next to St. James Cathedral.

The boys on the edicule are self-appointed cheerleaders for the enormous crowd. It is they who catch the first glimpse of the Greek patriarch in his white satin gown and golden crown as he leads the Greek Orthodox clergy into the church. The Armenian patriarch and his entourage follow. Behind them, in clearly defined pecking order, are the leaders and clergy of other Orthodox denominations, all in resplendent gowns and robes.

With the first sight of the highest representative of the Greek Orthodox Church in Jerusalem, the boys let out a grand roar that resounds through the stone rotunda. Responding, the crowd presses forward, excitedly. Worshipers hold their candles aloft to keep them from melting, not from fire, which is nowhere yet in the rotunda, but from the heat generated by the assembly.

Up on their perch the boys defy gravity and clap their hands in rhythm as they sing. The melody sounds strangely like the happy Jewish song, "Siman Tov, oo-Mazel Tov".

Then the crowd makes room for the Greek patriarch and his followers to march around the edicule, while the congregation joins in singing a stately melody.

When the procession comes around to the front of the edicule and its entrance to Jesus' tomb, the rotunda lights are turned off (in the bleakness of the rotunda, it comes as a surprise to realize that lights were on at all), and the church, gloomy on the best of days, falls into twilight in the early afternoon.

Ecumenically, the Greek and Armenian patriarchs duck their heads and enter the edicule, while the now-hushed congregation expectantly watches the two tiny windows on the structure's sides.

Suddenly, a jubilant cry rings from the crowd. A tongue of a fire, said to appear in the tomb through a miracle, is glimpsed through the windows. The patriarchs emerge carrying flaming brands, and worshipers surge forward, almost in a frenzy, to transfer the miraculous fire onto their fagots of candles. Adding to the excitement, the church bells ring wildly.

One after another, throughout the rotunda, candles spring to glowing life. Then, just when the sight becomes a bedazzling sea of burning candles, the crowd suddenly turns to rush out the nearest exit to follow the patriarch's procession through the streets of the Old City.

Watch out. This is "Be Careful Not To Be Trampled" time. Whichever way the crowd goes, go too. Be a lemming. Fighting the direction is useless and well could be dangerous. Even going with the crowd has its hazards. Few people escape the sting of hot wax dripping on their hands and arms as they are swept along the human tidal wave. Worshipers, everywhere, carry the benediction of white streaks of dried wax on their shoulders and hair, an unintentional decoration. It seems impossible to hope that before the Ceremony of the Holy Fire is over, only the candles will have burned. Yet, that almost always is the case.

Outside the church, for at least an hour the Old City is as jammed tight as a wine bottle with no corkscrew. However, by the time the Arab scout troops, with their bagpipes, drums and flags, have passed, it begins to be possible to choose your own direction to walk.

The Greeks have a liturgy service at 1 a.m. before the edicule on Easter morning and a grand procession into the Holy Sepulchre at noon; the Armenian have mass at 1:30 a.m. in the Church of the Holy Sepulchre.

If staying up that late and walking through the souk in the wee hours of the morning seem unwise (reportedly, there is plenty of security because of the holiday), the Procession Service of the Armenians at 3 p.m. Easter in the Cathedral of St. James, is a colorful alternative.

The service begins in the fairy-tale like St. James Cathedral with its ornate blue tiles and stalactite forest of innumerable hanging lanterns. The patriarch wears a gold-beaded cape, so heavy that men at either side of him help support its weight. Behind him, priests follow in bejeweled crowns and gold-and-wine-embroidered gowns.

Even the altar boys are richly dressed for this occasion.

The ceremony soon moves outdoors into the Armenian Quarter compound plaza. There, the men arrange themselves in a rectangle and sing chants antiphonally. The choreography emerges as the men cross from one side of the rectangle to the other. Finally, they move into the cathedral courtyard and later back into the cathedral for the service's conclusion.

For Armenians and Syrians, the holiday has one more day of observance after Sunday. They celebrate a last Easter mass on Monday.

As with Latin/Protestant Easter, complete schedules of events are available at the Christian Information Center and the Government Tourist Information Office.

Happy Birthday, Israel
(Independence Day)

Israel's Independence Day (Yom Ha'atzma'ut) celebration has a prologue. It is introduced by Memorial Day for soldiers who died for Israel. Memorial Day begins at sunset 24 hours before Independence Day starts on the fifth of Iyar, in late April or early May.

Israelis don't refer to their soldiers as having "died". Instead, they use the term "fallen". Despite the reality of modern warfare, the word conjures up an almost romantic image of a young warrior stopped in his tracks by the enemy with, not a messy bomb or bullet that leaves his entrails on the ground — but something neater. Perhaps a spear, as in ancient times.

On this day, places of entertainment close at sunset, and at 8:30 p.m., a mournful two-minute siren ushers in a brief ceremony at the Western Wall. Although thousands of people are present, many of them relatives and friends of soldiers killed in battle, the usually bustling plaza now is subdued. With the siren, the nation's flag is lowered to half-staff and the president lights a memorial candle. A few comments by officials follow, and the observance comes to an end with *Kaddish*, the Jewish praise to God chanted by mourners. The ceremony is especially poignant because of its simplicity and brevity — like so many of the lives it memorializes.

At 11 the next morning, another two-minute siren brings traffic and other activities to a halt as it did on Remembrance Day. Also, as on that day a week earlier, the radio plays only subdued music and television is appropriately programmed.

Buses follow their usual schedule, but at about noon, stores close and remain closed through Independence Day, which follows.

Ceremonies at military cemeteries, including one for Druse soldiers in the Israeli Army, take place throughout the country. The culmination is a torch-lighting just before sunset atop Mount Herzl. This event is by invitation only, but usually entrance to a rehearsal the night before may be obtained by registering with the Government Tourist Information Office.

Then, an unexpected thing happens on Mount Herzl. The quiet, somber observance concludes with a burst of fireworks. Suddenly, the solemnity of the previous 24 hours is replaced by an explosion of exultation that is Independence Day, itself. And thus, Memorial Day and Independence Day are linked, carrying out the Jewish tradition of remembering joy in sadness and sadness in joy.

With Yom Ha'atzma'ut festivities in full swing, a strange sound of clicking is heard in the land. No, giant crickets haven't invaded. The sound is more brittle than what crickets produce. It's closer to that of metal "frogs" you find in Crackerjack boxes and pinch to make a resounding clack. This sound is produced by plastic hammers. Kids and a lot of adults use them to bop your head! If you have the "misfortune" of being tall and blond, you may have an enormous headache by the time the night is over. You offer a challenge kids strive to reach. But no matter who you are, what your age or appearance, you're fair game.

Actually, the hammer game isn't as sadistic as it may seem. On impact, the hammer compacts and simultaneously clicks. The sound is far louder than the hammer is heavy. And no one really is trying to use force. It's the "I gotcha!" triumph that these hammer-wielders aim for.

So there you have it: your first impression of Israelis celebrating their nation's re-birthday could be the sight of swarms of people playfully bopping each other on the head. The sound of the accumulated clicks conjures a movie scene of an old-fashioned teletype office at crisis time.

But more remains to be seen, besides the head hitting: buildings and streets strung with lights, platforms in the heart of Jerusalem with entertainers singing and dancing and exuberant, light-hearted crowds filling the streets.

Among events all over the city that night are concerts in the Jerusalem Theater and from the carillon in the YMCA tower. This also is the night for private festivities, the closest Israeli equivalent of the West's New Year's Eve parties.

But the most joyous way to spend the evening is by dancing in the streets. And there are plenty of opportunities. Rehov King George is set aside for dancing until 11 p.m. Then the hardy continue in Liberty Bell Park until 2 a.m., after which the diehards carry on at one of the sports centers until the buses, which stopped for the night, start rolling again at dawn.

Don't worry about having a dancing partner. If you stand on the sidelines, it's by your own choice, for this is Israeli dancing — in a circle, drawing music and steps from Israel's many cultural influences, including Yemenite, Arabic and Eastern European.

Several circles fill the street. People move in and out of them, strangers holding hands, celebrating together. Kids, the elderly, and all ages in between, are out there kicking up their heels. And as exuberant as they are, the high spirits come from the heart, not from booze. Wholesomeness and innocence pervade the atmosphere.

Late in the night, fireworks blaze against the sky. They are contributed by the hotels. The audience is enraptured, and "ooohs" and "aaahs" fill the air with each colorful shower of lights. The shows last, perhaps, up to four minutes. Jaded Westerners might sniff at that, but please, no spoilsports. Israel is a poor country and fireworks are expensive. These shows are as appreciated as million-dollar blasts.

The next day, many people go picnicking. And again, a string of events are scheduled; concerts, government-sponsored outings and the mayor's reception at the Citadel. An invitation to the last is available from the Government Tourist Information Office.

By the time the morning after the morning after dawns, you can feel Jerusalem shifting out of party gear and into its business-as-usual (Middle Eastern style) gear once again. The party's over for now.

Armenians Remember
(Armenian Remembrance Day)

On April 24, virtually the entire Armenian community in Jerusalem takes part in a slow, solemn procession led by black-robed priests from St. James Cathedral in the Old City to their nearby cemetery.

Armenians, too, carry the memory of their mass annihilation. The march commemorates the end of 3000 years of Armenian life in their ancient land of Ararat. Today, that area is eastern Turkey and a small portion extending into the Soviet Union.

On April 24, 1915, Turks arrested Armenian intellectual leaders in Istanbul and later executed them. Afterwards, the Turks commenced mass deportation and systematic murder of these people whom they saw as siding with their enemies, the British and Russians. How much of the genocide had to do with the fact that the Turks are Moslem and the Armenians Christian has been a debated point. But some 1.5 million Armenians died in the process, including thousands of children — many of them thrown into the sea.

Descendants of the survivors who escaped to Jerusalem, and as many of the survivors themselves, who still live, are among the 2000 marchers in the procession.

The walls of the Armenian Quarter acquire graffiti close to this date. It is young Armenians' way of explaining the purpose of the procession. It isn't only to remember the dead; it also is to remind the world in general, and Turkey in particular, of what happened. Armenians strive for an acknowledgement by Turkey that the massacre took place.

At the cemetery, the marchers lay wreaths at a cenotaph memorializing Armenian soldiers who lost their lives fighting with the British against the Turks during the First World War.

Clip Joint
(Lag Ba'omer)

The big show in Israel on Lag Ba'Omer takes place on Mount Meron, near Safed, on the 18th of Iyar, usually in May.

On the evening that Lag Ba'Omer begins, pilgrims gather there at the graves of Shimon Bar Yochai, reputed author of the basic book of Jewish mysticism, "The Zohar", and his son, Elazar. But if distance and jostling with a crowd of more than 150,000 madly celebrating people puts you off, there are plenty of other ways to enjoy the day in Jerusalem.

Lag Bo'Omer largely is considered to be a 24-hour interlude in the midst of a 49-day period of semi-mourning. In Temple times, a measure of barley (an *omer*) was counted for 49 days beginning on the second night of Passover and ending on the 50th day with the holiday, Shavuot.

The counting joined an agricultural festival with Temple rites. It was a way of setting the date on which two events were to be marked: the ripening of the wheat crop, which happens at the end of those 49 days, and the anniversary of the day on which Jews believe God gave them the Torah.

After the destruction of the Second Temple, the 49 Days became a period of semi-mourning in which weddings and haircuts were forbidden. Many explanations have been offered, one as benign as that this was when people were needed in the fields and there had to be a reason to keep them from taking time out to go to wedding parties.

But Judaism is known for being considerate of human frailties. The people needed a reprieve, and so Lag Ba'Omer emerged on the 33rd day of counting. Its origins, too, are obscure. Often heard is that Lag Ba'Omer marks the end of a plague almost 2000 years ago that killed many students of the illustrious Rabbi Akiva.

For Ashkenazim, Lag Ba'Omer offers a one-day hiatus for weddings and haircuts. Sephardim, however, look on Lag B'Omer simply as the first day after Passover on which weddings and haircuts may resume.

Whichever way it is being marked and whatever its origina, Lag Ba'Omer is a big wedding day. Watch for cars chauffeuring newlyweds. The cars aren't hard to spot, not because of blaring horns and trailing tin cans, since these aren't traditions here, but because of vehicles bedecked with balloons and flowers.

After dark on Lag Ba'Omer, the Jerusalem sky takes on a red glow. Bonfires have been set in gardens, empty lots and parks. Just stroll around and see, instead of people dancing, flames dancing. The Vale of Rehavia (the Valley of the Cross) is dotted with fires. Around some of them, families gather and have cookouts.

One of the biggest fires is in Mea She'arim, the ultra-Orthodox neighborhood. There, local residents build a huge grotesque tower of kindling. If you are nearby before the tower begins to burn briskly, you will find Israeli flags going up in smoke. This can be a shocking sight. It is the work of a small, but vociferous group of Jews who believe that since modern Israel wasn't created by God, it must be destroyed. Bonfire watchers with Zionistic inclinations might skip this particular bonfire or visit it late in its fiery life.

The next morning at about 10, Orthodox Jews gather before the Tomb of Simon The Just, off Nablus Road in East Jerusalem, for the Halaka ceremony in which three-year-old boys receive their first haircut.

Calling it a haircut is a bit formal. What happens is that each family asks an admired rabbi to take the first snip from the young son's hair. Then a favorite relative takes the next snip and so on. While each lock of hair is returned to the parents, perhaps to be saved, the three-year-old boy usually cries with despair.

Sephardim women get the honor of snipping hair along with the men. But among Ashkenazim, as with so much else, it's men only.

If you go down the stairs into the man-made cave known as Simon's Tomb, you will find it jammed with people praying or milling about. Simon The Just, Hatzadik in Hebrew, is a revered figure. His best-known words were, "The world stands on three things — Torah, divine service and charity."

Over the heads of the people in the cave, many of whom are stuffing notes to God in crevices between the rocks, an assortment of anachronistic chandeliers hang from the stone ceiling. One looks as if it were meant to be an eternal flame.

Outside, after most of the three-year-old boys have had their hair haphazardly trimmed, the celebration continues. Sephardim throw confetti. Food appears everywhere, as if miraculously. Cakes, schnapps, candy, *bourekas* and boiled potatoes are some of the goodies passed around. The kinds of food served distinguishes each family's ethnic background.

Fathers lift their children, especially the now-smiling hair-cut boys, and carry them in their arms for a traditional circle dance. It is "the

Yeshiva two-step", the shuffle executed by yeshiva students at the Western Wall on Friday nights.

And now, with their tears gone, along with a lot of their hair, the little boys feel grown up. Traditionally, they now are ready to begin their religious studies.

JERUSALEM SCENE:

Only in Israel: when it was time to cut the hair of a new contingent of Israeli Defense Forces parachutists, all the young men complied with having their hair cut short as required — except one.

It wasn't that the Jerusalem teenager had objections to having his hair cut. After all, it was the patriotic thing to do. But he did have objections to anyone cutting his hair but his father, the barber.

The young man stood his ground and insisted to his commanding officers, "No one has ever cut my hair except my father, and no one ever will."

So what did the Israeli military do? It let the new parachutist go home to Jerusalem — so his father could cut his hair. Of course.

Reunited We Stand
(Jerusalem Saga)

If your dancing shoes haven't been worn out in the Golden City, Jerusalem Day (Yom Yerushalayim), which celebrates the reunification of the city by the 1967 Six-Day War, surely should do it.

Landing on the 28th of Iyar, less than two weeks after Lag Ba'Omer, this festivity includes so many events, you need to carry a program to keep track of where you'd like to be and when.

The events vary from year to year. In a typical year, a major feature is dancing at Liberty Bell Park (and since you had all that practice on Independence Day, you now know the Israeli dance-step basics, a "Yemenite right" from a "Yemenite left").

Other activities might be a parade and performances on Rehov Yafo by 2000 young dancers; a relay race run into the city by 10,000 school kids; a midnight march by *yeshiva* students to the Western Wall; a memorial service on Ammunition Hill where the stiffest fighting against the Jordanians took place; special free walking tours of the city; and free admission to the Israel and Rockefeller Museums.

The Rehov Yafo dance performances are an achievement in logistics. You, the viewer, can stay put on the sidewalk while the show, with a cast of thousands comes to you. Following directions given over a loudspeaker, the teenage dancers, divided into groups, each with its own costumes, music and choreography, rotate places. You get to see as many groups as you wish, without losing your spot at the front of the crowd. Moving an army may be simple compared to the way these dance groups are shifted about, up and down the street.

Again, Jerusalem is bedecked this day — its very own day — with flags and bright lights. But stores are open, buses roll and the dancing continues.

Fruits of Learning
(Shavuot)

Remember "teach-ins", the phenomenon of the '60s and '70s that usually dealt with the Vietnam War?

Well, they weren't a new idea. Jews have been having them for centuries.

Shavuot, on the sixth of Sivan in late May or early June, is the time of the Jewish teach-in. Some say the custom started in the Sinai, with the Hebrew people waiting all night for Moses to come down from the mountain with the Torah. Others say Ashkenazi Jews started it in the 12th or 13th centuries C.E.

One of the main aspects of the holiday is to celebrate the "giving of the Torah" to Moses on Mount Sinai. Orthodox Jews maintain that by implication, Moses not only brought the Ten Commandments down from Mount Sinai, but the entire body of Jewish teachings.

In memory of the night-long wait the Hebrews had for Moses, Jews gather to study and discuss the Torah all night. In the morning, the Book of Ruth is read, probably because the story takes place at the time of the spring harvest and tells of her loyalty to her adopted religion. Sessions end with a sunrise service at the Western Wall.

Study sessions abound all over Jerusalem and at the Wall, as well. At least two are conducted in English: the "Learn-A-Thon" at the Israel Center, and the "Study Marathon" at the Center for Conservative Judaism.

The other significance of Shavuot is that it is one of three agricultural festivals that were observed with a pilgrimage to Jerusalem. Shavuot celebrates the "first fruits" of the harvest.

The traditional Shavuot food consists of dairy dishes. Legend has it that after their long wait for Moses, the Hebrews discovered that the milk in their camp had gone bad, so they made cheese from it. Today, cheesecake and *blintzes* are a must on Shavuot.

One of the most charming aspects of this celebration is that the day before Shavuot, school children, looking like sprites, may be seen on city streets with garlands of flowers around their hair.

Shavuot is like Shabbat: the siren announces its beginning, no buses run, stores and schools are closed, and now that it is early summer, hotels and beaches are packed.

Hot Dog!
(The Fourth of July)

For better or worse, there's always a way of getting in touch with your American roots in Jerusalem, whether it's at a meeting of the Texans in Israel Club or a gathering to see a tape of the Super Bowl Game.

But the day for all Americans is (when else?) the Fourth of July. The Association of Americans and Canadians in Israel sponsors a celebration in Sacher Park in the afternoon. So dig out your baseball cap and your red, white and blue clothes. A baseball game, relays, a sing-a-long and a barbershop quartet performance are some of the events. The AACI advises people to B.Y.O.P.B. Not "Bring Your Own Powerful Bottle", but "Bring Your Own Picnic Basket".

The only thing missing is the fireworks.

After the hotdogs, remember to wipe the mustard off your chin.

Dirge Day of Summer
(Tisha B'av)

The dog days of summer are bereft of major holidays, Jewish or Christian (the constantly whirling Moslem calendar, however, may offer a surprise in the midst of Israel's sunbaked season).

Perhaps the patriarchs were too busy farming to concentrate on religion, or maybe they simply were too hot to think lofty thoughts. But for two months, there is a drought in religious activity parallel to the absence of rain.

Then Tisha B'Av arrives, usually in early August. It isn't a major holiday, but it does offer a change of pace to the long, sunny days.

Tisha B'Av, which means simply, "the ninth of the month of Av", is intensely solemn. This is a day of out-and-out mourning over the tragedies in Jewish history. It is the blackest day on the Jewish calendar. It is said that on this day, Nebuchadnezzar destroyed the First Temple in 568 B.C.E.; Titus destroyed the Second Temple in 70 C.E.; the Bar Kochba revolt against the Romans collapsed and Hadrian plowed under Jerusalem in 135 C.E.; and, in 1492, King Ferdinand and Queen Isabella signed the decree to expel all Jews from Spain.

Tisha B'Av concludes a three-week semi-mourning period with a fast. During those three weeks, the Orthodox avoid meat and wine and neither wear new clothes, not get their hair cut nor get married. Customarily, when the ninth of Av arrives, leather isn't worn. So out come the running shoes and rubber thongs, as a substitute.

The Western Wall is the focal point of the Tisha B'Av observance, for the Wall is the last original remnant of the Temple. On this day thousands of Jews converge there. Many sit on mats on the ground or on low benches. The readings are dirges and the Book of Lamentations.

Inside synagogues, the Ark and all decorations are draped with black cloth. Even the Torah Scroll may have black cloth covering its metal breastplate. The only light is from the "eternal light" that always burns in the synagogue.

Most of the city closes down. Radio and television broadcasts reflect the theme of mourning.

Weeks later, the spiky squill plant's tiny white flowers blossom, announcing that summer is almost over. The intense heat of the past months, with its dry, desert wind, called *hamsin*, wanes. Jerusalemites' energy picks up. Suddenly (it always seems to happen that way), the High Holidays are approaching. The sound of men practicing the *shofar* is heard. "Already?" people ask each other, just as they did last year and will again next year. There are preparations to be made. All sorts of things to do. Got to get busy.

And thus Jerusalem's cycle of holy days, celebrations and memorials begins all over again.

Part Three:
How to Succeed as a Sojourner in the City of Jerusalem

Chapter 15:
Basics: Children, Neighborhoods, and a Warm Home

The dictionary defines a "sojourner" as a person who "stays for a time, resides temporarily". This last part of the book is for those of you who are able to become sojourners in the city of Jerusalem. But it also is for those of you who dream of staying longer or who simply dream of knowing as much as possible about the Golden City.

However, sojourners fall through the crack between tourism and immigration. They have to figure out a lot about the city on their own.

This part of the book gives shortcuts — from how to rent an apartment to where to buy books, make new friends and find the movie theaters — so the process of savoring Jerusalem can begin as quickly as possible. This part of the book tells how Jerusalem lives, laughs and loves.

Children Will Have Their Day

If you are contemplating an extended stay in Jerusalem, your first consideration may be your dependent children. You may wonder how they would fit into the Israeli world. The following story should provide some insight.

I was lingering over coffee in a Rehov Rivlin restaurant during off hours, irresistibly watching a scene being played out in front

Careful! Ari may have more help than he needs as he carries eggs home from the store.

of me.

A lithe man, perhaps still in his 20s, was sitting in a chair against a wall holding his baby in his arms. Another man, about the same age, tall and broad-shouldered, entered. He saw the father and his baby and approached them. Smiling, he reached out and carefully took the gurgling infant into his arms. After giving the baby a hug, he held her at arm's length so the two could conduct a baby talk conversation. Then a third young man, only slightly less burly than the second, entered and he, too, stopped to entertain the baby. He jingled his keys and then leaned over to nibble her ear.

After several minutes of this play, the broad-shouldered man pressed the baby against his chest again and then gently returned her to her father. With that, he and the man beside him continued on their way. They apparently didn't know the father.

I never had witnessed a scene like this before. I had never seen men play with a baby, unless they were related or had some other close connection to it. I told my friend, Ezra, about the scene, adding, "That was the most beautiful thing I've seen here." He smiled, shrugged and said, "That's Israel."

Indeed. Israel is a veritable kiddieland where children truly are treasured. Here, it isn't a matter of mere talk about the importance of children. In Israel, outside his home, every child becomes everyone's child. Strangers give children adoring looks and simultaneously check on their safety. Not only does every child have an anonymous Big Brother watching over him, but Big Sister and substitute Mom and Dad. The only time I heard a child in Israel hollered and nagged at, it turned out that his parents were American.

Children are accepted here (some may say, "pampered") in many ways they aren't in Western countries. On a business day on which elementary schools are closed, a lot of children simply accompany their parents to work. A bus driver's son stands beside him and punches passengers' tickets. In a bank, a manager is busy talking with a client. When his phone rings, his 7-year-old daughter answers it. You can be sure the caller isn't affronted, and he probably praises her telephone manners.

All this is by way of assuaging those of you who might be concerned about taking your children out of their own familiar environment to live in Jerusalem for a while. Kids would be lucky to have such an opportunity!

What American city kids find in Israel, perhaps for the first time, is freedom. Not the "freedom" that comes from being indulged or ignored, but the freedom of physical movement that doesn't need to be circumscribed. Generally speaking, it is safe for children to be out on the streets, even alone. On holiday nights, such as when Independence Day is celebrated, children are out there enjoying the fun accompanied only by other children. It isn't that there are no creeps in Israel; it's that they haven't taken over. The streets still belong to the people, not the perverts. American parents, who more and more worry over their children's safety at home, can relax here.

The most important thing about bringing children to Israel for any length of time is to plan for them in advance. When the idea of a stay in Israel first flickers in your mind, you should begin to plan action. The best source of information on schools and day camps is the Association of Americans and Canadians in Israel, which puts out a pamphlet entitled, "The Jerusalem Education System". Write for it and enclose a donation. Mention particular educational needs in the letter.

The School System

The administration of the educational system is shared by the Israel Ministry of Education, Rehov King David 18, and the Jerusalem Municipal Department of Education. Registration for school and extra-curricular activities takes place at the Department of Education office at Rehov Yafo 35. You may write to either of these offices in advance for information. There is no guarantee of a response.

Within the public schools are two parallel systems. In the secular system, religion is taught as a cultural heritage. In the religious system, the point is to teach observance. Parents may choose either one. In addition, independent, strictly Orthodox schools are maintained by Agudath Israel and Hasidic groups. The schools receive subsidies from city and national coffers.

Private schools in which English is the language of instruction, such as at the Anglican Church School and St. Anthony's School, usually are run by churches. They are open to all.

Many facilities exist at the day-care level, but demand is great. Registration for the fall is made by the preceding February. A few nursery schools are bilingual (Hebrew-English) or English-speaking.

The space situation isn't as tight in kindergarten (part of the public school system, but often located in separate buildings), elementary, or junior and senior high schools.

Extra-Curricular and Summer Activities

Because the six-day school week has short days (from 8 a.m. to noon, 1 p.m. or 2 p.m., depending on the elementary school grade; to 2 p.m. or 3 p.m. in high school), extra-curricular activities especially for younger children abound: art classes at the Israel Museum, music lessons at the Rubin Academy, classes in a variety of arts at the International Cultural Center for Youth, outdoor activities with the Society for the Protection of Nature and a potpourri of offerings at Beit Hano'ar Ha'ivri and the YMCA.

In the summer, the municipality runs Hebrew-language *ulpanim* especially for children, and almost every neighborhood has a day camp, where activities can range from routine activities such as lanyard-making to specialization in sports or computers. Private day camps are run by institutions like the Jerusalem Biblical Zoo and the Natural History Museum. Registration closes the end of May at most places. Worse news may be that day camps last only two or three weeks.

Perhaps the most important thing to remember about the Israeli school day is that the 10 a.m. snack is sacred. Children all the way through high school arrive with theirs in hand, although in day camps, snacks are provided.

In any event, parents can rest assured that their children will learn Hebrew and make the cultural adjustment far faster than they, themselves, will. I have seen children, even teenagers, blend in with their classmates and be the ones to help steer their parents through the complexities of Israeli life.

While You're in the Neighborhood

Jerusalem is the sum of its parts. And its parts are many. It is a jumble of neighborhoods, some as small as a city block, others a massive construction of residential buildings that make up cities in themselves.

It's important to get a handle on the neighborhood names so you can find your way around, understand what people are talking about when they refer to them and decide where you would like to stay during your time in Jerusalem.

The Old City, Rehavia and Mea She'arim are the neighborhood names people learn most quickly. It may seem as if all the others are called "Moshe" Something. I know the problem, for there are many neighborhoods with the name, "Moshe" — and all for Sir Moses Montefiore. To get the lay of the land and be able to pin down the major areas, open your trusty city map, and we'll check brief descriptions against some of the names.

Rehavia: Old Ashkenazi Jerusalem in south-central part of city, but more and more becoming mixed. Everyone who was anyone in the establishment of Israel who resided in Jerusalem lived and still lives here. It was the first "garden suburb", founded in 1921. It has a snooty reputation, less and less deserved.

Talbia: Just south of Rehavia. Newer homes than in Rehavia, and the newer rich live here. Arab homes add grace to the neighborhood. Martin Buber lived at Rehov Hovevei Zion 3.

Kiryat Shmuel: East of Talbia, south of Rehavia. "It would like to be Rehavia," is a snippy comment often heard about the area. Founded in 1928 and named for Rabbi Shmuel Salant, it has pockets of very observant Jews.

Yemin Moshe: East and south of the King David Hotel. After the Six-Day War, artists lived here in the restored houses on the hillside opposite the Old City. But most of the artists sold their homes for six-figure (in dollars) sums, often to Americans. Separated from the rest of the city, it is an affluent island.

Old Katamon: South of Kiryat Shmuel. Also called "Greek Colony" for being the home of the Greek monastery, Saint Simon. Before 1948, it was strongly Arab. Several foreign embassies used to be located here. Big, old homes. It is in demand as a place to live.

Katamonim: Below Old Katamon. Also known as Gonen. The big apartment developments were for low-income families, and the area has come to symbolize the poor. Recently it has taken on an improved image.

Neve Granot: South of the Israel Museum. Its location close to Hebrew University's Givat Ram campus, and its newer buildings, make it a choice neighborhood.

Neve Sha'anan (Oasis of Tranquility): Sandwiched between the museum and university. Large academic population and pleasant atmosphere.

Nahlaot: A collection of small neighborhoods east of Sachar Park. It was a poor, Sephardi area before independence. The area below Rehov Bezalel has become fashionable, with art students leading the direction. Now undergoing gentrification, some of its property is more expensive than Rehavia's.

Sha'arei Hessed: South of Nahalat Ahim. A quiet neighborhood, but its very observant population and the less observant population of Nahlaot occasionally cause each other concern.

German Colony: Below Talbia. Founded in 1880 by German members of the Templars' Society (who were evacuated by the British during World War II), it has a suburban, sometimes bucolic, air and a particularly European appearance.

Abu Tor (named for an officer of Salah e-Din, who conquered Jerusalem in 1187), along Hebron Road, and **Baka** (Ge'ulim), below it: both were poor neighborhoods that have become upscale. Abu Tor, which at places intermingles with an Arab neighborhood, especially has become pricey, largely because of its gorgeous view of the Old City, now threatened by developers.

Beit Hakerem: West of Hebrew University's Givat Ram campus. Green, quiet and attractive, it was established in 1922. A good neighborhood.

Beit Vegan: South of Beit Hakerem and similar, although probably with a larger observant population. Its name means "house and garden", and that is exactly what its founders constructed in the early '20s.

Old Talpiot: South of Baka. Another "garden city" from the early '20s. The home of the Nobel Prize-winning author S.Y. Agnon, at Rehov Klausner 16, now is a museum.

Arnona: a somewhat newer continuation of Old Talpiot.

East Talpiot, east of Talpiot; **Gilo,** south of the main population area; **Ramot,** north of the city, and **Ma'aleh Adumim,** east on Jericho Road, are among the new development areas. The last three, especially, are like cities unto themselves. They are enormous hunks of stone. Ramot might be considered the spiffiest, since it includes villas, cottages and a swimming pool. Parts of it are attracting people who are strictly observant. Other big developments are **Kiryat Haovel,** an integral part of the city to the west, and **Neve Ya'acov,** north, both too often looked down upon as being for lower-income residents.

Mea She'arim: Northwest of the Old City. It is home to the ultra-Orthodox, for whom it was built.

Ge'ula: Northwest of Mea She'arim. Not as ultra-Orthodox, newer than Mea She'arim and offering good, varied shopping.

Mekor Baruch: North of the Central Bus Station. Has some lovely old buildings. Is becoming increasingly Orthodox.

Romema: West of Mekor Baruch. Parts are newer apartment buildings. Working-class population.

Ramot Eshkol and **French Hill**: both post-1967 developments on the northern fringe and largely inhabited by modern Orthodox or those not particularly observant. Why French Hill, officially named "Givat Shapira", is commonly called French Hill seems to be a mystery.

The Jewish Quarter: Old City. Predominantly a strictly observant community. Most of the buildings are reconstructions of what existed before the Jordanian occupation or were built to blend in with the original architectural style. Real estate here is very expensive.

Ein Kerem: On the western edge of the city and separated from it by a long bus ride and a few hills and valleys. It still retains its original character of a village. Picturesque, absolutely charming — and part and parcel of Jerusalem.

The view south from Rehov Metudela in Rehavia.

JERUSALEM SCENE:

Canadian-born Richard was living in Kiryat Hayovel in the thick of a community of Georgian Jews. The ways of the Gruzinim were far different from his. Their culture from the southern Soviet Union collided with his of modern Jerusalem.

Richard suffered housewives throwing their scrub water and garbage out the window which landed on his clean laundry. He heard loud talk and music day and night. He particularly was fed-up with the elderly "Gruzini" — the Georgian man who usually could be found sitting outside the building in which Richard lived. The old man spent his day sipping mint tea and acting as self-appointed monitor of everyone who entered or exited.

Then Israel was attacked. Richard joined his unit and went to war.

Weeks later, he could go home. Exhausted and dirty, too tired to appreciate his survival, he struggled to reach his building and return to his own four walls. He was overpoweringly anxious, finally, to wash the war away and separate himself from it by getting some sleep.

As he approached his building, he cringed as he heard the usual noise that emanated from it at every hour. And there, sitting as usual, placidly drinking his tea and watching everyone's coming and going, was the elderly "Gruzini".

Richard gave a perfunctory wave to the old man as he tiredly made his way past him and headed for his mailbox to collect the letters that had accumulated while he was fighting the enemy. He was eager for that contact with normal life — words from loved ones; even bills. But when he reached his mailbox, he was thunderstruck. It was smeared over by brazen brushstrokes of red paint.

This was too much. He was furious. He had risked his life for these people and they had vandalized his mailbox. Did the people in this building know nothing about common decency?

Richard turned and angrily stalked toward the self-appointed guard. "Who did this to my mailbox? Who vandalized it?" he shouted.

The "Gruzini" looked at Richard in astonishment. "Nobody hurt your mailbox," he said.

"No?" Richard frantically pointed. "Then what do you call that red paint?"

"That?" The old man was taken aback. In a quiet voice, he said, "We painted over your mailbox so while you were at war, the Angel of Death wouldn't be able to find you."

Relating that episode, Richard says it was the turning point of his acceptance of life in Israel. He realized that it wasn't only a matter of his neighbors learning his ways, but of his learning their ways.

And he still lives at Kiryat Hayovel.

A Room with a View — Maybe

All right, you know some basics about Jerusalem — the transportation system, store hours, night life and the best place for *falafel*. Now you must find a place to live.

First, some terms that need defining: "flat" is the name used locally, not "apartment". In Israel, most people own their own flats. You probably will rent from a flat owner. In a few cases, you could rent from the owner of the entire building. (For reasons of semantics, I arbitrarily will call him "landlord" to distinguish him from the owner. If the reference applies to both, I'll say "dwelling owner".) Renting from a landlord is less preferable. I will explain later.

You undoubtedly will look for a furnished flat. The degree to which it is furnished will depend on your needs and what you will be lucky enough to land. If you have the use of the flat owner's sheets, blankets, washing machine and TV, your stay will be a lot more comfortable, but your rent will be much higher. If you rent from a landlord, chances are these items won't be available, and you will have to buy or borrow them. For a stay in Jerusalem of only a month or so, you probably will need a flat with everything provided.

Rent Costs

How much you can expect to pay for a roof over your head depends on a lot of things: supply, demand, inflation and other variables beyond your control. Add to the equation your budget — another matter over which you may not have control — and the style of living you are willing to accept, which you can control. And you might as well know from the beginning: Jerusalem isn't the place for Jewish-American Princesses and Princes or their non-Jewish and non-American equivalents. Be prepared to gear down your living standards.

Generally, despite Israel's rampant inflation in the early '80's, Jerusalem rents are a minor miracle to anyone who has suffered through apartment hunting in New York or Los Angeles. Australians, however, scream in pain over them. For reasons we only can be grateful for (and pray will continue), Jerusalem rents haven't skyrocketed with the cost of buying a Jerusalem flat.

In any case, the shorter the rental period, the higher the cost per month.

Keep in mind when assessing rents that in Israel, bathrooms and kitchens aren't counted as rooms. A flat listed as having two rooms has two in addition to those basics.

What can make a prospective tenant quake in his running shoes, however, is the fact that Jerusalem dwelling owners ask for, and often get, rents for up to a year in advance. Three months in advance is the minimum, so expect to produce a lot of money up front, but not in dollars. Paying your dwelling owner in dollars is illegal.

On the Trail

If friends in Jerusalem are scouting flats for you in advance, don't let them commit you to anything. Wait until you arrive to decide. It is better not to sign on the dotted line before you, yourself, see your future abode, unless you are the sort never to kick yourself after you blunder into a mess or are totally oblivious to your surroundings.

However, ignore the preceding paragraph if you expect to stay in Jerusalem for only a month or two. In that case, you shouldn't waste a precious moment in the city looking for a place to live. Go ahead and trust a helpful friend or work in advance with a Jerusalem rental agent. Among rental agents are **Israel Bed & Breakfast, LTD**, P.O. Box 24119, Jerusalem 91-240, Tel. 817-001, and **Anglo Saxon Realty**, Rehov Hasoreg 2, Tel. 221-161. But still, insist on an on-site inspection before closing the deal.

If you plan on a longer stay and have no friends or relatives who could put you up while you go flat hunting, find a temporary place to hang your hat through options listed in Chapter 5, "A Place to Lay Your Head".

With that accomplished, you can scour the town for a flat. There are several ways of tracking one down.

Get Friday's *Jerusalem Post*. What you find there in the classified section also appears in the major Hebrew-language newspapers. So don't be surprised if you call up and discover yourself connected with someone who doesn't speak English.

Register at She'al, Rehov King George 21, or Dahof, Rehov Yafo 43. At both places, for about $5, you have access for two or three months to their listings of flats to rent or share.

Neither She'al nor Dahof do leg work for you. They merely hand you a list in Hebrew, English or French that gives a brief description of each flat available, what neighborhood it is in, usually a phone number to call and often notes if the flat is open only to Orthodox Jews. If there isn't a crowd on the premises, the attendant, out of the goodness of her heart, might help you locate neighborhoods and streets on a Jerusalem map that you will have clutched in your hands.

August and September are the height of the flat hunting season, so expect mobs at the agencies those months.

Go to the Association of Americans and Canadians in Israel (AACI), behind Rehov Pinsker 11. For about $2 you can join and, besides getting in on AACI social activities, you can check on its housing notices.

Go to a real estate agency that manages rentals. Agencies are especially good for locating short-term rentals. Some agencies are better than others, but even at the most highly recommended ones, an agent might not bestir himself to see if anyone else in the office has additional listings. A discreet nudge from you may be in order.

Going to an agency won't cost you money unless you conclude a deal. Then, both you and the dwelling owner will pay a fee each on each month's rent. Yours will be between five and ten percent. You will have to sign a contract with the agency before you will get even a scrap of information about vacancies.

Put your own ad in the *Jerusalem Post*. It will run in Hebrew papers, too. That was how an American filmmaker landed one of the loveliest flats in one of the most picturesque neighborhoods in town — and at his price.

Tell everyone you know that you are looking for a flat. I mean everyone: people you climb over on the bus, people who offer you assistance when they see you stopped on the sidewalk studying your map, and taxi drivers especially. Everybody. Almost everyone in Jerusalem seems to know someone with a place to rent. So don't be shy.

Deborah, a young Canadian, can be your role model. Knowing not one word of Hebrew, she stationed herself for days on a choice residential street and asked passersby if they knew of a flat for rent. She finally found just what she was looking for.

Not to be overlooked is the possibility of sharing a flat. In Israel, strangers, even of the opposite sex, think nothing of splitting a rental between two or more people. This way, you can live at bargain-basement rates in a place beyond your dreams. But there are ticklish business details and personal matters to be agreed upon. And your own room may be the only place where you can entertain company.

If you want to live in East Jerusalem, you face a whole different set of problems, for no rental agencies exist there. Everything is accomplished by word of mouth. Customarily, rather than renting a flat in East Jerusalem, one would rent a room with a family.

Ask at East Jerusalem churches about available rooms for rent. Church staff probably will have a personal connection with a family in their congregation renting out a room, which, in itself, could be a recommendation for them. Another route is to get into a conversation with a restaurant owner and let your wishes be known. Everyone in East Jerusalem has a cousin who can solve all problems. If you let people know what kind of work or study you are pursuing, it might meet a particular family's approval and someone will materialize to help you.

But, life in East Jerusalem is conservative. A person lives under constraints there he wouldn't experience in West Jerusalem. In a

Moslem family, the consumption of alcoholic beverages is forbidden. But with either Christians or Moslems, the impact, primarily, could mean a limited social life with the opposite sex.

Checking Out the Possibilities: What You See and What You Will Get

When you go to see rentals, what can you expect to find? Usually, in a flat that remains on the rental market, instead of one being absented temporarily by its owner, there will be a few pieces of old furniture dragged up from Aunt Esther's storage room. You will get a bed perhaps no wider than an army cot (considered standard in Israel), probably a free-standing closet and a table and a chair or two. If there is anything more than that, consider yourself lucky. Looking down on your few sticks of furniture from the ceiling will be a naked light bulb. That is the hallmark of Jerusalem rentals.

Typically, in this situation, the kitchen is devoid of even a can opener. But make sure it has a refrigerator and stove. The latter is most often a two-burner, table-top model. If there is an oven, your friends will o-o-oh and a-a-ah over your good fortune.

Before you say, "I'll take it," pin down exactly what furniture will be in the flat. You can't assume that what you see will be what you'll get. Also, find out how the place will be heated, how you will get hot water, if there is a phone on the premises and what kind of security exists.

The matter of heat may not seem like a concern if you are renting in sunny September. Besides, this is the desert, isn't it?

Just wait. Despite Jerusalem's palm trees, its winters can be wet and miserable much of the time, even snowy. Many flats have no heat. You simply will have to buy your own kerosene or electric heater to inspire yourself to get out from under the covers on a cold morning.

Some flats have an outlet for a plug-in gas heater (which hopefully is on the premises), for which you will have to buy cylinder ("balloons") of butane gas as the fuel source. Your flat might be small enough and the heater strong enough to do a reasonable job.

You might strike a flat in a building with central heating. Don't jump for joy. You will pay a steep price for probably no more than four hours of tepid heat per day. If you will be in your flat a lot during the day, with no heat until, say, 6 p.m., you may begin to see your breath as it hits the frigid air. Inevitably, you will buy your own heater, so you will end up paying two heating bills. Keep that in mind.

Getting hot water isn't as troublesome as keeping warm. A lot of buildings have solar water heating installations, which save on the high cost of electricity. You might encounter confusion over the word "solar". In Hebrew it refers to a type of heating fuel. In any event, every flat has its own water tank which you can heat whenever you choose by a flick of a switch.

If the flat doesn't already have a telephone — which is and will remain in its owner's name — you will have alternatives (described in Chapter 18, "Communication"), unless you choose to live as a recluse and miss that invitation to dinner.

As in most big cities, everybody knows somebody whose flat has been burglarized. Flats on the ground floor or close to it should have adequate window security, namely, metal bars. The American resistance to bars on windows doesn't exist here. Centuries of invaders have turned homes into fortresses.

Just about all windows have outside shutters that roll up and down with the sound of a shovel scraped along the sidewalk. They are no substitute for window bars on lower floors. They keep out daylight, but not uninvited guests.

It is a good idea to check the door locks of your flat. If they are flimsy, and the dwelling owner won't agree to replace them, pop for a deadbolt. It is a worthwhile investment.

Rent Money Is Only the Beginning

With the cost of rent in mind, remember the other housing expenses you could have:

- Central heat
- Water
- Electricity (your own meter will be in your flat)
- Telephone
- Municipal taxes
- Butane cylinders ("balloons") to supply fuel to that little stove of yours and to a gas heater, if you have one. So that there always is fuel, people keep pairs of balloons. When one balloon becomes empty, call the company that supplies your flat and have it replaced. Get the telephone number from your dwelling owner and his customer number before you move in.

These are the items that can drive your housing costs up, up, up. Be thankful that you know about them before you make a commitment. But now that you have checked on all these details and you have decided on the flat you want, a new set of agonies begins: contract negotiations.

Signing on the Dotted Line

Don't rush to see how your signature looks on the contract. Remember what Israelis say: everything is negotiable. And that includes rent.

Israelis rightly maintain that foreigners are at a huge disadvantage negotiating a rental contract, because they often don't understand the system. Some Israeli and non-Israeli veteran tenants insist that a foreigner shouldn't stumble through negotiations alone, that the best thing for him or her is to have a tough-minded Israeli along from the start. You should be so lucky.

Every detail of the contract should be gone over by you and the dwelling owner or the agent, if one is involved. Make sure you understand it all.

At this time, those expenses beyond the rental fee, such as water, will be ticked off by the dwelling owner. I was in an utter daze when I first went through this. I couldn't keep track of all these additional costs. *Shkelim* seemed to fly past my eyes.

Those additional expenses, as mentioned earlier, will include water and, probably, maintenance and municipality tax. Municipality tax isn't always passed on to the tenant, but the trend is in that direction. Maybe you can get the landlord to split it with you.

Another expense will be central heating (if there is any). You could be so unlucky as to get a landlord like one I had. His last name translated into the name for a precious gem, but I will call him "Mr. Selah". That means "rock". Like his head.

Mr. Selah insisted that fuel for his centrally heated building be paid for in advance. His argument was that he wanted to buy it before the price went up. There is logic to that, but then I never knew how much he actually used and what it really cost to heat my flat. It occurred to me plenty of times that my money was keeping him warm. It certainly didn't do much for me. The only defense against a Mr. Selah is to find out from as many people as possible what they pay for central heating. Then you will have a bargaining guide.

A lot of buildings are run by a resident committee that bills each flat monthly for communal expenses like central heating, water and maintenance. The committee only can give a ballpark figure in advance as to what these *"vad ha'bayit"* expenses might be. And these bills, usually called the *"vad"*, won't necessarily be cheaper in the summer, because the committee, like Mr. Selah, will want to buy fuel for next winter in advance, against any price increase.

With all things being equal, if you have a choice between a building run by a landlord or a resident committee, choose the one run by the committee. A committee should have no qualms about letting you see its bills. But try asking a landlord to show you what his fuel bill actually was.

After the monthly rent, given in a dollar figure, and those additionals have been agreed upon, you will have to settle the matter of how many months' rent you will pay in advance. The dwelling owner will want a year's worth or all of it, whichever is the larger amount. Consider that a moment: you will lose both the use of your money during the months ahead as well as the interest it might have earned you. So what will you get in return? Israelis suggest you ask for a ten to 15 percent discount on the rent.

One renter I know readily agrees to paying his rent a year in advance. But then he turns his baby blue eyes on his prospective landlord and says, "Of course, I know you aren't trying to make money off me, so you'll pay me the interest my money will earn this coming year, won't you?" He swears the demand for rent a year in advance is dropped like a slippery, wet fish every time.

Finally, there is yet another matter that will appear in the contract on your dwelling owner's behalf. He will want you to leave, preferably in his hands, money to cover any damages you may have caused and electric and phone bills to come in after you depart for distant lands. Mr. Selah asked for a whopping $400 on my $250 a month flat. This is where renting through an agent can be helpful, for it probably would be acceptable to leave a damage deposit with the agent. Otherwise, fight like crazy to leave the deposit in escrow with a lawyer or a trusted friend who can pay your bills after he or she sees them and will send you any balance.

Something to get into the contract specifically for your benefit is a statement that you can sublet the flat. Who knows the future? Something may require you to move out early, and you shouldn't have to walk away from all that money you plunked down.

There is in Israel a standard, printed legal form for tenants and landlords. Even with that, details can be altered by mutual consent, so long as they aren't forbidden by law. But don't be surprised if you run into a Mr. Selah, who laboriously writes out every contract by hand.

In any event, after all the haggling, unless you have gone through an agent who deals a lot with foreigners, you will find every detail of the contract spelled out in Hebrew. At least the numbers will be recognizable.

But even if the contract is in English, still keep that ballpoint pen hidden until you have shown the document to a lawyer. Find out in advance what he or she charges. By this time, you don't need any more surprises. Thirty to fifty dollars is standard.

Watching Out for No. 1

When all the nit-picking details are agreed upon, the contract is signed and you have relieved yourself of all the money weighing you down, itemize the contents of the flat and prepare a damage list upon moving in.

And watch for your dwelling owner's nervous reaction to your damage list if it is in English.

Get a meter reading on electricity and the telephone (telephone charges are by meter, too) shortly before you move in, so you know your starting point. Get another reading of both when you leave.

One more note: should you have a problem with your dwelling owner after you move into your flat, it is comforting to know that Israeli law very much favors tenants. Once they're in, it almost takes an act of God to oust them.

It is a cozy thought, but don't get too comfortable with it. If you should fall into a conflict, remember it is the dwelling owner who knows how to shut off the water, the electricity, the telephone — all of which Mr. Selah did to me. Never mind that such action isn't legal. What counts is how long you can live without a flushing toilet.

A quiet street in Me'a She'arim.

The Hard Facts

Want an idea of what your total living costs will be? Remember that costs can change quickly, depending on all sorts of things, including government subsidies of utilities. Mr. Selah charged me $250 a month for a dreary, ground-floor, two-room flat in green, choice, centrally located Rehavia. In addition, there was $500 for four months of lukewarm heat maybe as much as four hours a night, usually less, which, like rent, had to be paid in advance. Other advance payments were for water and municipality tax. They averaged about $15 and $6 a month, respectively.

I paid about $15 a month for electricity and $17 for the telephone, excluding international calls. One (albeit lengthy) conversation to the U.S.A. came to a staggering $75. Unfortunately, the bill comes in far after the pleasure has faded.

Some other rents: a couple from New York with three young children found a four-and-a-half room, pleasant, fully furnished flat in Rehavia in a building with a lemon tree outside the front door. Their monthly rent for a year's stay was $450, which they believed was unusually low for what they got. Their other expenses averaged $110 a month heat, $35 for *vad ha'bayit* maintenance and $50 each for water and electricity.

John, a doctor from Berkeley who stayed for two months, paid $450 a month for a two-and-a-half room, bright, fully furnished flat in Rasco (southwest of Kiryat Shmuel) with a view of the Judean Desert. He left a deposit to cover his utility bills. His was a shining example of how rents are raised for short stays.

Okay. The details are over. You are in your Jerusalem home. It may not have a view. It may not even get sunshine. But now you can begin living like a Jerusalemite.

Making It Seem Like Home

Now you are in your Jerusalem abode. And it may resemble a prison cell. To turn it into a home you'll need to use your ingenuity and pocketbook.

— A naked bulb can be made decent with an inexpensive paper globe shade imported from the Far East. Some of the china importers carry them, like Class at Rehov Yafo 57.

— For furniture and appliances, you may find what you need advertised on the bulletin board at the office of the Association of Americans and Canadians in Israel, in Friday ads in the Jerusalem Post, or in second-hand stores.

Most of the second-hand stores are concentrated in the Mea She'arim-Geula neighborhood. Several are located along Rehov Mea

She'arim between Rehov Strauss, Rehov Yehezkiel and Rehov Shivtei Israel. Shmontses is at Rehov Yehezkiel 6, and Hayad Hashniya is at Rehov Shivtei Israel 38.

— For rugs that you might want to take back overseas with you, the place to go is the Arab *souk* in the Old City.

— For new kitchen supplies and for clothes hangers, blankets and linens, scour Mahane Yehuda. If you aren't ready to buy on the spot, make a note of where you saw what. Mahane Yehuda can be every bit as confusing as the Old City, and finding your way back is a challenge.

— Do buy a *sirpella* — known in English as a "Wonder Pot". It is. It looks like an angel food cake ring, but is a stove-top oven. Your kitchen may not have an oven, and even if it does, baking in a *sirpella* is more economical. Make sure when you buy it that you get all three parts.

The *sirpella* works amazingly well. Just keep the flame low, and you will be able to bake potatoes, kugels, casseroles and cakes. Local advice suggests that, as a precaution, you should locate the safety valves for turning off fuel to your stove or heater and close them whenever you leave your flat. The *sirpella* may turn out to be your favorite item purchased in Israel and you will want to take it home with you.

Televisions, washing machines, refrigerators and other appliances may be rented from The Electric House, Rehov Aza 14. Tel. 632-977.

It is possible to obtain free posters to add cheer to your flat. Check at the Israel Information Center in the portico next to the Apartotel, Rehov Yafo 214. The center is open from 9 a.m. to 1 p.m. Sundays through Fridays. Another source is the Jewish Agency, corner Rehov Keren Hakayemet and Rehov King George. Ask at the information desk. The agency closes at 3 p.m. daily.

After all this, you will discover that your flat, which may have seemed user unfriendly at first, is welcoming you. You will have made a home in Jerusalem.

A Winter's Tale

The biggest shock about living in Jerusalem is the discovery that when winter comes you are convinced you might freeze to death. You will wonder, "Is this the desert I envisioned?" It certainly isn't.

When, in the beginning of November, you see a window display at the department store, Hamashbir, with kiddie-sized dummies modeling new snowsuits and fixed to look as if they are romping in a pile of white stuff, you can take that as a hint as to what's ahead.

Blame it on Jerusalem's altitude. The city ranges from an elevation of 2230 feet at Ein Kerem to 2700 feet on Mount Scopus. Remember, people "go up" to Jerusalem literally, as well as spiritually.

There can be months of cold, heavy rain. There can be snow. Snow normally falls about twice annually, but one year I gave up counting after 12 snowfalls. Beware: those beautiful stone buildings that reflect light so gloriously, keep the heat out in summer and the cold in, in winter.

A bitter, damp chill is trapped in those unheated or minimally heated buildings. Even my big, strapping Canadian friends have been reduced to crybabies, whimpering that they've never been so cold in their lives.

It isn't that the temperature drops so low. It rarely goes below freezing. It's that when it gets cold, especially when it gets cold and rainy or snowy, there is practically no place in Jerusalem to keep warm. At least not any place where you could be warm and also bring your bed.

Those mean days can be just the time to take a trip to Eilat, Jericho, Tiveria or even sea level and probably 10-degrees-warmer Tel Aviv. And this is the choice season for visiting Egypt.

But there you are in Jerusalem. What to do? To keep comfortably warm in a centrally "heated" flat, you will have to remain in perpetual motion. If your flat is equipped with a gas heater attached to a balloon of butane gas, the room in which the heater is located might be quite pleasant. But what happens when you go to the bathroom?

The goal is to be in charge of your own goosebumps. To do that, you will have to buy or borrow a means of keeping warm which you can control where and when you want. The choices are between an electric or kerosene heater. Their initial cost is about the same, depending on the sophistication of the model. But the cost of operation may be quite different. Usually, kerosene is far cheaper to run, but changes in government subsidies can alter that. Check before you purchase.

The likelihood is that electricity is the more expensive to use, but an electric heater is wonderfully simple to operate. If it uses more than two kilowatts, however, it might need a special plug.

The use of kerosene requires the practice of several safety precautions. The heater must be lit and extinguished outdoors or in a hallway outside the flat. When in operation, ventilation is required. Since "insulation" is a new concept in Israel, an old flat may have enough cracks under doors and around windows to give more ventilation than you need or care to have, but the proper procedure is to open a window slightly.

When I found it was too cold at night to sleep, I decided that rather than buy at least two additional blankets to keep warm, I would get a sleeping bag. It cost about as much as only one blanket. I opened it, spread it across my bed and it kept me heavenly warm

— so long as it didn't slip to the floor during the night. Finally, I wised up and sewed it to the blanket.

If you can afford to splurge and are an electric blanket devotee, you can buy the Israeli version — an electric sheet.

A great way of keeping your feet warm on cold tile floors is to envelop them in the sheepskin booties found in the Arab shops in the Old City *souk*. They also sell sheepskin mittens.

Make sure you come to Jerusalem prepared. A list of what to bring to face a Jerusalem winter appears in the Appendix. Don't laugh when you read "long johns". You'll be smiling when you can climb into them.

So if you expect to be in Jerusalem in winter — don't think "Middle East", think "Siberia". Cold air is the only thing that emigrates freely to Israel from the Soviet Union.

After studying this chapter, it might be your luck to hit a mild Jerusalem winter and wonder what I've been talking about. Look at it this way: expect the worst. If it isn't, you won't be disappointed.

The Russian church of St. Mary Magdalene stands on the slopes of the Mount of Olives.

Chapter 16:
To Health: Physically and Financially Healthy

"La Briyoot" — *To Health*

The thought of needing a doctor thousands of miles from home is enough to make a grown person reach for a security blanket. Feel comforted that Israel is an international leader in some medical areas, but it does have its medical peculiarities. Being forewarned isn't as good as being vaccinated, but it should help.

Jerusalem no longer is the disease-ridden city it was before World War I. These days, the city doesn't present any particular health problem.

The Israeli medical profession is well equipped to handle any major medical problem and can be excellent. But that isn't what gets most of us. It is the minor, annoying things like tummy aches, colds that won't go away and fingers caught in a door. What to do about them?

First you have to understand Israel's health setup. Briefly, Israel maintains a socialized medical system. The several health insurance plans that cover all Israelis are intrinsic to its socialized medicine. But because health delivery within that system sometimes moves like gears submerged in molasses, private medical practices exist concurrently, forming a separate health delivery system. Anyone who wants to pay out of his own pocket may avail himself of a private physician. The first time I needed to see a physician in Jerusalem, I asked the Association of Americans and Canadians in Israel to refer me to the best. I was able to arrange to see a man who was the head of his department at the renowned Hadassah Medical Center.

But both the costs and time involved turned out to be exorbitant. I later learned that I could have gone through Hadassah's clinic much less expensively, although at a higher cost than to an Israeli. I might have wasted just as much time, and I might have been seen by this same doctor.

Eventually, I worked out the best arrangement for my particular situation when I became the private patient of a conscientious Australian-born physician whose fees were reasonable and who gave me prompt attention.

The AACI remains a source of help in dealing with medical needs. But if you feel, because of its fine, international reputation, that Hadassah is the only place in Jerusalem for health care, the telephone number at Ein Kerem is 427-427; at Mt. Scopus, 818-111.

Anyone carrying health insurance should check with the company on its overseas coverage before leaving home. Blue Cross-Blue Shield says a patient should make payment in Israel and then send the bill with itemized charges translated into English (good luck) and the total figure converted into dollars. To expedite claims, bring your company's insurance forms with you to Israel, just in case.

More and more American firms are offering special overseas health insurance. Check with your travel agent about these before leaving home.

Almost anyone can get coverage in Israel from Shiloach Co. Ltd., Rehov Ben Yehudah 34, the City Tower Building, Jerusalem, Tel. 222-341. The company's policies have a few restrictions — mostly pertaining to age. You can write for details. An added attraction (only in Israel would you get a deal like this) is that subscribers of an insurance group like Shiloach also get reduced rates at various hotels in the country.

Other Health Tips

The water in Israel is fine in towns and cities. Practice caution elsewhere.

Don't underestimate the sun and heat. Wear a hat in the sun. Drink a lot of liquids when the temperature goes up.

Wash fresh produce with a small amount of dish detergent and plenty of water to remove insecticides and animal waste.

For dental care, AACI has referrals to American and Canadian trained dentists.

For information and counseling on contraception, sexuality and pregnancy, contact Shilo Pregnancy Advisory Service, a private organization, at Ben-Yehuda Mall 16, third floor. Tel. 248-412. Hours are 5 p.m. to 8 p.m. Sunday through Thursday on a walk-in basis. Legal abortions are restricted in Israel, especially to any woman between the ages of 17 and 40.

If you spend any time in the Jordan Valley, be aware of leishmaniasis, a skin infection caused by a parasite carried to people and rodents by sand flies. Leishmaniasis is called, locally, "the Rose of Jericho", after the scar it can leave. The disease was dying out until Israelis began to settle in the valley after the Six-Day War. Humans provide a link in the parasite's life cycle. Efforts at controlling the mouse population have helped reduce the disease's occurrence. Treatment has improved greatly, but if you have an insect bite that doesn't heal, get medical attention as soon as possible.

And lest the thought of dealing with the Israeli health delivery system seem too discouraging, listen to Rahel's story. From South Africa more than five years earlier, she had made, at best, a mixed-bag adjustment to Israel.

When she faced a major surgical procedure, she not only was fearful and depressed by the prospect, but felt overwhelmed by having to go through this in Israel and not in the meticulous, orderly South Africa she knew.

The outcome is a happy story. Rahel's hospitalization became the pivot of her complete acceptance of living in Israel. She said the kindness, attention and warmth she received were beyond all expectation. They touched her heart so deeply, she felt, at long last, that Israel was home.

JERUSALEM SCENE:

Jay Shapiro, the American-born Israeli physicist who has written a book on immigrating to Israel, tells this story of what happened when he joined the Israeli army.

He was excited about the prospect of becoming a soldier, for he felt that would make him a true Israeli. But he had one worry about an impediment to his goal: when he was called up for the American army years before, he had been turned down because of being nearsighted.

Not to worry. He passed the Israeli exam with flying colors. How did he accomplish that, he wanted to know.

He said to the doctor, "Look, how come Israel accepts me as a soldier when the United States didn't? And now yet! I'm 20 years fatter, slower and older. I'm more nearsighted than ever."

The doctor's face took on a serious expression. In a thoughtful tone, he answered, "Both America and Israel have enemies. The difference is, America's enemies are far away. Ours are close."

Money Talk

Among Anglo-Saxons, at least on their home turf, it is considered bad manners to talk about money. In Israel, it is the No. 1 topic of conversation. So we will do as the Israelis and talk money.

Of course, you will arrive with traveler's checks. Also arm yourself with a Visa card, which is accepted almost everywhere in Israel, even the supermarkets. Better yet, have two Visa cards from separate accounts. There could be problems establishing your credit overseas with one account, so at least you will have the other (we hope) to fall back on. I had that problem when I tried to use one of my two cards. The report on it constantly said I didn't exist, or words to that effect. Fortunately, I had the telephone number of the man in the United States who set up that account for me through his brokerage firm, as well as the Athens number of the firm's closest office to Israel. I called them both collect, which solved the problem like magic.

Not only will you be able to charge items with the Visa card when you shop, but, most importantly, you will be able to make cash withdrawals in *shkelim* (the plural of *shekel*) from banks. But this arrangement won't suffice for any length of time, because of the service fee and the time it takes for your credit card to be verified again and again.

To be financially functional during an extended stay, you will need to open two accounts with a Jerusalem bank. One will be a foreign currency savings account; the other a checking account. With the latter, get a plastic bank card to use for withdrawals from an automatic teller (some banks close their automatic tellers on Shabbat).

You can choose to set up your foreign currency account in French francs, German marks, English pounds or American dollars, or other available currencies. Americans usually opt for a dollar account, which is the simplest to follow. But depending on the strength of the dollar and how much time you want to spend "watching" your money, you might consider other currency options. You can get advice at your Israeli bank.

You can deposit money in your Jerusalem foreign currency bank account by personal check drawn on your hometown bank or savings institution. Israeli banks require 14 American business days for your check to clear — not much longer than a lot of American banks require.

Your deposit will earn interest. Technically, the money is locked up for three months, minimum. Don't worry: Israelis have an answer for everything. You are free to make a withdrawal from your foreign currency account as soon as your check clears; you simply lose interest on the amount withdrawn.

At the same time that you establish your foreign currency account, open a checking account, which will be in *shkelim*. When you need *shkelim*, the teller will transfer the amount you designate from the foreign currency account to the checking account. Should there be galloping inflation, try to transfer as small an amount into the checking account as possible.

To get your checks, you must find the person at the bank who issues them — probably a young man who looks about 17. Give him your checking account number and he will stamp it on a book of checks. No name, address, telephone number or picture of pretty mountains. About $1 will be docked from your checking account for ea_h book you order.

You can pay by check almost everywhere. You even can write the amounts in English. The clerk may not be able to read what you have written, but if the numbers on it agree with the bill, that's almost all that matters. The hardest part is to remember to write the date the way Israelis do, using numerals in this order: day-month-year.

After the front of the check has been filled out, write your name, Jerusalem address and telephone number on the back.

There is no need to be intimidated by the prospect of using your plastic card at an Israeli automatic teller, just because its directions are in Hebrew. There probably will be but one set of directions to learn, anyway: the one that orders the machine to spew forth money. If in doubt, hang around the automatic teller a few moments. Someone will come along to use it who probably can give instructions or will allow you to watch his transaction.

Find out what the service charge is for each check as compared with each mechanical withdrawal. It could be less expensive to withdraw from the automatic teller.

The branch bank where I do business also has a machine inside that gives me a print-out on my cleared checks when I simply slip this same card into it and punch the right buttons. The only problem is that the machine works only half the time.

After I opened my foreign and checking accounts, I found I was deluged by mail from both accounts and in duplicate, even triplicate. All in Hebrew. Ask to get the statements in English. Maybe you will. And once you chuck the duplicates and triplicates, keep the remainder in a safe place until you are sure, sure, sure you won't need them.

The statement can be baffling. Sometimes there are inexplicable charges, often infinitesimal in cost. When I asked my favorite bank employee, Harry, a young former Montrealer, about them, he advised me, "Never mind. It will be too complicated to find out."

All those bank statements coming through the mail won't include canceled checks, however. Should you ask to get them, your teller will faint dead away. Should you need them for the American IRS, tell the IRS to go argue with an Israeli bank. Your solution is to save important receipts.

Israeli bank service charges are relatively low. An American will find that overdrawing on an account will be a lot less expensive in Israel than back home. Israelis say that banks even look benignly on overdraws of one month's salary. One-and-a-half month's salary overdrawn, however, begins to make bank officials cranky.

If inflation is afoot in Israel, your bank quickly will become a second home. You and hordes of others will spend considerable time waiting in lines to take your money out of foreign currency savings accounts (dollars, marks, etc.) and change it into *shkelim* at the last possible moment. When Israel was suffering from 400 percent inflation, the value of the *shekel* shrank as you held it in your hand. If inflation has been nipped, the bank will be empty and employees may carry on a social chat. In either case, you get to see a lot of the staff.

All of them, from bank director on down, probably will be in shirt-sleeves. Running sweats are popular among the younger men. It may be that they are ready for their afternoon activity after the bank closes Monday, Wednesday and Friday afternoons. At regular intervals, a "coffee" woman will go from employee to employee with a tray of beverages, so while you transact business, your teller may be sipping juice or coffee.

If school is out, bank employees may have their children with them. That makes for another contribution to the homey scene. And so does the sight of dogs standing in line with their owners.

To celebrate Rosh Hashana, my bank serves its patrons wine, cookies, candies and gives out roses. I'm sure that isn't unique.

If all this informality seems unprofessional in an institution dealing with high finances and *your* money, relax. An American-born, top Israeli bank official, who has worked at his bank's branches in two American cities where employees were Americans, advised me not to be fooled by appearances. "These people here are brighter, more responsive and have more initiative than either of my staffs in the States." His very words.

Chapter 17:
Materialism: Shopping for Food, Toiletries, Clothes

Food for Thought

I confess. Perhaps the thing that scares me most about making my way in a country where I face a language barrier is shopping, especially for food. I want to purchase something, but I must struggle to communicate what it is I want. I feel helpless — as if no one can count on me to tie my shoes myself. Eventually, we all get the hang of things. This chapter is aimed at providing you with some short cuts. In Jerusalem, either dealing with specialty shops or tackling the supermarkets can seem daunting.

Specialty shops include greengrocers with fresh fruits and vegetables; the grocery (*makolet*) with emphasis on non-perishables, daily products and bread; butcher shops; fishmongers, who often also sell poultry; natural food stores; bakeries that abound more frequently than is good for one's dimensions; and shops selling cheeses, nuts or fresh-roasted coffee. The *shuk* at Mahane Yehuda and the Arab *souk* in the Old City are a gathering of specialty shops.

But the best way to get your bearings, and learn what Israeli food stores offer, is to explore the supermarkets. You can take as much time as you want to wander through the aisles and eye the products. You may get pushed, but it won't be to buy. While there are supermarkets throughout the city, you are more likely to find English-speaking shoppers to help solve a stumper at Super-Sol on Rehov

Agron and the Co-op Supermarket in the basement of Hamashbir.

As in the United States, supermarkets here carry a lot besides food, like household cleaning supplies, candles, matches, toiletries, even pots and pans and brooms.

The number of brands from back home come as a surprise. You want Tabasco? You can find Tabasco. You want Kellogg's Corn Flakes? You can buy Kellogg's Corn Flakes. But for a price. For the budget's sake, check out Israeli alternatives. In certain categories, they don't measure up in quality or taste; in others, they can be superior.

The glory of an Israeli supermarket is that it is possible to buy bread still warm from the oven, and at the delicatessen counter you can find fresh *houmus*, *tehina*, Turkish salad, *baba ganouj* and barrels of different kinds of olives — even with a carton next to them to dump the pits of olives you have tasted — a necessary part of the decision to buy.

The most frustrating thing about shopping in a supermarket is that the carts rarely push through the check-out counter. The result often is a mass of empty carts blocking the counter and through which you must weave your way, if you hope to get out. If a line of people also is trying to work its way through abandoned carts, tempers may flare.

On the plus side, you can put your bill on Visa, and the supermarket, like the *makolet*, will deliver your purchases, sometimes for a small fee. The delivery man should be tipped.

Wherever you food shop, remember to arm yourself first with your own big, plastic sacks or string bags if you are carrying your purchases home. And expect to do your own sacking.

The dairy department possibly is the most baffling in a supermarket, because of its variety. Since dairy food is so basic to Israeli cuisine, you need to become familiar with it. The manager of Super-Sol walked the length of the dairy counter with me one day and explained the products.

This is what he said: Cheeses are divided, roughly, into yellow or white cheese. Yellow are hard cheeses, white are soft. Almost all yellow cheeses are available in slices, but they are a lot less expensive purchased in bulk.

These are the Israeli names of yellow cheeses and their internationally known equivalents:

Emek — Dutch Edam. Made of cow's milk.
Gush Halav — Dutch Edam, but more expensive than Emek.
Gilboa — Semi-fat relative of Emek and Gush Halav.
Colbi — Gouda.
Tal Ha'emek — Emmenthal Swiss Cheese.
Bashan — Provolone (smoked).

Golan — like Bashan, but not smoked (great for *bourekas* and kugel.) Made of sheep's milk.

Gad — Danish Danbo.

Ein Gedi — Camembert.

Galil — Roquefort.

Gilead — Balkan *Kashkaval* (smoked). Sheep's milk.

Brie — Brie. (As if you didn't know.)

Also available is a form of Cheddar cheese. Specialty yellow cheeses, usually processed, may be found in sausage-like shapes. They may be smoked or sharp.

White cheese falls into several categories. Salty white cheese is Bulgarian style and packaged in plastic. They are popular to serve at a wine-and-cheese evening. In increasing amount of fat, brand names of some salty white cheeses are Gamad, Betit, Kafrit (may be substituted for Feta) and Hermon.

White spread cheese is made by different companies, but Tnuva, which tends to set the pace, has a picture of a blue cow on the top of the container for its cheese with no fat or salt; a purple cow with 5% fat cheese, and a green cow with 9% fat cheese.

White cheeses chosen by dieters are Canaan with only 1% fat and Canaanite with half a percentage point more.

Other cheeses are: Shanit, which is similar to cream cheese; Feta; Shumit, like Boursin with garlic and herbs; Pilpelit, also like Boursin, but with black pepper and spices; and Fromez, made from goats' milk. Popular Labane is Greek-style cheese from goats' milk.

Na'aman comes in a tub and is called a "cooking cheese" and is akin to cream cheese, but with far less fat (3% total). It is used widely here in cheesecake, though it wouldn't do for my favorite, sky-high caloric cheesecake recipe.

Close by in small tubs will be Co-tege, possibly the most delicious cottage cheese you will ever taste.

Yogurt-related by-products of milk come in plastic containers in either the squat 120-cc size or the taller 170-cc size. The larger containers can be used as drinking glasses, if you're desperate.

The unflavored variety starts (by the lowest fat content) with Gil (also known as Leban) in a container with blue lettering. Gil is thin enough that grocery shoppers often take a container of it out of the display case, shake it up and drink it down right then and there.

Next comes Eshel with red letters, and then Shemenet, like sour cream, which you can recognize by the Seven Dwarfs that appear on the container of one manufacturer. Eshel makes a tasty and less caloric substitute for sour cream.

Flavored and dessert-type yogurts include Prili with pieces of fruit; Yogli, without fruit, and Prigurt, which is fruit-flavored. Israeli yogurt is watery.

Chocoholics won't be able to resist Israeli chocolate yogurt. Ma'adon contains less than 2% fat (who counts sugar?). Dani is the most popular chocolate yogurt, but Milki is the same but for a dash of whipped cream.

Buying milk can be confusing, because of the different types of containers. The standard is the one-litre bag (3% fat), for which you must make the one-time purchase of a plastic case to set it in. Or, you can buy the same milk in a carton for about 10% more money.

Halav Amid is "long-life" milk. It comes in a carton and requires refrigeration only after opening.

Milk in bottles is parboiled and doesn't have to be refrigerated at all. Keep it in a cool place, and it should last ten days. The bottle with the blue top has more than 2% fat, with the red top it has only 1% fat. This milk also comes chocolate flavored.

Buttermilk lovers can find it in half-litre cartons. A name to recognize it by is Rivion. Fat content is less than 2%.

Cream for coffee comes in bottles.

If you are planning on whipping up a topping for the plentiful, succulent, inexpensive strawberries (*tootim*) found from January to June, whipping cream comes in a one-quarter litre orange carton or plastic bag. Sugarless *parve* (suitable to serve with meat meals) cream whip also is available.

The last knot to unravel in the dairy cases is the one that pertains to margarine and butter.

The standard margarine has a blue band around its paper wrapper or cup container and is made with soya. It is the least expensive and it comes with or without salt. It can be used for cooking.

Margarine with the gold band is made with milk and is better quality than the blue-band margarine.

A margarine product known as Margania is made of sunflower oil and tastes similar to butter.

Calorina margarine is a dietetic brand.

Another member of the family, Afical, wrapped in blue and silver paper, is used for making pastry dough.

Butter comes in three forms and tastes: the standard is wrapped in silver paper and has no salt; or in gold paper, indicating it is salted. Both of these are called "European-type" butter. The third is known as "Dutch" or "American" and is salty and deeper yellow.

Another goody not to be overlooked in the dairy case is individual-servings of chocolate mousse.

And now that all the above information is being digested (perhaps along with a Milki), we will deal with other food shopping matters.

Bread in Israel usually is sold unwrapped. The loaves simply are

A vendor in the Mahane Yehuda.

tossed on a shelf or left in the containers in which they arrived at the store. You may want to give a loaf a squeeze to check its freshness. The courteous way of doing this is by pulling off one of the plastic bags close by, slipping your hand into it and then fondling the loaf you have your eye on (you'll wish everybody did).

Israeli bread has a crunchy crust. But, surprise, a typical loaf is white. A marvelous black rye is available, but it isn't subsidized, so it is quite expensive. It's worth a splurge now and then. The same goes for the French-style *baguettes*. And don't miss still-warm, fresh from the baker, *lachmaniot* — small bread rolls.

Frozen chicken may be cheaper than fresh chicken. Fresh chickens must have a date of slaughter on their cellophane wrapping. A Ministry of Health regulation requires that fresh chicken be sold within three days of slaughter.

Meat cuts in Israel aren't the same as in the United States. You may find a butcher to whom you can describe how you want to prepare a piece of meat and he will know what to sell you. Mataam, a butcher shop on Rehov Agrippas near Rehov King George, is touted as having an English-speaking staff. They also will deliver.

Frozen schnitzel is available and cooked like veal, but actually is made of chicken or turkey. Also on the market is soy schnitzel. It can have an excellent taste.

In fresh produce, the selection is becoming more cosmopolitan. Iceberg lettuce and kiwi fruit are relatively new. Celery looks ratty. Artichokes appear to be undernourished, and you may never see a blueberry or raspberry. But the little tomatoes will make you yearn for their flavor forever, and the plentiful strawberries are ambrosia.

Custard apples are available in season. They look like green, bloated apples with brown or yellow marks and can be cooked with sugar, lemon and cinnamon.

A *carambola* is a waxy, star-shaped fruit suitable for salad decoration, but fit for making hair grow on your teeth if it is not very, very ripe. It should be brown on the outside.

Another "exotic" is that glorious fruit of Israeli winter, persimmons. Here they are bright colored, sweet and eaten like apples. But beware. They can be hazardous to your digestive system. It is advisable not to eat too many and to eat them when they are very soft. Otherwise, you could find yourself making a sudden trip to the hospital.

A drink you might overlook is Nesher Malt, a non-alcoholic black beer. Kids love it. Advertisements claim that it promotes muscle development — after consumers work off the fat Nesher Malt will give them, no doubt.

Israeli pastry shops are totally seductive, as are their Arab counterparts with their specialties of sticky, sweet, pistachio-filled goodies. You will find your own favorites. If you are in the Old City and want to treat yourself to something less heavenly and rich, but tasty in its own way, try a *beigele*, the soft, doughnut-shaped, sesame-seed covered bread that may or may not be an ancestor of today's hard bagel. When you do, ask for some *zaytar*. It, at no extra charge, will come wrapped in a piece of newspaper. It is a wild spice from the mountains, akin to a blend of oregano and marjoram. For a more flavorful taste, dip your *beigele* in it as you eat.

To get the best food prices, you have to shop around. The *shuk* at Mahane Yehuda often, but not always, is the cheapest place. According to a comparative price report, pasta, beans and lentils not only are cheaper at some supermarkets, but have fewer stones in them.

Even if the price is right, a drawback could be that Mahane Yehuda vendors hate to sell, say, one green pepper. They may renege on their opposition to selling small quantities if you tell them that you, too, loved Menachem Begin.

At Mahane Yehuda and the supermarkets, prices on fresh produce go down on Friday afternoons, before everything closes for Shabbat. But the scene becomes wild with people elbowing each other to reach the tomatoes. And by then, the fight may be over the dregs.

When you become familiar with Israeli food products, try patronizing your neighborhood small business. You will be able to get the food you want and make human contact at the same time. And there will be no arguments over abandoned shopping carts at the check-out counter.

JERUSALEM SCENE:

Malkah, Russian-born, British-raised and very proper, walked into a bakery to treat herself to a cake one summer day. But she was mortified at the sight of masses of flies crawling over the baked goods.

Enraged, she turned on her heels and stormed back out the door, even before the proprietor could ask for her order.

Startled, he ran down the sidewalk after her. "Giveret! (Madame) Giveret!" he shouted. "Why are you leaving?"

She hollered over her shoulders, "Because of the flies on the food. It's disgusting!"

"Giveret," he said in a cajoling tone, "but this is the Middle East."

Toothpaste, Toilet Paper and Diapers

All those favorite brand names from home — Colgate, Ponds, Clairol, Flex, Johnson's, Pampers, Nivea, Vaseline, Tampax and many more — are available in Israel, but at a price fit for grand larceny.

Israeli-made equivalents cost a lot less and often are as good. For hair shampoos and conditioners, I am a fan of those sold at Roots, Rehov Mesilat Yesharim 7, and I know Israelis in the United States who have Nekesheva soap sent to them.

A choice place to buy toiletries at a discount is Millstein's at Rehov Eliashar 5 (at the Revlon sign), off Rehov Yafo, parallel to Rehov Harav Kook. But be prepared to wait in line at this busy store. More items are tucked away in the back room than meets the eye in front, so if you don't see what you want, ask.

Ben-Ben Superzol, Rehov Yafo 44 and Rehov Ben-Hillel 3, and Kolbotek, Rehov Yafo corner of Rehov Strauss, are other establishments that have some of the better prices in town for toothpaste, shampoo, sanitary napkins, detergent, diapers and household cleaning supplies.

Among Israeli-made household cleaning items, Ritz Paz is for washing tile floors, Ram is a scouring powder and Limonite is a dish detergent. Some of the laundry detergents are specifically formulated for hand laundry — which you may find you are doing a lot.

Perhaps the most colorful household item made in Israel is toilet paper. Bright red and deep violet are among the riveting shades to be found. They may make your bathroom interior-decorator pretty, but they will have their impact on you, too. The color rubs off.

If there is a diaper wearer in your family, the Israeli-made versions of Pampers are Titulin, Tafnukin and Tako. Many mothers recommend a Spanish product, Doto, for price, elasticized legs and absorption.

A chain of stores that advertises itself as "American-style bargain stores" is Ayzo Metzia at Rehov Beit Ya'acov 2, Rehov Havatzelet 3 and Rehov Sulam Ya'acov 4 in Ramot. They sell diapers, toys and children's clothing.

To shop for the best bargain in Jerusalem, you need a notebook to jot down prices from one store to the next (even within the same chain), a calculator to figure out the cost per weight or unit price, and endless time.

Shopping Free-For-All

Buying clothes in Jerusalem is a commercial free-for-all. On any particular item made by any particular manufacturer, you can find as many prices as stores you visit. So if the best price is your goal, you must devote time and shoe leather.

Bargains, you are unlikely to find. Clothes are expensive and markdowns are minuscule. To an Israeli shopkeeper's big announce-ment that clothes are selling at a 10% reduction, an American or Canadian merely would shrug, big deal. Reductions increase at the end of the season, but still, for the best price, comparative shopping remains the order of the day.

The generalities — and they are only generalities — are that prices are higher in stores along Rehov Ben-Yehuda and Rehov King George and lower in the dumpy, little places along Rehov Yafo near Mahane Yehuda. Lower prices on the same merchandise tend to exist in East Jerusalem, where you shouldn't be discouraged by the clutter in the store window.

Rock-bottom prices — such as they are — may (please note that word, "may") be set by Ma'ayan Stub, a discount department store at the corner of Rehov Strauss and Rehov Yafo. After that, bargains can pop up in unexpected places — such as the big department store, Hamashbir Lazarchan, for ski jackets — and fail to materialize at expected places.

Ayzo Metzia (See "Toothpaste, Toilet Paper and Diapers") carries children's clothes at a reduction.

Another possibility for saving money is at factory outlets. The same items in Polgat's outlet in the Talpiot Industrial Area may sell for a third less than they cost at Polgat's retail store on Rehov Yafo. About the same goes for shoes bought at the Gali outlet in the Talpiot Industrial Area and at the factory, Na'alei Yerushalayim, in Romema, which is a short walk from the Central Bus Station.

An adventure in clothes shopping usually exists in second-hand shops. Among them is the Ezrat Nashim Thrift Shop at Rehov Ben Shoshan 5. It has clothes for men, women and children, and the income goes to the Ezrat Nashim Geriatric and Mental Hospital. Some commercial establishments are Od Pa'am, at Rehov Yehuda 5 at Derech Beit Lechem; Kolav (for women only) at Rehov Aza 28; and Tanya's Shop (which advertises that it has "class") in the French Hill shopping center.

Chapter 18:
Communication: Reading, Hebrew Classes, Phones, Postal Matters

People of the Book
(Reading in Israel)

Jerusalemites apparently devour books with the gusto of Texans downing chili. Bookstores abound in Jerusalem. They range from the brightly lit Steimatsky stores where never a spec of dust is to be found, to the dark, cluttered Stein Bookstore near Hechal Shlomo, which Saul Bellow wrote about adoringly in *To Jerusalem and Back*.

These numerous stores carry books in an array of languages. But the problem with English-language books is that, even in paperback, their high price-tag makes you think you no longer can read numbers.

At first I felt a great loss without access to a public library or a good bookstore where almost all the books I ever wanted could be found or ordered. Eventually, I found some comforting alternatives.

Among them are two semi-private British and American libraries where all the employees are English speakers. A drawback at both places is that holders of tourist visas aren't allowed to take out books unless they are students on a year's program or, possibly, if they can wrangle a letter from an impressive institution vouching for their serious purpose amidst the stacks. But even if joining is impossible, both libraries have amenities available nowhere else in town, and the collections of both may be used on the premises.

The British Council Library is on the second floor of the Terra

Sancta building at Rehov Keren Hayesod and Place de France. True to character, the British Library is in Spartan, white-washed quarters and in winter is yet another chilly place to be. If you qualify to join, for a modest fee, you can check out books, records and tapes. In any event, there is an extensive collection of British periodicals available for browsing.

Available free is the monthly schedule of the BBC broadcasts. You can find out when to listen to a recording of Cybill Shepherd and Peter Bogdanovich singing "But in the Morning, No" (which has to be a rare opportunity) or a radio adaptation of Henry Fielding's *Tom Jones*.

The American Library is nearby in the American Cultural Center, Rehov Keren Hayesod 9. As the British library is stark, this one is plush, the most comfy reading place in Jerusalem. Enter at ground level and the lobby and stairwell can be a powerhouse display of splashy art, perhaps of brilliantly colored Andy Warhol posters. The library itself, typically American, is overheated in winter.

The policy is the same as at the British Council Library, but many reference materials can be used on the premises, even by a person not allowed check-out privileges. Videocassettes on a variety of subjects may be viewed; the *New York Times Book Review; Rolling Stone* and other periodicals are available as are reference books, and the *Voice of America* schedule for six months. This schedule doesn't contain juicy details like the BBC's. It simply describes briefly and lists the times of specific programs.

To get your very own books at a reasonable price, check out the Book Stop at Rehov Yosef du Nawas 6, east of Rehov Yafo and a block north of Rehov Helena Hamalka. The little store is packed with English-language books, most of them used, American-published paperbacks. The store has new books, too. But you might have to deal with personnel that treats customers with disdain.

Similar establishments are the Book Store in the Clal Building, which some people insist has better prices than the Book Stop, and Yalkut in the City Cellar shopping arcade beneath City Tower (next to Hamashbir). As an added attraction, all three buy books back.

Then there is Sefer v'Sefel. Climb up the stairs at Rehov Yavetz 4, off Rehov Yafo and below Rehov King George. Once in the shop, you will be able to sit and drink coffee or eat ice cream, while you help yourself to a newspaper or used book to read at your leisure right on the spot. You're also free to buy.

Last of all, take advantage of the informal book swaps that go on between English readers. There is no need to be shy about asking a a friend, "Say, do you have any used books to swap or lend?" It happens all the time.

The man on the left stages a protest at the corner of Rehov Balfour and Derech Aza, as close as he can get to the prime minister's house.

None of this, of course, can replace even a fair B. Dalton or Waldenbooks. Nevertheless, Jerusalem might be in the Middle East, but intellectually, it isn't in a desert.

JERUSALEM SCENE:

Speaking of bookishness, the men at the meeting looked like blue-blooded Boston patricians. They wore suits and ties and spoke in modulated tones. The women were counterparts to their mates, the way some proper Bostonian women are — slightly scruffy, no makeup, mousey hair, but strong features. Both men and women took active part in the discussion of a procedural point.

It was difficult to remember that this scene was being played out in the Middle East — in Jerusalem, to be specific — and not in a building at Harvard Yard.

The men and women were attending a meeting in the modern rooms of the Hebrew Union College of the Harvard-Radcliffe Club of Jerusalem. They were discussing a problem and examining options for solving it.

"May I suggest," said one *eminence grise* rising to the occasion, "the Harvard-Radcliffe Club of Singapore has an excellent way of doing this". He then went on to explain.

When Jerusalem is described as the "navel of the world", it's not for nothing. We all know, everything catches in the navel, even a Harvard-Radcliffe Club.

Ulpanizatioln
(Learning Hebrew)

Non-Israelis usually insist that everyone knows English in Israel. It may seem that way, so long as you stick to Rehov King George in Jerusalem and Rehov Disengoff in Tel Aviv. But inevitably, the moment you stray or face a crisis, you can't find anyone who can say more than "America! Good!" in English. I remember my anguish when I had to change buses to Safed in Rosh Pina, and I didn't know on which side of the road I should wait. Shabbat was descending, and buses would disappear before the day's light. Could anyone understand my urgent question? I might as well have arrived from Jupiter. Oh, for a few basic words of Hebrew, I inwardly wailed.

Crises or not, if a person is going to do more than simply pass through a country not his own, he ought to know as much as possible of that country's language.

Fortunately, a marvelous way exists for even abject beginners to get a handle on Hebrew and for those who have familiarity with the language to improve their skills.

It is through that almost miraculous institution, the *ulpan*. An *ulpan* is a program of intensive Hebrew study.

The Israeli *ulpan* pioneered the teaching of a language through that language. Hebrew only is allowed in the room (although students who share the same language find ways of getting around that rule, especially when the teacher's back is turned).

To the uninitiated, little in the world can sound more like gobbledygook than Hebrew. Guttural gobbledygook, at that. And trying to learn the language is like memorizing gibberish. Few Hebrew words relate to any language Westerners know.

Despite that, the *ulpan* method is amazingly effective. The technique has a way of ingraining knowledge no matter what.

The method of teaching brings to mind what the Italians of Parma shouted to an unacceptable tenor after calling him out on stage for what seemed like encore after encore. Finally, he bowed and apologized that he was exhausted. The Parmans hollered, "You'll do it until you learn it." In *ulpan*, through drill, drill and more drill, you'll do it until you learn it.

And now comes what may be your first Hebrew lesson: *Ulpanim* (plural of *ulpan*, masculine ending) refers to classes that meet five mornings a week, usually from 8 a.m. to 1 p.m.; *ulpaniot* (plural, feminine ending) are classes that meet less frequently — three or two times a week, mornings, afternoons or evenings.

While the word *ulpan* is connected with the concept of kibbutz living, *ulpanim* and *ulpaniot* exist simply as day schools all over Jerusalem.

Classes begin in August or September and January or February. But so long as there is space, it is possible to join at any time and for as short as a month. Fees are modest. They don't include books or optional, but choice, outings organized by the school.

Enrollment in classes offers tremendous fringe benefits in addition to the opportunity of learning Hebrew for self-preservation and, let's hope, a better understanding of the country. The fact is, attending *ulpan* is the very best way to meet people in Jerusalem.

New immigrants, old immigrants who want to improve their Hebrew skills, temporary residents and Arabs share the same space for months on end. Your class may be a mix of Moslems, Christians, Jews and even a few stout atheists.

One *ulpan* I was in included a Syrian Orthodox priest from Iraq, a young Christian woman from Ethiopia, many young Arabs from Jerusalem, Bethlehem and Ramallah (who were the stars of the class), a Dutch gynecologist of Christian background who immigrated to Israel despite insisting she hated all religions, and Jews from Switzerland, Holland, Australia, Mexico, France, Tunisia and the United States. One of the latter was a man of Syrian background who startled the Arabs by speaking to them in their language. Among the Tunisians was a convert to Judaism. Just picture us all taking part in the class Chanukah program!

The best source of information about classes is from Hanhalat Halashon at Beit Ha'am, Rehov Bezalel 11, between 8 a.m. and 1 p.m. Sundays through Thursdays. Tel. 224-156. But remember that instruction method of using Hebrew exclusively? Don't expect anyone in the office to speak English.

Bells Are Ringing
(Telephone Matters)

When the chief of investigations, the detective responsible for all the undercover operations and special investigations in Jerusalem moved to a new apartment, he had to wait seven months for a phone to be installed.

During that time, messages would come over his beeper at all hours of the night. He'd have to get into clothes, put on his shoes, make sure he had supplied himself during the day with *assimonim* (telephone tokens) and then hike out to a pay phone to call the police emergency number.

He finally got a telephone when a story of his phoneless status hit the newspapers.

This should tell you something about the Israeli telephone system. But there's another side to the local (lack of) communications service:

while some people still are waiting after nine years (yes, years, not months) for a telephone, once they get it, should they desire an automatic wake-up call day or night, they may arrange that very simply by dialing the proper numbers. Great service — should these people ever get their phone.

And you, should you be lucky enough to rent a flat that has a telephone in it, must keep in mind that the number is and will be in the owner's name. Plead all you want — you won't be able to get it changed to yours. Information never will know from you. Learning to hang onto your friends' telephone numbers is a way of life here, for they, too, may be nonexistent to Bezeq, the telephone company.

Still, you have the responsibility of paying the monthly bill with its basic rental fee, charges for each call (Information, 14, charges for three calls if you ask for a name that appears in the telephone book), plus at least a double layer of taxes. Like all utility bills you pay, keep copies for your final settlement with your landlord.

If no phone exists where you live, all isn't lost. A telephone answering service may be employed. Check the "Golden Pages" (after all, this is the Golden City, not the Yellow City) for a listing of such services.

Never, never step out of your door without a few *assimonim* jingling in your pocket. You never know when you might need to make a call and there will be no handy place to buy tokens. They are available at post offices, hotels and some kiosks.

Directions for using pay phones are given in Hebrew and through diagrams. Pay phones are likely to be tender and sensitive, so treat them accordingly. The most complicated thing to remember is to push up on the finger hole on the bottom right side to get back your *assimon* if your call is not completed or you dial the operator.

Interurban calls may be made by pay phone, but *assimonim* are gobbled up in the process. Have a stack ready. Dump them in, in advance. What isn't used is returned. And don't expect any leeway between the time you hear the recorded message that your tokens are used up and the time you are cut off.

The rates for interurban calls are reduced at 1 p.m., even more between 9 p.m. and 8:30 a.m. The best rate, if not the best time, for calling the United States, Canada and Europe is between 1 a.m. and 7 a.m. Israel time. Israel is two hours ahead of Greenwich Time and seven hours ahead of Eastern Standard Time. Observance of Summer Time (Daylight Saving Time) in Israel can throw those differences off, because it might not coincide with saving-time schedules in other countries.

Anytime you call the telephone company, you may ask for an English-speaking operator. But if you must do business at Bezeq's office at the corner of Rehov Yafo and Rehov Yirmiahu, do not count on finding any employees who speak English. Russian, perhaps, but not English. And take a number to wait your turn.

That's at the main office. However, Bezeq has a store in the City Tower Building, which offers some of the same services, but faster. It is open 8:30 a.m. to 12:30 p.m. daily except Saturdays and also 4 p.m. to 6:30 p.m. Sundays and Thursdays. Since the main object of the store is to sell high-tech phone equipment, you are treated like a welcome customer and not a pest. Phone books are available there without a wait and so are repairs on the telephone itself.

Repairs on the telephone instrument is another surprisingly good service in Israel. If something disastrous happens to your telephone, take heart. While I was carrying on a lengthy conversation, the base of my phone was on the floor between me and my electric heater. Oh, panic! The phone melted! It simply caved in, as if it had been in the soup too long. But someone told me about the telephone company's repair service.

In exchange for my pathetic, lopsided phone, I received a bright new one. What it cost — if anything — I never figured out from looking at my next few bills, but at least I had nothing to try to explain to my landlord.

Time was when all of Israel fit into one telephone book. During those years, the phone book was available in English, which made life easy for a lot of people. When the telephone company had to produce phone books for different parts of the country, the English version fell by the wayside.

Plowing through the Hebrew phone book can present an enormous challenge. But what a sense of achievement when that sought-for name is located! Not long ago, help for Hebrew illiterates was on the agenda. A Jerusalem phone book came out in 1986 that purportedly was in English. But its first edition proved that wasn't so. It was in "Hebrish", a language closely related to Gibberish. For example, most married women's first names in it started with a "V". That was because in the Hebrew version a couple's names can be listed "Yitzchak v'Sarah" ("Isaac and Sarah" in English.) In translation — which was made by computer — Sarah's name came out Vsarah. So there was Vbatya, Vrahel and on and on. Until drastic corrections can be made, the so-called English phone book may offer more of a challenge than the Hebrew phone book. But it may be purchased for approximately $7 through outlets of the *Jerusalem Post* and Steimatzky Bookstores. Further information is available from Atlas, the distributor, at 247-746.

Some Important Numbers:

Police	100
Ambulance	101
Fire	102
Information	14
Operator-assisted overseas calls and rates	18
Collect call from pay phone	(03) 622-881
Complaints or problems with phone line	16 or 666-216

Playing Post Office
(Postal Matters)

Israeli mail service has a whimsical side. Usually mail arrives, but occasionally, it seems to take the alternate route to the moon. I've sent mail from Jerusalem to other Israeli cities which neither reached its destination nor was returned to me. I never received a letter a friend mailed to me in Jerusalem from Jerusalem. On the other hand, I did get a letter from Cairo addressed only with my name, Jerusalem and the wrong ZIP code. I forever marvel how it reached me — unless the fact that the return address, which read "American Embassy", had some influence on the efficiency of delivery.

The matter of Israel's equivalent of a ZIP code can be a problem with mail from the United States. Since the code numbers (*mikud*) for Jerusalem consist of five digits beginning with the number 9, American-sent mail swings through one of several places in California before heading east, unless something clever is done. Putting a hyphen after the first two digits solved the problem for me. Other people insist that merely making sure the numbers appear next to "Jerusalem" and not after "Israel" does the trick.

To learn your code number, ask your neighbor or check at the nearest post office. The telephone book carries the *mikud* listings, but I dare you to figure them out.

Mailboxes are red and may be located almost anywhere. Stuck into walls along a sidewalk is a favorite place.

Packages mailed to you, even small ones, aren't delivered. The postman simply leaves a note in your mail box telling at which post office the package may be picked up. Bring your passport to claim it. There is no duty on packages from overseas valued under $10. If you mail a package overseas, it should be brought to the post office unsealed for inspection.

The Central Post Office, Rehov Yafo 23, is open from 7:30 a.m. to 7 p.m. weekdays and until 3 p.m. Fridays. Closed Shabbat. Most of the major post offices are open continuously from 8 a.m. to 7 p.m. weekdays. Others break from 12:30 p.m. to 3:30 p.m. and close at noon on Wednesdays.

Stamps and air letters are sold also at newsstands and kiosks that display the post office emblem — a leaping white deer on a blue background. The Israelis joke that the deer really is a turtle — that's how slowly Israeli mail moves.

If there are frequent changes in postal rates, it doesn't pay to stock up on air letters or stamps. And anyway, every trip to the post office, where your business is everybody else's, can be interesting.

On one of my errands to the Rehavia post office, where the line often resembles a dog show with all the people who bring Fido to keep them company as they wait, I asked for 10 air letters. The clerk counted them out and then told me to count them, too. So I did. I got to "six, seven, eight ..." when a man at my elbow behind me suddenly bellowed at the clerk, "Nine! Only nine!" (in Hebrew, naturally). Well what else did my neighbor in line have to do except watch the dogs and look out for my interests? Now, he, the clerk and I, and anybody who could crane his neck to see, counted the air letters again. They still totaled nine, and the clerk dutifully handed me another one.

For anyone in a rush, express mail service to the United States exists through the post office. If mailed early, an expressed letter will get out the same day (they say).

An alternative service is Sherut Express, which operates out of the Association of Americans and Canadians in Israel's Jerusalem office. It serves 130 countries, is expensive, but it's there when you need it. Contact the AACI for details.

Be sure to bring stamps from home for the many times you can locate "courier service". Shoving letters into hands of countrymen returning home is a common practice. They drop your letters in a mailbox after they arrive, which speeds delivery enormously. But keep in mind that for security reasons, people may and should be leery of transporting anything from someone they don't know. Your request may be rejected. To avoid that, try offering your letters unsealed.

Members of the AACI may use a mail drop in the association office (this isn't the same as Sherut Express). Members, in a constant flow across the Atlantic, collect mail from the drop and squeeze it into their suitcase.

When word gets around that you are returning home, you'll be amazed at the people you hardly know who ask when your flight will be. Don't be touched by their interest. It isn't personal. It's purely pragmatic. Their next question will be, "Will you have room for a letter or two?"

There's always room for a letter or two.

Chapter 19:
Recreation in the
Land of Creation

Alone and Female in Jerusalem

Coming to Jerusalem alone, I had two major concerns: was it safe and would I have a social life?

Answers I found to the first question appear in the section on "Terrorism" in Chapter 2, "Facts of (Jerusalem) Life".

The freedom of movement I feel here day and night sometimes makes me feel like a carefree kid. Not completely, however. I know that purse snatchers prowl certain hotel areas and, perhaps as a carry-over from life in the United States, I always try to stay alert to my surroundings.

The few negatives that exist are a tiny aspect of life here. The general violence that has come to haunt women's lives in a country such as the United States doesn't exist here. For that reason, Israel can be a glorious, free, liberating experience for a woman.

As for social life, I thought that as a single woman living in Jerusalem — a male-female social life would be zero. Too many wars, I concluded. There can't be available men.

You know what? I was wrong. Israeli men make themselves available.

How many other places in the world can a Jewish woman run to the store for a loaf of bread and be followed home by, not only a Frenchman, but a Jewish Frenchman, who invites her to coffee?

As a woman goes about her business on bustling Jerusalem streets, she frequently finds herself approached by men in a casual, friendly way. Israeli men's standard opening line is, "Do you know what time it is?" or "Do you know where Rehov X is?" Now, they may actually want to know what time it is or where to find Rehov X. Few people in the city seem to own a watch or to have figured out the jumbled streets. (These questions are peculiar to Jerusalem. I don't recall ever being asked either one in Tel Aviv or Haifa).

But if there is another purpose in the question, a woman quickly will know after she gives her answer — any answer ("I don't know the time or the streets") will do.

One man's variation on the standard opener was, "Don't you come from Philadelphia?" He approached me twice, months apart, with the same line. And, oh, yes, I have been asked, "What is your sign?"

If finding out the time or where to find a certain street merely was an opening gambit, expect to hear next, "Where are you from?"; "Do you live alone?" (watch out for that one), and then an invitation "to drink the coffee".

What to answer? Most women can size up a creep before he's uttered a complete sentence. But drinking coffee with a man who is a stranger can be totally harmless and interesting, even if the man isn't Mr. Right.

Ami invited me to drink, not coffee, but cinnamon tea with him after we got in a conversation when he answered an ad I had placed to rent a flat. He was a bright graduate student in political science. I learned things from him about the experiences of Jewish Moroccan immigrants in Israel that I might otherwise not have known.

But for these encounters to remain pleasant, the woman has to retain control. As education students learn in college, they should start out in a classroom being firm with their pupils. They always can lighten up later, but if they begin by being easygoing, control of the class may slip out of their hands, and they may never get it back again.

Taking that as my cue, and after a few missteps, my answer to "Do you live alone?" became, "I live with my aunt and uncle and their five children." The choice was between honesty and self-preservation. Never underestimate the persistence of Israeli men, married or not. I figured I always could "fess up" later, if that seemed the thing to do. Meanwhile, the above answer dampened the enthusiasm of pesky pursuers.

And I told no male over the age of five my address, unless I didn't mind the recipient of that information dropping by whenever the spirit moved him. Unannounced visits are a custom in Israel, but some are inopportune, as well. Not to mention unwanted.

If I accept an invitation to "drink the coffee" or tea, I pay for what I order. As a wonderful American jazz singer advised, "Girl, you pay the cost and be the boss."

While dealing with Jewish men usually is relatively simple, dealing with Arab men can border on becoming an international incident. So let's talk frankly.

Invitations to "drink the coffee" or the mint tea are an integral part of Arab courtesy. It could seem inhospitable for a Western woman to refuse such an invitation. But by accepting, she inadvertently could be sending messages that she is agreeable to more than coffee or tea. Like, "me".

What actually is on her mind — the wish to be gracious, curiosity about the life of someone from one of Jerusalem's mosaics — may not matter at all to the man in question. The sight of Western women with their freedom to come and go as they please, their independence, makes most Arab men's hormones light up like a pinball machine.

If a woman wants to accept coffee or tea and chat with an Arab man for awhile, fine. But as with those Jewish men who want to know what time it is, she should stay in control of the situation. She should in no way feel she has to submit or even tolerate advances that could begin with arm patting and suddenly escalate to a man's pressing his private parts against her. But these incidents don't need the courtesy of coffee or tea to occur. They can happen if a woman merely steps into a shop to look around. While she is checking on the merchandize, the shopkeeper could be checking vigorously on her.

When Jordan occupied Jerusalem, shopkeepers who played feelies with their female customers were subject to stiff penalties by the police. But with the delicate international situation between Arabs and Israelis, these days, a woman has only herself for protection, unless things get rough.

Her being from another culture, and not understanding the innuendoes of a situation, should not make her free game. If she isn't treated with respect, she owes none.

The big difference I've found between Jewish and Arab men is that when I've told a Jewish man on the street who has attached himself to me, to buzz off, we part with a handshake, a smile and good wishes to each other. There is a light-heartedness about the Jewish approach, as if we both know it's all a game, anyway.

But a woman handing a firm "no" to an Arab man probably will hear in return, at the very least, an outraged cry about "friendship". The parting could include a string of obscenities shouted at her in public. The experience could be distressing and humiliating.

The truth is, I was a slow learner about all this. But learn I did.

One day I, now knowledgeable, looked for a *sherut* near Damascus Gate to take me to an Arab village some miles from Jerusalem. An Arab driver assured me his car was a *sherut*. Bargaining settled the fare at $4. According to local custom, as the only passenger, I took the seat next to his, and we were off.

Still in the city, he suddenly put his hand on my thigh. I pushed his hand away and demanded, "Keep your hands off me." Then I added, "You know that if a strange man did this to your sister, you'd kill him." The last line was bravado on my part, but he nodded in agreement.

I was about to tell him to stop the car and let me out, when he turned the car around and drove back almost to where we started. But not quite. Instead of taking me to Damascus Gate, he took me to a place across the street where, I discovered, there were genuine *sherut* loading stands. His car wasn't a *sherut* at all, but a private taxi.

He pointed out which *sherut* I should take to my destination and told me, "Don't pay the driver more than 50 cents." He would have charged me $4.

This episode had a peaceful outcome, and I even saved money. But problems like this one don't arise only between Western women and Arab men who are strangers. There can be problems with men a woman has known for a while.

Ibrahim was a shopkeeper I'd been introduced to through a mutual friend. For years, I had enjoyed drinking tea with him and listening to his poetry recitals and talk of his family.

Then, he decided our relationship should become cozier. I refused. He angrily shook his fist at me and shouted, "I won't open the shop tomorrow. You'll see."

I never went by to check on it.

Na-Eem Me-Od
(Meeting People)

"*Na-EEM Me-OD*" is the Hebrew equivalent of "Pleased to meet you." But in Israel, being the disorganized country it is, formal introductions are few. So how do you meet people in Jerusalem?

That was what I wondered when I arrived knowing no one. But as I said earlier when I told of how I fell in love with Jerusalem, out of my taxi ride from Ben-Gurion Airport to the city came a treasured and enduring friendship with Ezra, the driver, his wife and five children.

One week later, I stopped at the Jewish Agency to track down information on *ulpanim*. The receptionist sent me down the hall to talk with Morty. American-born, long-time Israeli, Morty invited me into his office, asked what I'd like to drink (coffee, tea or juice — the standard Israeli fare) and plied me with questions about who I was, why I was there and so on.

Before that day had ended, two visiting American men and I had gone with Morty to a wedding in Herodion — Herod's ruined fortress southeast of Bethlehem — had danced and feasted at the wedding party in the village of Tekoa and had been shaken up in Morty's ancient auto, as it bounced up and down the hills of the Judean Desert. When we returned to Jerusalem, Morty took us to Mount of Olives and Mount Scopus to see one gorgeous view after another of golden Jerusalem, still golden under its lights at night.

Later, when I wearily climbed out of the car, Morty asked, "Say, why did you come to my office today?" I struggled to remember. "To find out about *ulpans*," I finally recalled. With a tone of amazement, he said, "But I don't know a damn thing about *ulpans*." And so started another friendship important to me.

I met my darling friend, Malkah, a feisty septuagenarian journalist and early settler from the Soviet Union, when she and I shared snippy comments over the uncooperative behavior of a woman ahead of us in the supermarket check-out line. Friday afternoon tea in Malkah's tiny Arab house became a ritual — our own ceremony to usher in Shabbat.

So these are among the ways you meet people. Jerusalemites are curious, talkative, generous-hearted, unpredictable and spontaneous. Thanks to them, being a stranger in Jerusalem is but a transitory stage.

Granted, women should recognize that some of the red-carpet treatment they receive has sexual overtones. But suffice it to say that anyone in Jerusalem — male or female — who has a sense of adventure and humor will make friends rapidly. Anyone who is timid should pretend not to be, and the results will be the same as for a gregarious soul.

Serendipity works beautifully in Jerusalem, but there's no need only to trust to luck. You can take matters into your own hands.

First of all, you can be an initiator of conversation with a stranger. No one in Jerusalem will look at you peculiarly for doing so, since everybody does it.

Still, that can be a chancy tactic. More organized ways of meeting people exist. A newcomer to the city may join interest groups and clubs, enroll in *ulpan*, take classes, attend lectures and call Jerusalemites whose names he or she has gotten from mutual friends.

Organizations

The first order of business for anyone in Jerusalem for any length of time at all should be to join the **Association of Americans and**

Canadians in Israel, located at the rear of Rehov Pinsker 11, Tel. 636-932. A year's AACI membership costs only a few dollars and entitles you to members' parties and a slew of activities, some according to age group or marital status. AACI also has counselors with free advice for members on almost any problem they have. In addition, the organization has the most complete list of its kind of Americans and Canadians in the country. It could serve as the only means of tracking down that other Ann Arborite in Israel.

Another terrific organization is **Israel Academic Projects,** Rehov Dis Kin 3, Tel. 638-176. Don't be intimidated by its imposing title. You don't have to be in academia to join. Just pay the dues, about $4. That puts you on the mailing list to get the monthly announcement of seminars and study trips, which can cost about $25. They almost always are excellent.

One study trip, for instance, examined "Different Aspects of Minority Life in Israel." Led by an expert on Palestinian Arab Affairs from the Haifa Technion, it began at dawn for Jerusalem dwellers who were driven to Haifa for a briefing, then visited the first permanent Bedouin settlement in the Galilee, lunched with Arab dignitaries in Nazareth, toured a joint Arab-Jewish school project, attended meetings in the mixed Arab-Jewish city of Acco and stopped at an Arab village.

The IAC sponsors some four or five activities each month. You quickly become familiar with the other participants.

Lectures

Ashkenazi immigrants from Middle Europe brought with them to Israel not only their love of Brahms and Mozart, but their devotion to lectures and discussion groups.

Should you desire, you could be lectured to almost day and night (and that's in English, even). Talks could be on Israeli politics, the economic situation, Israeli politics, Arab propaganda, Israeli politics, aspects of Judaism and Israeli politics. They could be delivered by a member of the Knesset, the mayor of Jerusalem, a rabbi who used to be a Christian minister or a Hebrew University professor, all experts in their field.

Talks are scheduled most frequently in English at the **Israel Center** (Orthodox Union), Rehov Strauss 10, and the **Center for Conservative Judaism,** Rehov Agron 2.

And when they aren't listening to their choice of mental enrichment, lecture fans can provide another vehicle for human contact.

Classes

An entire section has been devoted to the rewards, both social and practical, of enrolling in an *ulpan*. See "Ulpanization" in Chapter 18.

Courses taught in English at **Beit Ha'am**, Rehov Bezalel 11, which begin after the High Holidays, can be tremendously rewarding. You may be extremely fortunate and discover that your Jerusalem sojourn coincides with Jeff Halper's courses on Jerusalem history or the culture of Afro-Asian Jews.

Clubs

For a person who still has unfilled time or needs, special interest groups exist: Overeaters Anonymous, bridge, yoga, aerobic dancing, folk dancing, Bingo, Emotions Anonymous, Singles 30-Plus, Rotary Club, Scrabble and Al-anon among them. Athletic groups are discussed later in this chapter. The Friday *Jerusalem Post* lists meeting times and places. Some of these events are conducted in English.

Friends of Friends

And last of all, you can pick up the telephone, which may seem a little scary at first, and call those names mutual friends have given you. This goes on all the time — and sometimes gets out of hand. Margo, from New York originally, won't let anyone except her immediate relatives west of the Atlantic have her telephone number —

Newer residences on Rehov Dubnov in Talbia, near the Jerusalem theater.

and then only with the strictest warning that if they pass it on to anyone else coming to Jerusalem, she will call them collect every week.

Margo isn't a grouch by nature, but circumstances turned her into one on this matter. She found that heretofore unmet American after American invited himself, family and friends over for dinner. Then, when some of these self-invited guests used her place as a crash pad for weeks at a time, enough was enough.

If mutual friends want you to deliver a message to a Jerusalemite, by all means do so. But don't force anything. If you'd like to meet the person, you can issue the first invitation. Invite the Jerusalemite to your place or a cafe (the treat's on you) for coffee and cake.

Evening social life usually doesn't begin until 9 p.m. And how can Israelis then roll out of bed to get to their jobs that often start at 8 in the morning? As one sabra earnestly explained to me, "Oh, Israelis don't need much sleep."

Hanging Out in Jerusalem

Hanging out in Jerusalem is more than a means of seeing and being seen. It is, first and foremost, a way of being involved in conversation.

Yes, there is a lot of prayer in Jerusalem, but talk comes first: talk about politics, the economy, the latest jokes, gossip — and religion. A constant hum fills the air as people earnestly, often emotionally, engage in their favorite social activity.

And since talking is more comfortable when participants sit down, drink some coffee and maybe eat a cake or two — so, why not?

Keep in mind that an order of tea brings you your average order of tea — which in Israel means served in a glass and often with mint or a piece of cinnamon — pronounced "kinnamon". But if you order "coffee", you usually get instant coffee, generally referred to as "Nescafe", or, simply, "Nes". If you order "black coffee", you get Turkish coffee. A slang term for it is *"botz"*, which translates as "mud", which speaks for itself. Another coffee term is *"longo"*, which is a large espresso with milk on the side.

This act of being kind to one's feet and tummy while exercising the mouth has made Jerusalem's focal point of talk (after the Knesset, of course) the Ben-Yehuda Mall and its cafes. What could be more pleasant? On a nice day, one can sit outside, discuss, eat, drink and watch the world go by in the canyon of conversation. On a bad day, one can be cozily jammed indoors while carrying on the same activities in warmth.

Almost any cafe on the mall is good for relaxing, but the **Cafe Atara** is special because it is rife with memories. It doesn't look too different from the way it did in the '30s to the '50s, when it was the center of Jerusalem's cultural and intellectual life. The same people who hung out there then may hang out here still. They could talk about how the Atara deliberately had no liquor license during the Mandate Period, so as to discourage British soldiers from patronizing the place and discovering members of the Jewish underground army who held meetings there.

Even today, the best Atara drink isn't alcoholic, but a cup of hot chocolate — rich and under a mountain of whipped cream.

Other top places for hanging out in Jerusalem are **Ta'am, La Belle, Fink's** and **Hatzarif**. Each is far different from the others. **Ta'am** is on Rehov King George opposite the old Knesset building, now the site of the Government Tourist Information Office. Knesset members used to sit in this tiny, narrow cafe and drink tea and plot political moves. Today, Ta'am faithful sit, drink tea and plot chess moves. Ta'am also was the birthplace of the Black Panthers organized by the Musrara neighborhood's impoverished youth. These days, a lot of the clientele are liberal Peace Now supporters.

Whatever their politics, presiding over them with kindly patience and humor is Mordechai Kop, a right winger and Gush Emunim supporter. He also is known as being full of a lot of useful information and the best walking referral agency if you need the name of a lawyer. But from the diversity of his customers, you'd think Kop would have to quash possible political explosions.

But, no. Old-time luminaries and current firebrands savor the fine cakes — small, sweet *challahs* on Fridays, delicious *Oznei Hamman* at Purim and *soofganiot* at Chanukah — play chess, even sip Israeli cognac and, of course, talk.

No one as colorful as Kop gives character to **La Belle**, near the southern end of Rehov Rivlin. The atmosphere is a lot tonier than at Ta'am. La Belle has a continental look to it with its solid wooden tables and white stucco walls hung with art. Around the corner from the *New York Times* Jerusalem Bureau and close to Beit Agron, where the foreign press checks in, La Belle often becomes a gathering place for journalists — notorious gossipers the world over.

Fink's at Rehov Hahistadrut 2, dates back to 1932 and is Israel's best-known social life institution. It is tiny (six tables and an 11-stool bar) resembles something from London's Fleet Street and usually is jammed. In 1985, the establishment was named by *Newsweek* magazine and Ballantine Scotch as among the 52 greatest bars in the world. Fink's fans have decorated the walls with contributions of humorous bar signs, drinking glasses and mugs from just about any place you can think of. Fink's attracts the glitterati, visiting international movie stars and the ubiquitous press. But Shmuel Azneli, who runs the place, isn't impressed.

He refused entrance to Henry Kissinger when Kissinger insisted on taking over the whole place. " Mooli" wasn't about to chase out his regular customers for anybody. He told me he wasn't interested "in the nouveau-riche or big shots."

The place is open only in the evening, but not on Fridays. Don't go for dinner without a reservation (Tel. 234-523). Goulash is a specialty. Escargots are also served. Needless to say, Finks' isn't kosher.

The last of the top choices for hanging out is **Hatzarif**, Rehov Horkenos 5. Here are Jerusalem's young, beautiful people and such celebrities as the controversial, often morose politician, Yossi Sarid, and the Druse journalist, Rafik Halabi — often seen with their heads together.

At night, Hatzarif is romantic. A floodlight illuminates greenery outside a glass wall, and on a winter's night, a roaring fire blazes in the fireplace. But the place has drawbacks. Usually crowded and with all the talk that goes on, the room achieves a noise level that ties with a jet at takeoff. Also, Hatzarif isn't kosher and serves ham, which puts it off limits for a lot of people. Still, it can be a great place for lingering over mint tea and catching a rare view of Jerusalem citizenry.

For less trendy, less historical, but still enjoyable places to hang out, there are the following:

The many establishments along **Rehov Rivlin** and **Rehov Yoel Salomon**. People go in and out of these until they find the kind of crowd they seek.

Savion, Rehov Aza 12. Located on an island between two busy Rehavia streets and hidden by shrubbery, Savion is venerable, but somewhat seedy. Since the restaurant is close to the prime minister's residence, foreign correspondents spend time here as they wait for a story to break.

Cafe Calderon, Rehov King George 4. Its cakes scream, "Eat me", from the display window. Look on time at Cafe Calderon as a reward for all the walking up and down hills one does in Jerusalem.

Cafe Rondo, Independence Park. The top of the round building that is Cafe Rondo can be seen from the sidewalk along Rehov King George. This is a place for a quiet retreat. You can sit outside under a canopy and enjoy the park's (shrinking) greenery — and daydream. The slow pace carries over into service. Cafe Rondo is recommended more for its peacefulness than its cakes.

The Zionist Confederation House, at the end of Rehov Emile Botta (in Yemin Moshe, behind the King David Hotel) has teatime from 4 p.m. to 6 p.m. You may munch pumpkin or rhubarb bread in this new building constructed on an historical site on a steep slope overlooking the Old City.

The Cinematheque Restaurant, off Derech Hevron. With its connection to the Cinematheque movie theater, the restaurant has become chi-chi for its intellectual aura, good food and glorious view.

Besides these, the Old City explodes during July and August days with young tourists hanging out in cafes, particularly in the Arab sector. They often stay in the Old City's many church hostels to absorb the area's colors, sounds and aromas. But at night, the Old City locks up tight.

Also in the summer — and this brings us back to the Ben-Yehuda Mall — entertained by street musicians from other countries performing here day and night, a person can hang out by sitting on the brick edge of one of the planters in the middle of the mall. From that spot, she can take it all in and surely find people with whom to carry on a conversation, even without the price of coffee, tea or cake.

For those occasional times when you'd rather see than be seen, there are the coffee shops at the **King David Hotel** and the **Jerusalem Skylight** restaurant at the top of the Eilon City Tower at Rehov Ben-Yehudah 34. At the hotel, you can sit on the terrace and peacefully observe the play of light on the walls of the Old City. Offhours, you can nurse a drink atop the city while you look down like an eagle on Jerusalem, watch the city change colors as the day progresses and, at the same time, keep an eye on all those people hanging out on Ben-Yehudah Mall below.

Digging for Roots

Jewish genealogy is well documented in the Bible. Jews don't refer to themselves as "members of the tribe" without good reason.

But what happened between those ancient Biblical days and now? Wouldn't we all like to know? Persons descended from Spanish Jews, who often kept track of their family history, or those whose ancestors lived in a nation of compulsive record-keepers, like Germany or Austria, have the best chance at uncovering some of those mysteries for a few hundred years back or even more.

But Jews whose background stems from what now is the Soviet Union — where most North American Jews came from — or from North Africa — where most Jews in Israel came from — realistically shouldn't expect to learn more about their families after a dig in the limited Jewish archives than they have learned already from elderly Aunt Sarah.

But, if one must dig while in Jerusalem (and who can resist?), there still may be possibilities at various archival collections in the city of acquiring some general knowledge of the area from which one's family came.

Before starting out, a person seeking his roots should resign himself to looking on the venture as a test of one's frustration level — for a lot of reasons.

To avoid the first stumbling block, it should be remembered that people who work at these archives speak a language most of us don't — and I don't mean a language like Serbo-Croatian. Their language is the terms of their trade. When they refer to "genealogy", they mean specifically birth, marriage and death records. The rest of the information they deal with is called "communal" — referring to places, not people, except when people had a connection with communal life. If an ancestor was a member of, say, a community board — or if that ancestor dealt with a community board — tidbits about that person may be uncovered.

But just because no one kept genealogical records in pre-Soviet Berezno on the Shlutz River, where Grandpa came from, doesn't mean that discovering an archive's communal record from Berezno — such as a local lumberman's receipt book — can't provide its own thrill.

The *Guide to the Archives in Israel* tells in English what information is located where in Israel. It is available at the Jewish National and University Library Archives (see below). It isn't easy for a novice to use.

Below are places in Jerusalem where you can try to unearth the hidden past. Keep in mind, however, that financial support for these archives is low on Israel's priority list, and helping the public isn't the employees' main job.

Central Archives for the History of the Jewish People

The Central Archives, crammed into a few tiny rooms on the Hebrew University Givat Ram campus, probably has the most extensive collection of documents concerning Diaspora Jews. Basically, the bulk of information at the Central Archives is drawn from France, Italy, Holland and Czechoslovakia. Except for Poland, there is little from Eastern Europe. As Hadassah, a staff person, commented to me, "We have information on places where most Jews don't come from."

According to Hadassah, because people wanting more information about their backgrounds seem to know that the Central Archives has an item from the 12th century, they often have hopes that the Archives will be able to trace their ancestry halfway back to Rabbi Akiva.

But the fact is, she said, that a particular item often consists of a microfilm of minimal importance. And this is an exception in the Central Archives. Most of the documentation there goes back only to the 17th century. And most of the material is communal.

Unfortunately, Jewish history contains little genealogically documented continuity — the very thing diggers of roots hope most to find. Hadassah wearily said she would appreciate it if people realized, "We don't keep papyrus and stone tablets here."

Something to remember before attempting to look through records in this or any similar institution is that, much to the surprise of many roots-diggers, English wasn't the language in which these records were kept. But the Central Archives offers a little help by listing place names in its catalogs, in Latin characters.

Specialists in various languages work on different days. They may be able to spare some time to offer a translation. But there are no promises.

The Sprinzak Building, which houses the Central Archives, is in a string of buildings to the right after entering Hebrew University gates. There may be a name on the exterior by now. If not, Sprinzak is after the Popick, Miami Buildings. Go downstairs and look for Room 13.

> Hours are 8:30 a.m. to 2:30 p.m. Sunday through Thursday; to 12:30 p.m. Friday. Tel. 584-258.

Jewish National and University Library

This may be the best place for genealogical information. The Jewish Archives, upstairs in the library, has *pinkassim* (registers) of births and deaths from a wide range of communities, including North Africa and the Soviet Union. But there aren't a lot. The Russian *pinkassim*, for example, come from only 17 towns and villages.

The archives is a convenient place to look through the "Guide to the Archives in Israel". If you find in it a listing of a document you would like to see, you must fill out an order slip and deposit it in the main room on the main floor. Then you wait (bring a book to read) for the requested material to surface (and hope that it will surface in an expected place).

Before saying farewell to the order slip, fix the color of its print in your mind. The color indicates the room in which the requested material ought to appear. Should the material not be where you were told to find it, you will be quizzed on the color of the print. If you can't answer, it's to the back of the line with you.

The Jewish National and University Library is the large building at the end of the walk that continues past the Sprinzak Building. To find its Jewish Archives, take an elevator to "comah bet" (when last seen, there weren't numbers on the elevator buttons), go left, then right. The door to the archives is on the right.

> Circulation hours are 9 a.m. to 6:50 p.m. Sunday through Wednesday, to 2:50 p.m. Thursday, to 12:50 p.m. Friday. Reading Rooms: 9 a.m. to 9:45 p.m. Sunday through Thursday, to 12:50 p.m. Friday. Tel. 585-027.

Yad Vashem Archives

As would be expected, most of the material in Yad Vashem's Archives Building deals with the German World War II slaughter of 6 million Jews. Also, as the archives director pointed out to me, the material really is for scholars.

But there is a collection of some 600 *yizkor* (memory) books. After World War II, survivors from the same communities got together to commemorate their former home and the people in it by recording their recollections. Some of the accounts go back into the 19th century. These *yizkor* books contain far more information on Eastern European Jewry than any other source. The reading room staff person may be helpful and find a *yizkor* book of interest to you. But don't expect it to be in English.

The archives building is at the right of the parking lot, opposite the base of the Avenue of the Righteous.

If you seek information about someone who may have died in the Holocaust, inquire at Yad Vashem's Hall of Names, where biographical data on victims are being compiled. It is located upstairs in the main building. There, you write the name of the person you are interested in on a slip of paper and give it to the attendant. He will disappear into a back room and return with a container resembling a shoe box. Then he silently will rifle through the papers inside it trying to find a name that matches the one you gave him. Considering the circumstances of the search, the wait can be excruciating. It may be the only time that a roots-seeker hopes not to find an ancestor's name.

> Hours are 9 a.m. to 4:45 p.m. Sunday through Thursday,
> to 1:45 p.m. Friday. Tel. 531-202.

Archives of the Sephardi Community

For tracking down information from Ottoman or British-Mandated Palestine, the Archives of the Sephardi Community, Rehov Havazelet 12a, is rich in communal material, but, again, poor in genealogy.

Hatefutsoth (Diaspora Museum)

The ease and help of a computer in searching family roots can be yours for a fee of approximately $50 and a trip to the University of Tel Avi Campus, Tel Aviv. But the list of names isn't extensive. Funds for the **Jewish Genealogy Center**, inaugurated at the Diaspora Museum in 1985, are so limited that estimates are it will take 200 years just to register all the Jewish names that exist today in Israel. Never mind the Diaspora.

Perhaps the newly established **Jerusalem Genealogical Society** will spur interest in the field. It is the first such organization in Israel. Check the Friday *Jerusalem Post* for its telephone number.

Be a Sport
(Athletics in Jerusalem)

Moshe, a Jerusalemite born in ultra-Orthodox B'nai Brak, is an Orthodox rabbi. You could pigeonhole him as such on first sight with his chest-long, graying beard, his black suit and little black fedora precariously perched on his head. But one thing about him — out of the ordinary in any circle — is that he is 6 feet 4 inches tall.

And then, it turns out, this Orthodox rabbi is a dedicated swimmer. He also is an expert scuba diver.

Now there's a picture to demolish a stereotype — a 6-foot-4 bearded rabbi wearing a snorkel.

A generality seems to be that Jewish men are myopic, 120-pound weaklings who never leave the library. I don't know about you, but I'll take brains over brawn anytime, but the generality doesn't stand up to facts.

Israelis love sports. And they love the outdoors. They combine both whenever they can. Those aren't tourists toe-to-toe on the Tel Aviv beach. They participate in sports and they adore watching them.

Within the city of Jerusalem, athletic activities from mountain climbing practice to horseback riding are open to anyone willing to bestir himself.

But the most consuming sports activity in Israel is soccer. Israelis play soccer, watch soccer, talk soccer, scream soccer. Soccer (called "football") is the national passion.

It isn't only a matter of kids getting together to play soccer after school in almost every park. Men who graduated from Rehavia Gymnasia more than 25 years ago, vault the fence on the school grounds every Friday afternoon to play an all-out soccer game whether it rains, hails, snows or their wives object. For them, there's no such thing as a soccer "season". It's something they do all year around.

But professional soccer lasts from October to May. During that time, the country is in a soccer frenzy. Soccer fans don't believe in repressing a single emotion the game arouses in them. And the game arouses plenty of emotions. Fans storm the field with little provocation on behalf of their favorite team, Betar or Hapoel.

Some people blame such bad behavior on the bad facilities. For many years, the YMCA has loaned its field, not really designed for these events. "The place is worse than a cattle pen," one soccer lover complained to me. A battle over where to put a permanent soccer field in Jerusalem has raged for many years. Meanwhile, the YMCA field has to do.

People who live across the street from the field — especially in flats on higher floors — discover on Saturday game afternoons that long-lost relatives suddenly have found them. Balconies are jammed with fans watching the game from on high.

But balconies aren't the only places for grabbing a free peek. Young boys sit in nearby trees or peer through any opening they find in the wall around the field. Police department metal barricades make excellent ladders when turned on end. Lots of boys, and men, too, stand on them to view the game where they can.

Inside, fans press transistor radios against their ears, for the field has no loudspeaker system, and this is the only way they can hear as well as see. Meanwhile, they nervously crack *garinim*.

Every so often, the powers that be in regard to the soccer games conclude that the ruffians in attendance would mind their manners better if only more women were at the game. So then, a woman accompanied by a man is admitted free.

But the rest of the time, women, like anyone else, need to buy a ticket in advance at the ticket outlets in the city center. The price is about $8.

Tennis

More and more, the hollow sound of a tennis ball being lobbed across a tennis court is heard in the land. Tennis is booming in the Holy Land. Two reasons explain why.

One is that it's an inexpensive way of getting slum kids off the streets. Another is that it's an inexpensive way for Israel to develop competitors in international athletic meets.

The Israel Tennis Center in Katamon beat out Tel Aviv as the largest tennis center in Israel when it opened in 1983 with 18 all-weather courts. But how long will Tel Aviv accept being second, especially to Jerusalem?

The center is open seven days a week. Children under 18 play free from 2 p.m. to 7 p.m. and may borrow equipment. Details on hours and costs are from the tennis center, Rehov Elmaliach 5, Tel. 413-866. Bus No. 4 gets you there.

Moadon Ha'oleh, Rehov Alkalai 9, has a tennis court, but it is open only to Moadon members. To be accepted as a member, you should expect to be in the country for at least a year.

The Moadon court, too, is available daily. Call 633-718 for details. The closest bus is No. 15.

Swimming

We've all seen those posters touting the glories of Israeli beaches, but the truth is, for anyone living in Jerusalem, going for a swim — even in a pool, let alone a beach — is a pain. Nearby pools are expensive and/or often crowded. Getting to the Mediterranean beaches is a *shlepp*.

Beaches really aren't so far away, but once ensconced in Jerusalem, it's amazing how quickly you pick up the landlocked mentality of the city and how your concept of distance shrinks to Israeli size.

Tel Aviv beaches are the easiest to get to, what with the city only an hour away by bus and buses running one right after the other.

But there, beaches can be crowded and the water can be dirty. A black flag on the beach tells you if water is unfit for swimming. What's more, thieves love the Tel Aviv beaches for the "easy pickin's" available. They aren't ordinary thieves, but specialists in their trade. Some specialize in spiriting away your belongings beside you on the sand. Some are experts in breaking into bathers' cars. They may even have a union that prevents one specialist from encroaching on the area of another specialist.

Don't assume there aren't thieves at other beaches. It's better to assume there are, so you take proper precautions.

A less convenient beach to get to, but worth exploring as a Tel Aviv alternative, is at Ashkelon, where the sand is great and the surf is gentle. By bus, you may have to travel up to two hours to get there.

As for swimming pools, most of the pools in the Jerusalem area are open from the beginning of May through September. Among those that are public are the **Jerusalem Pool** in Baka on Rehov Emek Refaim, north of Rehov Azarva; and pools in **Kiryot Hayovel** on Rehov Zangwill, some distance north of Derech Manahat, and in **Ramot**, where the pool is heated all year. Membership at **Shoresh**, in the Judean Hills, Tel. 538-172, includes admission to the Jerusalem Pool. The cost of admission everywhere is higher on Shabbat.

While public pools usually allow single day admission on weekdays, most pools, private and some public, require annual memberships ("subscriptions", as they are called here). Several private pools are out of town, but like just about everything in Israel, accessible by bus. Tennis courts and a separate children's pool can be on the grounds at many of them.

Among private pools ringing Jerusalem are those in the **Jerusalem Forest** (Tel. 416-060, 412-246), **Kibbutz Ma'aleh Hahamisha** (342-591) and **Ramat Rahel** (715-711). Subscriptions are available for weekdays only or for seven days a week.

Hotel swimming pools are another option. Most hotels invite you — for a price. That price could be at least $10 a dunk. The **Sheraton Jerusalem Plaza** cushions the cost by allowing a free day at the hotel pool for the cost of a lunch. Pay $10-$15 for the meal, and you get the whole day at the pool. But after gorging on *shwarma*, chicken, *shishlik* and endless orange juice, you could swim like a rock.

Hotel swimming pool subscriptions are expensive. Membership approaches $1,000 for a couple to have access seven days a week at the **King David** pool. It must be filled with champagne.

Persons who are swimmers rather than sunbathers should keep in mind that pools at **Ramat Rahel**, the **Laromme Hotel, Beit Ha'Noar Ha-ivri** on Sderot Herzog and the **YMCA** are open all year round.

A special feature of pools at the Jerusalem Forest, the Ramada Renaissance Hotel and the Laromme Hotel is that one afternoon a week is reserved for men only and another for women.

Not to be overlooked, should they still exist in spite of the pressure from the ultra-Orthodox to have the place closed, are the Turkish Baths in an old building at Rehov Yehaskel 36 in the Bucharan Quarter. Tel. 286-961. The Turkish Baths accommodate only one sex on its premises at a time.

This is the real thing. The narrow corridors, low ceiling and cloying dampness tell you you're in a genuine Turkish bath establishment. And this one dates back to 1890. Within its maze of rooms are three indoor pools and one outdoor pool, plus a place on the roof for tanning all over. There is a sauna, a "reducing salon" and a "hairdressing salon" to get the strands back together after all that. In a side room, camel-hair Arab carpets cover divans and floor where bathers may watch TV, play backgammon or even picnic on their own food, if there's nothing tempting at the snack bar.

Horseback Riding

For horseback riding across the desert, several options exist that cost between $10 and $15 an hour. Included are:

Jerusalem Forest Horse Farm, Tel. 533-585.

The Judean Desert Ranch near Kfar Adumin, Tel. 240-419, 241-769.

The Anatot Ranch, east of Pisgat Ze'ev, Tel. 352-755.

Amir's Ranch, Atarot, near the Jerusalem Airport, Tel. 852-190.

I'm familiar with **Amir's Ranch**. The easiest way to get there is to take a *sherut* for Ramallah at the *sherut* stand across the street from Damascus Gate. Get off at the turn to the airport.

At the ranch, you might find the owner, Roni, a burly, several-times-over war-scarred Israeli. His English is limited, but his enthusiasm isn't. His three children might be there, too. The boys handle the horses; the girl stands at the microphone in the corner of the large main room and pretends to be the latest hit pop singer.

Evenings, the ranch house becomes a "pub". The English term has remained in Israel, but there's never been an English pub like this one. The sound of Arab music and the sight of an undulating belly dancer fill the place. Customers at the pub are "Moslems, Jews, Christians — who knows?" says Roni with equanimity. "I don't check identity cards at the door."

Roni has a number of horses to choose from. They all look as if they are the objects of tender love and care. Riding them costs about $15 an hour. Trails offer a view of the heights of Nebi Samuel, the traditional burial place of the Prophet Samuel.

Getting back to Jerusalem from the Amir Ranch is more of a problem than getting there. On my last inquiry, Egged bus No. 70 from Ramallah ran only every one-and-a-half to two hours. An alternative is being able to hail a *sherut* with room for an additional passenger or two that is returning to Jerusalem.

For the dedicated equestrian, the **Society for the Protection of Nature in Israel** (SPNI) sponsors two-day horseback trips. The SPNI flyer says that on these trips, you will ride "among wildflowers, stone terraces of fields cultivated for thousands of years, visit mountain springs, historical sites" and enjoy "panoramic views". Are you hitching up your riding britches?

The SPNI recommends previous riding experience for these jaunts, which cost about $60. The trips are conducted in English. Details and dates are available from SPNI, Rehov Helene Hamalka 13. Tel. 222-357, 244-605.

The existence of riding stables seems to be a big mystery to people who deal with tourist information. The Israel Sports and Riding Association has a booklet of recommended stables. You may write for it at Mercaz Hapoel, Rehov Ha'arba'a 8, Tel Aviv.

Hiking

Thanks to the SPNI, Jerusalem and all Israel is a hiker's paradise. The SPNI has a clutch of walking trips in Jerusalem itself. Some examples: a walk through the Rehavia neighborhood guided by an architect; a walk into Kidron Valley and up the mountain side to the Arab village of Silwan.

Some of the SPNI walks last only a few hours, some for days. The SPNI brochure clearly indicates which are the tough ones and which are in English. Brochures are available from the SPNI or the Government Tourist Information Office on Rehov King George.

Cricket

For watching (admission is free and you have your choice of almost 20,000 seats) and playing, the **Hebrew University's stadium** in Givat Ram resounds with the thwack of leather on willow every other Saturday during the summer.

The British brought cricket here, and immigrants from England, South Africa and India, along with the generosity of the university, are keeping it alive.

The Body Beautiful

Now there no longer is any need for *falafel* to make more of you. Now you can eat and laugh, even in Israel, because health clubs and gyms have blossomed. Among them is the plush **Jerusalem Hilton Hotel Health Club** with 14 Nautilus machines in a room that looks like the Nautilus torture chamber you left back home. Not only will the trainers assist you, they will keep a chart on your progress and, occasionally, give you the pinch test.

A place for anyone who can do without the Hilton's sauna, whirlpool and fancy price is **Samson's**, at Rehov Yoel Salomon 1, Tel. 247-526. Men and women work out at separate times.

Mountain Climbing

The name may be an exaggeration, but the **Israel Alpine Club** is a group that gets out there and does its energetic thing Friday afternoons. Ah, well, there's all of Shabbat in which to recover.

The Alpine Club's trysting place is in the Hinnom Valley, below Mount Zion at 1 p.m., or so.

At various other times, intrepid souls can be found rappelling against Suleiman's Wall of the Old City between Jaffa Gate and the walk up to Mount Zion.

Running

The other strenuous event that takes place before the day of rest is the weekly meeting of the **Israeli Trail Blazers Running Club**. Members don their running shoes at 2 p.m. in Sacher Park, near the underpass below Rehov Ruppin. Runs are four kilometers and more, but Gabe Shamir, who oversees details, insists that if four kilometers might as well be 40 to a novice, he or she still is welcome to join. As proof, he promises homemade peanut butter as a treat after the run, courtesy of a local health-food store.

Annual membership is about $15. Fringe benefits are discounts on sporting goods equipment, a running club T-shirt, camaraderie and, of course, the peanut butter. Shamir may be reached at 669-494, or check at the office of the Association of Americans and Canadians in Israel (AACI).

Scrabble

You find all that physical exercise exhausting, and you'd rather exercise your brain?

There is plenty of opportunity. Membership in the **Jerusalem Scrabble Club** is among them. For about $20, members get access to tables and competition with other players with either English or Hebrew

Scrabble boards. But no peanut butter.

For variations in mental gymnastics opportunities, bridge clubs, backgammon clubs, poker clubs and a myriad of other such groups abound. Check with the AACI or read the Friday *Jerusalem Post* for information on how to get in touch with them.

Reel Life in Jerusalem
(Going to the Movies)

New York film critic Pauline Kael wrote a book entitled *"I Lost It at the Movies"*. In Jerusalem, a film critic could write a book entitled, *"I Couldn't Find the Movies"*.

The location of Jerusalem movie theaters seems to be classified information. You can read Israel's state secrets in any morning newspaper. That's more than you can do on the whereabouts of Jerusalem's picture palaces.

The *Jerusalem Post's* Friday edition, for example, carries more than a page of advertisements of what's playing in movie theaters in Jerusalem and every other city in the country.

The ads tell the name of the theater, the name of the movie, when it's playing, how many weeks it already has been playing — but not where to find the theater.

And because movie theaters in Jerusalem don't have the familiar exterior trappings of traditional movie theaters in Europe and the United States, a person wanting to catch a flick soon feels as if she is trying to fight her way into a secret society. True, the Edison, which used to be the place in town where everyone who was anyone stumbled over each other in the dark, does indeed resemble a classical movie theater as we knew them before the last picture show. But the Edison, being in the midst of a growing ultra-Orthodox neighborhood that doesn't look kindly on such frivolity, may have its own last picture show one day soon.

So if you hanker to go to the movies, you have to look sharp as you walk through the city, especially in the city center, where most of the movie houses are. Occasionally, photos of film scenes on outside walls give a hint that a theater is nearby. But once you figure out where the theater is, the next step is to find the ticket booth. Ticket booths usually aren't located where they logically (to us) should be — near the entrance. They could be — and sometimes are — around the corner.

The price can be about $3 for a first-run American movie. That may seem like a bargain, but wait until you find out what you get for the money.

In the lobby you may purchase soft drinks to spill and make the floor sticky and popcorn to crunch underfoot may be purchased. A

Rehov Hillel in the Jerusalem center. The billboard indicates a movie theater is in the vicinity.

sign before the entrance to the auditorium will plead in Hebrew: "Please don't drop *garinim* shells on the floor." Surprisingly for a country of compulsive smokers, smoking isn't allowed in movie theaters (not that the ban always is heeded).

The auditorium itself usually resembles a dark, dank cave. When my California friend, John, first stepped into a Jerusalem theater, he looked around in astonishment and then muttered, "I should have brought my penicillin." The pervasive style of Jerusalem movie theaters is "high raunch".

Take your seat — usually of hard wood — and try to make yourself comfortable. Before the feature film begins, some 10 to 15 minutes of commercials will extol the glories of consumerism.

While they drag on, shouts in Hebrew from other moviegoers will assuage boredom: "Shlomo! Shlomo! Over here! Hey, Rafi, get me another Coca-Cola." Chances are, the noise will fade when the movie starts. If it doesn't, you shouldn't hesitate to say nicely, *"Sheked, b'vakasha,"* which means, "Quiet, please." Even if the noisemakers are a row of young men in army fatigues and with their Uzis by their side, they probably will respond like contrite kids. You'll be most effective if you are an attractive female or very elderly.

Foreign films aren't dubbed in Israel. Robert Redford sounds like Robert Redford. An English-language movie has Hebrew and, perhaps, French subtitles. But if a movie is Israeli, it might have only French subtitles — no English. That probably is because Israeli movies are exported to France far more often than to the United States, which might explain why the French are more anti-Israeli than Americans are.

Now, just as the dramatic screws begin to tighten in the movie and the Spartan environment fades from your consciousness, a message abruptly flashes on screen announcing, *"Hafsakah"* (Intermission), and the houselights pop on.

Viewers leap from their seats and rush to the candy counter or rest rooms. Some 10 minutes later, the film resumes. Oh, yes, where were we now...?

When the film ends, don't hope to see the credits. As soon as the last word it uttered, the film blacks out and lights come on again. That handsome, unknown hunk in the carwash scene will have to remain anonymous.

In winter, sitting in a movie theater is like sitting on an ice floe. Bundle up. Bring a blanket. Some theaters have a radiator at the back. The choice may be between a good view of the screen or unbending your frozen legs after the show. On a cold night, some movie managements serve complimentary hot tea during the intermission, which warms the heart more than the body.

Such is reel life in Jerusalem's 17 commercial movie theaters, with another six on the way. Tel Aviv has 35, including a drive-in, by way of comparison. Don't be depressed. It's amazing what one gets used to.

Happily, several more pleasant places in which to see movies exist in Jerusalem. At these flicks, the seats cushion the body, the film won't screech to a halt in the middle for *hafsakah*, credits at the end of the film get their due, no popcorn lies underfoot and teeth won't chatter in winter.

These miracles occur at the **Jerusalem Theater**, the **Israel Museum, Beit Agron** at the bottom of Rehov Hillel and the **Cinemateque** off Derech Hevron, southwest of the Old City. Their schedules run in the Friday *Jerusalem Post*.

Now, to make movie-going easier, the following is indispensable and exclusive information on where to find Jerusalem's commercial theaters:

Binyenei Ha'Uma: Small auditorium to the left of large building of that name on Rehov Yafo, opposite Central Bus Station.

Centre 1: The new shopping center near the Central Bus Station is scheduled to open six theaters.

Cinema One: Rehov Uruguay in Kiryat Hayovel, up a steep hill from Derech Manahat and tucked into a shopping center at Kikar Sharet.

Eden: Rehov Agrippas 5, near Rehov King George.

Edison: Rehov Yesha'Yahu 14, near Rehov Prag.

Habirah: Rehov Shammai 19, near Rehov Hahistadrut.

Kfir: Clal Building, Rehov Yafo 97, Level PDI.

Mitchell: Rehov Strauss near Rehov Prag.

Orgil: Rehov Hillel 18, next to the former Orgil Hotel.

Orion Or: Between Rehov Shammai and Rehov Hillel, across from Habira. There are five screening rooms.

Orna: Rehov Hillel 19, across from Orgil Hotel.

Ron: Rehiv Harav Akiva 1, at Rehov Hillel.

Semadar: Rehov Lloyd George 4, off Rehov Emek Refaim.

Another way to find Jerusalem's movie theaters is to remember that the three theaters whose names start with "O" and the Ron are close to each together. Habira is across the street from the Orna, and the Edison and Mitchell are almost back-to-back.

Part Four:
Never Say Goodbye

Chapter 20:
Leaving

Leave-taking can be a painful unraveling of all the connections formed during your time in the Golden City. They can bind your heart with chains of love.

And in the midst of what may be a confluence of emotions, practical things must be attended to.

For those who have settled in, a good bit of activity will center on your flat. To get your last phone bill, you must go to the telephone company and leave a note saying that you want the phone meter read and on which day. After the designated day, call the phone company at 220-111 to make sure the reading was taken. The phone owner probably will want to withhold your damage deposit until he is sure that he has received the final bill for any long-distance calls you have made. This may take a month or more.

Arrange to have the electric meter read, also, or you may be able to do it yourself.

For clothes or other items you don't want to haul back home, remember the charity organizations.

Between these matters, expect a round of farewell dinners, lunches, coffees. Even with them, don't forget to reconfirm your departure flight reservation at least 72 hours in advance and to set aside the cost of your airport tax, so you will have it when it must be paid.

You may wonder: is leaving less painful if you take a flight in the

The Old City and new Jerusalem seen from Dominus Flevit on the Mount of Olives.

early morning, so that you will struggle all night with your departure and drive out of the city before it is awake — or — is it better to have one more day to feel close to Jerusalem and then depart for the airport at twilight, just as the sky takes on a glow?

I've done both and also been on planes that took off at hours in between. And I have no answer. I only know, at any time, leaving Jerusalem is a lonely matter.

Almost everyone who has spent time in Jerusalem has his own itinerary of places to see, even to touch, one last time. You may want to write a desperately held wish on a scrap of paper and then wedge it into a crack, side by side with other notes of desperately held wishes, between the huge building stones of the Western Wall.

You may choose to adopt the practice of the Hasids when they or someone they know departs on a trip: before you leave, give money to charity — perhaps to a street beggar and/or an organization of your choice.

And now you may want to cling to the kaleidoscope that is Jerusalem. It fills your senses. Your eyes have caught the sight of flowers everywhere, cats as ubiquitous as flowers, dogs snoozing in a quiet street, pomegranate trees drooping with ripe fruit, nursery-school children carrying tiny black violin cases, the torches flickering from a nighttime dark Mount of Olives during a funeral, a camel on city streets, the sunsets.

Your ears have heard the city's sounds of Hebrew chanting from synagogues, the *muezzin's* amplified call during the middle of the night on Moslem holidays, the sudden scrape of shutters being pulled up or let down, sonic booms, a musician practicing at home, the Shabbat siren, the beep before radio and TV news begins, church bells, "Ah-lo, ah-lo", before someone pushing a cart almost runs you down. You have heard the silence on the evening of Yom Kippur as the city comes to a halt to remember the 6 million.

Jerusalem's aromas, too, will be part of your memory: the perfumed air in spring, cumin and cardamon from Mizrachi restaurants, the brittle smell during a *hamsin* — the hot, dry wind in the rainless summer, the musty odor in old buildings during the rainy winter, hashish, urine and spices in the narrow lanes of the Old City, rosemary when it blossoms in the fall.

Your taste buds too have stored their memories — of crispy *falafel* balls, stinging hot *hariff*, crunchy bread, tangy olives and peppery Jerusalem kugel.

My parting gift to you is a recipe for Jerusalem kugel, your Jerusalem "madeleine" to taste and set you dreaming:

Jerusalem kugel:

8 to 12 ounces of fine egg noodles or very thin spaghetti
½ cup cooking oil
½ cup sugar
1½ teaspoons black pepper
3 eggs, beaten

Cook noodles until *al dente*. Drain well. Heat oil and sugar in suacepan. Stir constantly until sugar becomes almost black. Add noodles, pepper and eggs. Stir well. Taste. If not peppery enough, add more. Pour into greased casserole dish. Bake uncovered 1½ hours in oven at 350 degrees. The kugel cooks beautifully on top of stove in a *sirpella*. When firm, remove pan from oven, turn upside down and unmold. (*B'tayavon*.)

And as you leave, remember, in Hebrew, there is no such word as "goodbye". So you never can say goodbye to Jerusalem. Say, instead, "*Shalom, Yerushalayim*". "Peace to Jerusalem". Jerusalem always will be with you.

Appendix

TRACKING DOWN INFORMATION: A lot of information and various publications may be obtained in advance in the United States by contacting the Israel Government Tourist Office, 350 Fifth Ave. (at 34th St), New York, N.Y., 10118. Tel. (212) 560-0650.

What to Bring

A lot depends on your length of stay, your prospective living arrangements and how much you want to carry while you travel (you may be in a position to mail things to yourself in advance). Consider the following for convenience and to save on Israeli local costs:

- An ample supply of personal items like makeup, shaving equipment, shampoo, toothpaste, hair color, contraceptives, sunblock and panty hose.
- Extra contact lenses or glasses.
- Insect repellent.
- Medications you normally use and some you just might need, like antihistamines and something for diarrhea (especially for trips to Egypt).
- Health insurance forms in the event you will need medical attention.
- Additional passport photos of yourself for Egyptian visas, etc.

- An address book in which to keep the Jerusalem telephone numbers you will accumulate. It might be hard to find one in Israel in which the alphabet is in A-B-C, instead of "aleph-bet".
- A Hebrew phrase book.
- A Hebrew-English dictionary.
- Home-country postage stamps so people returning can mail your letters after they arrive, and thereby speed delivery.
- Home-country aerograms (should you want to include one as a stamped-self-addressed letter in a letter you send overseas).
- Such useful gadgets as a portable radio; electric current converters (Israel's power supply is 220 volts AC — 50 cycles) and plug adapters; a calculator (one that is a metric converter is ideal); extra batteries; camera; film in a lead-lined bag to protect it from airport X-rays; tape recorder and tapes; binoculars; scissors; sewing kit and a flashlight.
- A day and/or backpack for hikes and camping trips.
- Flannel night wear, long johns, waterproof boots, rain gear and umbrella for winter.
- For housekeeping, a can opener, a vegetable peeler, good knives, blankets, sheets, pillow cases and (if you really want to live comfortably) a 220-volt toaster-oven.
- A computer. I know someone who has used his in Israel on a converter for years with no trouble, but check on your particular model. Also find out about Israel customs regulations, because computers fall into a troublesome area for travelers. You may have to leave a deposit for your computer with customs upon entry. You will be able to collect it when you leave — with computer in hand.
- The children.
- An open mind.

What Not to Bring

- A 60-cycle electric typewriter.
- Preconceived notions.

Boning Up

Some suggested reading:

Adventure in the Holy Land - A Guide for Children and Their Families, by Marcia Kretzmer

Getting Jerusalem Together, by Fran Alpert

Jerusalem Architecture - Periods and Styles, by David Kroyanker

Jerusalem Atlas, by Gilbert Martin

Jerusalem, by Jill and Leon Uris
Jewish Wars, The, by Flavius Josephus
Mandelbaum Gate, The, by Muriel Speck
O Jerusalem, by Larry Collins and Dominique Lapierre
To Jerusalem and Back, by Saul Bellow
'Round Jerusalem Guide to Bus 99, The, by Steve Zorobnick
Walker in Jerusalem, A, by Samuel Heilman
And don't fail to purchase the Old City Map by Aharon Bier.

Jerusalem's Climate

Summers are hot and dry. Winter is the rainy season, which usually lasts from November to March and can be cold. It gets a chapter to itself. Spring and autumn can be glorious.

Below is a chart of Jerusalem's average monthly temperatures. Remember, averages can be deceiving.

MONTH	Average Minimum		Average Maximum	
	F	C	F	C
January	43	6.1	53	11.4
February	45	7.1	56	13.5
March	48	8.8	62	16.4
April	53	11.7	69	20.4
May	59	15.1	76	24.6
June	63	17.5	81	27.2
July	66	18.7	83	28.1
August	66	18.7	83	28.3
September	64	17.7	81	27.1
October	61	16.2	76	24.5
November	54	12.3	66	18.9
December	46	7.8	56	13.2

Visa Extension

For a visa extension beyond three months, apply in Jerusalem to the Visa Department, Ministry of the Interior, Rehov Shlomzion Hamalka 1. Hours are 8 a.m. to noon Sunday through Thursday and 2 p.m. to 3 p.m. Monday and Wednesday.

Climb two flights of stairs in this dingy building and find the Visa Department, which has no recognizable signs to tell you you have reached it, and where no one speaks English to help you. Somehow, you will muddle your way into an inner office, where the clerk who stamps your passport is likely to speak English and be surprisingly helpful, despite all appearances to the contrary.

You will need a passport photo of yourself. And expect to pay about $2.50.

Your passport now will be stamped. If you had planned on going to Jordan to see Petra, now you can forget it, unless you can figure out a way of getting another passport.

If you don't get your Israeli visa renewed, despite your extended stay, you will be subject to a fine when you leave. So plan your travels accordingly.

Hair

Women will find stylists as *au courant* in Jerusalem as back home. About barbers, I really can't say. But if men can't get their ideal haircut in Jerusalem, they at least can rest assured that they will be able to hear the best gossip in town while in the barber chair.

Hotel hairdressers and barbers usually are the most expensive, but **Roots**, Rehov Mesilat Yesharim 7, a unisex establishment behind Hamashbir, is tops for hair care in price and service. The staff either comes from England or is London-trained. **Roots** also carries its own excellent shampoos and conditioners, which seem to last forever. Appointments are necessary here.

The other elegant, but slightly less expensive, hair-styling salon is **Shampoo**, not far from Roots at Rehov Mesilat Yesharim 1, and also unisex. No appointment is necessary, but cash is, since neither checks nor credit cards are accepted.

Down the line in costs are the neighborhood beauty salons. Below them, and open on Saturdays, are beauty salons on Salah ed-Din Street in East Jerusalem. The least expensive places to get hair done is at "bootleggers" — hairdressers who work in their homes and out of tax collectors' sight. Needless to say, they don't advertise.

Tipping procedures are the same as in the United States. Beauty salons and barber shops close early Monday afternoons.

Laundry

Maybe you will be blessed with a washing machine in your flat. If so, you were born under a lucky star. Otherwise, except for the use of another wonderful, reliable washing machine known as your very own hands, it is expensive maintaining clean clothes and linens in Israel.

Cheaper than commercial laundries and dry cleaners are laundromats. Coin-operated dry cleaning machines usually are on the premises, too. But by the time you pay for detergent and water softener and run the dryer a cycle or two, one load of laundry could cost about $4. Cut expenses by supplying your own detergent and water softener and not buying the laundromat's. If you don't have the leisure to watch your clothes get clean, the attendant will take your laundry or dry cleaning through its paces for an additional charge.

Between the time and money involved, even at a laundromat, it seems that most people resort to handwashing at least a good portion of their things. That explains why an Israeli detergent is made expressly for handwashing.

Looking After Your Sole (Shoe Repair)

Jerusalem demands a lot of your sole. You can be sure that in the Golden City, your shoes will get a lot of wear. While at home, the soles of your shoes may have touched little, outside of work and home, other than the gas pedal of your car; in Jerusalem, they'll learn what work is.

The impact could be traumatic and, sooner or later, first aid will be required. Finding help in Jerusalem for an ailing shoe can be something of a mystery, for shoemakers are tucked away in unlikely places. Searching them out can be an exploration into the city's back lanes. You can find a shoemaker stuffed into a portable kiosk-like, green metal structure on Rehov Keren Hakayemet, west of the Post Office.

You can find two or three shoemakers on the right side of an unnamed lane that is the third right turn after the toy and vegetable vendors inside Damascus Gate. Other cobblers are burrowed in the Mahane Yehuda area on Rehov Yosef Schwartz, Rehov Meyuhas and Rehov David Yellin, and another is in the alleyway running along Cafe Atara connecting Rehov Shammai with the Ben Yehuda Mall. There is a father and son pair of shoemakers. The father is at Rehov Nahalat Shiva 2 and the son at Rehov Aza 26.

The Co-op Supermarket in the basement of Hamasbhir and in French Hill and Beit Hakerem conveniently include shoe repair centers. While you look for food for your soul, your soles needn't be neglected.

Addresses

Alliance Francaise de Jerusalem — Rehov Agron 8. Tel. 221-204.

American Library — American Cultural Center, Rehov Keren Hayesod 9.

Anglo-Saxon Realty — Rehov Hasoreg 2. Tel. 221-161.

Apartotel — Rehov Yafo 214, P.O. Box 13100, Jerusalem. Tel. 531-221.

Association of Americans and Canadians in Israel — Jerusalem Region: Rehov Mane 6 (or Rehov Pinsker 11). Tel. 636-932, 669-598.

Ayso Metzia — Rehov Beit Yaacov 2; Rehov Havatzelet 3; Rehov Sulam Ya'acov 4 in Ramot.

Beit Ha'am — Rehov Bezalel 11. Tel. 224-156.
Beit Hano'ar Ha'ivri — Rehov Herzog 105. Tel. 666-141.
Ben Ben Superzol — Rehov Yafo 44 and Rehov Ben Hillel 3.
Books — The Jerusalem Post, 120 E. 56th St., New York, N.Y., 10022, or P.O. Box 81, Jerusalem, 91000, Israel.
Bookstop — Rehov Yosef du Nawas 6.
Book Store — Clal Building, Rehov Yafo.
British Council Library — Terra Sancta, Rehov Keren Hayesod and Place de France.
Center for Conservative Judaism — Rehov Agron 2. Tel. 226-386.
Christian Information Center — Jaffa Gate. Tel. 287-647.
Church of Mary Magdalene — Mount of Olives. Tel. 282-897.
Church of the Redeemer — Muristan Road, Old City. Tel. 262-543.
City Cellar — Eilon City Tower, Rehov Ben Yehuda and Rehov King George. City of DavidOphel. Tel. 224-404.
Class — Rehov Yafo 57.
Consumer Protection Board (Matan Hatkanim) — 718-367, 715-485.
Diaspora Yeshiva — Mount Zion, Tel. 722-339.
Egged Central Bus Station — Rehov Yafo 224. Tel. 528-231/2, 534-596, 551-868. Egged Tours, Rehov Yafo 44a. Tel. 223-454, 224-198. Egged Jaffa Gate Terminal (Beit Tannous), 248-144, 247-783.
Electric House — Rehov Aza 14. Tel. 623-977.
El-Hakaawati — in former Nuzha Cinema behind Tomb of Kings in East Jerusalem.
Ety's Piano Bar — Kikar Remez.
Ezra Nashim Thrift Shop — Rehov Ben Shoshan 5.
Galilee Tours — Rehov Mea She'arim 21. Tel. 287-585.
Government Tourist Information Office — Rehov King George 24. Tel. 241-281/2.
Hadassah Medical Center — Ein Kerem, Tel. 427-427; Hadassah Hospital, Mount Scopus, Tel. 818-111.
Harmony House — Rehov Yoel Salomon 17. Tel. 227-719.
Hebrew Union College — Rehov King David 13. Tel. 232-444.
Homotel — Rehov Ben Sira 3, Tel. 225-062, 224-539.
International Christian Embassy — Rehov Ahad Ha'em and Rehov Brenner. Tel. 699-839.
Israel Academic Projects — First Floor, Apartotel, Rehov Yafo 214. Tel. 528-939, 536-405.
Israel Bed and Breakfast LTD. — P.O. Box 24119, Jerusalem 91240. Tel. 817-001.
Israel Government Tourist Office — 350 Fifth Ave., New York, N.Y., 10118. Tel. (212) 560-0650.
Israel Museum — Rehov Ruppin. Tel. 698-211.
Israel Tennis Center — Rehov Elmaliach 3. Tel. 413-866.
Jerusalem of Gold Nightclub — Rehov En Rogel 5. Tel. 716-668, 718-880.
Jerusalem Pottery — 14 Via Dolorosa, Old City.
Jerusalem (Sherover) Theater — Rehov David Marcus 20. Tel. 667-167.
Jewish Agency — corner Rehov Keren Kayemet and Rehov King George.

Khan Nightclub — Kikar Remez. Tel. 718-283, 721-782.
Knesset — off Rehov Ruppin. Tel. 554-111.
Kolav — Rehov Aza 28.
Kolbotek — Rehov Yafo and Rehov Strauss.
Kuzari — Rehov David (Habucharim) 10, Tel. 826-632.
Ma'ayan Stub — Rehov Strauss and Rehov Yafo.
Maskit — Rehov Harav Kook 12.
Millstein's — Rehov Eliashar 5.
Moadon Ha-oleh — Rehov Alkalai 9. Tel. 633-718.
Old Pa'am — Rehov Yehuda 5.
Old Yishuv Museum — Rehov Or Hahayim 6. Tel. 284-636.
Palestinian Pottery — 14 Nablus Road.
Pargod Theater — Rehov Bezalel 94. Tel. 228-819, 231-765.
Penny Lane — Rehov Hanevi'im 20 (entrance from the parking lot behind
    the building).
Railway station — Kikar Remez, Abu Tor. Tel. 717-764.
Rampart Walk — Old City. Tel. 224-403.
Red Brick House — Motza. Tel. 533-686.
Roman Square — by Damascus Gate. Tel. 224-403.
Roots — Rehov Mesilat Yesharim 7.
Rothschild (Alix de) Crafts Center — Rehov Or Hahaim.
St. Anthony's School — Rehov Redaq. Tel. 632-365.
Scandals — Rehov Dorot Rishonim 8.
Sefer Ve Sefel Bookstore — Rehov Yavetz 2 (off Rehov Yafa 47). Tel.
    248-237.
She'al — Rehov King George 21. Tel. 224-456/7.
Shilo (pregnancy and contraception counseling) — Ben-Yehuda Mall 16.
    Tel. 248-412.
Society for the Protection of Nature in Israel — Rehov Helena Hamalka
    13. Tel. 228-357, 244-605.
Tanya's — French Hill Shopping Center.
Taxi companies: David Hamelech, Tel. 222-510; Hapsigah, Tel. 421-111;
    Rehavia, Tel. 224-444; Nesher (for airport transportation), Tel. 633-333,
    223-000.
Telephone repairs: Rehov Yafo 187. Tel. 522-016. (Other repairs in City
    Tower office.)
Ticho House — Rehov Harav Kook 7. Tel. 244-186.
Tower of David (Citadel) — Jaffa Gate. Tel. 286-079. (Sound and Light
    (Son et Lumiere) Show. Tel. 286-511.
Tzavta — Rehov King George 38.
United Tours — King David Hotel Annex. Tel. 222-187/9.
Visa Department — Ministry of the Interior, Rehov Shlomzion Hamalka 1.
WIZO Shop — Rehov Yafo 34.
Yad Vashem — Har Hazikaron, Siderot Herzl. Tel. 531-202/191.
Yalkut Book Store — City Cellar, City Tower.

Glossary

Hebrew: God's Native Tongue

There is the story of the 87-year old Boston woman who began studying Hebrew. Her friends asked why in the world, at her ripe age, she would begin the study of a language. She answered, "Because if, after my death, I should be able to meet God, I want to speak to him in his native tongue." (Or did she say, "should she want to speak to 'her'?")

I can't teach you Hebrew, but I can give you a glossary of words frequently heard in Israel and pass on some information about the language as it is heard today.

assimonim — telephone tokens. The singular is assimon.

bima — the raised platform in a synagogue from which services are conducted.

chanukiah — the candelabra used exclusively during Chanukah. It has eight candles and a place for a "servant" candle.

chuppah — the canopy over a couple taking marriage vows.

givat — mount.

kashrut — refers to Jewish dietary regulations that prohibit mixing meat and dairy products and eating of pork and shellfish. In English the word is "kosher".

katubah — marriage contract

kfar — village

kipah — the head covering worn by Jewish men that is a small, round cap that fits closely to the head.

kiryat — district

menorah — a seven-branch candelabra

mikud — Israeli equivalent of a postal ZIP code.

parve — food that is suitable for either dairy or meat meals. Fish is *parve*.

ramat — hill

shekel — the Israeli unit of money. Plural is shkelim.

sherut — a seven-passenger taxi that travels between cities and operates seven days a week.

sherutim — lavatories (literally, "facilities")

tallit — a man's prayer shawl

Talmud — ancient rabbinic written commentaries on *Torah*, the Book of Prophets and the Writings, which include such books as Ecclesiastes and Ruth.

Torah — The five books of the Bible from Genesis through Deuteronomy. Also may refer to all the laws and teachings of Judaism, written and in oral tradition.

tfillin — phylacteries: two small leather boxes, each containing strips of parchment inscribed with quotations from Hebrew Scriptures. One is strapped to the forehead and the other to the left arm by observant Jewish men during morning prayers, except on Shabbat and holidays.

tzitzit — the fringed vest Orthodox Jewish men wear for symbolic reasons

The following Hebrew isn't necessarily useful, but is, I think, interesting from a curiosity standpoint. It's here for your edification. These Hebrew words and expressions either are Israeli slang, fall into the category of "Engbrew" — a colloquial combination of Hebrew and English or are "Hebrish" — a colloquial combination of Hebrew and Yiddish. As they sound in Hebrew, but mean in English:

Oof mi poh — Scram (literally, Fly from here).

tchik-tchak — fast (slang)

bek exil — Back axle

front bek axle — Front axle

shvitz (v.) — Shows off, an Israeli transformation of the Yiddish word that means, "sweats".

shvitzer (n.) — A show-off.

Rehov Penis — Rehov Pines (as in the tree), a Jerusalem street named for a famous, old Jerusalem family.

Among Israeli expressions I like is one that is translated as: "To be close to the plate." It means "to be close to where the goodies are," but it never refers to food. It often is used when talking about politicians' situations.

And these are among examples of fractured English I have seen on store signs and menus.
Toest
Welcom
Ich Cream
Coketails
MerryX-mas

And at the Government Press Office:
I.D.F. Spoke
Sman
Has moved

Index

PUBLICATIONS

Available at your local bookstore or directly from John Muir Publications.

22 Days Series $6.95 each, 128 to 144 pp.

These pocket-size itinerary guidebooks are a refreshing departure from ordinary guidebooks. Each author has an in-depth knowledge of the region covered and offers 22 tested daily itineraries through their favorite parts of it. Included are not only "must see" attractions but also little-known villages and hidden "jewels" as well as valuable general information.

22 Days in Alaska by Pamela Lanier (68-0) April '88
22 Days in American Southwest by Richard Harris (88-5) April '88
22 Days in Australia by John Gottberg (75-3)
22 Days in California by Roger Rapaport (93-1) Sept. '88
22 Days in China by Gaylon Duke & Zenia Victor (72-9)
22 Days in Europe by Rick Steves (62-1)
22 Days in Germany, Austria & Switzerland by Rick Steves (66-4)
22 Days in Great Britain by Rick Steves (67-2)
22 Days in Hawaii by Arnold Schuchter (92-3) Sept. '88
22 Days in India by Anurag Mathur (87-7) April '88
22 Days in Japan by David Old (73-7)
22 Days in Mexico by Steve Rogers & Tina Rosa (64-8)
22 Days in New England by Arnold Schuchter (96-6) Sept. '88
22 Days in New Zealand by Arnold Schuchter (86-9) April '88
22 Days in Norway, Denmark & Sweden by Rick Steves (83-4)
22 Days in Pacific Northwest by Richard Harris (97-4) Oct. '88
22 Days in Spain & Portugal by Rick Steves (63-X)
22 Days in West Indies by Cyndy & Sam Morreale (74-5)

Undiscovered Islands of the Caribbean, Burl Willis $12.95 (80-X) 220 pp.

For the past decade, Burl Willis has been tracking down remote Caribbean getaways—the kind known only to the most adventurous traveler. Here he offers complete information on 32 islands—all you'll need to know for a vacation in an as yet undiscovered Paradise.

People's Guide to Mexico, Carl Franz
$13.95 (56-7) 560 pp.

Now in its 12th printing, this classic guide shows the traveler how to handle just about any situation that might arise while in Mexico. ". . . the best 360-degree coverage of traveling and short-term living in Mexico that's going." — *Whole Earth Epilog.*

People's Guide to RV Camping in Mexico, Carl Franz $12.95   (91-5)   356 pp.

The sequel to *The People's Guide to Mexico,* this revised guide focuses on the special pleasures and challenges of RV travel in Mexico. An unprecedented number of Americans and Canadians have discovered the advantages of RV travel in reaching remote villages and camping comfortably on beaches. Sept '88

The On and Off the Road Cookbook, Carl Franz $8.50   (27-3)   272 pp.

Carl Franz, *(The People's Guide to Mexico)* and Lorena Havens offer a multitude of delicious alternatives to the usual campsite meals or roadside cheeseburgers. Over 120 proven recipes.

The Shopper's Guide to Mexico, Steve Rogers & Tina Rosa $9.95   (90-7)   200 pp.

The only comprehensive handbook for shopping in Mexico, this guide ferrets out little-known towns where the finest handicrafts are made and offers shopping techniques for judging quality, bargaining, and complete information on packaging, mailing and U.S. customs requirements. Sept '88

The Heart of Jerusalem, Arlynn Nellhaus $12.95   (79-6)   312 pp.

Denver Post journalist Arlynn Nellhaus draws on her vast experience in and knowledge of Jerusalem to give travelers a rare inside view and practical guide to the Golden City—from holy sites and religious observances to how to shop for toothpaste and use the telephone.

Guide to Buddhist Meditation Retreats, Don Morreale $12.95   (94-X)   312 pp.

The only comprehensive directory of Buddhist centers, this guide includes first-person narratives of individuals' retreat experiences. Invaluable for both newcomers and experienced practitioners who wish to expand their contacts within the American Buddhist Community. Sept. '88

Complete Guide to Bed & Breakfasts, Inns & Guesthouses, Pamela Lanier
$13.95   (82-6)   520 pp.

Newly revised and the most complete directory, with over 4800 listings in all 50 states, 10 Canadian provinces, Puerto Rico and the U.S. Virgin Islands. This classic provides details on reservation services and indexes identifying inns noted for antiques, decor, conference facilities and gourmet food.

All-Suite Hotel Guide, Pamela Lanier
$11.95   (70-2)   312 pp.

Pamela Lanier, author of *The Complete Guide to Bed & Breakfasts, Inns & Guesthouses,* now provides the discerning traveler with a listing of over 600 all-suite hotels. Indispensable for families traveling with children or business people requiring an extra meeting room.

Elegant Small Hotels, Pamela Lanier $13.95   (77-X)   202 pp.

This lodging guide for discriminating travelers describes 168 American hotels characterized by exquisite rooms and suites and personal service par excellence. Includes small hotels in 35 states and the Caribbean with many photos in full color.

Gypsying After 40, Bob Harris $12.95 (71-0) 312 pp.

Retirees Bob and Megan Harris offer a witty and informative guide to the "gypsying" lifestyle that has enriched their lives and can enrich yours. For 10 of the last 18 years they have traveled throughout the world living out of camper vans and boats. Their message is: "Anyone can do it'!!

Mona Winks, A Guide to Enjoying the Museum of Europe, Rick Steves $12.95 (85-0) 356 pp.

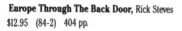

Here's a guide that will save you time, shoe leather and tired muscles. It's designed for people who want to get the most out of visiting the great museums of Europe. It covers 25 museums in London, Paris, Rome, Venice, Florence, Amsterdam, Munich, Madrid and Vienna.

Europe Through The Back Door, Rick Steves $12.95 (84-2) 404 pp.

Doubleday and Literary Guild Bookclub Selection.

For people who want to enjoy Europe more and spend less money doing it. In this revised edition, Rick shares more of his well-respected insights. He also describes his favorite "back doors"—less visited destinations throughout Europe that are a wonderful addition to any European vacation.

Europe 101, Rick Steves & Gene Openshaw $11.95 (78-8) 372 pp.

The first and only jaunty history and art book for travelers makes castles, palaces and museums come alive. Both Steves and Openshaw hold degrees in European history, but their real education has come from escorting first-time visitors throughout Europe.

Asia Through The Back Door, Rick Steves & John Gottberg $11.95 (58-3) 336 pp.

In this detailed guide book are information and advice you won't find elsewhere—including how to overcome culture shock, bargain in marketplaces, observe Buddhist temple etiquette and, possibly most important of all, how to eat noodles with chopsticks!

Traveler's Guide to Asian Culture, John Gottberg $12.95 (81-8) 356 pp.

John Gottberg, *Insight Guide* editor and co-author with Rick Steves of *Asia Through the Back Door,* has written for the traveler an accurate and enjoyable guide to the history and culture of this diverse continent. Sept. '88

Guide to Bus Touring in the U.S., Stuart Warren & Douglas Block $11.95 (95-8) 256 pp.

For many people, bus touring is the ideal, relaxed and comfortable way to see America. The author has had years of experience as a bus tour conductor and writes in-depth about every aspect of bus touring to help passengers get the most pleasure for their money. Sept. '88

Road & Track's Used Car Classics edited by Peter Bohr $12.95 (69-9) 272 pp.

Road & Track contributing editor Peter Bohr has compiled this collection of the magazine's "Used Car Classic" articles, updating them to include current market information. Over 70 makes and models of American, British, Italian, West German, Swedish and Japanese enthusiast cars built between 1953 and 1979 are featured.

Automotive Repair Manuals

Each JMP automotive manual gives clear step-by-step instructions, together with illustrations that show exactly how each system in the vehicle comes apart and goes back together. They tell everything a novice or experienced mechanic needs to know to perform periodic maintenance, tune-ups, troubleshooting and repair of the brake, fuel and emission control, electrical, cooling, clutch, transmission, driveline, steering and suspension systems, and even rebuild the engine.

How To Keep Your VW Alive $17.95 (50-8) 384 pp.
How To Keep Your VW Rabbit Alive $17.95 (47-8) 440 pp.
How To Keep Your Honda Car Alive $17.95 (55-9) 272 pp.
How To Keep Your Subaru Alive $17.95 (49-4) 464 pp.
How To Keep Your Toyota Pick-Up Alive $17.95 (89-3) 400 pp. April '88
How To Keep Your Datsun/Nissan Alive $22.95 (65-6) 544 pp.
How To Keep Your Honda ATC Alive $14.95 (45-1) 236 pp.

ITEM NO.		TITLE	EACH	QUAN.	TOTAL
	·				
	·				
	·				
	·				
	·				
	·				
	·				

Subtotals _____

Postage & handling (see ordering information)* _____

New Mexicans please add 5.625% tax _____

Total Amount Due _____

METHOD OF PAYMENT (circle one)   MC   VISA   AMEX   CHECK   MONEY ORDER

Credit Card Number   Expiration Date

☐☐☐☐☐☐☐☐☐☐☐☐☐☐☐☐   ☐☐-☐☐

Signature X _____
Required for Credit Card Purchases

Telephone: Office (___) _____ Home (___) _____

Name _____

Address _____

City _____ State _____ Zip _____

See reverse side for Ordering Information

ORDERING INFORMATION

Fill in the order blank. Be sure to add up all of the subtotals at the bottom of the order form, and give us the address whither your order will be whisked.

Postage & Handling

Your books will be sent to you via UPS (for U.S. destinations), and you will receive them in approximately 10 days from the time that we receive your order.

Include $2.75 for the first item ordered and add $.50 for each additional item to cover shipping and handling costs. UPS shipments to post office boxes take longer to arrive; if possible, please give us a street address.

For airmail within the U.S., enclose $4.00 per book for shipping and handling.

ALL FOREIGN ORDERS will be shipped surface rate. Please enclose $3.00 for the first item and $1.00 for each additional item. Please inquire for airmail rates.

Method of Payment

Your order may be paid by check, money order or credit card. We cannot be responsible for cash sent through the mail.

All payments must be in U.S. dollars drawn on a U.S. bank. Canadian postal money orders in U.S. dollars also accepted.

For VISA, Mastercard or American Express orders, use the order form or call (505) 982-4078. Books ordered on American Express cards can be shipped only to the billing address of the cardholder.

Sorry, no C.O.D.'s.

Residents of sunny New Mexico add 5.625% to the total.

Backorders

We will backorder all forthcoming and out-of-stock titles unless otherwise requested.

Address all orders and inquiries to:

JOHN MUIR PUBLICATIONS
P.O. Box 613
Santa Fe, NM 87504
(505) 982-4078

All prices subject to change without notice.